The Flora of
NORTHAMPTONSHIRE
and the Soke of Peterborough~

The Flora of NORTHAMPTONSHIRE and the Soke of Peterborough~

ISBN 0 907381 03 0 hardback
ISBN 0 907381 08 1 softback

Published for the
Kettering and District Natural History Society and the Northamptonshire Flora Group
by

ROBERT WILSON DESIGNS
23 Cecil Street, Rothwell, Northants NN14 6EZ   01536 711144

The Flora of
NORTHAMPTONSHIRE
and the Soke of Peterborough~

Gill Gent, Rob Wilson et al

4

*Dedicated to the memory of those botanists of the
Kettering and District Natural History Society
without whose early work this flora would never have been started.*

*Also to Peter Gent
for all his help and support over many years!*

*The Northamptonshire Flora Group would like to thank the following organisations for
their contributions towards the publication of this book:*

Botanical Society of the British Isles

Kettering and District Natural History Society

National Rivers Authority Anglian Region

Wildlife Trust for Northamptonshire

Printed by Unity Print Ltd., Corby, Northants

The Flora of NORTHAMPTONSHIRE
and the Soke of Peterborough~

Contents

The Flora of
NORTHAMPTONSHIRE
and the Soke of Peterborough~

Photographs

Diagrams and Maps

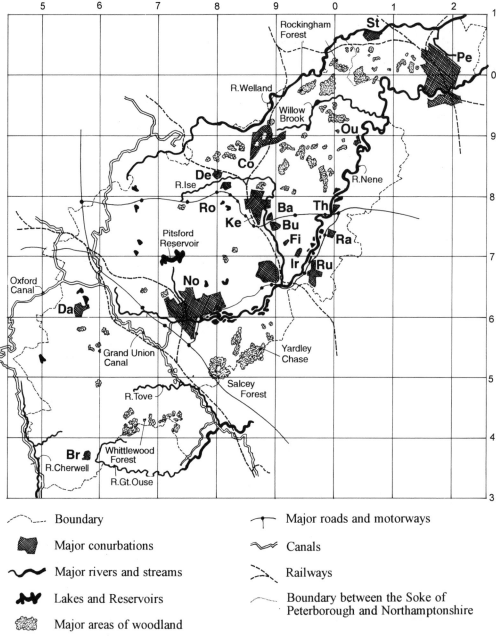

	Boundary		Major roads and motorways
	Major conurbations		Canals
	Major rivers and streams		Railways
	Lakes and Reservoirs		Boundary between the Soke of Peterborough and Northamptonshire
	Major areas of woodland		

Ba *Barton Seagrave;* **Br** *Brackley;* **Bu** *Burton Latimer;* **Co** *Corby;* **Da** *Daventry;*
De *Desborough;* **Fi** *Finedon;* **Ir** *Irthlingborough;* **Ke** *Kettering;* **No** *Northampton;*
Ou *Oundle;* **Pe** *Peterborough;* **Ra** *Raunds;* **Ro** *Rothwell;* **Ru** *Rushden and Higham Ferrers;* **St** *Stamford;* **Th** *Thrapston*

Figure 1 Northamptonshire and the Soke of Peterborough

The Flora of
ORTHAMPTONSHIRE
and the Soke of Peterborough~

Foreword

Miriam Rothschild

This is the ideal moment in which to publish a county Flora especially with distribution maps. It is useless crying 'biodiversity!' unless we have a sound knowledge of where and what we have left to save and protect. The authors have given us a thorough and balanced description of the flowering plants of Northamptonshire and both the amateur and scientist should be equally grateful for the wealth of factual information provided.

We are fortunate to have had Druce's Flora with which to compare the present work. He and Charles Rothschild were great friends and he lived at Ashton in my father's bachelor cottage whilst compiling much of his notes for this volume. Together they explored the "marshes of the White Water with its myriads of marsh orchids". . . and the country around Helpston, Barnack, Swaddiwell Field, the Bedford Purlieus, Eye and Peakirk, Salcey, Whittlebury, Monks Wood, Barnwell Wold and so forth. Druce named one of the nine species of roses he found at Ashton *rothschildii*, (now considered a cross between *R.canina* and *R.sherardii*), in my father's honour. But where are the myriad marsh orchids of White Water? Druce himself described the species as 'rare' 30 years after his stay at Ashton and today it is considered very rare. What has become of the pasque flowers and chalkhill blues of Swaddiwell Field, rated by my father as one of the most important botanical and entomological sites in the County? Vanished beneath a splendid crop of yellow rape! Helpston Heath in 1944 also disappeared under the plough and all but a fraction of Harlestone Heath has been lost to development.

To protect our countryside from thoughtless destruction, it is essential to have a careful and knowledgeable description of what remains. Plants - the green world - are of primary importance. The "Flora of Northamptonshire" is a valuable model of one of our basic needs if we are to succeed in well planned conservation. We are enormously indebted to Gill Gent and her co-authors for this stimulating and scholarly contribution.

The Flora of
NORTHAMPTONSHIRE
and the Soke of Peterborough~

Introduction

Gill Gent

The first thing that strikes you about Northamptonshire and the Soke of Peterborough is its length. It stretches some seventy miles from its border in the north-east with the East Anglian Fens towards the Cotswolds in the south-west. Even in 1995, when almost everyone has easy access to personal transport, a wealth of books and other sources to enable the accurate identification of the more difficult plant groups, it seems incredible that a small group of very amateur botanists based almost entirely in the north of the county should even contemplate the writing of a complete flora of the area, including some 1,200 species of plants. Probably we should have remembered the famous lines by Pope: 'For fools rush in where angels fear to tread'!

The only previous Flora of Northamptonshire, by Dr George Claridge Druce, had been published in 1930, with some of the data having been collected in the nineteenth century although it had been updated before publication. The publication of a new flora was originally discussed by the Kettering and District Natural History Society in 1953. Until 1969 progress was spasmodic, and at one stage interrupted by the need to collect records for the Atlas of the British Flora (Perring and Walters, BSBI, Thomas Nelson, 1962).

The collecting of records for the flora was originally an extension of the card index that had been kept by members of the society since the publication of Druce's flora of the county.

Initially it was decided that the records should be collected on a grid square basis but there is little record of progress and in 1965 it was decided to adopt a system of recording by parishes. Within three years of this decision record collecting reverted to a grid square basis and after a major controversy over whether records should be kept on a 2km or 5km square basis and trial recording for both sizes of square during 1969, from 1970 onwards the botany section of the Kettering and District Natural History Society has worked to record the flora of the county of Northamptonshire on a 5km grid. It was felt that the extra work involved in recording on a two kilometre grid would have put the new flora completely out of reach. Later experience has largely substantiated this, for the number of botanists who have been seriously involved in the project is very small in spite of efforts to draw others from outside the society into an involvement with the project. Initially the Soke of Peterborough, which had been lost to Cambridgeshire in the local government reorganisation of the 1970s, was not included in the project but it was later added to the work as it seemed unthinkable not to include it both as an update of Druce's flora and to provide a complete record of botanical Vice-county 32.

This flora has been a truly amateur effort from start to finish and to keep up the momentum of recording in one's spare time for nearly twenty-five years has not been easy and there have been times when enthusiasm has flagged. Often it seemed that this project would never be completed, but there always seemed to be new projects like the BSBI monitoring scheme in the late 1980s, and with the enlisting of new helpers from outside the county, once more enthusiasm was rekindled. We must not forget the help from visiting botanists over the years, they have been helpful in more ways than they perhaps realise.

We are told that in his later years Dr Druce recorded the flora from the back seat of his Daimler as he was driven around the countryside; the chauffeur being under strict instruction not to exceed 20mph, for below that speed he could recognise the flowers in the passing fields and verges.

At one point during the collection of data for the new flora I can proudly say that I emulated the great doctor, for during the 1970s quite an amount of country lane recording was done from the back seat of a Messerschmitt bubble car, as I was ferried through the countryside by fellow society member Bill Monck. I am sure that our slow and erratic progress caused a great deal of annoyance to other motorists, but fortunately the roads were quieter then!

After so many years of work in the field it was decided that publication should take place in 1995. As the inevitable 'cut-off' point approaches it still seems that there is much more that should have been done, by way of research and field recordings. But after such a long gestation period we would probably feel the same in twelve months time, or whenever we decided to publish this work, that has, for the people involved, been a mammoth undertaking.

Although we are extremely grateful for the help and criticism of professional botanists such as Dr Franklyn Perring - their comments have done much to improve the content of our work - it must be stressed that the whole project is primarily an amateur effort and has had to be completed within the spare time left after various other priorities such as earning a living, bringing up a family etc. and, of course, aspiring to be better botanists so that we could produce a worthwhile flora of the district. In the recent past whilst we worked towards the completion of the recording in the field, producing the written text and raising the finances needed for publication, many of these 'priorities' have had to take second place to work on the flora!

New computer techniques have meant that the task of producing the final text for the flora has been much simplified but even so we look forward to the publication, which will coincide with the ninetieth anniversary celebrations of the Kettering and District Natural History Society, with some sense of relief, and grateful thanks to all concerned.

The work does not end here however. From the committee that was formed in 1988 to steer the new flora through the final years towards publication, a Northamptonshire Flora Group has been formed. One of the aims of this group is to keep up to date records so that in the future a new county flora could be published within a year or two of it being thought necessary. That, however, is in the future although we would like to hear from anyone who would be prepared to involve themselves with this project. In the meantime we hope in presenting this work to you that our efforts will be of interest and use to both the amateur and professional botanist alike.

The Flora of
NORTHAMPTONSHIRE
and the Soke of Peterborough~

Acknowledgements

After several false starts, records for the new flora were collected from 1970 until 1994 but it was not until the late 1980s that a special committee was formed to oversee the final collection of data and the preparation of the text for publication.

At the time of publication the members of the Northamptonshire Flora Group committee were: Brian Adams, Phil Aldridge, Jeff Best, Joan Birch, George Crawford, Ray Cleaver, Gill Gent, George Hunnable, Seán Karley, Gwen Keech, Mike Miley, Andrew Robinson, Claire Williams and Rob Wilson.

The systematic flora has been a co-operative effort by the following authors: Brian Adams, Gill Gent, Seán Karley, Gwen Keech, Mike Miley, Andrew Robinson, Claire Williams and Rob Wilson, with Gill Gent assuming the role of author-in-chief and Rob Wilson that of editor. The section on *Rubus* was written by Alan Newton. The untimely death of Guy Messenger prevented him from fulfilling his promise to write the section on *Ulmus*. Authors in the other sections of the book are acknowledged at the head of each section, but our thanks are due to Jeff Best, Tony John Keech, Diana S.Sutherland and Ioan Thomas.

In recent years many of the records have been collected by committee members, but it is twenty-five years since a start was made on the collection of data and many other people have also been involved. Kettering and District Natural History Society members associated with the project who have, for various reasons, not been able to continue their involvement include the late Frank Adams, John Barker, Brian Chaplin, Elspeth Cooke, the late F.R.Dawkins, the late Tommy Downing, Derek Kilsby, the late Geoff Laundon, Jack Laundon, the late Marjorie Laundon, Geoff and Kay Lines, Ann Longhurst, Edna Marpur, the late Walter Mayes, Bernard and the late Jean Mitchell, Bill Monck, John Moore, Donald Payne and Derek Read.

Others who have willingly collected or given records include Tony Balbi, the late Sylvia Beale, Jeff Best, Ian and Kay Cameron, Perdita Cawthorne, the late John Chandler, Sara Chapple, Adrian Colston, Ann Conelly, Muriel and Bill Coulson, Betty Coxon, Ruth Dixon, Martin Dove, Peter and Alison Goodfellow, Geraldine Hunt, Mary Jackson, Ann Kennard, Brian Laney, Betty Latimer, Roy Maycock, the late Guy Messenger, Mike Miley, Rosemary Parslow, John Patrick, Dr Franklyn Perring, H.J.Phillips, R.C.Palmer, Chris Preston, Tony Primavesi, Patrick Rawlinson, Tim Rich, Tony Richardson, Rosemary Robson, Dorothy Rollit, Alan & Sheila Sheasby, Peggy Tuffs, Nick Turland, Angela Walker, Pat Wallis, Terry Wells, many members of the Botanical Society of the British Isles and the Wildflower Society who have visited the county on a number of occasions and have helped with recording, not forgetting the Northamptonshire Wildlife Trust habitat survey teams and others too numerous to mention.

Adrian Colston, Director of Conservation, Northamptonshire Wildlife Trust granted ready access to the Wildlife Trusts records and the records gathered by Linda Moore, Prime Sites Officer, Northamptonshire Wildlife Trust, during the prime sites project. These have done much to make this flora a complete record of the county.

The National Rivers Authority, Anglian Region allowed ready access to the considerable botanical data stored in their Rivers Environmental Database System.

Jeff Best, Adrian Colston, Rosemary Parslow, formerly with English Nature and now Director of Conservation, Cambridgeshire Wildlife Trust and Dr Franklyn Perring, Past President of the Botanical Society of the British Isles all freely gave their valuable time to comment on various drafts of the manuscript. Their suggestions have helped considerably.

Our thanks are due to Joan and Tom Birch for their assiduous checking of the final draft in an attempt to eliminate the numerous typographical errors and Andrew Gagg of Photo Flora for generously supplying photographs from his collection for our use.

This flora is entirely an amateur effort, but our grateful thanks must go to George Hunnable and the Kettering and District Natural History Society who provided some funding during its preparation and to the various organisations who helped towards the cost of publication. These are all duly acknowledged on page four. The remainder of the costs have been met by members of the committee.

All of the data collected for this flora was recorded on cards devised for the project, which listed the commonest species in the Vice-county. There was one card for each 5km square. This data was ultimately transferred from the recording cards to computer.

The computerisation of data was started in 1988, using the DRECS database and the DMAP distribution mapping program written by Dr Alan Morton whose help and advice was always willingly given when needed. Without these programs the production of this flora would have been much more difficult if not impossible. At this time the computer was an Amstrad 1512DD computer fitted with a 32Mb hard disk.

The first step was to digitise the boundary of the Vice-county by listing the six-figure map reference for every change of direction. Then plant records were transferred from recording cards which had been produced at a time when computer mapping was not commonly available and so it was necessary to produce an overlay which converted the names of the plants into numerical Biological Recording Centre codes. Entering this data took several months, with Rob Wilson and Claire Williams working on separate computers. This data was later combined. Throughout the preparation of the book many additional records have been added to the database. The data has easily survived changes to the computer system with no problems; first to a 386SX/16Mhz with a 40 Mb hard disk and later a major upgrade to a 486DX/33Mhz, now with a total of 320Mb hard disk capacity. At this point a tape back-up system was added for enhanced data protection. With the latter computer all of the maps used in the text were generated in DMAP for Windows and copied to Microsoft Word for Windows via the Windows Clipboard. The text was originally produced in PC-Write but was later transferred to Word for Windows and the final camera ready artwork was produced on an NEC Superscript 610 laser printer.

Thanks to everybody involved!

The '*Nats*' *Kettering & District Natural History Society*

Rob Wilson

After ninety years of existence the Kettering and District Natural History Society, known to members as the 'Nats', remains a group of friendly and enthusiastic naturalists committed to furthering their knowledge of the natural world.

It was formed in 1905, at a meeting attended by only eight people, but it quickly became an established part of local society. During the summers before the First World War exhibitions of wild flowers, all carefully labelled with their scientific and vernacular names, were very popular with the public and were revived during the inter-war years.

After the Second World War the society's membership reached its peak of between 150 and 200. Today, with many other calls on people's time, membership has declined but a regular programme of weekly lectures together with microscopical, ornithological, photographic and botanical meetings in the winter and field meetings in the summer still continues, offering members the opportunity to choose from over 100 meetings a year and members still enjoy the friendly association with people of similar interests that has been an important feature of the society throughout its history.

The botanical section has always been very active, and has kept a card index of the local flora since the early 1950s. Since 1970 the section has worked towards the publication of a new local Flora, the largest project ever undertaken by the society.

Throughout its existence naturalists of both local, national and international reputation have been associated with the Society. James Fisher, the prominent ornithologist and Miriam Rothschild have both held the post of vice-president. Prominent local botanists who were actively involved with the society include Albert Wallis, Walter Mayes, 'Billy' Becks, Marjorie Laundon, William Lee, Bill Warner, Frank Robinson, Miss Fairey, Frank Adams and Sir George and Lady Chester. Sir George Chester achieved professional recognition in fields far removed from natural history but in his early years he contributed significantly to the first *Flora of Northamptonshire*. It is appropriate therefore that the society's members should be largely responsible for the second *Flora* of the county.

This publication is not the first book that members of the society have been responsible for, either as individuals or as society members. These include *'The First Fifty Years'* (KDNHS 1955), a record published by the society in its Jubilee year, books of nature poetry by Herbert J.Hawthorn and George Harrison, the County books volume *'Northamptonshire'* by Tony Ireson (Robert Hale & Co., 1954) and 3 volumes of the Collins New Naturalist Series - *'Flowers of the Coast'* by Ian Hepburn (President in 1955); *'Fleas, Flukes and Cuckoos'* by Miriam Rothschild and *'The Fulmar'* by James Fisher.

The Flora of
NORTHAMPTONSHIRE
and the Soke of Peterborough~

Some Northamptonshire Botanists

Ioan Thomas

The earliest record for the flora of Northamptonshire comes from a manuscript of Friar Henry Daniel written about 1375. It is described by John Harvey in his book on Mediaeval Gardens (1981):

> *"and a Mallow (probably Malva neglecta Wallr.) which 'nowhere groweth but in woods....and about the midst of England in the Forest of Rockingham between Stamford and 'Cleve' [King's Cliffe] in the right hand of the highway under bushes...."*

Harvey suggests that Daniel spent some of his earlier years learning medicine and botany near Stamford. Later he went to London where he had a botanic garden in Stepney with 252 sorts of herbs.

The first comprehensive account of the plants of the County is in *The Natural History of Northamptonshire* by **JOHN MORTON** (1671-1726). It was published in 1712 in a folio book of 547 pages, and there are several copies in the County including one in Northampton Public Library. Morton took Plot's History of Oxfordshire as his model and spent about 18 years travelling all round the county collecting information. He was very interested in geology and especially in fossils and he comments on a great variety of topics. Sir Hans Sloane gave him much encouragement and some of the correspondence between them is published in Druce's *Flora of Northamptonshire* (1930). Sloane supported Morton's election as a Fellow of the Royal Society in 1703, when he was 32, so he must have established his reputation long before his book was published. Sloane also gave much help in finding subscribers. It must have been a difficult task to raise the funds needed to publish this great work from the small village of Oxendon near Market Harborough, where Morton was curate and then rector until his death.

Morton describes more than two hundred species of plants, many from his own observations, but he also enlisted the help "of several Persons of great Curiosity and Skill in Botany", mentioning by name those living in Peterborough, Oundle, Preston and Cosgrove. He writes "....did this County really yield any other kinds of new and undescribed plants...they could scarce have escaped us." This intention to be comprehensive is worth noting because one of the great problems in writing a County *Flora* lies in finding all the plants which should be included. He describes also many fungi, lichens and mosses - but considered the spangle galls on oak leaves to be a fungal growth. Druce records that Morton gives 197 new county records.

Morton's sources for correct names and previous county records include Gerard's Herball (1597) and William How's *'Phytologica Britannica'* (1650). How's book records mountain everlasting *(Antennaria dioica)* "on a goodly heath at Barnack", where it still occurs at one of its most southerly sites in Britain, and pasqueflower *(Pulsatilla vulgaris)* where over 10,000 plants were recorded. The uncultivated area around Barnack was probably much greater then than it is now. Morton was an acquaintance of John Ray and was inspired by him. Ray was 43 years older than Morton and he gave the same sort of encouragement which Druce had as a young man from the octogenarian Miles Joseph Berkeley.

GEORGE BAKER (1781 - 1851) had similar aims to Morton and even at the age of 13 had prepared a manuscript on the History of Northampton. Between 1815 and 1841 he produced five volumes on the History and Antiquities of the County of Northampton. He was ably assisted, especially with botanical and geological records, by his sister **ANNE ELIZABETH BAKER** (1786-1861). She was particularly interested in folk lore and published a *'Glossary of Northamptonshire Words and Phrases'* in 1854, after her brother's death and dedicated it to his memory. She records, among others, that lesser celandine *(Ranunculus ficaria)* was known as golden guineas, that angelica *(Angelica sylvestris)* was jack-jump-about, and that the bedeguar galls of dog rose *(Rosa canina)* were "placed by boys in the coat-cuffs as a charm to prevent flogging".

Detailed records of 423 species of plants in the neighbourhood of Daventry are in a paper written by **WILLIAM LOWNDES NOTCUTT** (died 1870) and published in The Phytologist in 1843, pages 501-508. The list is particularly valuable because he records what he had found over a three or four year period within a range of three and a half miles from Daventry. Some of the localities will have been lost due to road building and the extension of the town, but the records are sufficiently precise for an accurate comparison to be made with the present day. The list added 60 species to the County Flora, and establishes, for example, that rosebay willowherb *(Chamerion angustifolium)* was not present in the area. He mentions several plants, including grass-of-Parnassus *(Parnassia palustris),* which had been recorded previously in the district, but which he was unable to find.

Druce regrets that, though William Notcutt's son was one of his friends, he knew very little about the father. He was "either a Chemist and a Druggist or a Congregational Minister, but possibly both".

MILES JOSEPH BERKELEY (1803 - 1889) was a Northamptonshire botanist with an international reputation. But for many years he seemed to be a "prophet without honour in his own country". This is probably because he was a painstaking scholar whose busy life as curate and schoolmaster at Woodnewton near King's Cliffe did not leave much time for meetings with other scientists. Eventually at the age of 76 he was elected a Fellow of the Royal Society; a few years earlier he was given a government pension.

Berkeley's main interest was fungi and for fifty years he was the acknowledged British expert. In the 1840s he carried out detailed investigations into the cause of the potato blight, which was devastating Ireland and afflicting most of western Europe. Many of his contemporaries considered the fungus arose from the decay, but Berkeley became convinced that the fungus was causing the decay. With this conclusion he anticipated by about twenty years Pasteur's great work on the germ theory of disease.

Berkeley was born near Oundle, where his father was Resident Agent for the Biggin Estate. After being at school for a short time in Oundle, and then at Rugby, he went to Christ's College, Cambridge where he graduated as eighth senior optime in the Mathematical Tripos. He was a contemporary at Christ's with Charles Darwin's elder brother Erasmus, and this may be one of the reasons why Berkeley was asked to report on the fungi collected by Darwin during the voyage of the Beagle.

Berkeley's wife, Cecilia Emma, helped him greatly as she was an accomplished linguist and they were both skilled in making drawings and paintings of fungi. They had thirteen children and Berkeley became a schoolmaster as well as curate in order to support the family. Nevertheless he found time to write, among other books, the 'Introduction to the Study of Cryptogamic Botany' which became the standard text on fungi and mosses.

He became Editor of the *Journal of the Royal Horticultural Society* in 1865 and was responsible for the five volumes which came out between 1866 and 1879. He also contributed regularly to *The Gardeners' Chronicle*. In 1868 he was presented to the more valuable living of Sibbertoft near Market Harborough, and used to travel from there to London twice a week. Among other duties he examined in botany, and he once said that he had not set any questions for one examination in the subject which he could not have answered at six years old.

He contributed about a hundred of the records noted in Druce's *Flora of Northamptonshire*, including the first record for man orchid *(Aceras anthropophorum)* - at Barnack about 1850. And in 1884, at the age of 81, he contributed a paper on the flora of north Northamptonshire to a meeting of the Midland Union of Natural History Societies at Peterborough.

GEORGE CLARIDGE DRUCE (1850 - 1932) is the key name in any review of Northamptonshire's botanists. In 1879 he helped to found the *Journal of the Northamptonshire Natural History Society* and over the next thirty or more years regularly contributed articles on the flora of the county. These were brought together, and added to, in 1930 when he published the *Flora of Northamptonshire*. He was then in his eightieth year, and the delay can be explained by the fact that he had written Floras of Oxfordshire, and Berkshire and Buckinghamshire before returning to his first love, the *Flora of Northamptonshire*.

The Flora is a remarkable book. For each species he records the first County record, and its distribution in each of seven districts, with the authority for each record. Many of the records are confirmed by his own observations. He must have travelled many hundreds of miles in Britain and he was also botanising on the continent. In 1873 he added over 700 species to his herbarium. He must have been a prodigious worker and D.E.Allen notes in his book on *'The Naturalist in Britain'* that Druce wore unfashionable elastic-sided boots to save time as he went from fieldwork to his desk.

Druce, like Berkeley, was interested in wild flowers from an early age. He tells that by the time he was six years he could recognise four species of violets. He also collected

butterflies and moths, and became interested in the food plants of their caterpillars. He was apprenticed to the firm of P.Jeyes & Co., Chemists in Northampton, and in his twenty-first year he helped to found the Pharmaceutical Association and took part in their botanical walks.

Druce must have been something of a genius at getting people to work together. When the Natural History Society was founded in 1876 the town of Northampton was separated into many different social and religious cliques, but Druce and his friend Jecks managed to cross boundaries and create something entirely new. H.N.Dixon writes in an obituary "few gathered friends so easily".

In 1879 he bought a chemist's shop in the High in Oxford, and although he knew only one person in the city when he went there, within a year had founded the Oxford Natural History Society. He later became Mayor of the City of Oxford, and Curator of the University Herbarium. In 1903 he became the honorary secretary of the Botanical Exchange Club ("if the plant is too abstruse, pack it

off to Dr.Druce") and, in the words of D.E.Allen, "by a combination of charm, audacity, unsurpassable industry, even a certain deviousness", turned that flagging organisation into what has become the flourishing Botanical Society of the British Isles.

One of the young botanists who was greatly helped by the Botanical Exchange Club was **GEORGE CHESTER** (1886 - 1949). Ann Nicol has written about him in her dissertation for a degree and the notes which follow are based on her account. Sir George's herbarium was donated by Kettering Museum to Leicestershire in 1988.

George Chester attended elementary school in Kettering and at the age of 13 began employment in the shoe industry. He was one of the first members of the Kettering and District Naturalist's Society and Field Club and attended evening classes in botany from 1906-8. He took on positions of responsibility in the Trade Union movement, as a magistrate, and in the Kettering Urban Council, of which he became Chairman. He moved to London when he became General Secretary of the National Union of Boot and Shoe Operatives, and his reports have been described as "models of meticulous accuracy". Shortly before he died he was knighted and became a director of the Bank of England.

His love of natural history, which he had from a very early age, combined with a passion for learning and attention to detail, inspired his botanical collecting. His herbarium contains about 3,600 specimens, but only about a third of them were collected by him, and over three hundred specimens were donated to him by Druce. Many of the locality records for Northamptonshire in Druce's Flora were made by Chester.

The main contribution made to an understanding of the county flora by **IAN HEPBURN** (1902 - 1974) was in the writing of two papers published in the Journal of Ecology. In 1942 he wrote a detailed account of the 'Hills and Holes' at Barnack and in 1955 a similar paper on 'The Deeps' at Collyweston. In the Barnack paper Hepburn draws attention to the invading scrub - which was not controlled until the Northamptonshire Naturalists' Trust obtained a lease on the site in 1963. These two ecological papers were based on quadrat surveys in order to give accurate description of the sites, and they drew attention to the need for protection and management of the habitat.

Ian Hepburn was quintessentially an amateur. He was appointed to Oundle School to teach Chemistry in 1925, and for many years was a Housemaster and later Second Master. Botany was only one of the many interests he shared with pupils and colleagues, but he achieved a very high standard, as is evident in the book 'The Flowers of the Coast' which he wrote for the Collins New Naturalist series. His herbarium of Northamptonshire plants is in the biology department at Oundle School. He was President of the Kettering Natural History Society in its 50th anniversary year. The publication by the Society of this new *Flora of Northamptonshire and the Soke of Peterborough* would have given him great pleasure.

The Flora of
NORTHAMPTONSHIRE
and the Soke of Peterborough~

The Climate

Tony John Keech

Northamptonshire has on average a climate, moderately extreme in terms of temperature, with a light to moderate rainfall and rather less sunshine than average. Although the hills within the county borders are low, generally no more than 150 metres above sea level, they have a measurable effect on the climate, especially in respect of fog, local storms, and borderline cases between rain and snow, as temperature falls 1.1 degrees Celsius for every 180 metres gain in altitude. The remains of Rockingham Forest, and the nearby towns of Corby and Kettering, in the north of the county, Wellingborough, and the county town of Northampton a few miles to the south all have a local influence on the climate.

Temperature

The two warmest months in the county are July and August, both with average maximum temperatures of about 22 degrees Celsius. Occasionally June is the hottest month - coincidentally this occurred in the first year of each decade from 1930 to 1970 - but September is sometimes warmer than June. In May and June, sunny days with a cold

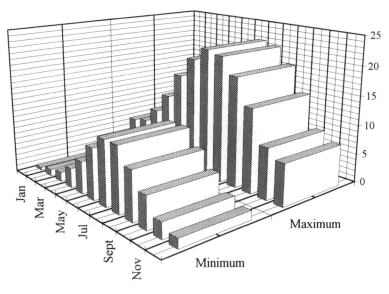

Figure 2 Average monthly maximum and minimum temperatures in degrees Celsius based upon 25 years of records taken at Kettering from 1967-1992

north-easterly wind can be followed by calm cold nights which can result in damaging late spring frosts. These are devastating to the vegetation, especially if they occur during a dry period. During the summer, temperatures above 27 degrees Celsius are quite common and for many years, the highest temperature recorded in Britain was one of 36.7 degrees Celsius, recorded at Raunds in Northamptonshire on August 9th 1911. This was exceeded in August 1990 in Cheltenham.

The coldest months are usually January and February, both with an average maximum temperature of 5.5 degrees Celsius, and average minimum temperatures of 0.5 degrees Celsius. In January 1987, minus 18 degrees Celsius was recorded in Desborough.

In addition wind chill can be an important factor, and there can be as many as 100 nights when there is an air frost, and 140 nights where a ground frost is experienced in the coldest winters, although a mild winter will have fewer.

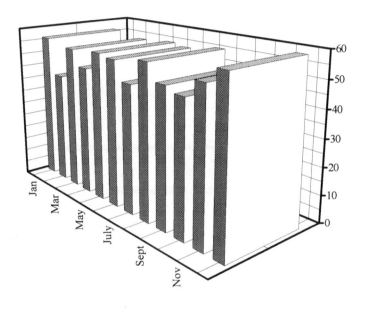

Figure 3 Average monthly rainfall in millimetres,
based upon 25 years of records taken at Kettering from 1967-1992

Rainfall

The higher ground in the south-west of the county tends to receive the highest annual rainfall - perhaps as much as 700 mm - while the average in Northamptonshire as a whole is about 630 mm, comfortably below the average of 850 mm for England and Wales and considerably below the average of 1000 mm for the whole of the British Isles. The rainfall is evenly distributed throughout the year, with little significant difference between the averages for any of the months, although there is often an enormous variation from year to year for individual months, and every month and season has been recorded as the driest or wettest of an individual year. There is a slight tendency, however, for Autumn to be wetter than Spring.

Monthly rainfall can vary from as little as 5.9 mm (May 1990), to as much as 134 mm (December 1978). The highest annual rainfall recorded in Kettering was 810 mm, recorded in 1992, while the lowest annual rainfall 422.4 mm, recorded in 1990.

In the summer the rainfall is generally more sporadic with heavy showers; while in autumn and winter the rainfall tends to be more prolonged and it rains at some time on about half of the days. Until 1992, recent years have had rather less rain than average, but this may only be a temporary fluctuation. The East Midlands and East Anglia are the parts of Great Britain that experience the most thunder, although the last few years have been very quiet, as a result of the recent drier summers.

It is unusual for any appreciable amount of snow to fall in the first half of the winter, and even in severe winters such as that of 1946-7, there was hardly any snow before January. Snowfalls are rarely severe, and generally seem to be less than in adjoining counties.

Sunshine

Northamptonshire does not do particularly well for sunshine, with an average of about 1400 hours annually, recorded at Nene College, Northampton, compared to an average of about 1600 hours for the British Isles. This is less than 35% of the hours of daylight in a year, giving a daily average of about four hours a day.

Wind

The most prevalent wind in Northamptonshire is from the south-west; blowing from this direction about 28% of the time. This wind is comparatively warm, even when it is blowing with some force. Northamptonshire gets its fair share of gales, but, as most originate in the Atlantic, the county's position at some distance from the western seaboard means that they have expended most of their fury by the time they reach us. The wind is strong enough for trees in moderately exposed positions to noticeably lean away from the prevailing wind direction and for the trees in small plantations to grow taller on the side away from the prevailing wind.

The Changing Climate

The climate of Northamptonshire seems to have changed a little in recent years, although whether this has any long term significance it is as yet impossible to say. The seasons all seem to start and end later in the year and temperatures fluctuate more in individual months. The average rainfall has also been appreciably lower than the long term average, with fewer rainy days although individual falls tend to be heavier, but 1992 and 1993 were both noticeably wetter. In recent winters snow has been scarce.

All of this may just be a short term variation, but if this general trend continues there are obvious implications for the county's flora, some of which would benefit from the change, while others would not.

The Flora of
NORTHAMPTONSHIRE
and the Soke of Peterborough~

Geology and Soils

Diana S Sutherland

The county is underlain by a great variety of older sedimentary rocks and much younger superficial deposits, giving rise to an intricate pattern of different soils. The older sedimentary rocks here are of Lower and Middle Jurassic age; they were formed largely under the sea between 185 and 160 million years ago, and were raised to become part of the landmass some 50 million years ago. The superficial deposits, glacial and fluvial, have been laid down on the land surface within the last two million years. To a geologist, all of them are 'rocks', whether they are soft clays and sands, or indurated sandstones and limestones. The overlying soils are closely related to the rocks from which they are derived, in terms of chemical content (e.g. lime) and physical characteristics (e.g. permeability), important factors in determining the flora that will thrive.

THE JURASSIC ROCKS

During the Jurassic most of Britain was covered by a shallow sea in which various types of sediment accumulated according to the depth of water, the distance from the land source, and local conditions; from time to time changes in sea level occurred, so that a succession of different sediments came to be deposited. Though individual rock units can be traced for many miles, they may vary in thickness and character or die out altogether. In general, though, the main rock units can be considered to have been originally a more or less horizontal pile, overlying Triassic and older rocks and overlain in turn by younger Jurassic and Cretaceous strata. In the subsequent uplift, the rock pile became slightly tilted to the south-east. Erosion of this landscape has removed the uppermost rocks, stripping the Cretaceous cover and the

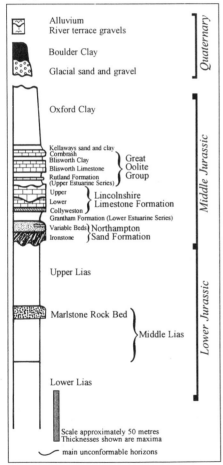

Figure 5: Geological succession in Northamptonshire

upper Jurassic from Northamptonshire; the rivers Welland, Nene, Tove and their tributaries have cut down through the layers of the Middle Jurassic to the Lias below, their outcrops on a geological map now resembling so many contours around each bluff and hillside. The gentle tilt to the south east, though, is responsible for the broad bands of outcrop of the successive rock units, from the oldest (Lower and Middle Lias) in the west to the youngest (the Oxford Clay) in the east of the county.

Lower Lias

The lowest beds, the Hydraulic Limestones, occur beyond the county boundary to the west and north-west, where they are quarried extensively for cement. As the sea deepened, mud deposition increased, only sporadically reverting to limestone or ferruginous limestone which form recognised layers or units within the clays. In Northamptonshire the Lower Lias, occurring around Braunston, Kilsby, Yelvertoft and west of Welford, with a narrow outcrop along the Nene valley beyond Weedon, comprises the Upper Clays, in which ammonites are characteristic, as well as concretionary nodules of the iron carbonate, siderite.

Middle Lias

The sea now became shallower, and some 20 metres of grey, micaceous silty mudstones were deposited, intercalated with several sideritic layers in which bivalves can be conspicuous. One of these ironstone layers is visible near the old railway bridge in the Wildlife Trust reserve west of Farthinghoe. A notably iron-rich and calcareous unit, the Marlstone Rock Bed, forms the upper division of the Middle Lias. It thickens to 9 metres in Oxfordshire, where it caps the escarpment of Edge Hill, and has been quarried as an ironstone and for building stone. In Northamptonshire it contributes a bench in the hilly landscape alongside the Nene westwards to Staverton, and overlooks the Lower Lias plain to the west. In some places it is full of fossil brachiopods: the ribbed rhynchonellid, *Tetrarhynchia tetrahedra*, and the smooth terebratulid, *Lobothyris punctata*, along with belemnites. These can be seen in the local building stones of Middleton Cheney, Byfield and Kings Sutton. The Marlstone thins northwards, disappears around Welford, and reappears, only a metre or so thick, towards Market Harborough, to thicken again into Leicestershire.

Upper Lias

This unit comprises mostly blue-grey clay or mudstone, 55 metres thick, though at the base are thin calcareous beds, containing the ammonites *Harpoceras, Dactylioceras* and *Hildoceras*. The clays occur in the valley bottoms of the main rivers and their tributaries throughout most of the county; they are partly covered by river gravel and alluvium. West of Northampton the Upper Lias occupies more of the hill slopes, capped by remnants of Northampton Sand. The clays were formerly dug in many places for brick-making. Crystals of gypsum (calcium sulphate) are common, produced by the weathering of pyrite in the clay.

Liassic soils

Soil maps show more detailed variation than geological maps, taking into account the parent geology (including remnants of former drift cover) and topographic development (including soil creep and downwash). The only soil survey map published so far for Northamptonshire (Reeve, 1978) covers the area around Long Buckby. Over Liassic rocks, soils are generally clayey to loamy and poorly drained (classification: 'pelostagnogley'); most tend to be acid (e.g. 'Long Load' series: pH 5.2 upper 25cm - 7.5 at 1 metre [Reeve, 1978, p84]). Over the Marlstone Rock Bed, the soil is a more permeable loam (classification: 'argillic brown earth'; e.g. 'Flore' series, pH 7.8 upper 20cm - 7.1 at 60cm [op.cit., p88]). Note also the possible occurrence of ironstone-bearing 'head', formed by solifluxion from overlying Northampton Sand, which gives a slightly acid, 'ferritic' silty clay loam over some outcrops of Upper Lias clay.

Northampton Sand Formation

In central Northamptonshire this widespread rock unit comprises two divisions: a lower Ironstone division 6-8 metres thick, and an upper division known as the Variable Beds, up to 7-8 metres. The ironstone was extensively quarried from the 1850s, locally until the 1970s, and a few of the old quarries remain as valuable nature reserves. The ironstone is an unusual sedimentary rock, containing about 30% Fe; originally this occurred in the reduced Fe^{2+} state in the green alumino-silicate, (berthierine) or the carbonate (siderite), but within about 10 metres of the land surface the rock has a rusty appearance and is composed largely of the hydrated oxide, limonite, in the form of soft ochre and hard brown seams produced by weathering. East and north of Wellingborough the Northampton Sand consists only of ironstone, with no overlying Variable Beds. These come in above the ironstone near Mears Ashby, and thicken towards Northampton. As the name implies they include several rock types; around Mears Ashby, Pitsford, Moulton, Boughton, Kingsthorpe and Weston Favell they consist largely of pale, sandy, ferruginous limestones or calcareous sandstones, but towards Duston and Harlestone the rocks are dominantly brown ferruginous sandstones with a discontinuous calcareous layer through the middle. All varieties have been quarried for building stone and field walling. West and south-west of Stowe-Nine-Churches the ironstone division disappears and the Northampton Sand comprises brown ferruginous sandstones, locally somewhat calcareous (e.g. near Newbottle). In the west of the county Northampton Sand occurs only as hilltop remnants. This rock is the first of the group known as Inferior Oolite; inferior in the sense of lying beneath the Great Oolite group, and in no way to be disparaged.

Northampton Sand Soils

A variety of soils has been mapped east and south-east of Long Buckby (Reeve, 1978). Most are shallow (e.g. 30cm), consisting of fine to coarse ferruginous sandy loam with rock fragments, freely draining, potentially acid (e.g. 'Frilford' pH5.4 and 'Harlestone' series, pH 4.2) and poor in potash. On ironstone areas fragments of limonitic ironstone are common, in a silty clay loam (for example, in the Haselbech area where a detailed soil survey was made by Smee, 1975). Such soils, free draining and acid, have been classified as 'ferritic brown earths' (e.g. 'Banbury' and 'Tadmarton' series with pH 3.8 and 6.1 respectively [Reeve, 1978]). However no soils would probably have more in common with Collyweston (see below) than with the survey has been published in areas that include calcareous Northampton Sand; such Northampton Sand of western Northamptonshire.

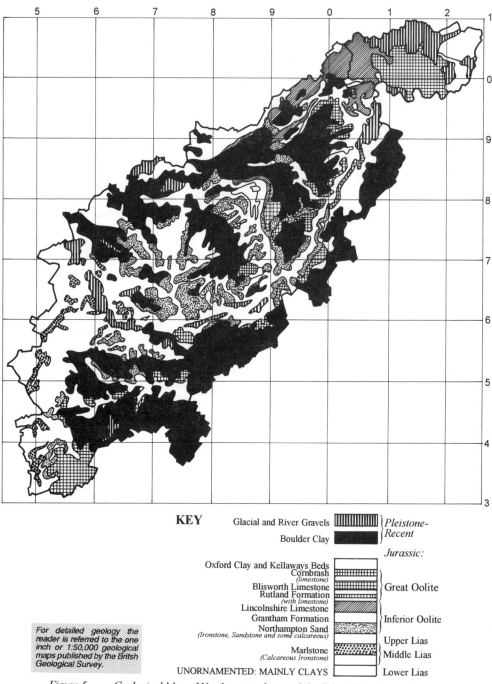

KEY

Glacial and River Gravels	*Pleistone-*
Boulder Clay	*Recent*

Jurassic:

Oxford Clay and Kellaways Beds	
Cornbrash *(limestone)*	
Blisworth Limestone	Great Oolite
Rutland Formation *(with limestone)*	
Lincolnshire Limestone	Inferior Oolite
Grantham Formation	
Northampton Sand *(Ironstone, Sandstone and some calcareous)*	Upper Lias
Marlstone *(Calcareous Ironstone)*	Middle Lias
UNORNAMENTED: MAINLY CLAYS	Lower Lias

For detailed geology the reader is referred to the one inch or 1:50,000 geological maps published by the British Geological Survey.

Figure 5   *Geological Map of Northamptonshire and the Soke of Peterborough*

'Lower Estuarine' (or Grantham Formation)

Overlying the Northampton Sand are 5-7 metres of various white sands, silty clay, and lavender grey and occasional carbonaceous clays, in which vertical carbonaceous rootlets of Jurassic horsetails can often be seen. These are the deposits of a marshy shore rather than an estuary. South of Kettering, where Lincolnshire Limestone is missing, the deposits mapped as 'Lower Estuarine' are now considered to be entirely 'Upper Estuarine' correlating with those which further north overlie the Lincolnshire Limestone.

'Lower Estuarine' soils

The soil survey for the Barnack area in the Soke of Peterborough (Burton, 1981) classifies these soils as 'typical brown sands' ('Frilford' series), with fine sand >70% and clay, 18%, non calcareous (pH generally 6-7 but locally <4.5), and with rapid drainage. Organic carbon content is generally low in surface layers and erosion can be a problem; rabbit burrows are common. These soils are found as narrow bands on hill slopes, following the outcrop of the parent rock.

Lincolnshire Limestone

This marine limestone is absent from much of Northamptonshire, a thin representative reaching as far south as Maidwell, Harrington and Geddington; it thickens in a north-easterly direction through Weldon to the Soke of Peterborough into Lincolnshire. The Lower Lincolnshire Limestone is sandy at the base (up to 30% fine sand, with mica flakes and shell fragments [Taylor, 1963], a fissile, cross-bedded unit that gives rise to Collyweston 'slates'. The lower beds, and horizons within the Lower Lincolnshire Limestone are often poorly cemented or decalcified, occurring as loose yellowish sand. The limestone itself is fine-grained and only sparsely oolitic. It contains some characteristic fossils, including an elongate screw-like gastropod (*Nerinea*). In the wide outcrop south of Stamford the limestone is used for rubble building and field walls.

The Upper Lincolnshire Limestone has a more restricted outcrop in Northamptonshire, extending in a belt some 3 miles wide from south-west of Corby through Stanion and Weldon to Apethorpe and Kingscliffe. Further outcrops occur in the area around Wittering, Barnack and Wansford, and the unit widens and thickens into Lincolnshire. The Upper Lincolnshire Limestone is oolitic, sometimes shelly, and locally well cemented by sparry calcite; it is the source of several well-known building stones.

Lincolnshire Limestone soils

Soils on the Collyweston base of the Lower Lincolnshire Limestone are described (Burton, 1981) as 'pararendzina', a lithomorphic soil in which the top A horizon rests directly on calcareous bedrock. It consists of fine sand (60-200µm) with some platy fragments of limestone, but the pH is quoted as 5.2 (op.cit., p38). A widespread soil characteristic of the limestone plateau is less sandy, a shallow (30cm) 'brown rendzina, Sherborne series' (again rarely having a B horizon), in which clay-size material forms more than 18%. Limestone fragments occur and the pH quoted is 8.3. All these soils drain rapidly.

The Great Oolite Group: 1. 'Upper Estuarine Series' (Rutland Formation)

Overlying the Lincolnshire Limestone is a varied succession up to 12 metres thick; over a thin basal ironstone horizon the lowest beds are usually white or grey silts with plant rootlets, formed on a marshy shore. They pass up into a repetition of rhythmic units, each generally comprising the sequence: laminated clays with marine bivalves; oyster marls or limestone; silts and sands with burrows of shallow-water organisms; and an uppermost rootlet horizon marking temporary marine recession. South of the Lincolnshire Limestone outcrop one such unit is dominant, its limestone bed conspicuous and mapped as the Upper Estuarine Limestone; it is 1-2 metres thick and is locally sandy and fissile, full of shell debris and echinoid spines, or with layers of algal deposits. In south-west Northamptonshire, this limestone thickens to more than 3 metres and a wider outcrop is found around Helmdon, Culworth and Farthinghoe.

'Upper Estuarine' soils

In the north-east, the soils include clay or clay loam (classified as 'pelo-stagnogley') of low permeability. For 'Denchworth' series the pH is 8.1 (Burton, 1981, p42). Also on this variable geology is silty clay loam ('Ufford Complex'), non-calcareous, with pH 6.1-6.7 (op.cit., p69). Towards the south the outcrop of the limestone unit will have produced more calcareous soils.

2. Blisworth Limestone (Great Oolite Limestone)

This limestone, up to 7 metres thick, crops out in eastern Northamptonshire on the upper slopes of the Nene valley; on higher ground away from the valley, and in the south, it is generally overlain by superficial glacial deposits. It varies from fine-grained (micrite) to spar-cemented shelly limestone; it is not commonly oolitic, but smooth superficial ooliths are often present, which are grains with a micrite coating. Brown marly partings are common between beds. The lower beds contain the small brachiopod *Kallirhynchia sharpi*, and bivalves include *Modiolus, Pholadomya* and the ubiquitous oyster (*Praeexogyra hebridica*). Limestones are typically thinly bedded or flaggy within a metre or so of the surface, due to frost action and weathering.

Blisworth Limestone soils

The upland soil is classified by Burton (1981) along with that developed on the Lincolnshire Limestone (see above) as 'brown rendzina (Sherborne series)', a thin (25-40cm) calcareous stony soil resting on fissured limestone.

3. Blisworth Clay

A variable thickness of grey clay, some 6 metres around Stanion but thinning away south-eastwards, overlies the Blisworth Limestone. The outcrop forms narrow belts on the uplands alongside the Nene valley, from Nassington to Rushden, with remnants on high ground near Irchester, south of which it becomes hidden beneath glacial deposits.

Blisworth Clay soils

Heavy, poorly drained soil is characteristic. The 'Denchworth' series, classified as 'pelo-stagnogley', is a firm clay, slightly calcareous, with pH 8.1-8.4 (Burton, 1981, p42).

4. Cornbrash

The Lower Cornbrash is a thin, rubbly limestone with marl, overlain by a more massive or flaggy Upper Cornbrash having a basal bed of rolled limestone pebbles indicating contemporaneous erosion.   Only about 2 metres thick, it occurs along the uplands east of the Nene beyond Wellingborough, and as outliers to the west, the outcrop often restricted by a capping of Boulder Clay.   *The soil is classified with other limestones (see 'Sherborne' series, above).*

Kellaways Clay and Kellaways Sand

The clay, about 2 metres thick, overlies the Cornbrash east of the Nene, for example near Raunds, and is in turn overlain by about 3 metres of silty Kellaways Sand. *They give rise to acid soils (pH 4.1): 'pelo-stagnogley (Long Load)' and 'stagnogley (Langley)' respectively, the underlying clay having low permeability (Burton 1981).*

Oxford Clay

The eastern margin of Northamptonshire is occupied by Oxford Clay, a thick marine clay containing abundant ammonites and bivalves which is exploited for brick-making at Peterborough. *At outcrop it gives a dark 'pelo-stagnogley' soil ('Denchworth' series pH 8.1 [Burton, 1981, p42]).*   Much of this area, though, is overlain by Boulder Clay.

PLEISTOCENE AND RECENT DEPOSITS (DRIFT)

For part of the last 2 million years the landscape of Britain was covered by ice-sheets which extended southwards in extreme cold periods and decayed by melting in intermittent temperate periods.   Around the fringe of the ice sheets the rocks were affected by permafrost, accompanied by severe frost-shattering and mechanical disruption by frost-heave.

There is evidence for four glacial advances in Britain, but the last one (the Devensian (26,000-10,000 years BP) did not reach Northamptonshire, which lay in a zone of permafrost. Earlier glacial advances however had brought with them enormous quantities of rock material scoured from distant sources including the Jurassic of Yorkshire, the chalklands of Lincolnshire, the Carboniferous of Derbyshire, Triassic sandstones and igneous rocks of Leicestershire, as well as the widespread variety of local clays and ironstones. Decay of the ice sheet left thick deposits of glacial till, consisting of dark grey clay containing assorted pebbles and derived fossils; the Northamptonshire Chalky Boulder Clay includes pebbles of chalk, flint and brown quartzite, as well as fossils such as *Gryphea*, ammonites and belemnites. Boulder Clay occupies wide areas of the county east and west of the Nene north of Thrapston, and caps the relatively high ground of the interfluves around Wellingborough and Northampton, where it is more dissected. Extensive areas occur again around the Tove in the south.

Boulder Clay Soils

These are mostly heavy, poorly drained 'stagnogley' and 'pelo-stagnogley' soils; they are calcareous ('Hanslope' with chalk fragments has pH 7-7.8 [Reeves, 1981]) or they may be acid where leached ('Ragdale' is described as non-calcareous, leached of carbonate to 40cm, though chalk remains in the lower profile and pH increases from 5.7 to 7.8 at 80cm depth [Burton, 1981, p91]).

Sand and Gravel

Some of the glacial material was deposited by meltwaters in the form of washed sands and gravel; they occur in irregular but extensive areas beneath and within the boulder clay, for example on the high ground above the Nene at Wollaston, further west around Old and Scaldwell, and quite widely around West Haddon, Long Buckby, and Great Brington. Very extensive continuous tracts of gravels are mapped along the upper course of the Nene north-west of Nether Heyford. To the south, sand and gravel deposits are associated with Boulder Clay around Milton Malsor and Collingtree and are widely distributed south of Towcester. Pebbles are similar to those found in the Boulder Clay, with less chalk.

Along the Nene valley north-east of Northampton gravels form a series of river terraces and underlie the silty-clay alluvium. There are extensive gravel workings and flooded pits in the valley.

Soils of the glacial gravels and fluvial deposits

These are permeable sandy loam soils with flint and quartzite, potentially acid ('Sutton' series), or also with ironstone ('Dodford' series) which can be calcareous below 70cm (Reeve, 1978); some are calcareous throughout (Burton, 1981, p105).

The valley alluvium, though, gives rise to humic clayey soil (e.g. 'Fladbury' series) with pH 6.1 increasing to 7.5 below 66cm (Reeve 1978).

Peat and Tufa

Since the end of the Devensian glacial period, about 10,000 years BP, the sea level has generally risen, but with fluctuations that caused the development of peat beds, particularly near and to the east of Peterborough. The peat soils are often wet unless drained; some are calcareous in limestone valleys (Burton 1981).

Tufa is not uncommon, but deposits are seldom large enough to be depicted on published maps. It is formed where calcareous groundwater springs emerge and precipitate calcium carbonate in the form of a soft paste or a hard, porous limestone. Such deposits are found especially at springs near the base of the Northampton Sand (e.g. near Northampton, Haselbech, and Wellingborough), and locally where limestone overlies clay.

References [and further reading]

Burton R.G.O.,, Soils in Cambridgeshire II Sheet TF00E/10W (Barnack). Soil Survey Record No 69 1981

[Hains B.A. and Horton A.,, British Regional Geology: Central England. HMSO 1969]

[Horton A.,, Geology of the Peterborough district. Mem. British Geol. Surv. 1989]

Reeve M.J.,, Soils in Northamptonshire I Sheet SP66 (Long Buckby). Soil Survey Record No. 54 1978

Smee D.K.,, Soil mapping: a case study at Haselbech Northamptonshire. Compton Russell 1975

[Sylvester-Bradley P.C. and Ford T.D.,, Geology of the East Midlands. Leicester Univ. Press 1968]

Taylor J.H.,, Geology of the country around Kettering, Corby and Oundle. Mem.Geol.Surv.GB 1963

Geological Maps:

(1:50,000)

Sheets 157 (Stamford), 158 (Peterborough), 170 (Market Harborough) (1in.), 171 (Kettering), 184 (Warwick), 185 (Northampton), 186 (Wellingborough), 201 (Banbury), 202 (Towcester) (1in.)

(1:250,000)

52N 02W East Midlands

The Flora of
NORTHAMPTONSHIRE
and the Soke of Peterborough~

The Landscape

Rob Wilson

It has been said that no traveller will visit Northamptonshire for its landscape, that its beauty spots are few and there is no coast or spectacular range of hills. Others have stated that it is as completely representative of our green and pleasant land as Shakespeare's Warwickshire. There is a degree of truth in both points of view. There is no dramatic scenery but for the most part it is a countryside where a more subtle beauty can be found by those who can appreciate it and there is a great variety to be discovered within the gently rolling hills and fenland.

Northamptonshire, which in this context is taken to include the Soke of Peterborough, runs diagonally from north-east to south-west across the heart of England. It has a length of about seventy miles but a width of no more than twenty-six miles, and in some places it is as narrow as seven miles; it covers an area of about 1000 square miles.

The landscape of much of the county is formed by the Northamptonshire Uplands, a countryside of low, undulating hills separated by valleys. They run from the northern extremity of the Cotswolds in the south-west to join the limestone scarp lands of Lincolnshire that extend a few miles inside the county border in the north-east. Confined within the county's borders, these low hills stand above the Fens in the north-east and the Midland Plain in the west. They are responsible for the individual look of the county, and make its landscape distinguishable from that of adjoining counties, even those where ranges of low hills predominate. Beyond Peterborough, in the extreme east of county, a small area of fenland is contained by the Nene and Welland valleys. It is the lowest land in the county, barely above sea level.

At the end of the last ice age the site where Peterborough now stands was on the shore of a vast inland lake that stretched from the Humber estuary as far south as the present site of Cambridge and east to the present coastline. It was formed by ponded river water trapped by the still frozen North Sea. Sediment from this lake formed the level land that we know as the Fens. This is one of the youngest landscapes in the country, created from swamps, winding rivers and mud flats by mediaeval engineers. Their irregular grid of drainage channels, often between banks well above the level of the adjoining land, have made the area that, for the present, is amongst the richest farming land in the country, although the continued drying of the land and the subsequent soil erosion must mean that its productive days are limited. This small area of the county has more in common with East Anglia than with the rest of Northamptonshire.

Within the uplands, the land tilts down to the south, leaving the highest hills in the north-west. Here is Arbury Hill, the highest point in the county, which stands 734 feet above sea level. The average height of the hills is only some 300 feet. Outcrops of clay and limestone combine to form a rich marl that adds greatly to the quality of the land;

which is extensively used for mixed farming and can still be a patchwork of differing colours in the summer - golden acres of ripening grain contrasting with the lush green of pasture land, unfortunately interspersed with the harsh yellow of oil seed rape. Unfortunately agricultural advances have had a detrimental effect on the landscape. While enclosure hedges still border many fields, more hedges have been removed than is often thought desirable, although the fields are often still small enough to impart a human scale to the countryside. Where the hedges have disappeared though, the countryside once more approaches the appearance of the 18th century pre-enclosure landscape.

Trees are as much a part of the landscape as the hedges and fields. Much of Northamptonshire was once part of the great Royal Forest that stretched from Oxford to the edge of the Fens at Stamford. By 1580, though, woodland clearances meant that large wooded areas were confined to three large districts: Whittlebury, Salcey and Rockingham Forest. Large woods still exist in these areas today, while smaller woods and plantations are to be found in most other areas. These range from small game coverts to ancient woodlands covering many acres. Rockingham Forest, in the north of the county between the village of Rockingham and the current county boundary near Stamford, contains the largest areas of woodland. Unfortunately many areas now contain modern conifer plantations, but much ancient broad-leaved woodland still remains.

From its central location in the country, Northamptonshire is a watershed for midland rivers. From the hills around Daventry the Cherwell flows south to join the River Thames at Oxford, the Nene and the Welland flow east through the Fens to the Wash and the Avon flows through Warwickshire to the Severn estuary near Tewkesbury. The larger river valleys, especially those of the Welland and Nene, are still commonly used as pasture land. Some of these pastures in the two main river valleys still serve as flood meadows during the winter when the faster flow of water from the hills within the county backs up behind the slower flow of water across the fens. In recent years many of the flood meadows in the Nene valley between Northampton and Thrapston have disappeared beneath the advancing tide of gravel extraction.

In the north of the county, quarrying for ironstone has left a different sort of scar, with some of the older quarries left as abandoned spoil heaps thinly disguised by alien plantings, or occasionally abandoned to nature. More recently quarried land has been restored but here the idiosyncrasies of the original landscape are replaced by bland, man-made countryside.

Before 1964 Northamptonshire shared a border with nine counties, more than any other in England. Along the borders of Warwickshire, Lincolnshire, Buckingham, Bedfordshire Huntingdonshire, Cambridgeshire, Rutland, Leicestershire and Oxfordshire, some trace of the character of these adjoining areas can be discerned; less obvious than the Fenland character, but it is there for anyone to see. Because of the handiwork of man, the county does have a distinctive character of its own, with ironstone villages set amongst rolling enclosure farmland, the ironstone quarries of the north and the gravel pits that now form a series of lakes along the Nene valley. Renowned nationally as the county of Squires and Spires, the character of the landscape is more subtle than the admitted beauty of its country houses and churches and is unfortunately not appreciated even by many people who have spent their lives within the area.

Arable Land

(Top left) common poppies in an arable field at Rothwell; *(top right)* arable weeds on disturbed ground beside the Brixworth by-pass; *(bottom left)* venus's-looking-glass at the edge of a sugar beet field; *(bottom right)* scentless mayweed dominating a field of rape.

(Top left) a decreasing weed of stubble fields, round-leaved fluellen; *(top right)* night-flowering catchfly, a scarce weed of unsprayed calcareous fields; *(bottom)* a set-aside field near Corby.

Churchyards

(Top left) hoary plantain in Woodnewton churchyard; *(top right)* fiddle dock in Bozeat churchyard; *(bottom left)* meadow saxifrage in Weldon churchyard; *(bottom right)* white butterbur in Castle Ashby churchyard.

Grasslands

(Top left) autumn gentian at Collyweston Deeps; *(top right)* adder's-tongue, a typical plant of unimproved pasture; *(bottom)* Barford Mead, a species rich meadow that is now a Wildlife Trust reserve.

(Top left) early-purple orchid and pasqueflowers; *(top right)* knapweed broomrape; *(bottom left)* dropwort and *(bottom right)* cowslips; all found at Barnack Hills and Holes.

(Top) An extremely rare example of a flood meadow in the Nene valley; *(bottom left)* cuckooflower in Yardley Chase; *(bottom right)* greater tussock-sedge, an uncommon plant of marshland.

Heathland

Hedgerows

(Top left) petty whin is found at Harlestone Heath; *(top right)* heather is also a rare heathland species in the county; *(bottom)* goat willow in a hedgerow at Harrington

(Top) blackthorn in flower in Geddington Chase; *(bottom left)* spindle on the edge of a wood near Ufford; *(bottom right)* wild roses at Rothwell Gullet nature reserve.

Quarries

(Top left) hart's-tongue and *(top right)* common spotted-orchid at Rothwell Gullet nature reserve; *(bottom)* a typical abandoned Northamptonshire ironstone quarry.

Walls

(Top left) tower cress growing on a wall in Gayton churchyard; *(top right)* ivy-leaved toadflax, a common plant on walls; *(bottom)* black spleenwort on a limestone wall at Isham.

Waste Places

(Top left) rosebay willowherb dominates a railway bank at Corby; *(top right)* bee orchids on the abandoned airfield at Harrington; *(bottom left)* colt's-foot on waste land at Ringstead; *(bottom right)* deadly nightshade, more commonly found on calcareous soils.

Water

(Top left) celery-leaved buttercup in a pond in Kingswood, Corby; *(top right)* water-violet beside Borough Fen duck decoy; *(bottom left)* water chickweed at Maidwell; *(bottom right)* arrowhead, a common plant of rivers and canals in the county.

(Top) lesser water-plantain, a rare plant of fen ditches in the Soke of Peterborough; *(bottom)* the upper reaches of the River Ise at Desborough.

(Top) wood vetch at Mantles Heath; *(bottom)* primrose and woodruff in High Wood Wildlife Trust reserve.

(Top left) herb-paris, an indicator of ancient woodland, in Vivian's Copse; *(top right)* wood spurge, first discovered in Yardley Chase in 1989; *(bottom)* bluebells in coppiced woodland, Stoke Wood.

(Top left) bird's-nest orchid in Stoke Wood; *(top right)* fly orchid in Wakerley Spinney; *(bottom)* yellow star-of-bethlehem in Badsaddle Wood.

Plant Habitats

Arable Fields Gill Gent

Whereas the arable areas in the county have steadily increased since the Second World war, the diversity of weed species has declined dramatically. With cleaner seed and effective herbicides many have been all but eliminated. Cornflower *(Centaurea cyanus)* and corncockle *(Agrostemma githago)* have completely disappeared from our fields, although the sudden appearance of the latter at Lyveden New Bield when a hedge was removed in 1993 leads one to suppose that the seed may lie dormant for many years. Other species have, perhaps, not declined so drastically and it is still possible to find scarlet pimpernel *(Anagallis arvensis)*, scentless mayweed *(Tripleurospermum inodorum)* and field pansy *(Viola arvensis)* along the perimeters of most fields and occasionally a colourful field of poppies *(Papaver rhoeas)*.

Spraying with herbicides against broad-leaved species may have led to a decline in the number and variety of arable weeds, but it has created opportunities for invasive narrow-leaved species such as common couch *(Elytrigia repens)* and black-grass *(Alopecurus myosuroides)* which have increased.

The limestone areas to the north and east of the county still have odd fields where venus's-looking-glass *(Legousia hybrida)*, night-flowering catchfly *(Silene noctiflora)* and dwarf spurge *(Euphorbia exigua)* occur but the two fluellens - *Kickxia spuria* and *Kickxia elatine* - once a feature of autumn fallow fields in this area - are found but rarely now.

As a contrast, on the more peaty fields of the area to the north-east of Peterborough the following species can be seen where the sprays do not reach - large-flowered hemp-nettle *(Galeopsis speciosa)*, field woundwort *(Stachys arvensis)* and treacle mustard *(Erysimum cheiranthoides)* - species which are very uncommon throughout the county.

The lighter sandy soil areas to the west and north of Northampton have a few weeds typical of such areas, such as corn spurrey *(Spergularia rubra)* and field bugloss *(Lycopsis arvensis)* and the striking corn marigold *(Chrysanthemum segetum)*, although the latter is more likely to be seen now on new road verges and other disturbed ground.

Sadly the list of arable weed species is a fast declining one, although the recent introduction of set-aside, a scheme whereby for a cash incentive a farmer takes 15% of his land out of cultivation for a three to five year period, has led to a surprising reappearance of many cornfield species. One field near Newborough, in the Soke of Peterborough was full of rarely seen weeds including large-flowered hemp-nettle, field woundwort and night-flowering catchfly *(Silene noctiflora)* and yet another yielded corn parsley *(Petroselinum segetum)* a Red Data Book species. One can only hope that this change in farming policies will arrest to some extent the serious decline in our arable weeds.

Churchyards Gill Gent

Although this habitat be classified under grassland, churchyards throughout the county are becoming very important in their own right as a last refuge for some of our grassland species. The churchyard represents the original communities of plants present when the area was enclosed. These may have been altered by grave plantings which have spread into the community but in the main they have a complement of grasses that were present in old hay meadows - sweet vernal-grass *(Anthoxanthum odoratum)*, downy oat-grass *(Helictotrichon pubescens)* and crested dog's-tail *(Cynosurus cristatus)*. Buttercups *(Ranunculus sp.)* common sorrel *(Rumex acetosa)*, bird's-foot trefoil *(Lotus corniculatus)*, salad burnet *(Sanguisorba minor subsp. minor)* and burnet saxifrage *(Pimpinella saxifraga)* are also very typical, with lady's smock *(Cardamine pratensis)* in the damper areas.

In many churchyards, meadow saxifrage *(Saxifraga granulata)* is quite common and assured of a haven while it has been disappearing from our meadows. Churchyards are also a haven for species such as fiddle dock *(Rumex pulcher)* and wild clary *(Salvia verbenaca)*. Both species are fairly resistant to continuous mowing as are the rosettes of hoary plantain *(Plantago media)*, which are often a feature of late summer.

Grasslands Andrew Robinson

There are now fewer acres of grassland in the county than 50-60 years ago since much has been ploughed to provide land to grow extra cereals. Much of the remaining grassland has been 'improved' by adding fertilisers, herbicides to remove unwanted herbs, and some has been ploughed and re-seeded with rye-grass *(Lolium perenne)* and white clover *(Trifolium repens)* mixture. This 'improved' grassland is of little interest to the botanist. Over 95% of all grassland has been treated in this way.

It is worth remembering that there is no natural grassland in this part of England and that what we have is only maintained by the activities of man and his animals removing any trees and shrubs which occur. The other three types of grassland are determined by the nature of the soil - calcareous, neutral and acidic. Calcareous soils are formed on limestone in Northamptonshire and hence are slightly alkaline. Many of the sites still remaining are on former quarries. These are in the south, as at Charlton and Cosgrove and in the north as at Weldon and Collyweston. The best known of these is at Barnack where the famous 'hills and holes' is now a National Nature Reserve. The vegetation is based on a grassland of upright brome *(Bromus erectus)* and tor-grass *(Brachypodium pinnatum)* with yellow oat *(Trisetum flavascens)*, red fescue *(Festuca rubra)*, quaking grass *(Brizia media)* and many more. There is also a rich and varied display of orchids at Barnack and Collyweston but not at the other sites. However all are characterised by a profusion of flowers including salad burnet *(Sanguisorba minor)*, fairy flax *(Linum catharticum)*, bird's-foot-trefoil *(Lotus corniculatus)*, wild carrot *(Daucus carota)*, lady's bedstraw *(Galium verum)*, hedge bedstraw *(Galium mollugo)*, harebell *(Campanula rotundifolia)*, clustered bellflower *(Campanula glomerata)*, common knapweed *(Centaurea nigra)* and greater knapweed *(Centaurea scabiosa)*. The latter is often parasitised by knapweed broomrape *(Orobanche elatior)*. One of the characteristics of limestone grassland soils is that they are thin, quick-draining soils of the types known as rendzinas.

The commonest type of grassland is on the neutral alluvial river valley soil. These are rich in mineral salts, well drained yet remaining fairly moist throughout the year. They are high yielding for grass crops e.g. hay and silage and flesh on the hoof. Common grasses include perennial rye-grass *(Lolium perenne)*, cock's-foot *(Dactylis glomerata)*, sweet vernal-grass *(Anthoxanthum odoratum)*, crested dog's-tail *(Cynosurus cristatus)* and timothy *(Phleum pratense)*.

Meadows that have traditionally been left to be mown at the end of June or the beginning of July have a later maturing seed crop than those kept for summer grazing. These hay-meadow plants include greater burnet *(Sanguisorba officinalis)*, bulbous buttercup *(Ranunculus bulbosus)*, common vetch *(Vicia sativa)*, yellow rattle *(Rhinanthus minor)* and common knapweed *(Centaurea nigra)*. Wetter areas of river valley meadows often include glaucous sedge *(Carex flacca)*, meadowsweet *(Filipendula ulmaria)*, southern marsh-orchid *(Dactylorhiza praetermissa)* and lady's-smock *(Cardamine pratensis)*.

In Northamptonshire the main acidic soils are the estuarine sands and gravels situated mainly in the west where they are often arable or leys. They are quick draining soils and the few mineral salts are soon leached out so that white sand and grains of quartz stand out. These impoverished soils such as at Harlestone and Lings, have been frequently planted with coniferous trees. The main grasses are the bents *(Agrostis sp.)* with wavy hair-grass *(Deschampsia flexuosa)* and the early flowering annual silver hair-grass *(Aira caryophyllea)*. Associated with these are: heath bedstraw *(Galium saxatile)*, tormentil *(Potentilla erecta)*, sheep's sorrel *(Rumex acetosella)* and whitlow-grass *(Erophila verna)*.

Heathlands Gill Gent

True heathland is a habitat lacking in Northamptonshire as very few acid-soil types occur.

The area known as Harlestone Firs, once part of the larger Dallington and Harlestone Heaths near Northampton, approaches a heathland habitat, but it is only a shadow of former times.

Here only, where areas of conifer plantations planted about the turn of the century are clear-felled, does a remnant of the original vegetation return. In these areas heather *(Calluna vulgaris)*, harebell *(Campanula rotundifolia)*, gorse *(Ulex europaeus)*, broom *(Cytisus scoparius)*, tormentil *(Potentilla erecta)* and wavy hair-grass *(Deschampsia flexuosa)* occur and in some areas bell heather *(Erica cinerea)*, wood cudweed *(Gnaphalium sylvaticum)*, and wood sage *(Teucrium scorodonia)* have occurred sporadically.

The sandy ridings provide habitats for a number of creeping species, in particular bird's-foot *(Ornothopus persupillus)*, tormentil, knotted clover *(Trifolium striatum)* and sand spurrey *(Spergularia rubra)*. Apart from tormentil these species are very rare in the county.

There is a small area of original heathland left where no trees were planted and here the rare petty whin *(Genista anglica)* grows along with marsh pennywort *(Hydrocotyle vulgaris)* and heath bedstraw *(Galium saxatile)*.

One other former heathland, Billing Lings, was once home to many sand loving plants, but in the main these have disappeared with the planting up of the area with assorted conifers.

So called heathlands occur at Sutton and at Castor in the Soke of Peterborough. These are in limestone areas and vary greatly from those in Northamptonshire, but they too are only a relic of their former selves.

Hedges   *Seán Karley*

This County has had a network of hedges as far back as human memory goes. However it is as well to remember that many of these date from the Enclosure Acts of the 18th and 19th centuries, and are not actually very ancient. Some go back for 500 or a thousand years or more, for instance on parish boundaries, or beside old roads such as the Banbury Lane, and these can usually be picked out by the great number of different species of shrubs present. If a hedge has more than about four species in each 30 yard length then it is most probably ancient. The Enclosure Act hedges were almost always planted with "pure" hawthorn; actually these were usually common hawthorn *(Cratageus monogyna)*, but often midland hawthorn *(Cratageus laevigata)* was also present, and so of course were hybrids. In some stretches it may be difficult to find a bush that is not a hybrid!

Traditionally hedges in this area were managed by laying at intervals of ten to twenty years. When the hedge had grown fairly tall and was beginning to show signs of thinning at the base it would be cleared of most of the poorer bits, the taller stems would be cut part way through and then pressed down to one side of the hedge and enmeshed with each other, the whole being held secure with a series of middling thickness upright stakes and a twisted line of thin whippy stems along the top. In due course the base would make new growth and form a new hedge with a strong bottom to keep farm animals in (or out!). For many years this practice was neglected, but recently many farmers have re-introduced it, having realised that as well as being an important part of our traditions it is also a cost effective boundary maintenance technique.

Botanically the more recent hedges are usually fairly dull, although of course they are very important for mammals and birds. The older hedges however often contain more of interest. Gradually other species of shrubs come in to change the hedge proper; blackthorn or sloe *(Prunus spinosa)* is usually one of the first, field maple *(Acer campestre)*, ash *(Fraxinus excelsior)*, oak *(Quercus robur)*, guelder rose *(Viburnum opulus)*, wayfaring tree *(V. lantana)*, wild cherry or gean *(Prunus avium)*, purging buckthorn *(Rhamnus cathartica)* etc. can follow. Elder *(Sambucus nigra)* and rose *(Rosa sp.)* are frequently present, although usually not as part of the hedge itself. Under the hedge the sweet violet *(Viola odorata)* and cuckoo pint or lords-and-ladies *(Arum maculatum)* get their flowering done early before the coarser plants like jack-by-the-hedge or garlic mustard *(Alliaria petiolata)* and cow parsley or keck *(Anthriscus sylvestris)* overtop them. Later in the year white bryony *(Bryonia dioica)* and black bryony *(Tamus communis)* clamber up. They can cover large stretches first with their large leaves but rather insignificant flowers, later with their spectacular berries.

Many hedges still contain trees, which have been allowed to grow unmolested by the hedge laying. Most of the elms *(Ulmus sp.)* have died long since, but in many places their suckers now form a major part of the structure of the hedge itself. oak and ash are often noteworthy, and occasionally others such as gean, rowan *(Sorbus aucuparia)* and even wild service-tree *(Sorbus torminalis)* occur. The field maple sometimes also forms a small tree, as at Ramsden Corner Nature Reserve.

Quarries Seán Karley

Northamptonshire has been subjected to much quarrying, particularly over the last 300 years. In earlier times the main target for the larger quarries was building stone, from the Lincolnshire, Great Oolite and Blisworth limestones, and from the Northampton Sand series. Most such quarries were fairly small scale operations with only a minor impact on the botany of the county, although the Barnack limestone quarries were extensive and active for many centuries. Some iron was also extracted from the Northampton Sand series in Iron Age times, the Roman settlement and later, but the major period of quarrying activity was from Victorian times onwards when great swathes of the landscape were ripped out to feed ironworks at Kettering, Wellingborough and, from the 1930s, at Corby. These quarries left behind them many acres of "Hill and Dale", roughly parallel series of steep ridges of ten to twenty or more feet in height over the intervening troughs. Later operations were required to restore this land to agriculture, so they were levelled and eventually became mediocre pasture or arable fields. Many quarries however were planted up with conifers before this happened and the Hill and Dale was preserved. The other principal feature was a large Gullet along the remains of the working face, usually showing a large steep slope of loose overburden on the worked out side, the exposed but undisturbed strata above the face, and in the bottom often a deeper section where the ore was removed and a flat topped bed of ironstone left behind. This is in many cases now hidden below the growing talus formed from the gradually crumbling face. All of these features can be seen clearly at Irchester Country Park.

The botany of our quarries is dominated by the poor quality of the soils. Often these were initially devoid of any humus and over-endowed with clay. Frequently the drainage was inadequate so they were wet and heavy, but in dry periods prone to severe cracking and desiccation, making them almost impervious to roots. They were only fit for colonisation by some of our toughest, most vigorous plants, i.e. the "weeds". Even after forty or more years of growth they still often have a very open vegetation, particularly on the slopes. Most sites develop first a thin scattering of small herbs such as common bird's-foot-trefoil *(Lotus corniculatus)* and smaller grasses, then a closer cover of coarse grasses containing some of the bigger herbs, and eventually shrubs such as hawthorns *(Crataegus monogyna)* invade and slowly expand to cover the ground. Tree species are not usually important here, but probably will be in another century or so. In essence, our quarries are active examples of the early stages of progression from bare ground to oak-ash *(Quercus robur - Fraxinus excelsior)* woodland.

Against this background of rough vegetation some notable species also find niches. In the early stages of colonisation these often include wild strawberry *(Fragaria vesca)*, blue fleabane *(Erigeron acer)*, common centaury *(Centaurium erythraea)*, common spotted-orchid *(Dactylorhiza fuchsii)* and especially the bee orchid *(Ophrys apifera)*. Within the county this is almost totally confined to old quarries and similar disturbed ground. In the conifer plantations ploughman's-spikenard *(Inula conyza)* is frequent. As the open areas close over the woolly thistle *(Cirsium eriophorum)* is often prominent. It has even been known for this thistle to be exported to Scotland from a Northamptonshire source.

Another type of quarrying operation which is probably at its peak activity now is the extraction of sand and gravel from the Nene valley. The drier parts of these workings develop in much the same manner as the deeper quarries except that the scrub species invading are usually various willow species.

Walls *Joan Birch*

Northamptonshire is often referred to as the county of spires and squires and thanks to these assets, we have hundreds of miles of stone walling enclosing the churchyards in the villages and encompassing the estates of the county landowners. The walls are built of Oolitic limestone or ironstone, both from local quarries, and provide supportive plant habitats. The railway network across the county used brick or stone for bridge supports and it is surprising what will grow on these. All these areas are still largely as they were at the time of Druce although many of the railway tracks are no longer in use for trains.

A wall is an inhospitable place for a plant to grow, mimicking a stark, sheer quarry face, but where there is even a tiny crack in the stone or mortar, and a water supply, a plant will survive.

Lichens are the first colonisers of a wall. They have no roots and often seem like an encrustation on the surface of the stone or brick.

Mosses are important pioneers of rock and brick structures where little else will grow. They hold moisture in their leaves and form humus in which seeds of other plants can germinate.

Many ferns are found growing in limestone crevices or mortar in old walls e.g. an occasional maidenhair spleenwort *(Asplenium trichomanes)*, the commonly occurring wall-rue *(Asplenium ruta-maria)* and rustyback fern *(Ceterach officinarum)*. All grow together on a wall in Isham and there is a wonderful display of common polypody *(Polypodium vulgare)* at Titchmarsh and Castle Ashby. Black spleenwort *(Asplenium adiantum-nigrum)* is fairly commonly seen.

The most frequently recorded plant on a wall must be the ivy-leaved toadflax *(Cymbalaria muralis)*. In towns and villages throughout the area, wherever there is a wall, this alien appears. According to Druce it was first recorded in the county in 1787.

Another common plant recorded everywhere is the perennial pellitory-of-the-wall *(Parietaria judaica)*. It is particularly associated with churchyard walls.

Chickweed *(Stellaria media)* and thyme-leaved sandwort *(Areneria serpylifolia)* commonly occur on south facing walls as does that lover of sunny walls, biting stonecrop *(Sedum Acre)*. The crane's-bills *(Geranium sp.)* grow well in stony places. These calcicoles often appear on wall tops; herb robert *(G. robertianum)* and shining crane's-bill *(G. lucidum)* are common on the county's walls.

Fairly common plants on walls in the county are red deadnettle *(Lamium purpureum)*, common whitlow-grass *(Erophila verna)*, thale cress *(Arabidopsis thaliana)* and the tiny rue-leaved saxifrage *(Saxifraga tridactylites)*.

Uncommon wall dwellers include early forget-me-not *(Myosotis hispida)* which flowers very early; a wonderful display can be seen on some churchyard walls e.g. Walgrave and Brixworth. The lesser chickweed *(Stellaria pallida)* is on walls in Kingsthorpe and Collyweston whilst Navelwort *(Umbilicus rupestris)*, which according to Clare "once grew on every stone", and was recorded by Druce at Peterborough Cathedral, now only occurs at three sites: Litchborough, Canon's Ashby and Eydon.

Ivy *(Hedera helix)* is the commonest climbing plant on walls: it roots in the soil at the foot of the wall and its assimilatory branches are supported by the wall. Its flowers appear in the sun at the top of the wall.

Fern grass *(Desmazaria rigida)* likes dry places and is fairly common on wall tops whilst Wall barley *(Hordeum murinum)* was, at the time of Druce, and still is common in all parts, particularly at the base of the wall.

One plant which is now naturalised throughout the county and common on walls is the yellow corydalis *(Corydalis lutea)* .

Waste Places Phil Aldridge

Like many of the counties in Britain, Northamptonshire has a large number and wide variety of waste places. These areas are often quite small but, nevertheless, may exhibit a varied and interesting flora ranging, taxonomically, from the field horsetail *(Equisetum arvense)*, to various members of the orchid family *(Orchidaceae)*.

A distinctive and unmistakable feature of newly disturbed ground, particularly alongside many of the new roads being built through the county, is the colourful display of the various poppies *(Papaver sp.)*. These include, in decreasing order of frequency but increasing persistence, the common poppy *(P. rhoeas)*, the long-headed poppy *(P. dubium subsp. dubium)* and the prickly poppy *(P. argemone)*. These will grow alongside the lace white of various members of the carrot family *(Apiaceae)* particularly cow parsley *(A. sylvestris)* and the bright yellow flowers of oil-seed rape *(Brassica napus subsp. oleifera)* and, in a few places, the paler yellow of evening primrose *(Oenothera sp.)*

Ruderal communities in and around towns often develop where the hard, dry and bare ground suits a few species while discouraging many of the normally more dominant varieties. Mousetail *(Myosurus minimus)* now a nationally rare plant which had all but disappeared from the county, recently turned up in the Northampton and Peterborough areas. Where the ground has been cleared by fire, rose-bay willow-herb *(Chamerion angustifolium)* and sticky groundsel *(Senecio viscosus)* may thrive.

Finds on roadsides and other waste places near towns and villages may include medicinal and kitchen garden plants. Two members of the goosefoot family, good king henry *(Chenopodium bonus-henricus)* and fat hen *(C. album)* may be found as relics of earlier cottage garden cultivation. Notable in the medicinal plant category is the greater celandine *(Chelidonium majus)* which was grown for use as a purgative and as a remedy for skin disorders. This is easily identified by its orange juice and can be found in and around villages throughout the county.

Relatively undisturbed by people, unpolluted by fertilisers and, in the past, regularly cleared by small fires from steam engines, railway lines, embankments, cuttings and bridges can offer a haven for plants. Well known in this category (and common in Northamptonshire) is the oxford ragwort *(Senecio squalidus)* which, in a comparatively short time, has spread widely along railways from Oxford. The main text describes a similar story, on a smaller scale, for members of the mouse-ear chickweed genus *(Cerastium sp.)*. Maidenhair fern *(Adiantum capillus-veneris)* was recorded from an old railway bridge in the 1970s, but has since disappeared, as has the limestone fern *(Gymnocarpium robertianum)*, formerly found in a railway cutting. Holly-fern *(Polystichum lonchitis)*, normally known from northern Britain, occurred on a railway bridge during the 1970s.

Finally, rubbish tips, both in and away from towns, are good places to look for plants that have been introduced with industrial, household or garden refuse. Dyer's rocket *(Reseda luteola)* and more rarely woad *(Isatis tinctoria)* may be well established where wool was dyed. Larkspur *(Consolida ajacis)*, hollyhock *(Alcea rosea)*, honesty *(Lunaria annua)*, sweet alison *(Lobularia maritima)* and opium poppy *(Papaver somniferum)*, for example, occur on disturbed ground but rarely persist for long. Hemp *(Cannabis sativa)* used to be commonly found from bird seed but has become considerably less so (the last confirmed Northamptonshire record being in the 1950s), whilst amaranth *(Amaranthus retroflexus)* and the bristle-grasses *(Setaria sp.)* and canary-grass *(Phalaris sp.)* found in bird seed, are not uncommon. Root beet *(Beta vulgaris subsp. vulgaris)*, rhubarb *(Rheum x hybridum)*, garden strawberry *(Fragaria ananassa)*, garden cress *(Lepidium sativum)*, cabbage *(Brassica oleracea)* and horse-radish *(Armoracia rusticana)* may also be found.

Don't overlook waste places when botanising around the county as there are many unexpected plants to be found. Unusual finds might include deadly nightshade *(Atropa belladonna)*, pokeweed *(Phytolacca sp.)*, apple-of-Peru *(Nicandra physalodes)* and mintweed *(Salvis reflexa)* while hairy buttercup *(Ranunculus sardous)*, extremely rare within the county, has been recorded from various tip sites across the county although it has, for the time being at least, disappeared. Even on the edges of disused airfields surprises may be found. At one such lime-rich site near Kettering over three hundred bee orchid *(Ophrys apifera)* plants were found flowering in 1991.

Water   Brian Adams

Since the time of Druce, new aquatic habitats have been created; gravel workings have left large flooded areas in the Nene Valley, several reservoirs have been constructed, and the 'ugly miniature mountain regions' which were the disused ironstone workings described by Beeby Thompson, have matured into fine sheltered areas of water, helping to replace field ponds which are disappearing fast, either by being filled in by man or through neglect. However, the most interesting aquatic habitats, the fen ditches in the north east of the county are decreasing. This is all that remains of an extensive valley fen area that existed around Peterborough up to the 1800s. Due to excessive drainage over the years a number of fen ditches are drying up and may soon be filled in. In 1993 Cat's Water on the eastern boundary of the Soke was almost dry in some places. Druce's vivid description of these fen ditches held good in the Peakirk area until the early 1970s when herbicide spraying destroyed large stands of water-violet (*Hottonia palustris*) and other rare aquatics from which it has never recovered; even so this is still an area worth looking at and small pockets of relatively unspoiled fen ditches remain to this day, much as Druce must have seen them: Car Dyke, a drainage channel dug out by the Romans, is particularly rich in aquatic species.

Canals, once a premier location for aquatics have seen an upsurge in holiday traffic in recent years. This has had a detrimental on a number of habitats, although marginals have not been affected, and without this traffic it is doubtful if the canal system would still be in operation.

Rivers and streams are an important habitat in the county. Recently the water quality has improved, particularly the Rivers Nene and Ise, after many years of effluent discharge. This has led to a significant improvement in plant life. Marshland by rivers and streams may sometimes form what can be best described as wet woodland, consisting mainly of alder (*Alnus glutinosa*) willows (*Salix sp.*) and ash (*Fraxinus excelsior*) Most of the remaining habitats of marsh-marigold (*Caltha palustris*) are here as they are relatively undisturbed. One or two of these sites have formed true fen carr with fairly extensive peat depths, notably White Water near to Burghley Park and Birch Spinney near Loddington. True marshland, is best described as waterlogged areas without appreciable amounts of peat. If appreciable peat deposits do exist it is called fen. Marshland therefore can sometimes be easy to drain, the fate a large number of sites have suffered in the past. The drier ones in river plains are often grazed where the danger of flooding makes them unsuitable for draining and really extensive marshland is not present in the county.

There are no acid bogs in the county, although small areas on heathland at Harlestone might have qualified for this title during the past century, but they have long since gone. The 'bogs' referred to in the text are mostly calcareous flushes where some peat has formed, these are very fine areas botanically and some of our rarest aquatic plants are to be found here.

Gravel pits, particularly the older ones, are fine aquatic habitats, being relatively free from pollution as most are only connected to rivers by small dykes if at all. The marginal species, however, need a number of years before becoming established.

Reservoirs are also very good habitats but suffer from fluctuating water levels which can lead to sterile shorelines. Some of the older, unused ones are particularly good with an extensive marginal flora.

The lakes attached to most large estates must still be as Druce would have seen them, and we are indeed fortunate in this county to have so many of them. The osier beds close to a number of them have unfortunately been neglected for many years

Aquatic plants are very sensitive to pollution and disturbance, but unfortunately do not have the same impact on conservationists as do some more flamboyant flowers such as orchids. Therefore some of the most important aquatic sites have suffered damage in the past. Perhaps a more enlightened view may prevail in the future.

Woodlands - ancient and modern   Rob Wilson

The small blocks of woodland   scattered across   the county and the Soke of Peterborough are both ancient - that is they have existed in some form continuously from before 1600AD, and secondary, that is they have evolved or have been planted since that date.   The ancient woodland is confined to the north, where wooded remnants of the ancient, royal Rockingham Forest are to be found east from Corby; and to the south, where a series of ancient woodlands includes Yardley Chase, Salcey Forest, Whittlewood and the group of woodlands south of Daventry.

The land covered by ancient woodland now only accounts for about 5% of the county's area (compared to a national average of 8%), and much of this has changed greatly since the 1950s, when the Forestry Commission began a large scale replanting programme, replacing the indigenous trees with faster growing softwoods.

In recent years this trend has been reversed and our remaining woodland heritage is being managed with greater sensitivity, and in some woods, notably those managed by the Wildlife Trust and the Woodland Trust, (but there are others), a regime of clearing or coppicing has been re-introduced, with consequent benefits to the ground flora and the tree layer.

All of these woodlands still harbour plants that are generally accepted as indicators of ancient woodland, including wood anemone *(Anemone nemorosa)*, nettle-leaved bellflower *(Campanula trachelium)*, yellow archangel *(Lamiastrum galeobdolon)*, herb paris *(Paris quadrifolia)*, greater butterfly orchid *(Platanthera chlorantha)*, early purple-orchid *(Orchis mascula)*, wood sorrel *(Oxalis acetosella)* and lily-of-the-valley *(Convallaria majalis)*. Not all of these are in every ancient woodland and some grow in very small numbers and at very few sites, maintaining a tenuous foothold in their chosen habitat, and it is usually the more common flowers that carpet the woodland floor each Spring and provide much of their emotional attraction.   Short Wood, near Oundle and Badby Wood, near Daventry are both famous for their displays of bluebells *(Hyacinthoides non-scripta)* while striking displays of these and other spring flowers can be seen at most of the woodland reserves as well as within some of the Forestry Commission woodland.

Even where the old order of trees has been totally replaced by foreign species, the native flora of the ancient woodlands, including some county rarities, still manages to survive along the edges of rides and in some cases in the deep shade beneath the canopy of pines.   Possibly the largest colony of bird's-nest orchids *(Neottia nidus-avis)* in Northamptonshire now grows beneath the conifers in the heart of Hardwick Wood.

Much of the ancient woodland of Northamptonshire consists of a mixture in various proportions of oak *(Quercus robur)*, ash *(Fraxinus excelsior)* and hazel *(Corylus avellana)*, with the latter formerly grown for coppicing.   Occasional stands of birch *(Betula pubescens)*, alder *(Alnus glutinosa)* and willow *(Salix sp.)* grow where the soil conditions are suitable. Less common woodland trees such as holly *(Ilex aquifolium)*, field maple *(Acer campestre)* crab apple *(Malus sylvestris)* and wild cherry *(Prunus avium)* can be found scattered through many woodlands. There is a fine display of wild cherry at High Wood, near Daventry, a wood which is also noted for its primroses *(Primula vulgaris)* in the spring. The rarer native trees such as wild service-tree *(Sorbus torminalis)* are generally found in the calcareous areas in the north of the county.

The secondary woodlands rarely contain as much of interest as the ancient woodlands. Nevertheless the older examples are far from dull. The few beech *(Fagus sylvatica)* woods in the county are all secondary woodland or replanting within ancient woodland.

The newer woodlands and plantations, planted for the timber or game cover, are rarely managed in a way sympathetic to plants. Botanically they are uninteresting, and the ground cover often contains only poor examples of the adjoining hedge flora that will survive as long as the tree canopy is incomplete.

Within most deciduous woodlands the dominating understorey plants are hawthorn *(Cratageus monogyna)* and bramble *(Rubus sp.)*, although in some small woodlands planted for game cover, snowberry *(Symphoricarpus albus)* can be quite common. These newer blocks of woodland are often surrounded by fields and pasture where there is little variety of plant life, too far separated from blocks of ancient woodland for woodland plants to cross the open ground between. The same is true of plantations on old quarry sites, common in the ironstone area around Corby, which are often densely planted and leave little room for other plants to establish themselves.

Finally a special mention must also be made of Bedford Purlieus, which is the remnant of a much larger ancient wood standing outside Rockingham Forest. Described by Druce as 'the most flower-rich wood in England', this description is probably still true although some woods outside the county contain more plants specifically associated with ancient woodland. Its survival after threats of ironstone mining may be taken as an indication that much of the woodland in the county now faces a more certain future, although the threat to privatise the Forestry Commission could once more jeopardise those parts of our woodland heritage that fall within their ownership.

References
Marren P. *The Wild Woods, David & Charles 1992*
Pollard E., Hooper M., Moore N.W., *Hedges, Collins New Naturalist 1974*
Colston A. & Perring F. (Eds.) *The Nature of Northamptonshire Barracuda Books 1989*
Laundon J.R. *Semi-natural Vegetation in Northamptonshire, Journal of the Northamptonshire Natural History Society and Field Club, Volume XXXIV June 1964*
and of course
Druce G.C. *The Flora of Northamptonshire T. Buncle and Co. 1930*

The Flora of NORTHAMPTONSHIRE *and the Soke of Peterborough~*

'What time hath stole away'

Jeff Best   *(from Remembrances by John Clare)*

Recent years have seen the appearance of several accounts of the origin and historical development of the vegetation of Northamptonshire, as listed under *References* below. Rather than attempt to needlessly duplicate what is already available, this essay is wholly directed towards consideration of change since the publication of the first Flora in 1930.

For that benchmark study we are indebted to George Claridge Druce, who finally saw it to bed in his eightieth year. Notwithstanding his many other achievements, including no less than five other Floras, this was truly the culmination of his life's work. In retrospect one can only marvel that he managed to assimilate so much information, the majority of which he personally collected, and actually saw through so monumental a venture. Given that the present Flora is the arduous product of the co-ordinated efforts of a Committee, a network of active fieldworkers and the convenience afforded by modern information processing technology, the more remarkable the accomplishment of its predecessor.

Nonetheless, all that can reasonably be expected of each generation is that it endeavours to address the issues of its time, in the sure knowledge that the work, however grand, will be superseded - as both the character of the objects of study and the questions asked of them change.

That Druce was well aware of this inevitability is revealed by the brief verse in his prelude,

> *When Finis comes, the Book we close,*
> *And, somewhat sadly, Fancy goes*
> *With backward step from stage to stage*
> *Of that accomplished pilgrimage...*
> *The thorn lies thicker than the rose!*
> *There is so much that no one knows,*
> *So much unreached that none suppose;*
> *What flaws! what faults! on every page*
> *When Finis comes.*

In order to do justice to both the past and the present, more than literal changes concerning the flora between the first and second Floras is called for. The intervening years have witnessed changes in the approaches to study that is just as important as the changes in the status of plants themselves. It is against this background that subsequent advances are briefly reviewed, before proceeding to consider what has happened to the plantlife of the county in the meantime.

There are few glimpses in Druce, of recognition of 'plant communities' as units of significance. Whilst the present Flora perpetuates the format whereby individual species are treated separately, it does so knowing that the traditional focus upon species as discrete entities, has given way to contemplation of assemblages or 'associations' of species as functional entities - the generic relationships and dynamics of which are now seen as the proper foundation for assessment of status. Sir Arthur Tansley's pioneering work towards this end did not appear until several years after Druce's death in 1932, and further considerable refinement, in the form of the National Vegetation Classification, is only now becoming available, some fifty years later. In response, there have been a few 'ecological' Floras, of for example the Breckland, and it seems likely that the absorption of the message of the N.V.C. will stimulate others to map vegetation in terms of associations, a task so far confined to selected areas of interest, mainly in upland Britain.

There have been many fundamental shifts too, in regard to the way in which the continuity of vegetation cover is subdivided into territorial units. The 'botanical districts' of the first Flora , determined by river catchments, now look archaic and inappropriate as frames of reference for either recording or monitoring. In their place, the adoption of a grid square basis for plotting and comparison may be less evocative of the pleasures of field botany, but furnishes a more objective and practically useful system of spatial organisation to meet today's needs.

As for the process of recording, though field by field survey has supplanted the 'parish visit', the goals of comprehensiveness and reliability remain as elusive. Druce's caution, "However keen one's observation may be, there is sure to be some spot unvisited or but too slightly investigated, and there are all the difficulties of variations in seasons and the unexplained plant periodicity which necessitates visiting the same spot again and again", still has currency today. Against all the odds 'high value' sites continue to be 'discovered' - ostensibly for the first time - within supposedly well worked districts. This is demonstrated by the hitherto overlooked forest grassland species suite recently 'found' within the unlikely setting of Corby's municipal parkland. Similarly, the first record of swamp meadow-grass *(Poa palustris)* for the county, found at several places around Pitsford Reservoir in the summer of 1994.

Increased use of remote-sensed images, obtained by aerial photography and satellite - which, whilst still requiring field work to calibrate false colour images against the 'ground truth', offer exciting prospect of better 'access' to the totality of the ground than the strenuous and incomplete fieldwalking, and more economical means for regular monitoring of the character and dynamics of vegetation, albeit at a comparatively coarse scale of resolution. However, as the examples cited suggest, they ought never to oust the latest mark of the human, first hand, field surveyor.

There are hints in Druce's Flora, of awareness of the implications of history in his characterisation of the kaleidoscope of wildflower distributions. For example, he writes, "The woodlands have been greatly changed in character. A great portion now consists of blackthorn thickets or plantations of small trees and larch . . . . . so shady that there is a poor and singularly unvarying vegetation, and it is chiefly with nettles, herb mercury, creeping dog rose or enchanters nightshade that these thickets are now covered. It is only in the remains of the older woods. . . that there is any variety of woodland plants to be found". Compare this statement with the stance of the late-twentieth century botanists, whose regard for plant occurrences through space and time is now better informed of the relationships between vegetation development and sequential progress of land use via emergence of the sub-discipline of Historical Ecology. One of the distinctive features of the 'inter-Flora' period is the major advances that have been made in unravelling and interpreting the earlier character and development of the county's vegetation thanks to the application of landscape archaeology and palaeoecology. Druce perceptively remarked that, "The Willow Brook district has the woodland species excellently represented, and much work is needed before the treasures of this part of the county can be said to be sufficiently ascertained . . .". Indeed, as a result of the work of those taking up this challenge, many fascinating aspects of the floristic development of woodland within and without historic Rockingham Forest have come to light, including the perhaps unpalatable notion that the majority of the woods to be seen today are actually of secondary origin, developed upon the abandoned lands of Romano-British farmers during the inter-regnum before Dark-Age control was re-asserted on the landscape. Much detail is still imperfectly understood about the origin of these 'ancient secondary' woods, and may regrettably remain so, because of the subsequent impact of grazing upon the Forest woods' flora - itself an artefact now recognisable thanks to recent research. Why else the abnormal abundance of wood sorrel *(Oxalis acetosella)*, burdock *(Arctium sp.)* and ground ivy *(Glechoma hederacea)* in King's Wood?

Such methodological considerations aside, just how has the flora of the county changed during the sixty-five years since Druce's publication? What one suspects would be the all too ready answer should heed the reality of the situation documented by Druce himself. To begin with, it has to be acknowledged that the majority of plants described as 'rare' or 'local' were actually rare or local in his time too. To be sure, others have now declined, but rarity is not entirely a consequence of changes in modern times.

Similar provisos should also condition our presumptions regarding 'recent' reduction in extent and quality of several of the major habitats of especial botanical appeal. For example most of the damaging changes in the fenland portion of the county had already happened before Druce's Flora. As he observed." . . . . the country which was at one time marsh or fen with its rich sedge and reed vegetation, or of bog-land over which cotton grass waved its plumes, is now a vast extent of cornfields with their rippling waves of wheat . . . . ". Or, with reference to the opposite end of the spectrum, "The absence of heathland is well nigh complete and, where it exists, it is only in patches and usually on basic soil . . . . Dallington and Harlestone heaths, with Castor and Ailsworth, are poor representatives of such habitats . . . .". Whilst not wishing to deny the consequences of further attrition in recent decades, these changes do need to be viewed in the wider context of the dynamics of earlier times.

Marren has recently emphasised the appalling losses of ancient woodland in the county since 1920, but that also needs to be appreciated against the background of even more traumatic and extensive dislocation and reduction following disafforestation, during the nineteenth century when the long extant patchwork of the old Forest woodlands was unsentimentally done away with.

One should also be cognisant of Druce's comment, ". . . . . nor is there any great extent of aboriginal turf, such as clothes the Cotswolds, on the limestone formation of Northamptonshire. . . . ." For several reasons one might now object to the term aboriginal, and what there used to be of this habitat has undoubtedly been seriously compromised by subsequent changes, but it is necessary to go back several centuries to find genuine, substantial occurrence of limestone grassland on an extensive scale - principally in the guise of the 'heaths' that fell victim to agricultural 'improvement' before Druce was born. One aspect that has not changed very much over the intervening years is the importance ascribed to grassed-over quarry sites as refuges for limestone flora. A few have since been lost but the key sites not only survive but, as at Collyweston, appear to have been spared the difficulties anticipated by Druce. For him, neglect of management was thought likely to lead to deterioration of floristic interest, as succession occurred. Happily, this process has been kept at bay, thanks to the purposive intervention of modern conservation management. Moreover, as suggested later, there have even been some unexpected additions to the stock of 'aboriginal' limestone grassland. The most remarkable omission from Druce's overview is any mention of mesotrophic grassland as a focus for concerned attention. Other than the obvious floristic attractions posed by 'limestone' and 'acid' swards, there was evidently no conception of the wide span of 'neutral' associations that are now recognised. Again, such reorientation had to await Tansley's seminal publication of 1939. The widespread and penetrating damage wrought by intensive, industrial agriculture could not have been envisaged by Druce, for whom such characteristic species as marsh-marigold *(Caltha palustris)*, great burnet *(Sanguisorba officinalis)* and green-winged orchid *(Orchis morio)* were all still widely distributed and locally abundant. Such indicators - and the many more associated species of herbs and grasses once so commonplace as not to warrant especial regard - are depressingly recorded as 'much reduced' and 'declining' in the present Flora. As such, the rapid diminution in area and floristic integrity of the county's meadow and pasture grasslands has to be seen as one of the most significant events of the past sixty-five years.

The situation in Northamptonshire mirrors the experience of the country as a whole in this respect, as is also the case of the plants associated with arable fields. Druce observed that, "There are many causes which prevent the flora of Northamptonshire being a rich one. The chief of these is the great expanse of the county which is under cultivation". Well, in the light of what has since transpired, many would probably have gratefully accepted that 'great expanse', the arable acreage in 1928 being a mere 163,390 acres amid 370,000 acres of 'permanent' pasture and meadow.

What is curious is that there is no comment upon the dramatic shifts from one to the other, which independent sources advise us took place in Druce's lifetime. In comparison with his early botanising, which coincided with the golden age of 'corn before horn', the picture by the time his Flora was revised half a century later, surely displayed substantial shrinkage in the amount of tillage as a result of the great agricultural depression. One can only surmise that, in keeping with the present contemporary thought, the tumbledown fallow and emergent grass was viewed as only a temporary condition.

Be that as it may, Druce did positively highlight the contribution of long established arable weeds to the species complement of the county. Sixty-five years ago poppies, fumitories and the like were widespread and abundant, although interestingly, corncockle *(Agrostemma githago)* was then only 'locally common', corn marigold *(Chrysanthemum segetum)* 'local', cornflower *(Centaurea cyanus)* 'local and decreasing' and corn buttercup *(Ranunculus arvensis)* 'common in all districts, but I think a decreasing species'. The equivalent entries from today's Flora testify to the subsequent drastic decline of this most colourful accompaniment of cultivation. The corn buttercup only occurs as a casual of disturbed ground, corn marigold is rare and both corncockle and cornflower are now deemed extinct (though occasionally planted nowadays).

However a positive if incidental outcome of the recent spate of building development in the county has been the reappearance of many 'lost' arable weed species, upon upcast and remodelled soil. The seeds have lain concealed but vital, in some cases since the 1930s, until triggered to grow by renewed disturbance. Amongst the tell-tale flush of red poppies *(Papaver rhoeas)* enjoyed by motorists travelling along the new highways, bypasses and edge of town developments, careful search has resulted in the rediscovery of a venerable suite of species inherited from the less intensively managed arable of Druce's day. Although all too quickly suppressed by sown grasses, or doomed beneath absurd tree plantings, a proportion ought to have produced seed capable of springing another welcome surprise to botanists and passers-by should there be a future dislocation of the ground. There is even the possibility of return to their ancestral habitat, given reduced use of chemical sprays, encouragement for farmers to leave untreated headlands around persistent arable plots, and maybe in some instances, on rotational set-aside land. One current concern echoed by Druce is that of, "the alterations for the change of traffic" as he so delightfully puts it. Roadside verges were seen to be under threat from a variety of disturbances. Modern times have seen damage caused by harsh chemical and mechanical management treatments, before financial strictures forced widespread neglect of control, apart from the requisite, close mown visibility margins - and consequent spread of false oat-grass, hogweed and cow parsley. Druce's spectre of succession has thereby obscured the floristic interest of many roadside sections. The network of previously grazed 'green lanes' has suffered too, and now has to contend with 'recreational' vehicle use.

The impact of new, major road construction is predominantly a feature of the present age. There seems to be a peculiar affinity between national road development proposals and tracts of floristically rich ground, which the introduction of Environmental Impact Assessment has so far only partly checked. Further damage can be anticipated, in line with continued expansion of road programmes, albeit defiantly recompensed by transitory flourish of erstwhile field annuals - as adjacent to the A1-M1 link road at the time of writing. Incidentally, it is to be wondered what Druce would have thought of the locally encouraged practice of deliberately seeding the fringes of the new highways with wildflower seed mixtures. On another tack, he would probably have been amused by the spread of reflexed saltmarsh-grass *(Puccinella distans* subsp. *distans)* following the use of salt on the roads, having categorically asserted that the inland position of the county effectively precluded such elements from its flora.

Druce was one of the first to appreciate the botanical benefits associated with railway lines, commenting that, "The railway lands often give one a better idea of the native flora than the surrounding ground which is under cultivation, as our competing grasses and other strong species have not had time to exert their overcrowding properties, while the drainage and the sunny exposure often give plants which are fond of an open situation facilities which the more uniform sheltered, shaded, and highly cultivated arable or pasture country no longer affords". Today, this continues to be true, as testified by the several Sites of Special Scientific Interest (S.S.S.I.), Wildlife Trust Reserves and Sites of Nature Conservation Value (S.N.C.V.) situated within railway land, including enhanced opportunities unforeseen by Druce, whereby abandoned railway lines, although threatened by landfill and other 'restoration' processes, now harbour many species that could not otherwise maintain a foothold.

Surprisingly, the similar prospect afforded by the increasing extent and scale of ironstone quarries was not deemed worthy of a mention sixty-five years ago, nor would it be now, but for the contribution of the 'landscapes of the moon' in the years between. Just like the raw railway cuttings before them, derelict ironstone gullets have been colonised by interesting assemblages of species for which there is no place in the conventional countryside. Mouse-ear-hawkweed *(Pilosella officinarum)* and wild strawberry *(Fragaria vesca)* often attain exceptional abundance on the softer spoil, blue fleabane *(Erigeron acer)*, bee orchid *(Ophrys apifera)*, yellow-wort *(Blackstonia perfoliata)*, ploughman's-spikenard *(Inula conyza)*, basil thyme *(Acinos arvensis)*, pyramidal orchid *(Anacamptis pyramidalis)* and burnet rose *(Rosa pimpinellifolia)*, or carpets of bird's-foot-trefoil *(Lotus corniculatus)* elsewhere, whilst in the larger, now mature unreclaimed examples, good quality limestone grassland redeems the destruction of the original vegetation involved. Where shaded rock faces persist, hart's-tongue *(Phyllitis scolopendrium)* has found unlikely stronghold in a county not climatically suited to the needs of ferns. Remote and generally inaccessible quarry pools often support more fringing and aquatic plant interest than any denuded or enriched field ponds nearby. It is certainly ironical that the demise of large-scale opencast extraction of ore in 1980 terminated a most worthwhile means of habitat diversification in what is otherwise often botanically dull terrain. Sadly, few naturally revegetated ironstone gullets are likely to be sustained as evidence of the significance of this phase of landscape development. There are a few reserves and more S.S.S.I.'s but most are under pressure from landfill operations.

Damage to the flora predicted in advance of development can sometimes, in hindsight, be found to have been exaggerated though. Druce was rightly concerned about the enclosure of the ". . . .so small an acreage of common or waste ground" possessed by the county. However, his assertion that ". . . .the few patches that are left are almost submerged by the 'golf stream' . . .", embodies a joke that may yet rebound. The recent abandonment of the Northampton Golf Club course has been followed by a truly astonishing re-emergence of a rich mosaic of dry grassland associations. This flora was evidently well established upon the 'hills and holes' created by stone working, at the time of acquisition by the Club a century ago and has actually been protected by their particular use of the site. Similarly, reports of the demise of interest of the adjoining Kingsthorpe Scrub Field when shamefully ploughed a few years ago, were evidently premature. Today both the structure and the species composition of the regrown sward are almost indistinguishable from that which elicited so much concern at the time. Indeed several notable rarities appear to have been positively revitalised and are more abundant than before. The semi-natural associations best suited to the awkward soils there have returned with fitting vengeance. Moreover, the fleeting appearance of the two species of fluellen *(Kickxia sp.)* amidst other unexpected dryland annuals during the early years of recovery, embarrassingly suggest that 1985 was not the first time the ground in question had been disturbed.

Unfortunately such lessons cannot easily be translated to the present rash of new golf course construction across the county. Although a few incorporate elements of unimproved grassland, the majority are being developed on arable and ley, but they deserve monitoring to see what might emerge upon the novel fairways and roughs. Another timely example is that of Borough Hill. For Druce, ". . . .its flora, though less interesting than formerly from the encroaching hand of cultivation and wireless stations, has still many local species". With the removal of the radio station and moves afoot to obtain access to this major tract of ancient landscape, there is once again the possibility of future generations enjoying the sight of plants probably much less damaged than if the place had not been 'developed' thus in the inter-war period.

The extent and pace of urban development experienced by the county during the past thirty years has of course involved substantial material loss of established plant communities. It is not however, a simple equation, for much of the countryside foregone had already been deprived of botanical interest long before the onset of construction - as arable, improved, or recently established grassland of indifferent worth. Some key sites have been destroyed, for example a species-rich tract of ridge and furrow and accompanying mead within the built-up area of Kettering, which gave way to a superstore, garden centre and petrol station complex. In that case and other instances of genuine loss, it has sometimes been because the botanical interest has not been sufficiently recognised or brought to the attention of the decision makers in time to affect the outcome. Hopefully, the days when such damage came about by default are now over, thanks to overdue advances in survey, evaluation and assimilation of the legitimate conservation interest within the development control system. Paradoxically, whilst potentially damaging changes in husbandry in the countryside at large continue to remain outside effective control, the prospects for maintenance of the flora can sometimes be better nowadays when large scale development looms. There are real dangers implicit but, combination of sympathetic planning, increasingly aware developers and professional representation of the conservation argument can now result in appropriate protection alongside approved development.

This is a manifestation of one of the most important changes to have occurred since the publication of the first *Flora*, a shift in position from being merely mute onlookers, to one of influence to deflect or mitigate threats to the flora. Concern for the plight of the county's wildflowers has necessarily quickened in the face of onslaught from so many quarters during the middle years of this century. Parallel with the emergence of 'flower power' of a different sort, has come intervention on behalf of the dependent plant communities by committed botanists, on a scale which Druce would have applauded but could hardly have imagined possible. A whole new category of land-use has come into being - that where conservation of established botanical (and other wildlife) interest is, to varying degrees, formally acknowledged. Thanks to Sites of Special Scientific Interest, Local Nature Reserves, Wildlife Trust Reserves, a constellation of Sites of Nature Conservation Value, plus some Country and Pocket Parks, a substantial proportion of the county's wildflower heritage now enjoys at least a modicum of protection. Whether this rearguard action will ultimately prove to have been sufficient, or an instance of 'shutting the stable door. . . .' it is too early to judge, but whilst the jury is out, the suspicion must be that without it, our flora would be even poorer today.

If the tide appears at last to be turning in our favour, there are of course lamentable aberrations. One pending test case would have been of particular interest to Druce, who was aware of, ". . .a small but very special piece of bogland, known as Fox Hall bog, but the riches will probably ere long be lost, as willows *(Salix sp.)* have been planted in it which will probably destroy the marsh plants which made it so interesting a feature of our well drained county."

Against all logic, Birch Spinney and Mawsley Marsh S.S.S.I. has more to contend with today than the shadow cast by the willows, in the form of a preferred site for a new village development hard up against it.

Woodland, perhaps the premier habitat in the county, has suffered further loss by removal, as in the case of Gib Wood, and conversion to plantation, as at Hardwick Wood, both sites known to Druce. Once again though one cannot help but sense his wry appreciation of the selective advantage thereby conferred upon an otherwise uncommon saprophytic orchid species *Neottia nidus-avis* within the predominant gloom of the latter place.

In response, the principal surviving woods of presumed antiquity are at least now recognised in the Ancient Woodland Inventory produced by the former Nature Conservancy Council. Although that alone does not guarantee their future, it is a step in the right direction and there is now a general presumption against planning applications posing threat.

'Paintball' wargames present localised hazard, but greater contemporary concern is rather, how such archaic woodlands are to be maintained, with the limited incentives available to their owners above goodwill or neglect. Cessation of coppice management a decade or so after Druce's time would probably not have surprised him, for traditional woodsmanship was in an advanced state of decline during his lifetime. As a result many of the relict ancient woods have deteriorated in quality of their springtime floristic display, though not it is believed, beyond reach of recovery. Druce's distress at the condition of county woodland reflected the clumsy asset-stripping of the hiatus period before new positive roles for such woods were identified. The consequences of management indifference upon primrose *(Primula vulgaris),* wood anemone *(Anemone nemorosa)* and other coppice associates, is an issue that has only become clear during our time. Today, in a small but increasing number of instances, notably Wildlife Trust Reserves at Short Wood, King's Wood, Thorpe Wood and High Wood, positive steps are being taken to arrest dysfunctional change and the primroses are blooming again where feared lost. The practical means whereby this turnaround has been accomplished, did not exist in Druce's time and the contribution of purposive 'conservation management' to the sustenance and enhancement of the county's woodland and other habitats is another notable aspect of change since than. The present generation has obtained unprecedented opportunity to redirect the management of botanically worthwhile sites, by direct action on the equally novel reserves, and on land managed on behalf of both public and private sector owners elsewhere, and nowhere is it clearer than with regard to woodland. The benefits of turning back the clock are evident for all to see and there are the first hopeful signs of diffusion and adoption of such practices in other woodlands too.

Grassland preserves also receive deliberate treatment according to the requirements of the plant communities selected for maintenance, and the diversity of other habitats and communities on other sites are 'looked after' in appropriate fashion - often by dedicated volunteers with only a passing interest in botany.

The present agricultural depression and reactions to it by policy makers, regulatory authorities, landowners, land-using enterprises and interest groups, heralds a further source of change for the county's flora. Although some initial adjustments to the onset of surplus farmland are already visible, there is no clear consensus as to either the future character of the countryside or the manifold implications for its associated plantlife. Now, given that so much farmland has lost the bulk of its non-recreatable floristic quality, from a strictly botanical point of view there is little to fear from substitution of dwellings or business parks for redundant arable, should it be released for development. It is conceivable but hardly likely, that much of the land will simply be abandoned to nature. Suitably subsidised extensification would relieve vestigial plant communities from damaging pressure and allow the opportunity for local reversion to more semi-natural associations; a phenomenon poorly researched but apparent in fields where 'improvement' has not been reinforced in recent decades. Retreat from economically and ecologically marginal fringes might also permit the re-establishment of 'natural' communities. In the case of river valleys, withdrawal of cultivation and relinquishment of associated intensity of drainage, could quite quickly be followed by welcome return of much that has recently been lost. Overall, withdrawal from low capability soils and topography ought to be followed by progressive re-expansion of more appropriately adapted plant communities from island refuges. In all these possibilities though, much depends upon resolution of fundamental questions including compensation payments and future management arrangements over the medium and long term. Set-aside, in its currently preferred rotational form, is widely regarded as presenting the least benefit with respect to the flora, but more enlightened 'permanent' Set-aside would have attractive potential.

The justification for the re-establishment of woodland is strong, but either *via* natural succession or deliberate planting, anticipated botanical gains are likely to be limited to the most robust and already well represented species. Grudging release of realistic payments from the wealth of agricultural support funds, to landowners prepared to manage surviving tracts of established floristic value sympathetically,. would perhaps increase safeguards for already 'protected places' and maybe secure a sounder future for the lesser tier of Sites of Nature Conservation Value. Experience is accumulating from the pilot phase of the Countryside Stewardship and Environmentally Sensitive Area schemes, which ought to further permeate the wider countryside in due course. Such issues reflect nationwide needs and opportunities. Peculiar to the county the 'new' Rockingham Forest Project has undoubted promise, for the re-establishment or simulation of the distinctive complex of Forest habitats and associated floras, but calls for far-sighted, imaginative - and expensive - commitment at a time of deep general recession.

It having become conventional wisdom to attribute changes in the flora solely to the impact of human activity, events of the recent past demand that consideration for entirely 'natural' change should also be shown. Significant episodes during the period of this review include several major droughts and winter storms of abnormal ferocity, and of course the havoc wrought by Dutch Elm disease in the 1970s. The effects upon the plantlife of the county, though superficially obvious at the time, will not become truly apparent until many years hence, particularly in the case of woodland. It is now understood that the natural history of temperate woodland is - contrary to popular concern - accustomed to such periodic events, and may need them to ensure the long term maintenance of diversity. Unfortunately, fragmentation, reduction in size, increase in isolation and the multiplicity of other, unnatural stresses impinging upon relict stands (including well meaning but misplaced clearance of storm debris and replanting) may mean that future adjustment can no longer replicate past rhythms - with all that entails for the associated flora.

Then overshadowing all else at the moment, is the mounting fear of environmental change initiated by 'global warming', and the complex interactions between this trend and the opposing processes during the latter part of the current inter-glacial period. Significant effects are now believed to be with us, in terms of the earlier nesting dates of some species of birds, with more to come before the next sixty years have passed - although what precisely they might be is still uncertain. One scenario predicts a northward shift of climate/vegetation zones of approximately 600 kilometres. If correct, this would have the most intriguing consequences for the flora of Northamptonshire. Overall, there ought to be increase in the number of species, but offset by loss of some of the presently cherished elements. Gains might include return of the early spider-orchid *(Ophrys sphegodes)*, autumn lady's-tresses *(Spiranthes spiralis)*, burnt orchid *(Orchis ustulata)* and other southern European species. If the past is any guide, greater preparedness to accept additional limestone extraction could suitably prepare the way for welcoming such prodigals.

What future though for the mountain melick *(Melica nutans)*, giant bellflower *(Campanula latifolia)*, alluvial grassland communities and our characteristically wet boulder clay woodlands? To speculate further at this time is not profitable, but the various possibilities certainly deserve attention with regard to present and prospective conservation strategies.

As to what Environmental changes bring, it is for the next *Flora* to report and comment upon, but in conclusion, as we approach the millennium, what is the judgement of the myriad changes that have taken place since Druce's foundation study? In the author's opinion, of greater concern than either the diminution of particular species or floristically interesting habitats, is the depressing uniformity and dullness of much of the county's vegetation cover today. There is much that is still 'green' but it is so bland and devoid of diversity and sensual appeal. Maybe it is an exaggeration to hearken back to an imagined time when 'every parish' could boast a representative array of wildflowers, but the current reality of having to travel to enjoy a marshy pasture enlivened with kingcups *(Caltha palustris)*, or a dry bank scented with cowslips *(Primula veris)*, is no figment. From the perspective of knowledge of other places and other times, the feeling is akin to that upon entering an historic country house only to find that it contains precious little in the form of ornament or furniture for the visitor to benefit from as was the pleasure of previous generations. Rachel Carson powerfully drew attention in a less enlightened age to the onset of this condition as afflicting the status of the countryside in the United States. The indictment of my generation must be that we allowed it to happen here. The largely undramatic, progress towards an equivalent 'silent spring' throughout the greater extent of the vegetation of Northamptonshire has been beyond our means to curb, but there have been significant if belated, manifestations of a counter movement. I count myself lucky for having been privileged to have grown up in a poorer yet richer countryside and trust that those who follow will heed the message embodied in the present *Flora* to deplore and resist further avoidable deterioration with as much vehemence.

References

Colston A. & Perring F. (Eds.) *The Nature of Northamptonshire Barracuda Books 1989*
Marren P. *The Wild Woods David and Charles 1992*
The Wildlife of Peterborough Peterborough Wildlife Group 1992
Best J.A. *King's Wood Corby Nene College 1983*
Best J.A. *Kingsthorpe Scrub Field NNHS&FC 1984*
Best J.A. *Lost and Found - Neutral Grasslands of Conservation Value NNHS&FC 1986*
Best J.A. *The Greatest Show on Earth NWT Newsletter 1991*
Best J.A. & Logue W.L. *The Grasslands of Thoroughsale and Hazel Woods, Corby NWT 1991*
Best J.A. *Reaping the Benefits NWT Newsletter 1993*
Best J.A. *The Past, Present and Future of Rockingham Forest NWT 1994*
and of course
Druce G.C. *The Flora of Northamptonshire T. Buncle and Co. 1930*

Crested cow-wheat and navelwort (drawings by Gill Gent)

The Flora of
NORTHAMPTONSHIRE
and the Soke of Peterborough~

The Systematic Flora

Introduction

The arrangement of families, genera and species within the systematic flora follows that of the 'List of Vascular Plants of the British Isles' by D.H.Kent *(Botanical Society of the British Isles, 1992).* The English names follow the 'English Names of Wild Flowers' by J.G.Dony, S.L.Jury and F.H.Perring *(Second Edition, Botanical Society of the British Isles, 1986),* and the 'New Flora of the British Isles' by C.Stace *(Cambridge University Press 1991).* Additional English names are included if they are more commonly used and understood locally than the standard English name. These are given after the standard English name.

Synonyms are generally given only where the current name differs from that given in 'The Excursion Flora of the British Isles' by A.R.Clapham, T.G.Tutin and E.F.Warburg *(Second Edition, Cambridge University Press, 1968)* or where it is necessary for easy understanding and where it is necessary for an accurate reference to be made to the earlier *'Flora of Northamptonshire'* by George Claridge Druce *(T. Buncle & Co., 1930).* In the former instances the synonyms are listed after the current accepted name, whilst in the latter case they are given in brackets in the last line of text, after the word *'Druce'.*

The number in brackets, generally at the end of the first line after the species name, gives the number of five kilometre squares where the plant was found during the field survey work for the flora, from 1970 to 1994. This is followed by the origin and local habitat of the plant; and a description of the status and distribution within Vice-county 32.

The final two paragraphs detail the date and recorder of the first county record where known; and the status of the plant as given in the previous county flora. Where there is no data these lines are omitted. The first records by John Clare, the poet from Helpston in the Soke of Peterborough are as determined by Druce and some are open to question. Any comment that has been added by the authors after the status in Druce (and which is generally based on information contained within the text of Druce's Flora) is enclosed in square brackets.

The systematic flora includes all the plants that are thought to be native to the Vice-county, and can be found growing in the countryside. Plants that were present when Druce wrote his flora and were described by him are included, whether they are native to the county or were introductions and whether they are still present in the county or not. Plants that have been recorded in the countryside during the course of the present survey are all included whether native or introduced, intentionally or otherwise. Records of garden throw-outs and other introductions that have not established themselves are included where there are any records, but inevitably many of these must have been missed. The systematic flora does not generally include trees, shrubs or flowers planted in parks or gardens (unless these plants have naturalised themselves and are self supporting), or municipal planting on housing and industrial estates, and urban roadsides. Trees and shrubs that are constituents of woodland and hedgerows are included, whether they are present as wild plants, or due to the action of man, as are any other trees and shrubs that are significant features of the broader countryside.

The terms which are used in reference to the species status refer to Watsonian Vice-county 32 only and may not be consistent with any terms used for the same species in other areas. The following terms have been used throughout the systematic text, with the following meanings:-

ORIGIN

Native	*A species generally taken to be a present in the Vice-county since pre-historical times.*
British	*A species which is native to other parts of the British Isles, but has only arrived in the Vice-county within historical times, generally by human intervention, either intentional or accidental.*
Adventive	*A foreign species which arrived here by inadvertent human action. It may be well established in the wild or it may persist for short time only.*
Introduction	*A foreign species that was originally intentionally planted. It may be well established in the wild as an escape from cultivation, or it may persist for a short time only as a throw-out.*

STATUS

Common	*Found abundantly in the majority of the Vice-county or within a specific area or habitat as stated.*
Frequent	*Found in reasonable numbers in the Vice-county or within a specific area or habitat as stated.*
Occasional	*Scattered throughout the Vice-county or within a specific area or habitat as stated but usually not in large numbers.*
Rare	*Found in only a few parts of the county and then usually in fairly small numbers. Appendix 3 lists plants in this category which occur at no more than fifteen individual sites within the Vice-county, and which do not fall into the extremely rare category.*
Extremely rare	*Generally only used for species found at no more than three individual sites within the Vice-county. A list of native plants falling within this category is given in Appendix 2.*
Extinct	*Not reported in the county since 1970 or missing from its only recorded sites, even after deliberate searching. A list of native plants falling within this category is given in Appendix 1.*

All of the above terms for distribution and status are qualified where it was felt that the basic description did not, in the opinion of the authors, accurately reflect the true position within Vice-county 32.

Distribution Maps

Distribution maps included in this section are generally of all the species recorded during the survey for this flora, unless they occur only as planted specimens, as non-persisting escapes or throw-outs, or rare plants which occur at few localities within the Vice-county, although there are exceptions to this. Distribution maps are not included for species where our knowledge has proved insufficient to determine the various micro-species, notably members of the Rosa, Rubus, Taraxacum and Hieracium genera. In a few cases subspecies have been lumped together and sometimes a map is shown which gives an overall idea of the general distribution of the species. Where this is the case it is made clear in the accompanying text.

Each dot indicates at least one record in a five kilometre square, but can also represent many thousands of plants at different sites distributed across the square, thus the maps only give a general idea of the distribution within the Vice-county and not the quantity of the plants occurring there. It is important, therefore, that the maps are read in conjunction with the text in the systematic flora.

Although the data for this flora has been collected between 1970 and 1994, every effort has been made to produce maps that show the current status of plants within the county for within this period of time many habitats within the county have been destroyed and distribution patterns have changed.

It has been our aim that the coverage across the Vice-county should be as even as possible, even though the majority of the people involved live in the northern half of the area. The squares with the highest numbers of records generally coincide with known botanical 'hot-spots', and those with the lowest numbers of records, apart from a few part squares on the boundary which are often intensively farmed, are almost all concentrated in the central western area, a part of the county which Druce noted as less interesting botanically. The rest of the county consistently produces in the region of 400 different species per 5km square. The coincidence map below gives an approximate idea of the quantity of records for each square. The larger the dot, the more records per square, with the largest dots equating to approximately 550 species.

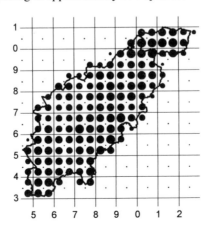

The Flora of NORTHAMPTONSHIRE and the Soke of Peterborough~

Systematic Account

LYCOPODIOPSIDA
(LYCOPSIDA)
1 LYCOPODIACEAE
3 LYCOPODIUM L.
1 L. clavatum L.
Stag's-horn Clubmoss
Native. Heathland.
Extinct. Only previously recorded by H.N.Dixon at Harlestone Firs in 1885.
First record: H.N.Dixon 1885
Druce: Very rare [only H.N.Dixon's first record is quoted].

EQUISETOPSIDA
(SPHENOPSIDA)

4 EQUISETACEAE
1 EQUISETUM L.
4 E. fluviatile L. (42)
Water Horsetail

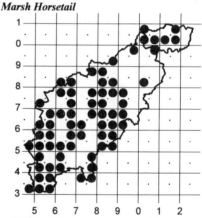

Native. In shallow water, streamsides etc.
Frequent in suitable water bodies.
First record: Baker 1822
Druce: (E. limosum) Locally abundant.

5 E. arvense L. (122)
Field Horsetail, Common Horsetail
Native. Fields, roadsides and gardens.

Common in many habitats - roadsides and quarries - often as an aggressive weed.

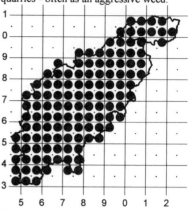

First record: Beesley 1841
Druce: Common in all districts.

7 E. sylvaticum L. (2)
Wood Horsetail
Native. Shady places, often on acid soil.
Extremely rare. Confined to three localities: Ramsden Corner, High Wood and Church Wood, in the south of the county.
First record: Morton 1712
Druce: Very rare.

8 E. palustre L. (68)
Marsh Horsetail

Native. Marshy areas, stream sides etc.
Frequent in marshy areas and very shallow water.
First record: Gulliver 1841
Druce: Locally common.

9 E. telmateia Ehrh. (48)
Great Horsetail

Native. Damp shady places.
Occasional. Scattered throughout the county but commoner in the west. It is often in large stands where it grows.
First record: E.Forster jun. 1805
Druce: (E. maximum) Local.

PTEROPSIDA
(FILICOPSIDA)
5 OPHIOGLOSSACEAE
1 OPHIOGLOSSUM L.
1 O. vulgatum L. (36)
Adder's-tongue

Native. Grassland in well established meadows.
Occasional. Scattered throughout the county in suitable habitats although these are diminishing due to so-called improvements. It

occurs around Corby in the King's Wood local nature reserve and in Great Oakley Meadow nature reserve. It also is found in Bedford Purlieus, Yardley Chase SSSI, Pipewell Woods and many other places.
First record: Baker 1822
Druce: Local.

2 BOTRYCHIUMSw.
1 B. lunaria (L.) Sw.
Moonwort
Native. Dry grassland.
Possibly extinct. The last record for this species is from Thornhaugh, in 1954, by Ian Hepburn.
First record: Morton 1712
Druce: (Lunaria minor) Very rare.

6 OSMUNDACEAE
1 OSMUNDA L.
1 O. regalis L.
Royal Fern
Native. Boggy places.
Extinct. The only record of this plant, from Moulton, is in *The History and Antiquities of the County of Northampton*, by George Baker, published in 1822.
First record: Baker 1822
Druce: Extinct.

7 ADIANTACEAE
3 ADIANTUM L.
1 A. capillus-veneris L.
Maidenhair Fern
British. Walls and bridges.
This was recorded from an old railway bridge near Daventry in the 1970s. It has since disappeared.

9 MARSILEACEAE
1 PILULARIA L.
1 P. globulifera L.
Pillwort
Native. Ponds or their margins.
Extinct. The first record, from Borough Fen is the only known record.
First record: Sir John Hill 1746
Druce: Almost certainly extinct.

11 POLYPODIACEAE
1 POLYPODIUM L.
1 P. vulgare L. (44)
Polypody
Native. Tree trunks, walls etc.

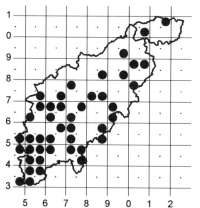

5 6 7 8 9 0 1 2

Fairly common on old walls and sometimes in woodland in the south west of the county and scattered through the rest of area.
First record: Baker 1822
Druce: Rather common.

2 P. interjectum Shivas (6)
Intermediate Polypody

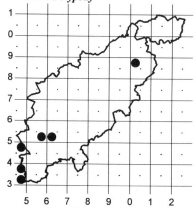

5 6 7 8 9 0 1 2

Native. Shaded limestone walls and banks. Rare. Occurs in a few places, mainly on walls, in the south-west area of county.
Druce: [Not recorded by Druce as the different species of Polypodium were not recognised until the 1950s].

13 DENNSTAEDTIACEAE
(HYPOLEPIDACEAE pro parte)
1 PTERIDIUM Gled. ex Scop.
1 P. aquilinum (L.) Kuhn (80)
Bracken
Native. Woods etc. usually on acid soils.

A common species on sandy soils and heathy areas, it is quite well distributed throughout the county. Occasional plants can be found on the brickwork of old railway bridges.

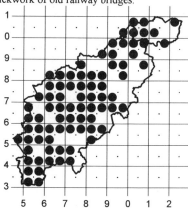

5 6 7 8 9 0 1 2

First record: Gibson 1695
Druce: (Eupteris aquilina) Locally abundant.

14 THELYPTERIDACEAE
1 THELYPTERIS Schmidel
1 T. palustris Schott
(*T. thelypteroides* Michaux *subsp. glabra* Holub)
Marsh Fern
Native. Bogs.
Extinct. The last record is from between Thornhaugh and Stamford, between two and three miles from the former place, prior to 1930.
First record: Baker 1822
Druce: (Dryopteris thelypteris) Very rare.

3 OREOPTERIS Holub
1 O. limbosperma (Bellardi ex All.) Holub
(*Thelypteris oreopteris* (Ehrh.) Slosson)
Lemon-scented Fern
Native. Acid soils.
Extinct. The last record is from Badby Wood prior to 1930.
First record: Baker 1822
Druce: (Dryopteris oreopteris) Very rare and probably extirpated.

15 ASPLENIACEAE
1 PHYLLITIS Hill
1 P. scolopendrium (L.) Newman (47)
(*Asplenium scolopendrium* L.)
Hart's-tongue

Native. Old quarries, walls, shaded and moist areas.

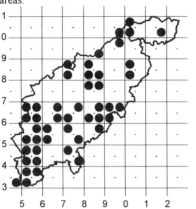

5 6 7 8 9 0 1 2

Fairly common on old brickwork. It is scattered through the county but is more frequently found in the southern half. It is quite a feature of the old quarry face in the Rothwell Gullet nature reserve.
First record: Morton 1712
Druce: Local and decreasing.

2 ASPLENIUM L.
1 A. adiantum-nigrum L. (42)
Black Spleenwort

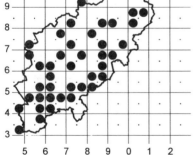

5 6 7 8 9 0 1 2

Native. Walls.
Occasional throughout the county on stone walls, brickwork, railway bridges etc.
First record: Morton 1712
Druce: Local.

5 A. trichomanes L. (42)
Maidenhair Spleenwort
Native. Walls etc.

Occasional throughout the county, mainly on limestone walls. It is more often found along the south-eastern side of the county and although it is usually found as a single plant it can sometimes occur in large quantities such as on the wall of Easton Maudit church.

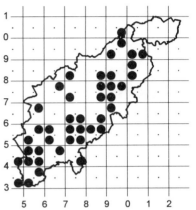

5 6 7 8 9 0 1 2

First record: Druce 1878
Druce: Local and rare.

7 A. ruta-muraria L. (78)
Wall-rue

1
0
9
8
7
6
5
4
3

5 6 7 8 9 0 1 2

Native. Walls etc.
Common in the county, particularly on railway bridges and stone walls with a preference for the south and the east.
First record: Morton 1712
Druce: Local.

3 CETERACH Willd. (29)
1 C. officinarum Willd.
Rustyback

Native. Limestone walls, or brick walls with limestone mortar.

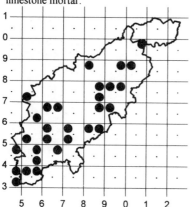

5 6 7 8 9 0 1 2

Occasional and seeming to be commoner in the western half of the county. Often well established not only on limestone walls but in the brickwork of old railway bridges.
First record: Rev M.J.Berkley 1860
Druce: (C. ceterach) Local and rare.

16 WOODSIACEAE
(ATHYRIACEAE)
3 ATHYRIUM Roth
1 A. filix-femina (L.) Roth   (40)
Lady-fern

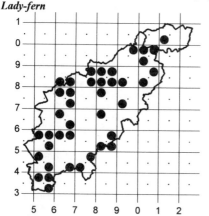

5 6 7 8 9 0 1 2

Native. Shaded localities, damp woods etc. Occasional in damp woodland where suitable sites occur throughout the county.
First record: Baker 1822
Druce: (A. filix-foemina) Local.

4 GYMNOCARPIUM Newman

1 G. dryopteris (L.) Newman
(Thelypteris dryopteris (L.) Slosson)
Oak Fern
Native. Damp woodlands.
Possibly extinct. This was discovered in Bucknell Wood in 1973 by Mrs K.M.Stevens. Subsequent searches have failed to locate it.
First record: Mrs K.M.Stevens 1973

2 G. robertianum (Hoffm.) Newman
(Thelypteris robertiana (Hoffm.) Slosson)
Limestone Fern, Limestone Polypody
British. Limestone scree.
Extinct. The only record is from Roade railway cutting where it was recorded in 1896.
First record: H.N.Dixon 1896
Druce: (Dryopteris robertiana) Very rare.

5 CYSTOPTERIS Bernh.
1 C. fragilis (L.) Bernh.
Brittle Bladder-fern
Native. Walls.
Possibly extinct. Recorded from the churchyard walls at Lower Benefield by J.Rees during the 1960s but not seen since - this is the only recent record.
First record: Morton 1712
Druce: Very rare.

17 DRYOPTERIDACEAE
(ASPIDIACEAE pro parte)
1 POLYSTICHUM Roth
1 P. setiferum (Forsskål) T.Moore ex Woynar
          (8)

Soft Shield-fern

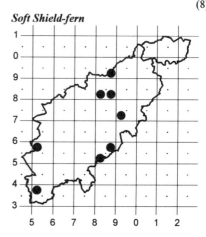

5 6 7 8 9 0 1 2

Native. Woodlands and shaded hedge-banks in moist situations.

A rare species occurring at eight sites in the county, mainly woodland as at Newbottle Spinney, Horton Woods, Bedford Purlieus, Old Pastures and Dane Hole. It also occurs at Finedon on an old mineral railway. It was recorded from Bedford Purlieus prior to 1970.

First record: Druce 1878
Druce: Very rare.

2 P. aculeatum (L.) Roth (7)
Hard Shield-fern

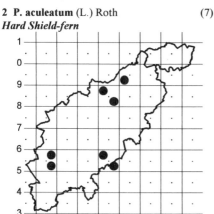

Native. Woodland.

Very rare and only occurring in seven separate locations in woodland in the county: near Canon's Ashby, Yardley Chase, woodland near Stoke Albany and the Old Water Mill, Desborough.

First record: Baker 1822
Druce: (P. lobatum) Local and decreasing.

3 P. lonchitis (L.) Roth
Holly-fern

British. Walls.

A most unusual occurrence of this species was recorded by Colin Legge on a railway bridge at Wellingborough in 1973. Unfortunately it did not survive for more than a couple of years.

First record: Colin Legge 1973

3 DRYOPTERIS Adans.
2 D. filix-mas (L.) Schott (113)
Male-fern

Native. Woodland.

Very common in woodland and on old brickwork throughout the county.

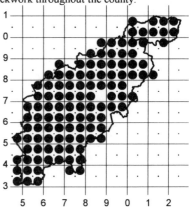

First record: Beesley 1842
Druce: Rather common ...but suffering from the rapacity of vagrants.

3 D. affinis (Lowe) Fraser-Jenkins
Scaly Male-fern

a subsp. **affinis**
Native. Woodland.
No recent records.
Druce: (D. filix-mas var. affinis) [No status given but only six localities listed].

c subsp. **borreri** (Newman) Fraser-Jenkins (5)

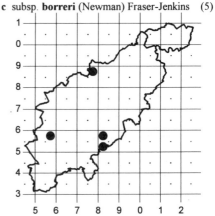

Native. Woodland.

Very rare. It is only found at five localities: Yardley Chase, Mantles Heath, Dingley, Salcey Forest and at Horton..

Druce: (D. filix-mas var. paleacea) [No status given but only five localities listed].

8 D. carthusiana (Villars) H.P.Fuchs (14)
(*D. spinulosa* Kuntze)
Narrow Buckler-fern

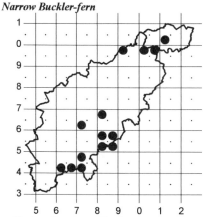

5 6 7 8 9 0 1 2

Native. Damp woodlands.
Very occasional. Found mainly in the Whittlebury and Yardley Chase woodlands in the south-east and in Wakerley Woods and Bedford Purlieus in the north. It is also found in Harlestone Firs and Sywell Wood.
First record: Baker 1822
Druce: (D. spinulosa) Rare.

9 D. dilatata (Hoffm.) A.Gray (80)
Broad Buckler-fern

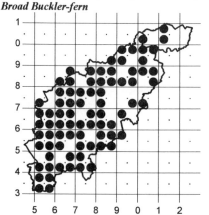

5 6 7 8 9 0 1 2

Native. Shaded woods, hedge-banks etc.
Fairly common in woodland throughout the county, although Druce considered this to be a rare species.
First record: Morton 1712
Druce: (D. aristata) Rare.

18 BLECHNACEAE
1 BLECHNUM L.
1 B. spicant (L.) Roth (2)
Hard-fern

Native. Woods and heathland.
Extremely rare. Usually a fern of acid heath areas, this has been rediscovered in cleared woodland at Harlestone Firs. The only other site is at Bedford Purlieus in the Soke of Peterborough, although Druce gives several localities.
First record: Morton 1712
Druce: Very local and rare.

19 AZOLLACEAE
1 AZOLLA Lam.
1 A. filiculoides Lam. (7)
Water Fern

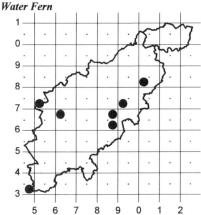

5 6 7 8 9 0 1 2

Adventive. Naturalised in rivers etc.
Very occasional. Since it was first noticed in a pond in Long Buckby in 1981 it has been found in several localities. It was recorded from the River Nene at Irthlingborough in 1986 from where it has spread downstream to Wadenhoe and upstream to Earls Barton. Other separate sites are in a pond at Onley in the north and at Aynho Wharf on the Oxford Canal, from where it was recorded in 1992. It will be interesting to see if it survives so far north.
First record: Angela Walker (Long Buckby) 1981

PINOPSIDA
(GYMNOSPERMAE)

Many species of conifers that are found within the county are planted as forestry crops. For this reason the distribution of these species has not been recorded but the more important species are recorded below.

20 PINACEAE
2 PSEUDOTSUGA Carrière
1 P. menziesii (Mirbel) Franco
Douglas Fir
Introduction. Plantations.

3 TSUGA (Antoine) Carrière
1 T. heterophylla (Raf.) Sarg.
Western Hemlock-spruce
Introduction. Plantations.

4 PICEA A.Dietr.
1 P. sitchensis (Bong.) Carrière
Sitka Spruce
Introduction. Parkland and plantations.
The commoner spruce planted in the wetter areas of the county.
Druce: A planted tree.

2 P. abies (L.) Karsten
Norway Spruce
Introduction. Plantations, parks and gardens.
The commoner spruce planted in the drier areas of the county.

5 LARIX Miller
1 L. decidua Miller
European Larch
Introduction. Plantations.
Common throughout the county in plantations, reclaimed quarries etc.
Druce: (L. larix) A planted tree. Occurring in all districts.

1 x 2 L. decidua x L. kaempferi = L. x marschlinsii Coaz
(*L. x eurolepis* A.Henry, nom. illegit.)
Hybrid Larch
Introduction. Plantations and parks.
This may occur as a natural cross, but it has rarely been recorded as this and most records are of planted specimens.

2 L. kaempferi (Lindley) Carrière
Japanese Larch
Introduction. Plantations and parkland.

7 PINUS L.
1 P. sylvestris L.
Scots Pine
Introduction. Plantations.
Planted in several of the local forests and occasionally elsewhere. Occasionally self-set seedlings are found.
First record: Morton 1822
Druce: Not common.

2 P. nigra Arnold
First record: Druce 1928
Druce: A planted tree.
a subsp. **nigra**
Austrian Pine
Introduction. Woodland.

b subsp. **laricio** Maire
Corsican Pine
Introduction. Plantations.
Commonly planted in most of the local woodlands. This is the commonest of the varieties of *P. nigra* to be planted.

TAXODIACEAE
TAXODIUM Rich.
T. distichum (L.) Rich.
Swamp Cypress
Introduction. Wet places.
Planted at Wadenhoe.

21 CUPRESSACEAE
X CUPRESSOCYPARIS Dallimore (CUPRESSUS X CHAMAECYPARIS)

X C. leylandii (A.B.Jackson & Dallimore) Dallimore (*Cu. macrocarpa x Ch. nootkatensis*)
Leyland Cypress
Introduction. Planted for screening.

2 CHAMAECYPARIS Spach
1 C. lawsoniana (A.Murray) Parl.
Lawson's Cypress
Introduction. Parks and gardens, rarely planted in plantations.

3 THUJA L.
1 T. plicata Donn ex D.Don
Western Red-cedar
Introduction. Plantations.
Frequently planted in a number of local woods for its valuable 'cedar' wood.

4 JUNIPERUS L.
1 J. communis L.

Common Juniper

Native. Formerly in heathy, bushy places. Extinct as a native plant, it is now present only as a planted species.
First record: Morton 1712
Druce: Very rare.

23 TAXACEAE

1 TAXUS L.
1 T. baccata L. (42)
Yew

British. Churchyards and parkland. Frequent and scattered across the county. It is present in many of the county's churchyards, often as the upright bush cv. *Fastigiata*, but many trees are to be found. The ancient tree at Helmdon has been stated to be 1700 years old although there is no proof of this. Bird-sown seedlings are fairly frequent.
First record: Paley 1860
Druce: Rare, a doubtful native to the county.

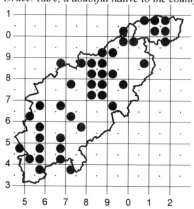

MAGNOLIOPSIDA
(ANGIOSPERMAE)

MAGNOLIIDAE
Dicotyledons

25 ARISTOLOCHIACEAE
2 ARISTOLOCHIA L.
1 A. clematitis L.
Birthwort

Introduction. Damp habitats.
It was recorded between Lowick and Drayton House in 1953 by Marjorie Laundon.
Druce: An unconfirmed record.

26 NYMPHAEACEAE

1 NYMPHAEA L.
1 N. alba L.
White Water-lily
a subsp. **alba** (35)

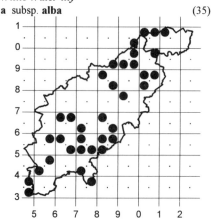

Native. Rivers and lakes.
Rare. Found mostly as a planted species in lakes, ornamental waters and ponds although it is to be found at one or two locations on the River Nene and River Welland.
First record: Hill 1773
Druce: Locally common.

2 NUPHAR Smith
1 N. lutea (L.) Smith (76)
Yellow Water-lily

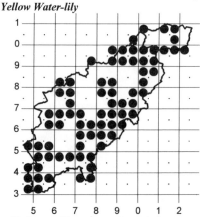

Native. Rivers, canals and large water bodies.
Common and widely distributed in all suitable habitats.
First record: Hill 1773

Druce: Rather common and generally distributed.

27 CERATOPHYLLACEAE
1 CERATOPHYLLUM L.
1 C. demersum L. (38)
Rigid Hornwort

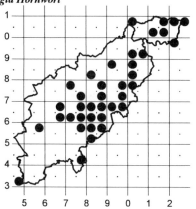

Native. Rivers, lakes, canals and large water bodies.
Frequent in the River Nene, less common in the canals, occasionally in lakes and reservoirs and even ponds.
First record: Morton 1712
Druce: Local.

2 C. submersum L.
Soft Hornwort
Native. Slow waters particularly near to coasts.
Extinct. One record by Druce from near St. James' End, Northampton in 1878.
First record: Druce 1878
Druce: Rare.

28 RANUNCULACEAE
1 CALTHA L.
1 C. palustris L. (78)
Marsh-marigold, Kingcup
Native. Marshy places.
Occasional. Once widely distributed throughout the county but decreasing owing to drainage of suitable habitats.
First record: Clare 1821
Druce: Locally abundant and widely distributed.

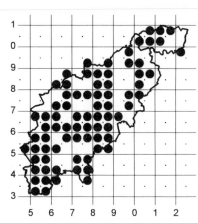

3 HELLEBORUS L.
1 H. foetidus L. (11)
Stinking Hellebore

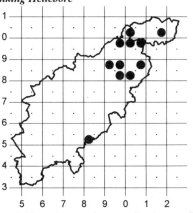

Probably native. Ancient woodland, generally on calcareous soil.
Very rare and mostly confined to ancient woodland in the north of the county; particularly Bedford Purlieus, but it was frequent in the quarry at Ring Haw in 1994. A recent find in Yardley Chase confirms an old record and it still occurs at Lyveden where George Chester recorded it.
First record: Pitt 1797
Druce: Rare.

2 H. viridis L.
Green Hellebore
a subsp. **occidentalis** (Reuter) Schiffner (4)
Native. Damp calcareous woodland scrub.

84

Very rare and only known with any certainty from two sites in the south of the county, including Walton Grounds nature reserve. Otherwise introduced on country estates as at Castle Ashby, Brockhall etc.
First record: Parkinson 1629
Druce: Rare.

4 ERANTHIS Salisb.
1 E. hyemalis (L.) Salisb.　　　　　　(19)
Winter Aconite

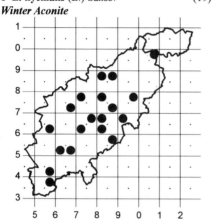

　　5　6　7　8　9　0　1　2
Introduction.　Woods and scrub on moist soils.
Occasional but well established throughout the county, mainly in churchyards and on country estates. It is often quite a feature of such areas.
Druce:　(Cammarum　hyemale)　Now established in a few places, but originally an escape from, or a relic of, cultivation.

6 ACONITUM L.
1 A. napellus L.
Monk's-hood
Introduction. Damp grassland and spinneys.
Naturalised in a few areas on large estates and sometimes establishing itself as a very poisonous garden throw-out.

7 CONSOLIDA (DC.) Gray
1 C. ajacis (L.) Schur
(*C. ambigua* (L.) P.Ball and Heyw.)
Larkspur
Introduction.　Mainly on tips and waste ground.
Often occurs on disturbed ground as a garden escape but never persists for long.

9 ANEMONE L.
1 A. nemorosa L.　　　　　　(65)
Wood Anemone

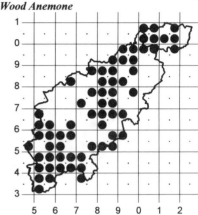

　　5　6　7　8　9　0　1　2
Native.　Woodland　rides,　scrub　and hedgerows.
Frequent on lighter soils in woodland throughout the county; it does sometimes occur in woodlands on heavier soils.
First record: Clare 1821
Druce: Locally common, and too widely distributed in all districts to need special localities.

2 A. apennina L.
Blue Anemone
Introduction. Woodland margins and hedge-banks.
Naturalised in shrubberies at Castle Ashby and other estates.
First record: Miss J.Tebbs 1953

3 A. ranunculoides L.
Yellow Anemone
Introduction.　Deciduous woodland, scrub and hedge-banks.
Naturalised　on　estates　and　sometimes escaping.

11 PULSATILLA Miller
1 P. vulgaris Miller　　　　　　(1)
Pasqueflower
Native. Short turf on thin calcareous soil.
Extremely rare, but recorded in large numbers at Barnack Hills and Holes. It has also been recorded from nearby Southorpe Roughs and Southorpe Paddock, where it may reappear under a new management regime.

First record: Dr Bowles 1650
Druce: (Anemone pulsatilla) Very local.

12 CLEMATIS L.
1 C. vitalba L. (62)
Traveller's-joy, Old Man's Beard

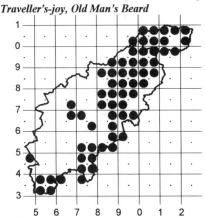

Native. Woodland margins and hedgerows.
Frequent. Common on calcareous soils and
quite a feature on the limestone areas in the
north-east; it is also found throughout much
of the eastern half of the county, in the
extreme south and a few other areas. It is
absent from the lighter soils in the west.
First record: Morton 1712
Druce: Locally common on calcareous soils.

13 RANUNCULUS L.
1 R. acris L. (126)
Meadow Buttercup

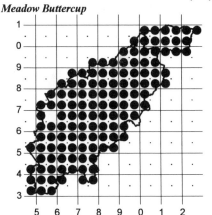

Native. Damp meadows and pastures.
Common and well distributed.
First record: Clare 1821

Druce: Abundant and generally distributed.

2 R. repens L. (133)
Creeping Buttercup

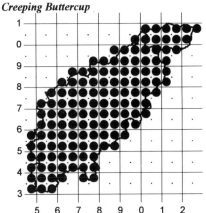

Native. Wet, heavy calcareous or slightly
acid grassland.
Extremely common throughout in damp
situations, and a troublesome garden weed.
Occasionally double forms are recorded.
First record: Gulliver 1841
Druce: Common and generally distributed.

3 R. bulbosus L. (115)
Bulbous Buttercup

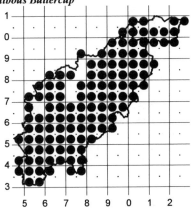

Native. Grazed meadows and hayfields.
Frequent, but preferring drier pastures than
the preceding two species. Decreasing due to
grassland improvement.
First record: Pitt 1813
Druce: Abundant and generally distributed.

4 R. sardous Crantz
Hairy Buttercup

Probably native.   Damp grazed valley meadows.

Possibly extinct. Not really considered a species in the county by Druce, this plant turned up in dozens on the old tip at Finedon in 1981 and at Northampton in 1982. There is also a record of it growing on dumped soil near the River Nene lock, Wellingborough in 1983. All of these sites have since been destroyed.

7 R. parviflorus L.   (6)
Small-flowered Buttercup

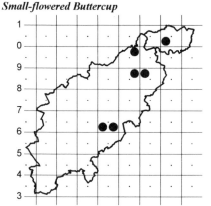

```
5   6   7   8   9   0   1   2
```
Native. Dry grassy banks, roadsides etc.

Very rare. It was more common in Druce's day, when it was scattered through the north and east of the county. It is now found at Fineshade and has been recorded from Lyveden, Cogenhoe and Grendon in recent years. It was also recorded at Castor Hanglands but it has not been seen there recently. The Grendon site was destroyed by ploughing.

First record: 1875
Druce: Very local.

8 R. arvensis L.   (15)
Corn Buttercup

Native. Arable land, especially cornfields on calcareous or clay soils.

Occasional. Once considered a common cornfield weed, it has declined drastically over the last 30 years and now only occurs

casually on recently disturbed ground.

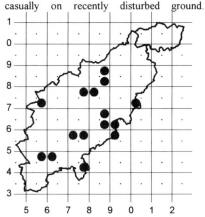

```
5   6   7   8   9   0   1   2
```
First record: Lightfoot 1835
Druce: Common in all districts but ....a decreasing species.

10 R. auricomus L.   (54)
Goldilocks Buttercup, Goldilocks

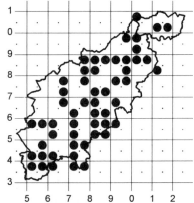

```
5   6   7   8   9   0   1   2
```
Native. Meadows, woods and hedgerows.
Occasional in woodland and along lanes throughout the county, and a feature of some old churchyards.
First record: Notcutt 1843
Druce: Locally common and a distinct evidence of present or past woodland.

11 R. sceleratus L.   (83)
Celery-leaved Buttercup, Celery-leaved Crowfoot

Native. Mud or shallow water, beside ponds and streams.

Occasional throughout the county, but can be

common in some areas, especially where gravel pits are being developed.

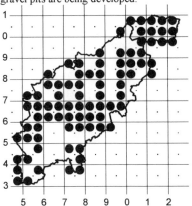

First record: Druce 1872
Druce: Locally abundant and widely distributed.

12 R. lingua L.
Greater Spearwort
Native. Marshy ground, ponds and ditches, in shallow water.
Often introduced and naturalised in ornamental waters, as at Maidwell and Castle Ashby, but otherwise there is only an occasional sighting, as on the old railway at Ringstead. There are no recent records from the fen district near Peterborough which was the main stronghold of this species.
First record: Morton 1712
Druce: Wet places in fenny districts. Very local.

13 R. flammula L.   (34)
Lesser Spearwort
a subsp. **flammula**
Native. Wet flushes in woodland, pool and stream margins.
Occasional. It is scattered through the county but may be very common in some woodland grasslands or ridings and around old ponds as in Hazel Wood, Corby, Yardley Chase and Weldon Park Wood. It is also recorded from the old Golf Links at Northampton.
First record: T.Beasley 1873
Druce: Local.

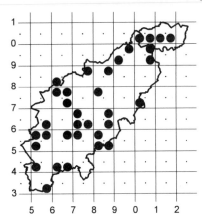

17 R. ficaria L.
Lesser Celandine
a subsp. **ficaria**   (127)
Native. Deciduous woodland, hedgerows etc.
Extremely common throughout the county in woodlands, hedge-banks, and other moist places.

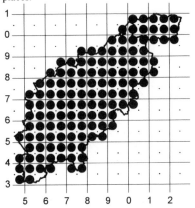

First record: Clare 1835
Druce: Common and generally distributed.

b subsp. **bulbilifer** Lambinon   (11)
Native. Shaded habitats, frequently on disturbed ground.
Less common than subsp. *ficaria* but very much overlooked.

18 R. hederaceus L.
Ivy-leaved Crowfoot
Native. Muddy habitats and shallow water.

88

There are several records of this plant, mainly from the west of the county, but no up-to-date sightings until 1993, when it was recorded at two separate sites - Borough Hill, which confirms an old record, and the Nene valley north of Kingsthorpe. The scarcity of records is probably due to the increasing drainage of wet areas.
First record: Baker 1822
Druce: Local and not common.

21 R. baudotii Godron
Brackish Water-crowfoot
British. Ditches and pools with brackish water.
Druce records this in Farming (Fermyn) Woods in 1876, but it is now thought to be an incorrect identification.
First record: Druce 1876
Druce: Very rare.

22 R. trichophyllus Chaix   (30)
Thread-leaved Water-crowfoot
Native. Ponds and ditches.
Occasional. Found throughout the county, particularly in small ponds.

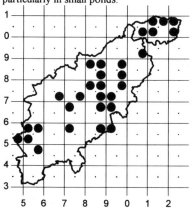

First record: Druce 1877
Druce: Local.

23 R. aquatilis L.   (42)
Common Water-crowfoot
Native.   Ponds, ditches and small water bodies.
Frequent in suitable habitats throughout the county, often producing land forms when the water level changes. It has decreased due to the filling in of ponds.

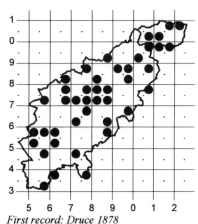

First record: Druce 1878
Druce: (R. heterophyllus) Local.

24 R. peltatus Schrank   (8)
Pond Water-crowfoot
Native. Mostly still waters.
Rare. Recorded at one or two locations in the Soke, in the River Welland and a few other localities within the county.
First record: E.B.Bishop 1933.

25 R. penicillatus (Dumort.) Bab.
Stream Water-crowfoot (5)
b subsp. **pseudofluitans** (Syme) S.Webster (5)

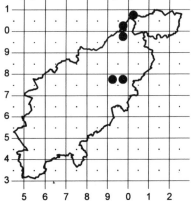

Native. Fast flowing water.
Extremely rare, with records only from Harper's Brook, the River Ise and the River Welland where it is abundant downstream from Wakerley. It is probably overlooked.
First record: Brian Adams 1955

26 R. fluitans Lam. (16)
River Water-crowfoot
Native. Fast flowing waters.

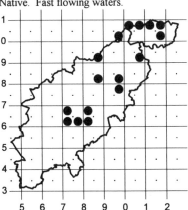

5 6 7 8 9 0 1 2

Frequent in the cleaner faster streams and rivers especially the upper reaches. It is also fairly common in the River Welland in the most northerly part of the area.
First record: Druce 1878
Druce: Local.

27 R. circinatus Sibth. (24)
Fan-leaved Water-crowfoot

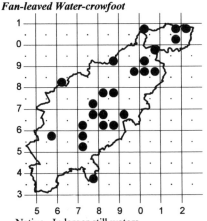

5 6 7 8 9 0 1 2

Native. In larger still waters.
Occasional in canals, lakes and reservoirs, rarely in flowing water.
First record: Gulliver 1841
Druce: Locally common.

14 ADONIS L.
1 A. annua L.
Pheasant's-eye

Adventive. Arable land and disturbed ground.
There are only two recent records of this species, from the Soke of Peterborough by J.H.Chandler and from Cranford Quarry, in 1976.
First record: Blaby 1878
Druce: Very rare.

15 MYOSURUS L.
1 M. minimus L.
Mousetail
Probably native. Bare and waste habitats, path margins.
Extremely rare. It has all but disappeared from the county. It was present on the gravel drive of a Northampton school in the 1970s and fields near Spratton during the same period. It is recently recorded on the new road verges in the Peterborough area.
First record: Morton 1712
Druce: Very local.

16 AQUILEGIA L.
1 A. vulgaris L.
Columbine
Native. Open woods and scrub.
Rare. Probably native in the ancient woodland in the north-east of the county. Found sporadically throughout the rest of the county but mainly as a garden escape.
First record: Morton 1712
Druce: Very local.

17 THALICTRUM L.
3 T. flavum L. (21)
Common Meadow-rue

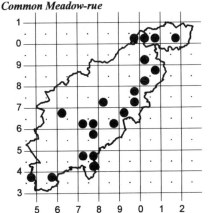

5 6 7 8 9 0 1 2

Native. Wet, grassy habitats, now especially on roadside verges.
Rare. It was once much commoner in the county but changes in agricultural practices have decreased its distribution. The river meadows where it once flourished have nearly all disappeared.
First record: Pitt 1813
Druce: Local.

4 T. minus L.
Lesser Meadow-rue
Introduction. Calcareous scrub.
It was recorded in 1959 near Easton Hornstocks in the Soke of Peterborough, where it was in all probability an escape from cultivation.

29 BERBERIDACEAE
1 BERBERIS L.   (12)
1 B. vulgaris L.
Barberry
Introduction. Hedgerows, woodland and scrub on calcareous soils.
Occurs in a few places as a bird-sown species, mainly occurring as a hedgerow shrub.

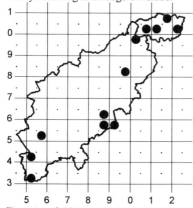

First record: Notcutt 1843
Druce: Local.

2 MAHONIA Nutt.
1 M. aquifolium (Pursh) Nutt.   (47)
Oregon-grape
Introduction. Woods and hedge-banks in semi-shade.
Occasional. Found as a bird-sown species, or garden throw-out.

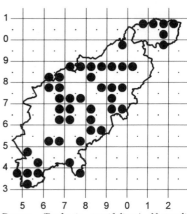

Druce: (Berberis aquifolium) Naturalised and sometimes bird-sown in woodlands etc.

30 PAPAVERACEAE
1 PAPAVER L.
1 P. orientale L.
Oriental Poppy
Introduction. Cultivated and waste land.
Occasionally found as a throw-out or escape.

3 P. somniferum L.
Opium Poppy
a subsp. **somniferum**
Introduction. Cultivated and waste land.
Often occurring in large numbers in quarries and rubbish tips etc. as a garden escape.
First record: Druce 1874
Druce: Rare.

4 P. rhoeas L.   (119)
Common Poppy, Field Poppy

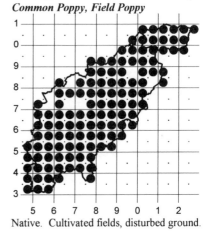

Native. Cultivated fields, disturbed ground.

Frequent. Occurring less as a cornfield weed, but springing up in vast numbers where soil is disturbed such as during pipe laying in roadside verges etc.
First record: Morton 1712
Druce: Abundant in light soils.

5 P. dubium L. (84)
a subsp. **dubium**
Long-headed Poppy

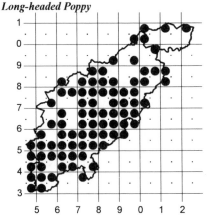

Native. Waste places.
Frequent. Locally common in disturbed ground etc., as with *P.rhoeas,* but it is by no means as common as that species.
First record: Notcutt 1843
Druce: Locally common.

b subsp. **lecoqii** (Lamotte) Syme (19)
(*P. lecoqii* Lamotte)
Babington's Poppy

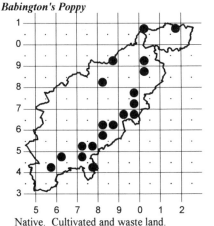

Native. Cultivated and waste land.

Occasional. Occurring mainly along the eastern edge of the county.
First record: Druce 1871
Druce: Very local.

6 P. hybridum L.
Rough Poppy
Possibly native. Arable fields.
Probably extinct. It was recorded by J.L.Gilbert, in a cornfield at Yarwell in 1934.

7 P. argemone L. (20)
Prickly Poppy, Prickly-headed Poppy

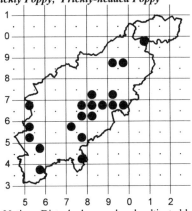

Native. Disturbed ground and cultivated land on sandy soils.
Occasional, scattered throughout the county on the lighter soils, often persisting for many years in the same area.
First record: Morton 1712
Druce: Local.

2 MECONOPSIS Viguier
1 M. cambrica (L.) Viguier
Welsh Poppy
Introduction. Shaded habitats.
There is one record of a garden escape from 1965, but it is probably under-recorded.

5 CHELIDONIUM L. (70)
1 C. majus L.
Greater Celandine
Native or introduction. Moist semi-shaded habitats.
Widely distributed through the county, mainly near habitation as a relic of cottage cultivation. It is frequently found on or close to walls. *C. majus var lacinatum* Mill. was found by Sylvia Beale in Northampton in

1968, and it has subsequently spread around the area.

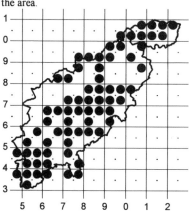

5 6 7 8 9 0 1 2

First record: Baker 1822
Druce: Locally common.

6 ESCHSCHOLZIA Cham.
1 E, californica Cham.
Californian Poppy
Introduction. Tips and roadsides.
A few records as garden escapes or throw-outs.

31 FUMARIACEAE
2 CORYDALIS DC.
1 C. solida (L.) Clairv.
Bird-in-a-Bush
Introduction. Shrubberies, parkland etc.
Introduced and naturalised in parkland or churchyards at Castle Ashby, Denford and Lamport.
First record: G.Adams 1903
Druce: (Capnoides solida) [No status given].

2 C. cava (L.) Schweigger & Koerte
(*C. bulbosa* auct., non (L.) DC. nom. illegit.)
Hollow-root
Introduction. Shrubberies and parkland.
Known only from the village of Clipston, in a wood on the outskirts of Cranford, where it was still growing in 1993 in part of a spinney that was formerly a rectory garden and from Castle Ashby.
First record: Frank Adams (Cranford) 1956

3 PSEUDOFUMARIA Medikus
1 P. lutea (L.) Borkh.   (55)
(*Corydalis lutea* (L.) DC.)
Yellow Corydalis

Introduction. Walls and stony places.
Occasional, mainly in villages. Well distributed throughout the county on stone walls, in old quarries etc. It occurs at Harpole with white flowers.
Druce: (Capnoides lutea) No status given.

5 FUMARIA L.
5 F. muralis Sonder ex Koch
Common Ramping-fumitory
a subsp. **muralis**
Native. Arable ground and hedge-banks.
Extinct. A single plant of this species was found on waste ground at Duston in 1978. This species would appear to be on the verge of extinction in the British Isles.

7 F. officinalis L.   (81)
Common Fumitory
a subsp. **officinalis**

```
1 -
0 -
9 -
8 -
7 -
6 -
5 -
4 -
3 -
    5  6  7  8  9  0  1  2
```

Native. Cultivated and waste ground.
Common in all areas as a weed of cultivated ground.
First record: Clare 1827
Druce: Common and generally distributed.

b subsp. **wirtgenii** (Koch) Arcang.
Native. Cultivated and waste ground.
A single record from Cottingham quarry in 1988. This sub-species is probably much overlooked in the county.

8 F. densiflora DC.
(*F. micrantha* Lagasca)
Dense-flowered Fumitory
British. Arable land.
Extremely rare. This species was recorded from an arable field near Collyweston in

1988. This was the first record for the county.

First record: 1988

33 ULMACEAE

In the early autumn of 1993 Guy Messenger agreed to write the text for the section on the Elm family. His sudden death in November of that year meant that he was unable to fulfil his promise and the Elms have consequently not been covered in as much detail as we had hoped. We apologise for this, and hope this inadequate text will stand as a reminder of how much Guy Messenger will be missed.

1 ULMUS L.

1 U. glabra Hudson   (116)
Wych Elm
a subsp. **glabra**
Native. Woods and hedgerows, and planted in parks.
Frequent throughout but more common in the east. Often originating as a planted tree. Hybrids between *U. glabra* and *U. plotii* have been recorded but not in recent years.

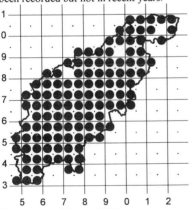

First record: Morton 1712
Druce: (U. montana) Scattered throughout the county, but usually, if not always, a planted tree.

1 x 3 U. glabra x U. minor = U. x vegeta
(Loudon) Ley   (11)
(*U. glabra* Hudson var. *vegeta* Loudon)
Huntingdon Elm
Native. Parkland and hedgerows.
Occasional. Only recorded in the north of the county.

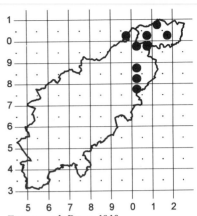

First record: Druce 1910
Druce: Rather frequent.

1 x 3 x 4 U. glabra x U. minor x U. plotii = U. x hollandica Miller
Dutch Elm
Native. Villages.
This hybrid appears to be extinct in the county.
Druce: Rare.

2 U. procera Salisb.   (107)
English Elm

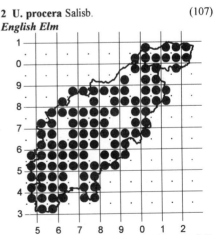

Native. Hedgerows and fields, especially where the soil is well drained.
Frequent. Still occurs reasonably often, although all elms have been decimated in recent years by Dutch Elm disease. As with others of this genus, many of the recent records are of young suckers around trees killed by the disease. These are now under

threat from a new outbreak of the disease in England.
First record: Clare 1827
Druce: (U. sativa) Abundant throughout the county.

3 U. minor Miller
Small-leaved Elm, Smooth Elm
a subsp. **minor**   (31)

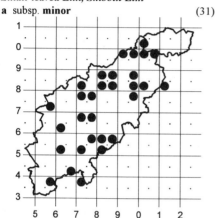

Native. Hedges, fields and woodland edges.
Occasional. Now absent from much of the county, being found, with few exceptions, through the middle of the county from north to south.
First record: Druce 1880
Druce: (U. carpinifolia?) Rather common and widely spread.

b subsp. **angustifolia** (Weston) Stace
(*U. angustifolia* (Weston) Weston)
Cornish Elm
British. Hedgerows and parkland.
Occasional. Found on scattered sites in the western half of the county. Always occurs as a result of planting.
First record: Druce 1879
Druce: (U. minor var. sarniensis?) Probably planted.

4 U. plotii Druce
Plot's Elm
Native. Hedgerows.
Extremely rare. It was thought to be extinct, a victim of Dutch Elm Disease, but in the spring of 1992 five young trees that showed definite features of *U. plotii* were found in a farm gateway at Laxton, previously one of the best known sites for this species. Until this time it had been supposed that Dutch Elm Disease followed by a ruthless grubbing out of hedges wherever regeneration might have been successful had eliminated the species from this site. There is also a well grown tree and several juveniles on the edge of a farm, adjacent to a roadside hedge, in Bulwick, about one kilometre from Laxton.
First record: Druce 1911
Druce: Locally common.

34 CANNABACEAE
1 CANNABIS L.
1 C. sativa L.
Hemp
Adventive. Rubbish tips and places where birds are fed.
Occasionally recorded, the last known instance being in 1960s from birdseed but it has probably occurred sporadically since then.
Druce: No status given.

2 HUMULUS L.
1 H. lupulus L.   (68)
Hop

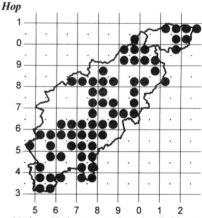

Native. Hedgerows and scrub, climbing over surrounding shrubs and trees.
Occasional. Generally as solitary plants, often as a cottage garden relic.
First record: Clare 1827
Druce: No status given.

36 URTICACEAE
1 URTICA L.
1 U. dioica L.   (134)
Common Nettle, Stinging Nettle

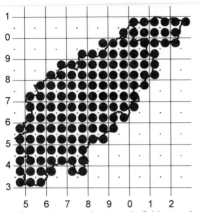

5 6 7 8 9 0 1 2

Native. Waste places and field margins. Extremely common, especially near dwellings, as it prefers nitrogen rich soils.
First record: Clare 1820
Druce: Abundant and generally distributed.

2 U. urens L.   (72)
Small Nettle, Annual Nettle
Native. Cultivated ground and waste ground.

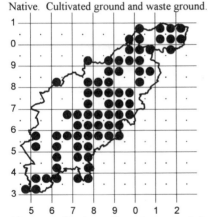

5 6 7 8 9 0 1 2

Almost totally absent from the west of the county, it can be common in the east, although even here it never occurs in the same quantity as *U. dioica*.
First record: Gulliver 1841
Druce: Locally common throughout the county, but much less frequent than U. dioica.

U. pilulifera L.
Roman Nettle
Adventive. Waste places.

Not recorded for many years.
First record: Lewin 1880
Druce: Very rare. Probably extinct.

2 PARIETARIA L.
1 P. judaica L.   (84)
Pellitory-of-the-wall

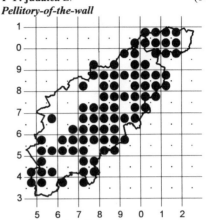

5 6 7 8 9 0 1 2

Native. Old walls.
A common feature of church and churchyard walls, predominantly in the eastern half of the county. It is sometimes found on the brickwork of lockgates and has also been locally dominant on waste ground at Wollaston since the 1980s.
First record: Pitt 1813
Druce: (P. ramiflora) On walls of villages, churches etc. Locally common.

3 SOLEIROLIA Gaudich.
1 S. soleirolii (Req.) Dandy
Mind-your-own-business
Introduction. Damp, shaded walls. Occasionally found as a naturalised plant.

37 JUGLANDACEAE
1 JUGLANS L.
1 J. regia L.   (24)
Walnut
Introduction. Generally planted.
Occasional. Predominantly recorded on sites in the east of the county. Rarely found as other than a planted tree, it can nevertheless establish itself in the wild, as with the example growing in the canal towpath hedge near Braunston which has survived repeated 'coppicing' to keep the towpath clear. It

occurs in reasonable numbers close to the Stamford to Peterborough railway line.

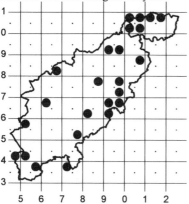

First record: E.B.Bishop (Barnack)1933

39 FAGACEAE
1 FAGUS L.
1 F. sylvatica L.   (101)
Beech

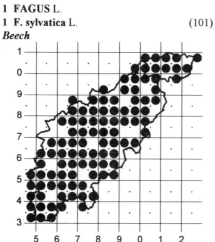

British. Woods on calcareous and sandy soils.
Common. Found throughout, but often as a result of earlier planting. Almost always it occurs as a solitary specimen, but planted beech woods are occasionally found. The best example of this is the Bedlams at the northern end of Bedford Purlieus, but other examples do exist, such as the small plantation in Coton Park which, with the exception of a few *Larix decidua* (European Larch) and *Ilex aquifolium* (Holly) is a pure beech wood, rare in this county. A large,

solitary, pollarded beech in Wakerley Spinney may be the most northerly medieval beech extant. Occasionally varieties such as *'forma pendula'* and *'purpurea'* are found in parks or gardens.
First record: Morton 1712
Druce: Scattered throughout the county, but somewhat doubtfully native.

3 CASTANEA Miller
1 C. sativa Miller   (59)
Sweet Chestnut
Introduction. Woods and parkland.
Occasional. Widely planted in parkland and some woods and can become naturalised in the right environment, especially on light soils.
First record: Morton 1712
Druce: Very local.

4 QUERCUS L.
2 Q. cerris L.   (48)
Turkey Oak

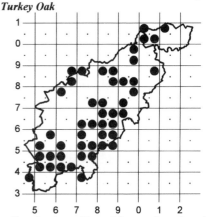

Introduction. Planted in woods and parks and occasionally naturalised.
Occasional. It is usually found in Victorian parkland or plantations, or planted during that era in older woodland, as at King's Wood, Corby. It can become an invasive species as at Barnack Hills and Holes, with seedlings from the adjoining woodland in the grounds of Walcot Hall.

3 Q. ilex L.
Evergreen Oak, Holm Oak
Introduction. Parks, gardens and hedgerows.

Recorded at a few sites, where it is always planted. There are good examples beside the main A6 near Desborough and it is recorded from Broughton Spinney.

5 Q. petraea (Mattuschka) Liebl. (12)
Sessile Oak

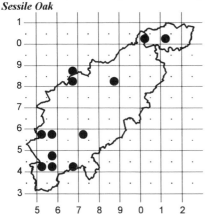

Native. Woodland and hedgerows on poorer soils than *Q. robur*. Occasionally planted. Rare. Found at a few sites which are mostly in the south-west, with a few isolated examples across the north and into the Soke.
First record: Druce 1884
Druce: (Q. sessiliflora) Rare and usually as a planted tree.

6 Q. robur L. (132)
(Q. borealis Michaux f.)
Pendunculate Oak

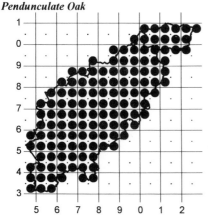

Native. Woodlands and hedgerows, but also widely planted in parks.

Common. Found throughout the area, often as a solitary tree in hedgerows but it is also a feature of old woodland, where it can be locally common although it is rarely the dominant species.
First record: Morton 1712
Druce: Common and widely distributed.

7 Q. rubra L.
Hungarian Oak
Introduction.
Known to be introduced in a few woodlands.

40 BETULACEAE
1 BETULA L.
1 B. pendula Roth (115)
Silver Birch
Native. Woodlands, parks and gardens. Frequent. Often a planted tree, it is found scattered throughout the county. As a woodland tree it is more common in woodlands with poor soil. On the sandy soils across the middle of the county, self-sown trees are frequently found.

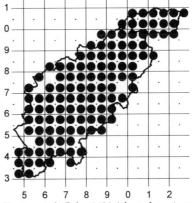

First record: Coles 1651 (planted specimen.)
Druce: (B. alba) Rare as a native tree.

2 B. pubescens Ehrh. (32)
Downy Birch
a subsp. **pubescens**
Native. Woodland.
Occasional, but can be fairly common in the right habitat. It is confined to woodland sites across the county. It will grow with *B. pendula* but it replaces this species on badly drained soils. Near Old Pond Close (Yardley

Chase) and at Birch Spinney near Loddington there are good stands of this species.

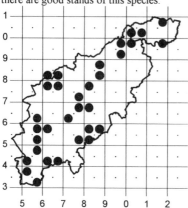

First record: Druce (no date)
Druce: [No status given].

2 ALNUS Miller
1 A. glutinosa (L.) Gaertner (98)
Common Alder

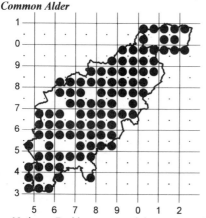

Native. Beside water and in wet woods, often planted.
Frequent. In the right environment it can become common, although it is rarely a dominant species. Its bark was formerly used by the local leather industry as a tanning agent.
First record: Morton 1712
Druce: Widely spread.

2 A. incana (L.) Moench
Grey Alder
Introduction. Deciduous woodland.

Very rare. It is known at only four sites, Irchester Country Park, Titchmarsh Heronry, a disused quarry south of Corby, and Yardley Chase where it is almost certainly planted.

3 CARPINUS L.
1 C. betulus L. (66)
Hornbeam
British. Woods and hedgerows.
Occasional. It is found at scattered sites across the county. It is almost always planted, being native only in southern Britain. It was formerly favoured for its very hard wood which was used in cogs and spindles.
First record: Gerard 1597
Druce: Rare and usually as a planted tree.

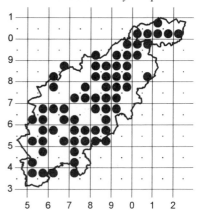

4 CORYLUS L.
1 C. avellana L. (115)
Hazel

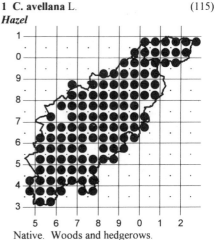

Native. Woods and hedgerows.

Common. In the right environment it can become a dominant feature of the understorey in deciduous woodland. It was previously one of trees commonly coppiced in the county, and it is found in all ancient woodlands.
First record: Morton circa 1716
Druce: Locally abundant. Specially abundant in Whittlebury Forest, whence quantities of nuts were brought to Northampton Market, 1870-1890.

2 C. maxima Miller
Filbert
Introduction. Woodland
Planted in Borough Fen Duck Decoy.

41 PHYTOLACCACEAE
1 PHYTOLACCA L.
P. americana L.
American Pokeweed
Introduction.
There are two records of this plant. It was recorded in the churchyard at Chipping Warden, where it was an escape from cultivation and in a garden on a housing estate in Wellingborough in 1993, by Joan Birch.

43 CHENOPODIACEAE
1 CHENOPODIUM L.
4 C. bonus-henricus L.   (32)
Good King Henry

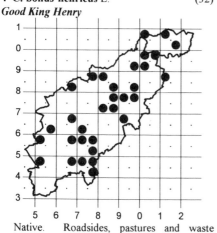

Native. Roadsides, pastures and waste ground.

Occasional, particularly near villages, where it is possibly as a relic of cottage garden cultivation.
First record: Gulliver 1841
Druce: Widely distributed.

6 C. rubrum L.   (53)
Red Goosefoot

Native. Cultivated and waste ground, and tips.
Fairly common on dumped soil, around old farmyards; and often a feature of reservoir margins in late summer when the water levels drop.
First record: Gulliver 1841
Druce: Rather common and widely distributed.

8 C. polyspermum L.   (24)
Many-seeded Goosefoot, All-seed

Native. Waste and cultivated ground.

Occasional throughout the county, but mainly found in the eastern half.
First record: Morton 1712
Druce: Very local

9 C. vulvaria L.
Stinking Goosefoot
Possibly native. Waste places.
Extinct. The last record is from Northampton Sewage Works prior to 1930.
First record: Morton 1712
Druce: Very rare. A decreasing species.

10 C. hybridum L.
Maple-leaved Goosefoot
Probable introduction. Waste and arable ground.
Very rare. It is only recorded in the north of the county from Wothorpe and Collyweston where it has persisted for several years; and in the south from Thrupp Grounds, and a farm near Grendon.
First record:Rev. Berkeley 1850
Druce: Very rare.

11 C. urbicum L.
Upright Goosefoot
Extremely rare. Occurred previously in the Soke of Peterborough and recorded from there by J.H.Chandler. More recently there is a record of this species in a garden at Grendon by George Crawford.
Druce: Doubtful if this was correctly recorded.

13 C. ficifolium Smith (18)
Fig-leaved Goosefoot

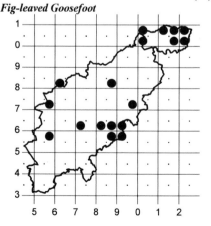

Native. Waste and arable ground.
Occasional. Present mainly in the north and east of the county.
First record: Druce 1879
Druce:Locally common.

14 C. opulifolium Schrader ex Koch & Ziz
Grey Goosefoot
Adventive. Waste ground and tips.
No recent records.
First record: Druce 1919
Druce: Rare.

15 C. album L. (121)
Fat Hen

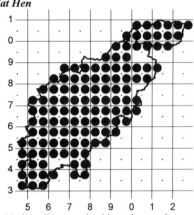

Native. Waste and cultivated ground.
Very common on disturbed ground throughout the county.
First record: Gulliver 1841
Druce: Common and generally distributed.

C. desiccatum Nelson
(C. pratericola Rydb.*)*
Adventive. Tips and waste ground.
No recent records.
Druce: (C. leptophyllum) Rare.

C. capitatum (L.) Asch.
Strawberry-blite
Introduction. Waysides, cultivated ground.
No recent records. *
First record: Curtis 1898
Druce: Very rare.

C. foliosum (Moench.) Asch.
Adventive. Waste ground.
No recent records.
First record: 1875

Druce: (C. virgatum) No status given.

2 BASSIA All.
1 B. scoparia (L.) Voss
(*Kochia scoparia* (L.) Schrader)
Summer-cypress
Adventive. Tips and waste places.
Recorded in Wellingborough in the 1970s.

3 ATRIPLEX L.
1 A. hortensis L.
Garden Orache
Introduction. Tips and waste places.
Recorded by Sean Karley from the roadside
near Irchester in 1975, and by R.C.V.Warren
at Stanwick in 1993.

2 A. prostrata Boucher ex DC.   (53)
(*A. hastata* auct. non L.)
Spear-leaved Orache

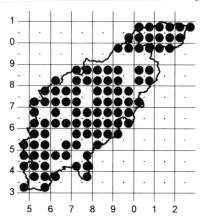

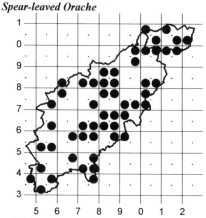

Native. Waste places and cultivated ground.
Less common than *A. patula* but widely
distributed.
First record: Druce 1876
Druce: (A. deltoidea) Local (A. hastata)
Common and widely distributed. [Druce
treated A. deltoidea as a separate species but
this is now no longer accepted].

7 A. patula L.   (99)
Common Orache
Native. Disturbed and waste ground.
Very common and widely distributed
throughout the county.
First record: Baker 1822
Druce: Common and generally distributed.

4 BETA L.
1 B. vulgaris L.
Root Beet
c subsp. **vulgaris**
Introduction. Cultivated and waste ground.
Occasional. Occurs sporadically as a relic of
cultivation.
First record: 1882
Druce: Alien. A relic of cultivation.

8 SALSOLA L.
1 S. kali L.
Prickly Saltwort
a subsp. **kali**
British. Waste places.
Extinct.
Druce: [no status given].

AXYRIS L.
A. amaranthoides L.
Russian Pigweed
Introduction. Waste places.
No recent records.
First record: Goode 1917
Druce: [no status given].

44 AMARANTHACEAE
1 AMARANTHUS L.
1 A. retroflexus L.
Common Amaranth
Adventive. Waste places and tips.
Occasional. Scattered throughout the area,
possibly as a result of birdseed scatterings.
Druce: [No status given].

A. hybridus L.
Green Amaranth
Adventive.
There are two records of this species, one from a garden in Rushden in 1989 and one from a garden at Collingtree where it was growing with other alien species such as *Amaranthus albus*
First record: K. Cheasman and Seán Karley (Rushden) 1989

A. albus L.
White Pigweed
Adventive.
A single plant came up in a garden at Collingtree with other alien species in 1994, possibly from bird seed.

45 PORTULACACEAE
2 CLAYTONIA L.
1 C. perfoliata Donn ex Willd.
(Montia perfoliata (Donn ex Willd) Howell
Springbeauty
Introduction.
Recorded at a few sites in the vicinity of Northampton, at Grendon, Cottesbrooke and a few other localities. All records are of garden escapes.
Druce: [No status given].

2 C. sibirica L.
(Montia sibirica (L.) Howell)
Pink Purslane
Introduction.
It was well established in the grounds of St. Andrew's Hospital, Northampton, by the 1960s, where it still persists and it has also been recorded along the Wilby Brook and in Daventry Country Park in the 1980s.
First record: H.J.Allen (St. Andrew's Hospital, Northampton) 1960s or earlier.

3 MONTIA L.
1 M. fontana L.
Blinks
Native. Damp places.
Presumed extinct as there have been no sightings despite searches at Honey Hill, Badby Downs, Hunsbury Hill, and Elkington, its former habitats. It is possible that it has been overlooked, but all the records date from prior to 1930.
First record: Morton 1712

Druce: (M. verna)Local.

46 CARYOPHYLLACEAE
1 ARENARIA L.
1 A. serpyllifolia L.
Thyme-leaved Sandwort
a subsp. **serpyllifolia** (101)

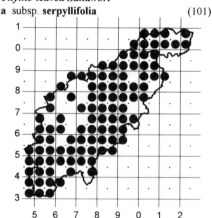

Native. Open, well drained ground.
Very common on wall-tops, quarries and cultivated ground.
First record: Gulliver 1841.
Druce: Common and generally distributed.

c subsp. **leptoclados** (Reichb.) Nyman (32)
(*A. leptoclados* (Reichb.) Guss.)

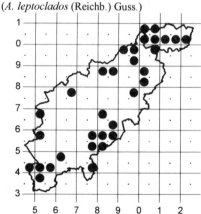

Native. Open, well drained ground, limestone walls etc.
Occasional. Much less common than subsp. *serpyllifolia* but scattered through the southern and eastern sides of the county,

mainly on village walls. An easily overlooked species.
First record: Druce 1874
Druce: Locally common.

4 A. balearica L.
Mossy Sandwort
Introduction. Walls.
This was recorded on the churchyard wall in Guilsborough in 1983. It was still there in 1994.
First record: Gill Gent and Andrew Robinson c1983

2 MOEHRINGIA L.
1 M. trinervia (L.) Clairv. (92)
Three-nerved Sandwort

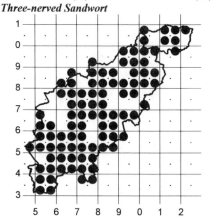

Native. Woodlands and hedgerows.
Fairly common in suitable habitats such as hedgerows and especially dense woodlands and thickets with little ground cover.
First record: 1841
Druce: (Arenaria trinervia) Widely distributed, but not very common.

4 MINUARTIA L.
5 M. hybrida (Villars) Schischkin
Fine-leaved Sandwort
Native. Bare patches in grassland.
Extremely rare, it has only recently been recorded from Barnack Hills and Holes national nature reserve. Prior to this it was last recorded from near Salcey Forest in 1956, by D.E.Allen and A.S.Harris.
First record: Morton 1712
Druce: (Arenaria tenuifolia) Very rare.

5 STELLARIA L.
2 S. media (L.) Villars (130)
Common Chickweed

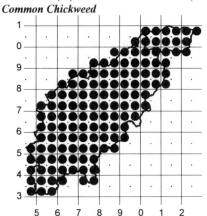

Native. Cultivated and open ground.
A very common weed of cultivated ground. One of the most common weeds.
First record: 1841
Druce: Common and generally distributed.

3 S. pallida (Dumort.) Crépin (7)
Lesser Chickweed
Native. Walls.
Rare or overlooked. Occurs mainly on walls at Collyweston, Easton on the Hill and Pilsgate. There are also records from Kingsthorpe and Braunston.
Druce: (Stellaria media var. apetala) [No status given].

4 S. neglecta Weihe
Greater Chickweed
Native. Shady damp localities.
Extremely rare. Only known from a small wood near to Easton on the Hill during the period of this survey. In addition there is an unconfirmed record from the grounds of Wollaston Hall dating from 1969.
First record: R.C.Palmer (Easton Hillside) 1972

5 S. holostea L. (70)
Greater Stitchwort
Native. Woods and shaded hedgerows.
Common in woodland, hedgerows and other suitable habitats throughout most of the county.

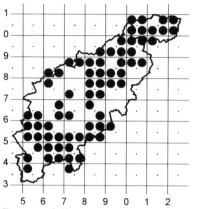

First record: Notcutt 1843
Druce: Locally abundant and generally distributed.

6 S. palustris Retz.
Marsh Stitchwort
Native. Marshes and fens.
Extremely rare. It has disappeared from all of the localities recorded by Druce, probably due to drainage and it was thought to be extinct. The last records were from Salcey Forest where it was present until the 1950s, at Ashton and Biggin, where it was recorded by J.R.Rees. More recently, during the late 1980s, it was recorded by Rosemary Parslow at Trafford Bridge Marsh.
First record: Baker 1822
Druce: (S. dilleniana var. palustris) Local.

7 S. graminea L. (96)
Lesser Stitchwort

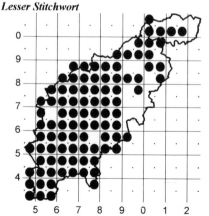

Native. Especially where the soil is quick draining and acidic.
Occasional in grassy places, woodland rides and heathy areas.
First record: Notcott 1843
Druce: Locally common

8 S. uliginosa Murray (45)
(*S. alsine* Grimm, nom. inval.)
Bog Stitchwort

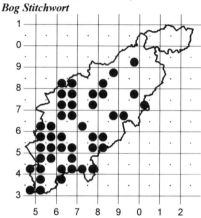

Native. Streamsides and ditches.
Occasional in wet boggy places, often in damp woodland rides. Druce considered it rare but it may have been under-recorded in his day.
First record: Baker 1822
Druce: (S. alsine) Rare.

7 CERASTIUM L.
2 C. arvense L. (25)
Field Mouse-ear

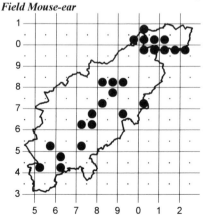

Native. Dry grassland.
Rare, and often confined to railway banks and old quarries. Quite a feature of the old limestone quarry at Collyweston and the old golf course at Northampton.
First record: Morton 1712
Druce: Local

3 C. tomentosum L.
Snow-in-Summer, Dusty Miller
Introduction. Naturalised in dry places.
Occasional. Naturalised as a garden escape in a few places, by roadsides and on railway banks etc.

7 C. fontanum Baumg.
Common Mouse-ear
a subsp. *vulgare* (Hartman) Greuter & Burdet
(127)

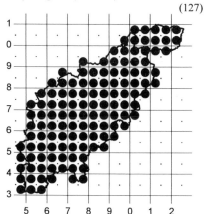

Native. All types of open grassland, walls etc.
Very common in all areas, on lawns, grassy places, walls etc.
First record: Gulliver 1841
Druce: (C. vulgatum) Abundantly and generally distributed.

b subsp. *holosteoides* (Fries) Salman, van Ommering & de Voogd
Native. Wet places.
A single record but may be under-recorded.

8 C. glomeratum Thuill. (98)
Sticky Mouse-ear
Native. Open ground.
Very common, liking dry areas such as wall-tops, gravel paths and disused railway lines.

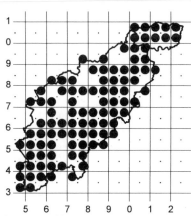

First record: 1841
Druce: (C. viscosum) Common and generally distributed.

9 C. brachypetalum Pers.
Grey Mouse-ear
British. Fairly bare grassland.
First found by Dr. and Mrs. Dony in 1973 on the main railway line just south of Irchester, having spread from the site in Bedfordshire, where it was first found in 1947. This plant is a British Red Data Book species.
First record: J.G. Dony (Irchester) 1973

10 C. diffusum Pers. (7)
(*C. atrovirens* Bab.)
Sea Mouse-ear, Dark-green Mouse-ear
Native. Dry, open, sandy or gravelly ground.
Rare, and almost always confined to areas near the railway, as at Finedon Pits, on the dismantled railway line at Braunston and the old furnace site at Kettering. It has also been found on the canal bank at Aynho.

11 C. pumilum Curtis
Dwarf Mouse-ear
Native. Bare calcareous ground.
This species was first noticed by Dr John Dony on the railway near Wellingborough in 1950 . Two subsequent sightings on a branch railway near Wellingborough (now dismantled) in 1970 and 1980, have not been substantiated.
First record: J.G. Dony 1950.

12 C. semidecandrum L. (13)
Little Mouse-ear
Native. Dry calcareous soils.

106

Rare. Found in scattered localities in quarries and on railway embankments. It has recently been found in the sand pit near Harlestone and at Kingsthorpe. It may be overlooked.
First record: Druce 1876
Druce: Local and rather rare.

8 MYOSOTON Moench
1 M. aquaticum (L.) Moench   (92)
Water Chickweed

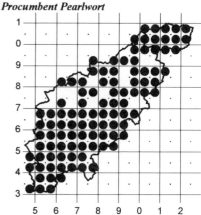

5 6 7 8 9 0 1 2
Native. Stream banks and marshes.
Very common by water and damp places.
First record: 1841
Druce: (Stellaria aquatica) Local.

9 MOENCHIA Ehrh.
1 M. erecta (L.) P.Gaertner, Meyer & Scherb.
Upright Chickweed
Native. Bare, sandy or gravelly ground. Presumed extinct. Considered very rare by Druce, the last record is from Harlestone Firs in 1877.

10 SAGINA L.
1 S. nodosa (L.) Fenzl
Knotted Pearlwort
Native. Damp, open peaty ground.
Extremely rare. It was thought to be extinct because it had not been seen since it was recorded at Castor Hanglands national nature reserve in the Soke of Peterborough, during the 1960s, but has been recently recorded by Linda Moore on the Brampton Valley Way.
First record: Goodyer 1633
Druce: Very rare.

3 S. subulata (Sw.) C.Presl.
Heath Pearlwort

Recorded from Borough Hill in the *History and Antiquities of Northampton* by George Baker. *Druce: Error? or extinct.*

5 S. procumbens L.   (102)
Procumbent Pearlwort

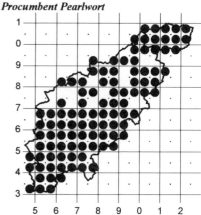

5 6 7 8 9 0 1 2
Native. Paths and lawns.
Very common as a weed on paths and other suitable dry areas.
First record: Notcutt 1843
Druce: Common and generally distributed.

7 S. apetala Ard.
Annual Pearlwort
a subsp. **apetala**   (3)
Native. Dry bare ground on heaths.
Extremely rare, or possibly overlooked.
First record: Druce 1876
Druce: (S. ciliata) Very rare.

b subsp. **erecta** F. Herm   (50)

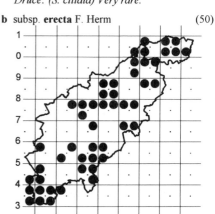

5 6 7 8 9 0 1 2
Native. Paths, walls and cultivated ground.

Common on suitable dry areas.
First record: Druce 1874
Druce: (S. apetala) Local.

11 SCLERANTHUS L.
1 S. perennis L.
Perennial Knawel
a subsp. **perennis**
Native. Sandy heathland.
Probably extinct. Considered by Druce to be probably extinct, but there was a reported sighting on a wall in Wellingborough about 1974.
First record: Morton 1712
Druce: Very rare or probably extinct.

2 S. annuus L.
Annual Knawel
a subsp. **annuus** (3)
Native. Dry, open, sandy soil.
A rare species of sandy soils recorded mainly from old sand pits and more rarely as a weed of cultivation.
First record: Notcutt 1843
Druce: Locally common.

16 SPERGULA L.
1 S. arvensis L. (15)
Corn Spurrey
Native. Sandy, cultivated ground.

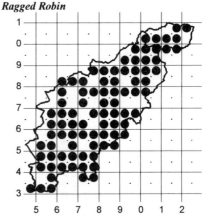

Occasional as a weed of cultivation, but can be common in the more sandy soils around Overstone, Harlestone, Spratton and Hollowell areas and in the west of the county.
First record: Beesley 1841
Druce: [Regarded by Druce as two different species] S. arvensis: Gregariously abundant

but *absent from large areas; S. sativa: Very rare.*

17 SPERGULARIA (Pers.) J.S.Presl & C.Presl
4 S. rubra (L.) J.S.Presl & C.Presl
Sand Spurrey
Native. Sandy or gravelly ground.
Extremely rare, and only known from a few places on sandy soils: the canal towpath at Winwick, Church Brampton golf course and from Great Doddington in early 1950s.
First record: Notcutt 1843
Druce: Local.

18 LYCHNIS L.
1 L. coronaria (L.) Murray
Rose Campion
Introduction.
A garden escape persisting only a few years.
First record: Seán Karley (Irchester) c1970

2 L. flos-cuculi L. (88)
Ragged Robin

Native. Damp fields and grassland.
Occasional, but may be common in damp places in woodland and other damp areas by rivers, canals etc. Distribution has been reduced by the drainage of its habitat.
First record: Morton 1712
Druce: Common.

19 AGROSTEMMA L.
1 A. githago L.
Corncockle
Adventive. Cultivated and waste ground.
Extremely rare. Thought to be extinct apart from deliberate sowing on roadsides etc., but

in 1993 it was discovered at Lyveden by Ted Faulkner. Three plants flowered, presumably from dormant seed, in ground that had been disturbed when a new hedge was set at the edge of land that had probably never been sprayed. It appeared again in 1994 but must inevitably disappear as the hedge grows. Prior to this the last sightings were in the early 1950s before crop spraying became universal. *First record: Pitt. 1813* *Druce: (Lychnis githago) Locally common.*

20 SILENE L.
1 S. italica (L.) Pers.
(*Cucubalus italicus* L.)
Italian Catchfly
Adventive.
Recorded by Claire Williams growing in Geddington as a garden weed in 1993.

2 S. nutans L.
Nottingham Catchfly
Native. Dry grassy places.
Recorded by Morton in 1712. Thought by Druce to be an error for *S. noctiflora*.

4 S. vulgaris Garcke
Bladder Campion
a subsp. **vulgaris** (78)
(*S. cucubalus* Wibel, nom. illegit.)

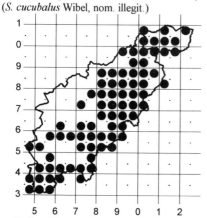

Native. Waste ground, and rough grassland. Common throughout the county except in the western area bordering Warwickshire.
First record: Morton 1712
Druce: (S. angustifolia) Common and generally distributed.

8 S. noctiflora L. (9)
Night-flowering Catchfly

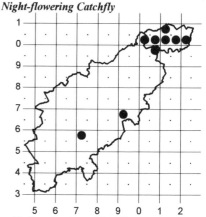

Native. Sandy, arable soils.
Rare. A very much less common species now due to the decline in cornfield weeds. It still occurs in the north around Collyweston and Barnack. It also occurs sporadically in the Irchester and Wellingborough areas on disturbed soil and it was recorded in a garden in Collingtree in 1991.
First record: Irvine 1838
Druce: Local.

9 S. latifolia Poiret
(*S. alba* (Miller) E.H.Krause, non Muhlenb. ex Britton)
White Campion
a subsp. **alba** (Miller) Greuter & Burdet (120)

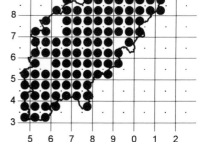

Native.Banks, roadsides etc. on lighter soils. Very common throughout the county on roadsides, waste places etc.

First record: 1841
Druce: Commonly distributed.

9 x 10 S. latifolia x S. dioica = S. x hampeana
Meusel & K. Werner
(*S. x intermedia* (Schur) Philp, non (Lange)
Bocq.)
Pink Campion
Native. Banks, roadsides etc.
Locally common where the two parent
species occur together, usually on roadside
verges.
First record: Druce 1916
Druce: [Three localities given].

10 S. dioica (L.) Clairv. (84)
Red Campion

5   6   7   8   9   0   1   2

Native. Woods and hedgerows in shaded
places.
Common in the west of the county,
occasional throughout the rest but absent
from the most easterly areas, although it is
present in the Soke of Peterborough.
First record: 1841
*Druce: Locally abundant, but absent from
large areas.*

11 S. gallica L.
Small-flowered Catchfly
British. Waste places and cultivated land.
No recent records.
First record: Notcutt 1843
Druce: (S. anglica) Very rare.

S. dichotoma Ehrh.
Forked Catchfly
Adventive. Waste places.

Recorded by Druce in about three areas
during the early 1900s but there are no more
recent records.
First record: Chester 1900
Druce: Rare.

22 SAPONARIA L.
1 S. officinalis L. (33)
Soapwort

5   6   7   8   9   0   1   2

British or introduction. Dry grassland etc.
Occasional on roadsides near villages, on
dumped soil and on railway lines, but can be
quite prolific where it does occur. Many
colonies are double-flowered.
First record: Gerard (Herbal) 1597
Druce: Very rare.

23 VACCARIA Wolf
1 V. hispanica (Miller) Rauschert
(*V. pyramidata* Medikus)
Cowherb
Adventive. Tips and waste ground.
No recent records.
Druce: (Saponaria vaccaria) Rare.

25 DIANTHUS L.
1 D. gratianopolitanus Villars
Cheddar pink
British.
The only record is in Druce, naturalised on a
bridge at Rush Mills - presumably a garden
escape.
*Druce: (D. caesius) [a single record as
detailed above].*

3 D. plumarius L.
Pink
Introduction. Old walls.

Formerly at Barnwell Castle.
First record: Marchioness of Huntley 1883
Druce: [First and only record given].

6 D. barbatus L.
Sweet-William
Introduction.
A single record, in Old Sulehay Forest.

47 POLYGONACEAE
1 PERSICARIA Miller
(Polygonum)
3 P. wallichii Greuter & Burdet
(Polygonum polystachyum Wallich ex Meissner)
Himalayan Knotweed
Introduction. Grassy places and roadsides.
Long cultivated in large gardens. It is not as
frequent as an escape or throw-out as might
be expected, the only record being on the
roadside at Upton.

6 P. bistorta (L.) Samp.   (3)
(Polygonum bistorta L.)
Bistort
Native. Grassland.
Extremely rare, and it would appear to have
gone from most of the old localities. It now
only occurs in one marshy meadow not far
from Corby and it is naturalised at Castle
Ashby from whence it has spread to the
roadside in that area.
First record: Morton 1712
Druce: Rare.

7 P. amplexicaulis (D.Don) Ronse Decraene
(Polygonum amplexicaule D.Don)
Red Bistort
Introduction. Grassland.
The only recent record is from Charlton, in
1981, where it was recorded by Ian Cameron.
Druce: (Polygonum amplexicaule var.
speciosum) [No status given, but only one
record from the grounds of Finedon Hall].

9 P. amphibia (L.) Gray   (89)
(Polygonum amphibium L.)
Amphibious Bistort
Native. Slow and still waters and wet banks.
Fairly common, particularly in canals, ponds,
lakes and some of the older reservoirs.
First record: Beesley 1842
Druce: Common and widely distributed in
all the districts.

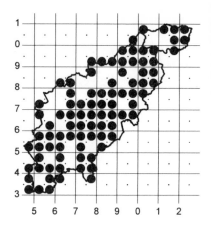

11 P. maculosa Gray   (127)
(Polygonum persicaria L.)
Redshank, Persicaria

Native Cultivated land, waste ground etc.
Very common throughout the county in
waste places and as a weed of cultivation. It
can be particularly common in broken land at
the early stages of gravel digging.
First record: Pitt 1813
Druce: Common and generally distributed.

12 P. lapathifolia (L.) Gray   (60)
(Polygonum lapathifolium L.)
Pale Persicaria
Native. Cultivated and waste land, especially
if damp.
Common throughout. Mainly found as a
weed of cultivation by streams and other
similar areas, but also in waste places and at
sewage works.

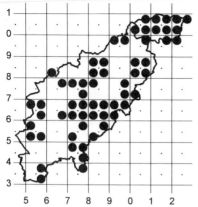

First record: 1841
Druce : [Regarded by Druce as two species]
P. scabrum: Locally common; P. petecticale:
Local - [seven localities recorded].

14 P. hydropiper (L.) Spach (59)
(*Polygonum hydropiper* L.)
Water-pepper

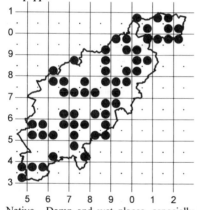

Native. Damp and wet places, especially in shade.
Occasional by water and in damp woodland rides throughout the county.
First record: Hill 1773
Druce: Locally common.

15 P. laxiflora (Weihe) Opiz
(*Polygonum mite* Schrank)
Tasteless Water-pepper
Native. Wet and damp places.
Probably extinct. There is no recent record of this species. Druce considered it very local

in 1930 when it appears to have been found only in a few areas in the Soke.
First record: Watson 1851
Druce: (Polygonum mite) Very local.

16 P. minor (Hudson) Opiz
(*Polygonum minus* Hudson)
Small Water-pepper
Native. Damp fields and ditches.
Extinct. Druce considered this very rare and there are no recent records of the species.
First record: Baker 1822 (doubtful record)
Druce: (Polygonum minus) Very rare.

3 FAGOPYRUM Miller
1 F. esculentum Moench
Buckwheat
Introduction. Waste ground.
A few isloated records of this former crop plant.

4 POLYGONUM L.
3 P. arenastrum Boreau
(*P. aequale* Lindman)
Equal-leaved Knotgrass
Native. On tracks and in cracks in footpaths.
Common. It can stand a good deal of trampling, more so than P. aviculare. Much under-recorded.
Druce (P. equale (sic)) [No status given].

4 P. aviculare L. (129)
Knotgrass

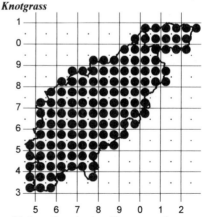

Native. Grassland and bare ground.
Very common in bare places, as a weed of cultivation etc.
First record: Clare 1827

Druce: Very   common   and   generally distributed.

5 FALLOPIA Adans.
(Reynoutria Houtt.)

1 F. japonica (Houtt.) Ronse Decraene   (35)
(Reynoutria japonica Houtt.   *Polygonum cuspidatum* Siebold & Zucc.)
Japanese Knotweed

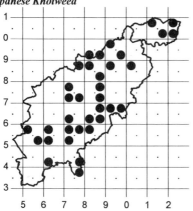

5   6   7   8   9   0   1   2

Introduction. Roadsides and wasteland. Fairly frequent. Scattered through the county as a garden escape and establishing itself successfully.

2   F. sachalinensis (F.Schmidt ex Maxim.) Ronse Decraene
(Reynoutria sachalinensis (F.Schmidt ex Maxim.) Nakai)
Giant Knotweed
Introduction. Waste land and road verges. Uncommon. Established on the roadside at Great Harrowden, Upton and a few other localities.

3 F. baldschuanica (Regel) Holub
(F. aubertii (L.Henry) Holub.)
Russian Vine
Introduction. Rubbish tips and hedges. Occasionally well established as a garden escape.

4 F. convolvulus (L.) Á.Löve   (103)
(Polygonum convolvulus L.)
Black Bindweed
Native. A frequent weed of arable and waste land.
Common, often on field margins, frequent in gardens.

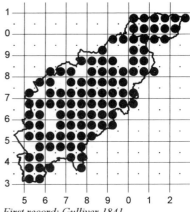

5   6   7   8   9   0   1   2

First record: Gulliver 1841
Druce: Common and generally distributed.

7 RHEUM L.
R. rhaponticum L. x **R. palmatum L. = Rheum x hybridum** Murray
(R. rhaponticum auct., non L., *R. rhaponticum* L. x *R. palmatum* L.)
Rhubarb
Introduction. Waste ground, rubbish tips etc. Found as a throw-out on tips and similar areas; common in abandoned allotments.

8 RUMEX L.
1 R. acetosella L.   (50)
Sheep's Sorrel

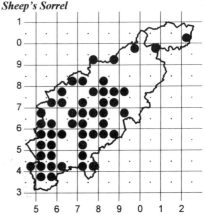

5   6   7   8   9   0   1   2

Native. Heath and grassland.
Occasional on light sandy soils, furnace waste and old railway lines.
First record: Notcutt 1843
Druce: Locally abundant.

3 R. acetosa L.
Sorrel
a subsp. **acetosa** (125)

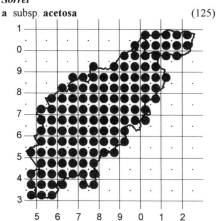

Native. Grassy places.
Common in old meadows, woodland rides, green lanes, etc.
First record: Pitt 1813
Druce: Common and generally distributed.

10 R. hydrolapathum Hudson (41)
Great Water Dock

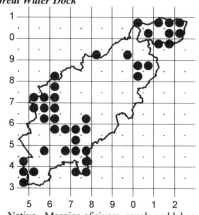

Native. Margins of rivers, canals and lakes.
Fairly common by rivers and streams etc. but by far the commonest habitat in the county is by the canals.
First record: Beesley 1842
Druce: Common and widely distributed.

13 R. crispus L.
Curled Dock
a subsp. **crispus** (126)

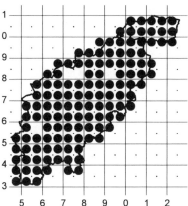

Native. Waste land and rough grassland.
Very common and widely distributed in waste places. An aggressive weed of cultivation.
First record: Pitt 1813
Druce: Common and generally distributed.

14 R. conglomeratus Murray (104)
Clustered Dock, Sharp Dock

Native. Damp, grassy places.
Occasional in damp places, along grassy lanes, in woodland and other similar places.
First record: Baker 1822
Druce: Common in all districts.

14 x 20 R. conglomeratus x R. palustris = R. x wirtgenii G. Beck
Native. Damp grassy places.
A single record from near Earls Barton by the River Nene in 1983.

15 R. sanguineus L. (104)
Wood Dock

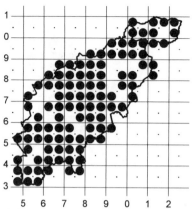

5 6 7 8 9 0 1 2

Native. Damp shady places, mainly in woods.
Occasional in woodland and ditches etc.
First record: Druce 1880
Druce: (R. viridis?) Locally common.

15 x 19 R. sanguineus x R. obtusifolius = R. x dufftii Hausskn.
Native. Damp, shaded grassland in woods.
Recorded in the grounds of Upton Hall.
Druce: [No status given, but only one record, from Ashton, near Oundle].

18 R. pulcher L. (19)
Fiddle Dock

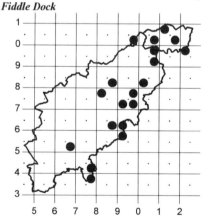

5 6 7 8 9 0 1 2

Native. Dry grassy places.
Rare. Mainly restricted to old churchyards and dry pastures, often around villages, in the east of the county. It is particularly well established by Wadenhoe church.
First record: Baker 1822
Druce: Very local.

19 R. obtusifolius L. (131)
Broad-leaved Dock

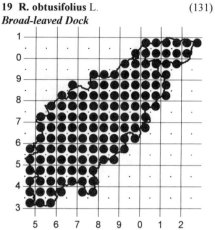

5 6 7 8 9 0 1 2

Native. Grassland and rough ground, especially near water.
A very common weed, found everywhere.
First record: Druce 1874
Druce: Common and generally distributed.

19 x 20 R. obtusifolius x R. palustris = R. x steinii A.Becker
Native. Damp grassland.
A single record near Earls Barton in 1983.

20 R. palustris Smith (21)
Marsh Dock

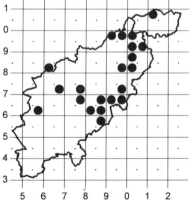

5 6 7 8 9 0 1 2

Native. Edges of ponds, ditches, rivers etc.
Frequent by the River Nene and around reservoirs in the county.
First record: Druce 1909
Druce: Rare.

21 R. maritimus L. (10)
Golden Dock

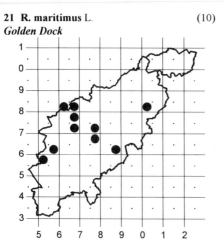

Native. Edges of ponds, rivers etc.
Rare, but well distributed by open stretches of water at Pitsford, Ravensthorpe and Welford reservoirs, Titchmarsh Heronry, and by the ponds at Grendon and Church Charwelton.
First record: Ray 1670
Druce: Rare.

51 CLUSIACEAE
(Guttiferae, Hypericaceae)
1 HYPERICUM L.
1 H. calycinum L.
Rose-of-Sharon
Introduction. Hedgebanks and shrubberies. Established at one or two sites as a relic of cultivation.
First record: Harlestone Firs, 1875
Druce: Established in a few places.

3 H. androsaemum L.
Tutsan
Native. Damp woods and hedges.
A rare plant in the wild, it is recorded mainly as a garden escape. It was recently recorded for Easton Hornstocks, where it appears to be native. Other sightings are from Old Pastures Wood and King's Wood, not too far from habitation.
First record: Morton 1712
Druce: Very rare.

6 H. perforatum L. (102)
Perforate St John's-Wort, Common St John's-wort

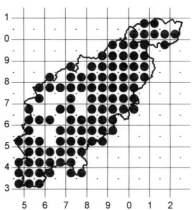

Native. Open woods, hedgebanks and grassland.
Common and distributed throughout the county.
First record: Ray 1662
Druce: Locally abundant.

6 x 7 H. perforatum x H. maculatum = H. x desetangsii Lamotte
Des Etangs' St John's-wort
Native. Damp grassland.
Extremely rare. Only recorded at Aynho in 1974.
First record: Aynho 1974

7 H. maculatum Crantz (16)
Imperforate St John's-wort

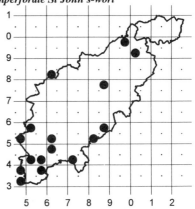

Native. Damp places, wood margins etc.
Very occasional. Recorded at several localities within the county, but mainly in the south and west. Most of the sites are on

disused railway banks but a large stand was discovered in part of Yardley Chase in 1990. This has been recorded as an aggregate species, but there have been a few records specifically attributed to subsp. *obtusiusculum*.
First record: Druce 1876
Druce: (H. quadrangulum) Rare.

9 H. tetrapterum Fries   (99)
Square-stalked St John's-wort

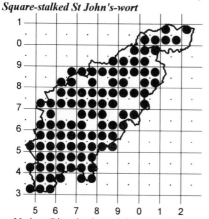

Native. River banks and damp meadows. Frequent throughout the county in its habitat.
First record: Parkinson 1640
Druce: (H. acutum) Rather common and widely distributed.

10 H. humifusum L.   (14)
Trailing St John's-wort
Native. Open woodland and hedgebanks on dry, sandy, usually acidic soils.
Rare. Recorded in a few such woodlands throughout the county and the Soke of Peterborough, where conditions are suitable, but it is never common.
First record: Morton 1712
Druce: Local

12 H. pulchrum L.   (16)
Slender St John's-wort
Native. Dry woods and rough grassland on non-calcareous soils.
Rare. Found mainly in Wakerley Great Wood and Bedford Purlieus, woodland areas bordering on the Soke of Peterborough, in the Whittlebury area in the south, at

Harlestone Firs and at Badby Woods in the west of the county.

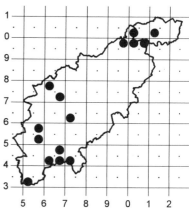

First record: Morton 1712
Druce: No status given.

14 H. hirsutum L.   (73)
Hairy St John's-wort

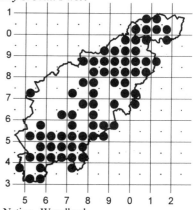

Native. Woodland.
Abundant in woodland throughout the county.
First record: Baker 1822
Druce: Locally abundant and generally distributed.

15 H. montanum L.
Pale St John's-Wort, Mountain St John's-wort
Native. Woods and scrub on calcareous or gravel soils.
Extremely rare and possibly extinct. There is no recent record of this plant although it was

seen by Andrew Robinson near Bedford Purlieus in 1951, confirming the earlier records of George Chester and J.H.Chandler.
First record: 1915
Druce: Very rare.

52 TILIACEAE

1 TILIA L.
1 T. platyphyllos Scop.
Large-leaved Lime
Introduction. Woods, coppices and parks on limestone.
Rare in the county but planted on estates and other similar areas.
First record: Elwes. Tree at Burghley planted. Queen Elizabeth 1
Druce: Rare.

1 x 2 T. platyphyllos x T. cordata = T. x vulgaris Hayne (112)
Common Lime

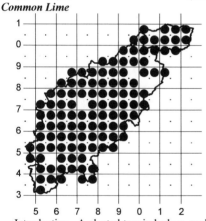

Introduction. A planted tree in hedges, parks etc.
Very common and widely planted as an ornamental tree throughout the county and often planted to form avenues, as at Boughton Park and other great estates.
First record: M.J. Berkley 1836
Druce: (T. europaea) Planted in avenues etc. throughout the county.

2 T. cordata Miller (20)
Small-leaved Lime
Native. Woods on limestone soils.
Common in woodlands in the north of the county including Easton Hornstocks and Collyweston Great Wood where it was

formerly coppiced. Otherwise it occurs sporadically in other woods as at Yardley Chase, Aynho and Force Leap. It is also occasionally found as a single tree in parkland, as at Burghley House.

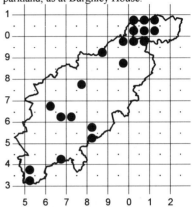

First record: Gerard 1597
Druce: Locally common.

53 MALVACEAE

1 MALVA L.
1 M. moschata L. (46)
Musk Mallow

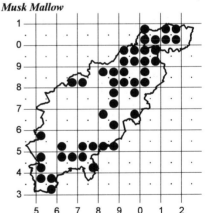

Native. Hedgebanks, waste places.
Occasional throughout but more common on the limestone soils in the north-east.
First record: Baker 1822
Druce: Local.

3 M. sylvestris L. (121)
Common Mallow

Native. Roadsides, hedgebanks and waste ground.

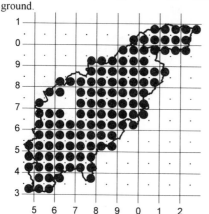

5 6 7 8 9 0 1 2

Very common, occurring throughout the county.

First record: Parkinson 1640

Druce: Common and generally distributed.

7 M. neglecta Wallr. (89)
Dwarf Mallow

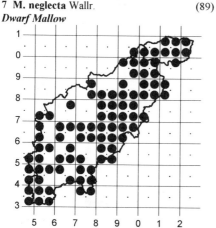

5 6 7 8 9 0 1 2

Native. Roadsides, wasteground.
Common and well distributed throughout the county.

First record: Gulliver 1841

Druce: Common.

3 ALTHAEA L.
1 A. officinalis L.
Marsh-mallow
Introduction.
One record, probably an introduction.

4 ALCEA L.
1 A. rosea L.
(*Althaea rosea* (L.) Cav.)
Hollyhock
Introduction.
An escape or throw-out on tips etc.

55 DROSERACEAE
1 DROSERA L.
1 D. rotundifolia L.
Round-leaved Sundew
Native. Wet, peaty, acid bogs.
Druce considered this species to be extinct for his only records are from the 18th and 19th centuries. It was formerly present in the area known as Harlestone Firs
First record: Morton 1712
Druce: Very rare, probably almost extinct.

56 CISTACEAE
2 HELIANTHEMUM Miller
1 H. nummularium (L.) Miller (8)
Common Rockrose

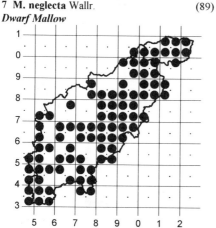

5 6 7 8 9 0 1 2

Native. Basic grassland and scrub.
Rare now due to the destruction of calcareous grasslands over the past forty years, and only present in the limestone areas around Collyweston, Barnack and Wakerley.
First record: Morton 1712
Druce: (H. helianthemum) Locally abundant but absent from the clay soils.

57 VIOLACEAE
1 VIOLA L.
1 V. odorata L. (106)
Sweet Violet

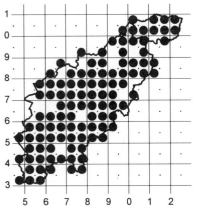

5 6 7 8 9 0 1 2

Native. Hedgebanks and wood borders.
Common. Occurs widely in suitable habitats.
First record: Morton 1712
Druce: Rather common and widely distributed.

1 x 2 V. odorata x V. hirta = V. x scabra L.
Native. Hedgebanks and woodland margins.
Probably extinct, no recent records.
Druce: (V x permixta & V x sepincola) No status given, and only four records listed.

2 V. hirta L. (53)
Hairy Violet

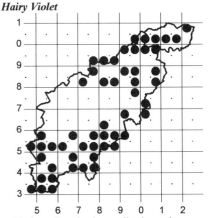

5 6 7 8 9 0 1 2

Native. Grassland, woodland margins.
Occasional on calcareous soil, being more commonly found in the north and the south.
First record: Morton 1712
Druce: Locally common.

2 V. rupestris F.W.Schmidt
Teesdale Violet

Recorded by Druce as *V. rupestris* var. *glabrascens*, but all glabrous records from this country are errors. Almost certainly a mis-identification of *V. hirta.*

4 V. riviniana Reichb. (86)
Common Dog-violet, Dog Violet

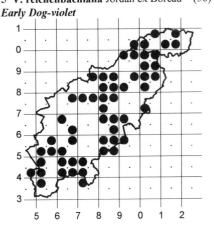

5 6 7 8 9 0 1 2

Native. Woods and hedgebanks.
Frequent in most of the county in suitable habitats.
First certain record: Druce 1877
Druce: Common and widely distributed in all districts.

4 x 6 V. riviniana x V. canina = V.x intersita
G. Beck
Native. Woods and hedgebanks.
Probably extinct, no recent records.
Druce: [No status given, a single record.]

5 V. reichenbachiana Jordan ex Boreau (56)
Early Dog-violet

Native. Woods and hedgebanks.
Frequent and fairly widely distributed.
First record: Druce 1877
Druce: (V. silvestris) Local, but widely distributed.

6 V. canina L.
Heath Dog-violet
a subsp. **canina**
Native. Dry sandy heaths.
Very rare. Recorded in four localities only, one being Harlestone Firs, where it was recorded by Druce.
First record: Druce 1879
Druce: Rare.

V. x wittrockiana Gams ex Kappert
Garden Pansy
Introduction. Cultivated and waste ground.
A few recent records of garden escapes or throw-outs.

12 V. tricolor L.
Wild Pansy
a subsp. **tricolor**
Native. Cultivated and waste ground.
Extremely rare. Recorded near Ringstead in 1992, and on the edge of an arable field adjoining Bonemills Hollow in 1993.
Druce: Widely distributed. [Druce included several 'micro-species' including V. arvensis, which was probably always the most common species].

13 V. arvensis Murray   (103)
Field Pansy

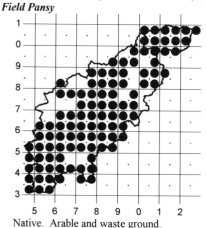

5   6   7   8   9   0   1   2
Native. Arable and waste ground.

Frequent in arable fields, especially in crop margins despite modern farming practices.

60 CUCURBITACEAE
1 BRYONIA L.
1 B. dioica Jacq.   (99)
White Bryony

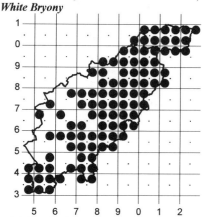

5   6   7   8   9   0   1   2
Native. Hedgerows and scrub.
Occasional throughout the county, but can be frequent in the east, especially in and around the Soke of Peterborough and the south. Generally seen as a solitary plant overgrowing hedgerow plants it can occasionally be prolific enough to cover whole hedges.
First record: Pitt 1797
Druce: Rather frequent.

61 SALICACEAE
1 POPULUS L.
1 P. alba L.
White Poplar
Introduction. Often planted in hedgerows and coppices and often naturalised.
Frequent. Scattered through the county but more commonly found in the Soke of Peterborough.
First record: Morton 1712
Druce: Rare.

1 x 2 P. alba x P. tremula = P. x canescens
(Aiton) Smith
(*P.canescens* (Aiton) Smith)
Grey Poplar
Introduction. Planted in hedgerows and plantations in damp locations.
Very occasional. Scattered throughout the county.

First record: Druce 1878
Druce:(P. canescens) Local.

2 P. tremula L. (63)
Aspen

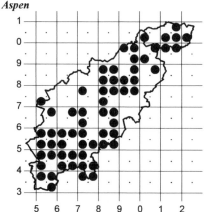

5 6 7 8 9 0 1 2

Native. Woods and hedges.
Occasional. Found in most of the woods throughout the county, although it is perhaps more common in the south.
First record: Gulliver 1841
Druce: Local.

3 P. nigra L.
Black-poplar
a subsp. **betulifolia** (Pursh) W.Wettst. (6)
Native. In fields and hedgerows in damp situations.

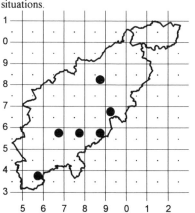

5 6 7 8 9 0 1 2

Now a very rare species in lowland England and most of these trees appear to be getting towards the end of their lives. There are two or three on the roadside near Stanford reservoir and two have been recorded near Yardley Hastings. There were odd trees in Wellingborough and Kislingbury but these have been cut down. The only other records are of three on the roadside near Little Houghton, two or three obviously planted on the Boughton Estate and a very fine pollard on the county boundary near Brackley.
First certain record: Druce 1886
Druce: Rare.

'Italica'
(*P. nigra var. italica* Muenchh.)
Lombardy Poplar
Introduction. Planted for screening.
Commonly planted, often in rows around farms as shelter belts.
Druce:(P. italica) no status given.

P. nigra x P. deltoides Marshall = **P. x canadensis** Moench (50)
(*P. euroamericana* (Dode) Guinier ex Piccarolo, nom illegit.)
Hybrid Black-poplar, Black-Italian Poplar

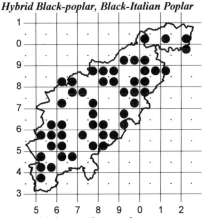

5 6 7 8 9 0 1 2

Introduction. Grown for ornament and screening.
Occasional. Scattered throughout the county. The most common variety of this hybrid is *var. 'Serotina'* which is easily recognised by its habit of late flowering - Serotina means late flowering - but *var. 'Eugenii'* (Carolina Poplar) and *var. 'Marilandica'* are both occasionally planted for ornament and screening. All of these trees are planted as the trees are unable to set seed, being only of one sex.
First record: Gulliver 1841

Druce: (P. deltoides) Common and widely distributed; (P. marilandica) rare.

4 P. trichocarpa Torrey & A.Gray ex Hook
Western Balsam-poplar
Introduction. Planted for ornament and screening.
It is recorded from Broughton Spinney and Weekley Wet Beds.

5 P. candicans Aiton
(*P. gileadensis* auct., non Roul.)
Balm-of-Gilead
Introduction. Planted in parks, hedgerows etc. for ornament.
Recorded at isolated sites, where it has become naturalised, as at Irchester Country Park..
Druce: (P. tacamahacca) [No status given].

2 SALIX L.
1 S. pentandra L. (3)
Bay Willow
British or native. Wet places.
Extremely rare, nearly always an introduction, but it may be native (and it is certainly naturalised) at White Water and Borough Fen Duck Decoy. It is also recorded from other localities within the county where it is probably planted. There are five trees beside the River Nene at Peterborough.
First record: Druce 1875
Druce: Very rare.

2 S. fragilis L. (107)
Crack-willow

Native. Wet places, especially streamsides.

Frequent in suitable habitats throughout the county.
First record: Anderson 1835
Druce: Common and widely distributed.

2 x 3 S. fragilis x S. alba = S. x rubens
Schrank
Native. Wet places and streamsides.
Probably extinct. Recorded in three places by Druce, but no recent records.
First record: Druce 1888
Druce: (S. alba x S. fragilis =S. viridis) Local.

3 S. alba L. (113)
White Willow

Native. Wet places, especially streamsides.
Common in suitable habitats; widely planted and formerly much pollarded by rivers. Var. *caerulea* (Cricket-bat Willow) is occasionally found planted, notably at Wicksteed Park, Kettering. Var. *Vitellina* (Golden Willow) is sometimes planted for its decorative twigs.
First record: Morton 1712
Druce: Common and widely distributed.

4 S. triandra L. (41)
Almond Willow
Native. Wet places and hedgerows.
Occasional at scattered localities, often as a single specimen. Sometimes planted as an osier; it is often found in hedgerows as a result of it being used as a hedge-stake in former times.
First record: Morton 1712
Druce: Not uncommon.

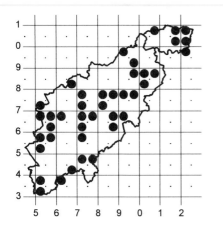

4 x 5 S. triandra x S. purpurea
Introduction or native. Wet places.
A single record from the south west of the county, beside the Oxford Canal, dating from 1979.

5 S. purpurea L.   (18)
Purple Willow
Native. Wet places, streams and riversides. Fairly rare, although good stands occur at Wadenhoe, Lyveden and Maidwell Dales. It also occurs in a few other wet areas throughout the county and has recently been found in Sare Copse, Yardley Chase and at Grendon.

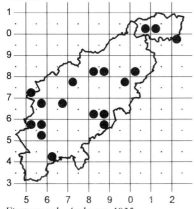

First record: Anderson 1835
Druce: Locally common.

5 x 9 S. purpurea x S. viminalis = S. x rubra
Hudson

Native. Wet places.
There is a single recent record from Welton Marsh; by Linda Moore in 1989.

5 x 11 S. purpurea x S. cinerea = S. x pontederiana Willd.
(S. x sordida A. Kerner*)*
Native. Wet places.
A single record from Wansford in 1959, by John Gilbert.

9 S. viminalis L.   (93)
Osier

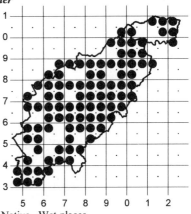

Native. Wet places.
Common, particularly in old osier beds. Sometimes found in hedgerows, due to its use as a hedge-stake.
First record: Clare 1821
Druce: Common.

9 x 10 S. viminalis x S. caprea = S. x sericans
Tausch ex A. Kerner
Native. Woods, hedges and streamsides.
Extremely rare. Recorded once by Druce. Recorded twice in recent years - at Hogs Hole, Moulton in 1979 and at Hinton-in-the-Hedges in 1966. The earlier record was by R.C.Palmer.
Druce: (S. mollissima) [No status given]

9 x 10 x 11 S. viminalis x S. caprea x S. cinerea = S x calodendron Wimmer
Holme Willow
Native. Dyke sides.
Extremely rare or under-recorded. Recorded in a few places by Druce, there is currently only one recent record from Peterborough, but it is probably overlooked.

First certain record: Druce 1902
Druce: Very local.

9 x 11   S. viminalis x S. cinerea = S. x smithiana Willd.
Silky-leaved Osier
Native. Wet or waste places.
Rare or overlooked.   Only two recent records.
First record: Druce 1876
Druce: Not uncommon.

9 x 12   S. viminalis x S. aurita = S. x fruticosa Doell
Shrubby Osier
Native. Wet fens.
Recorded by Druce in the Soke of Peterborough, but no recent records.

10   S. caprea L.
Goat Willow
a subsp. **caprea**   (124)

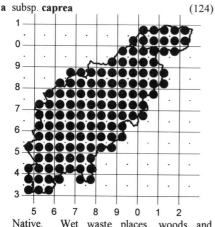

     5   6   7   8   9   0   1   2
Native.   Wet waste places, woods and hedgerows.
Very common in all parts of the county.
First record: Clare 1835
Druce: Common and generally distributed in woodland rides.

10 x 11   S. caprea x S. cinerea = S. x reichardtii A. Kerner
Native.   Wet waste places, woods and hedgerows.
A single record but it is probably under-recorded

10 x 12   S. caprea x S. aurita = S. x capreola J. Kerner ex Andersson

Introduction or native. Wet places.
A single record from Horton in 1986, by Dr Franklyn Perring

11   S. cinerea L.   (107)
Grey Willow

     5   6   7   8   9   0   1   2
Native. Wet places, woods and hedgerows.
Common, but recorded as an aggregate species.   Subsp. *oleifolia* is frequently found; subsp. *cinerea* has been recorded from at least half a dozen sites including near Eye, Peterborough, Mawsley Marsh, Sywell Woods, Hollowell reservoir, and Hogs Hole but is certainly under-recorded.
Druce: [Three records only, no status given].

11 x 12   S. cinerea x S. aurita = S. multinervis Doell
Native. Woods, thickets and wet places.
Probably extinct. Recorded by Druce but no recent records.
Druce: [No status given].

12   S. aurita L.   (4)
Eared Willow
Native. Wet places.
Very rare, but possibly overlooked in some of the acid areas.   Found in Yardley Chase, Whistley, Bucknell and Sywell Woods and Old Pastures near Yardley Hastings.
First record: Druce 1874
Druce: Local.

62   BRASSICACEAE
(CRUCIFERAE)

1   SISYMBRIUM L.
3   S. loeselii L.
False London-rocket

Adventive. Waste ground, tips etc.
Only known from one site in the county;
beside the main London (St. Pancras) railway
line at Irchester in 1988.
First record: Gill Gent (Irchester) 1988

5 S. altissimum L.
Tall Rocket
Adventive. Waste ground.
An uncommon plant of waste areas, railway
sidings and old furnace sites, mainly in the
eastern half of the county.
First record: Jackson 1906
Druce: Local.

6 S. orientale L.   (20)
Eastern Rocket
Adventive. Waste ground.
Fairly common in areas near the railway and
other waste places.
First record: Chester 1910
Druce: Rare.

7 S. officinale (L.) Scop.   (125)
Hedge Mustard

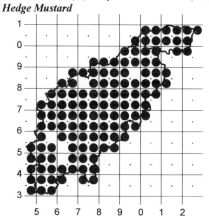

Native. Hedgerows, rough and cultivated
ground.
Very common and generally distributed
throughout the county.
First record: Gulliver 1841
Druce: Abundant and generally distributed.

2 DESCURAINIA Webb & Berth.
1 D. sophia (L.) Webb ex Prantl   (119)
Flixweed
Possibly native. Rough and waste ground.
A fairly uncommon species of waste places,
old quarries, railway lines etc., it is mainly

concentrated along the eastern side of the
county around the Wellingborough, Kettering
and Northampton areas with a couple of
records in the Soke of Peterborough.

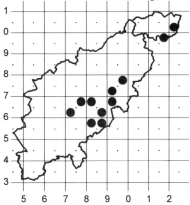

First record: Pitt 1813
Druce: (Sisymbrium sophia) Local.

3 ALLIARIA Heister ex Fabr.
1 A. petiolata (M. Bieb.) Cavara & Grande
                                                              (129)
Garlic Mustard, Jack-by-the-hedge

Native. Rough ground, hedgerows and shady
places.
An abundant hedgerow plant throughout the
county.
First record: Gulliver 1841
*Druce: (Sisymbrium alliaria) Locally
abundant and generally distributed.*

4 ARABIDOPSIS (DC.) Heynh.
1 A. thaliana (L.) Heynh.   (63)

126

Thale Cress
Native. Cultivated ground, banks etc.
Fairly common on railway banks and waste ground and very often occurring as a garden weed on gravel paths etc.

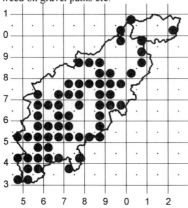

First record: Pitt 1813
Druce: (Sisymbrium thalianum) Local.

5 ISATIS L.
1 I. tinctoria L.
Woad
Introduction. Waste ground.
This species was established for a few years at Oundle during the 1960s, otherwise it is now an extremely rare plant, although it was once extensively cultivated as a dye plant.
First record: Baker 1854
Druce: [No status given].

6 BUNIAS L.
1 B. orientalis L.
Warty-cabbage
Adventive. Rough grass and waste places.
No recent records.
First record: Chester 1910
Druce: Rare.

B. erucago L.
Southern Warty-cabbage
Adventive. Waste ground, rubbish tips.
No recent records.
First record: Druce 1884
Druce: [One record].

7 ERYSIMUM L. (Cheiranthus L.)
1 E. cheiranthoides L. (17)
Treacle Mustard
Introduction. Cultivated or waste ground.

An occasional plant of waste ground, old railways, quarries, etc. It occurs sporadically, but mainly in the northern area of the county, tending to be more common in the Soke of Peterborough as an arable weed.
First record: Gulliver 1841
Druce: Local.

2 E. cheiri (L.) Crantz (25)
(*Cheiranthus cheiri* L.)
Wallflower
Introduction. Walls etc.
Still established on old walls as it was in Druce's day, at Kirby Hall and other places.
First record: Druce 1874
Druce: Local.

8 HESPERIS L.
1 H. matronalis L. (38)
Dame's Violet
Introduction. Waste ground.
Naturalised on some roadsides, quarries and other suitable places in the county.
First record: T. Beasley 1843.
Druce: [No status given].

11 BARBAREA R.Br.
1 B. vulgaris R.Br. (103)
Winter-cress

Native. Road verges, hedges etc.
Very common throughout the county in damp areas. Often occurring in profusion for a few years on verges where the soil has been disturbed.
First record: Miss Lightfoot 1835
Druce: (B. barbareae) Common and generally distributed.

2 B. stricta Andrz.
Small-flowered Winter-cress
Adventive. Waste ground, rubbish tips.
No recent records.
Druce: [No status given, but only two records, one of which was seen from a train and a subsequent search failed to detect it].

3 B. intermedia Boreau
Medium-flowered Winter-cress
Introduced. Waste, open and cultivated land.
Very rare. It has been twice recorded, from
Ditchford in 1961 by D. Payne and from near
Southwick in 1977 by Dr Franklyn Perring.
First record: D.Payne (near Ditchford) 1961.

4 B. verna (Miller) Asch.
American Winter-cress
Introduction. Cultivated ground.
Only recorded as naturalised at Stoke
Pavilions in 1985.
First record: Druce 1875
Druce: Rare.

12 RORIPPA Scop.
(Nasturtium R.Br.)
1 R. nasturtium-aquaticum (L.) Hayek (108)
(Nasturtium officinale R.Br.)
Water-cress
Native. Margins of water bodies.
Common in shallow water throughout the
county.

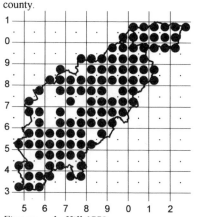

First record: Hill 1778
Druce: (Radicula nasturtium) Generally distributed.

1 x 2 R. nasturtium-aquatica x R. microphylla
= R. x sterilis Airy Shaw (3)

Hybrid Water-cress
Native. Margins of water bodies.
Recorded only from the Soke of
Peterborough.

2 R. microphylla *(Boenn.) N.Hylander ex Á. Löve & D. Löve* (25)
(Nasturtium microphyllum (Boenn.) Reichb.)
Narrow-fruited Water-cress, One-rowed Water-cress

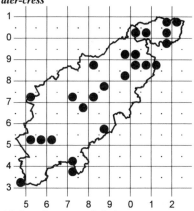

Native. Streams and ditches.
Occasional. Less common than *R. nasturtium-aquaticum.*
First record: Slater (Thornhaugh) 1902.

4 R. palustris (L.) Besser (53)
Marsh Yellow-cress

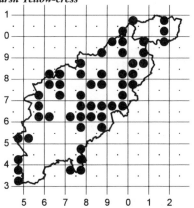

Native. Stream and pond margins
Very common in wet areas, by gravel pits,
rivers etc. and often an early colonising
species of such places.

First record: Baker 1822
Druce: (Radicula islandica) Locally common.

5 R. sylvestris (L.) Besser (13)
Creeping Yellow-cress

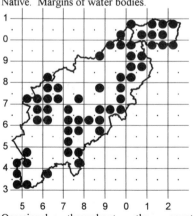

Native. Damp or disturbed ground.
Rare, sometimes found as a garden weed and sometimes beside water.
First record: Paley 1860
Druce: (Radicula sylvestris) Local.

6 R. amphibia (L.) Besser (58)
Great Yellow-cress
Native. Margins of water bodies.

Occasional throughout the county, particularly beside canals and rivers. It is scattered along eroding banks of the upper River Welland near Ashley and is very common beside the River Nene and the canals.

First record: Morton 1712
Druce: (Radicula amphibia) Locally common.

13 ARMORACIA P.Gaertner
1 A. rusticana P.Gaertner (105)
Horse-radish

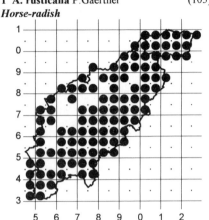

Introduction. Grassy places and waste ground.
Frequent on roadsides and waste places, but always as a garden throw-out. It does not spread by seed.
First record: Druce 1930
Druce: (Cochlearia armoracia) Now completely naturalised.

14 CARDAMINE L.
3 C. amara L. (16)
Large Bitter-cress

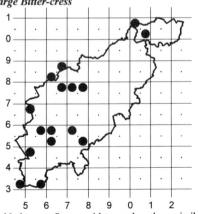

Native. Stream-sides and other similar locations.

Rare. Scattered in a few wet places including beside the canal near Northampton and Welford. It is also found on the Northamptonshire bank of the River Welland at Theddingworth Bridge and by a stream at the base of Easton Hillside. It is still in the Maidwell Dales where it was recorded for the first time in the county in 1712, by Morton.
First record: Morton 1712
Druce: Local.

4 C. raphanifolia Pourret
Greater Cuckooflower
Introduction. Shady places.
One record from Wellingborough in 1982, possibly a garden escape but the site is now destroyed.
First record: Wellingborough 1982.

5 C. pratensis L.   (122)
Cuckooflower, Lady's Smock

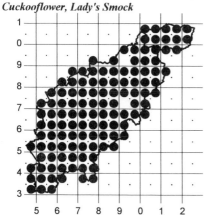

Native. Damp ground in meadows and woodland rides.
Common in damp places, woodland, old churchyards and meadows and beside water throughout the county.
First record: John Clare 1821
Druce: Common and well distributed.

6 C. impatiens L.
Narrow-leaved Bitter-cress
Native. Damp woods and river banks
Extinct. A single record from an allotment near Kettering in 1914.
First record: Chester 1914
Druce: [No status given. A single record].

7 C. flexuosa With.   (68)
Wavy Bitter-cress, Wood Bitter-cress

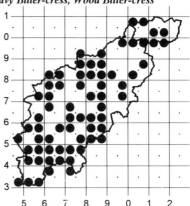

Native. Damp or cultivated ground.
Occasional. Occurring in damp places - woodland, riversides and canals.
First record: Baker 1822
Druce: Local.

8 C. hirsuta L.   (108)
Hairy Bitter-cress

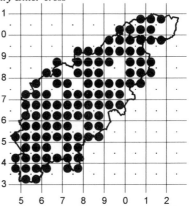

Native. Cultivated or other open ground.
Very common on cultivated land, gravel paths and other suitable habitats. Three plants with double sterile flowers occurred at Wollaston, in 1979 and a specimen was exhibited at the Botanical Society of the British Isles Exhibition Meeting in that year. They did not survive
First record: Morton 1712
Druce: Local common.

15 ARABIS L.

3 A. turrita L.

Tower Cress

Introduction. On old walls.
In 1985, during the churchyard survey, this was found in Gayton Churchyard, where it still flourishes. A nationally rare plant otherwise only known from Cambridge where it grows on the walls of St. John's College.

5 A. caucasica Willd. ex Schldl.

Garden Arabis

Introduction. On walls.
Occasionally recorded as a garden escape.

6 A. hirsuta (L.) Scop.

Hairy Rock-cress

Native. Bare grassland.
Extremely rare and only occurring in the limestone areas in the north of the county at Collyweston, Easton on the Hill and Barnack Hills and Holes. It was formerly present in the Thrapston area, where it was last recorded in 1955 in the old quarries.

First record: Morton 1712

Druce: Local and rather uncommon.

16 AUBRIETA Adans.

1 A. deltoidea (L.) DC.

Aubrieta

Introduction. Waste ground etc.
A very occasional escape, generally on walls, but well established in a sand-pit near Easton Maudit.

17 LUNARIA L.

1 L. annua L.

Honesty

Introduction. Waste ground etc.
An occasional escape but not persisting.

18 ALYSSUM L.

1 A. alyssoides (L.) L.

Small Alison

Introduction. Waste ground etc.
No recent records.

First record: Druce 1876

Druce: Very rare.

20 LOBULARIA Desv.

1 L. maritima (L.) Desv.

Sweet Alison

Introduction. Walls and dry places.
Occasional as a garden outcast on tips.

22 EROPHILA DC.

2 E. verna (L.) DC.   (86)

Common Whitlowgrass, Spring Whitlowgrass

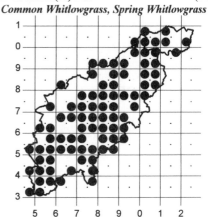

Native. Walls and gravel paths.
Very common on walls and gravel paths etc. throughout the county.

First record: 1841

Druce: Abundant. [Druce also recorded E. boerhaavii: No status given, and E.praecox: Rare. None of these are now recognised].

23 COCHLEARIA L.

5 C. danica L.

Danish Scurvygrass

British. A native of coastal areas.
Previous to the late 1980s this species had only been recorded rarely, from railway ballast as at Finedon sidings and as a garden weed in Wollaston and Northampton. It has recently become very well established on the A45 dual carriageway near Northampton due to salt gritting of our roads, and looks likely to spread furthur, together with other coastal species such as *Puccinellia distans* etc.

24 CAMELINA Crantz

1 C. sativa (L.) Crantz.

Gold-of-pleasure

Introduction. Tips, formerly arable fields.
A rare introduction that has not been recorded recently in Northants.

First record: Morton 1712

Druce: Rare.

25 CAPSELLA Medikus

1 C. bursa-pastoris (L.) Medikus   (131)

Shepherd's-purse

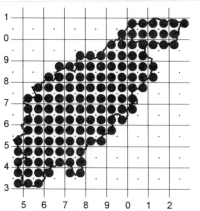

5 6 7 8 9 0 1 2

Native. Cultivated and open ground.
Very common throughout on disturbed soil.
First record: Pitt 1813
Druce: (Bursa pastoris) Abundant.

27 TEESDALIA R.Br.
1 T. nudicaulis (L.) R.Br.
Shepherd's Cress
Possibly native. Sandy soils.
Extinct. It has not been seen since Morton's
day,when it was recorded near Little Creaton.
First record:Morton 1712
Druce: Very rare if not extinct.

28 THLASPI L.
1 T. arvense L. (66)
Field Penny-cress

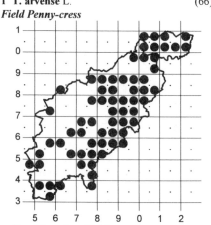

5 6 7 8 9 0 1 2

Possibly native. Fields.
Common as a weed of cultivation on richer
soils, often able to survive herbicides.
First record: Morton 1712

Druce: Locally common.

29 IBERIS L.
2 I. amara L.
Wild Candytuft
Introduction. Calcareous grassland.
No recent records.
First record: Beesley c1850
Druce: [No status given, two localities].

30 LEPIDIUM L
1 L. sativum L.
Garden Cress
Introduction. Rubbish tips.
Occasionally turning up on rubbish tips etc.
Druce: Not permanently established.

2 L. campestre (L.) R.Br. (19)
Field Pepperwort

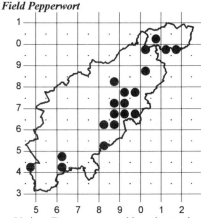

5 6 7 8 9 0 1 2

Native. Dry pastures, arable and waste land.
Occasional, but tending to be commoner in
the eastern areas of the county.
First record: Druce 1875
Druce: Local.

3 L. heterophyllum Benth.
Smith's Pepperwort
Native. Dry pastures, arable and waste land.
Extremely rare. Recorded on disturbed
ground near Bedford Purlieus during the
1970s but not seen since. Druce also
recorded it from the same area.
First record: Druce 1877
Druce: (L. smithii) Very local.

4 L. virginicum L.
(*L. densiflorum* Schrader)
Least Pepperwort

Introduction.
No recent records.

5 L. ruderale L.
Narrow-leaved Pepperwort
Probable introduction. Casual on waste places, tips etc.
Recorded from a few places in the county mainly on rubbish tips and waste ground.
First record: Blaby 1880
Druce: Alien. Likely to spread.

6 L. latifolium L.
Dittander
British. Damp, bare ground.
This essentially saltmarsh plant was established on the side of the A47, near Collyweston Great Wood, for a number of years on dumped soil. This has now disappeared with road widening operations.

8 L. draba L.
(Cardaria draba (L.) Desv.)
Hoary Cress
a subsp. **draba** (36)

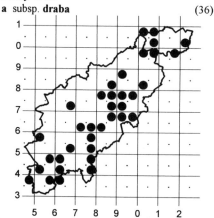

Introduction. Waste ground.
A fairly common species of roadsides and waste places particularly near to houses.
First Record: Druce 1876
Druce: Established and likely to increase.

b subsp. **chalepense** (L.) Thell.
(Cardaria draba (L.) Desv. subsp. *chalepensis* (L.) O.Schulz)
Adventive.
Found on railway sidings in Peterborough in 1988 by T.C.E.Rich.

31 CORONOPUS Zinn (106)
1 C. squamatus (Forsskål) Asch.
Swine-cress

Probably native. Waste ground and paths etc.
Quite common throughout the county, having a liking for well trodden areas such as gateways and cultivated ground.
First record: Baker 1822
Druce: (C. coronopus) Scattered throughout.

2 C. didymus (L.) Smith (15)
Lesser Swine-cress

Adventive. Cultivated and waste ground.
Uncommon and scattered throughout the area on disturbed ground, gravel pits, rubbish tips etc., persisting for a few years only.
First record: Doddington 1943.

33 DIPLOTAXIS DC.
1 D. tenuifolia (L.) DC. (4)
Perennial Wall-rocket

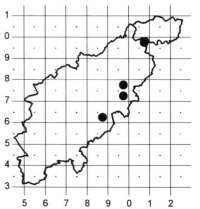

5 6 7 8 9 0 1 2

Probable introduction. Dry waste places. Very rare and only recorded from four sites in the county. During the 1960s it was recorded from disused railways at Irthlingborough and Woodford. More recently there are records from the Grendon and Wansford areas.
First record: Druce 1877
Druce: Very rare and now extinct.

2 D. muralis (L.) DC.   (13)
Annual Wall-rocket, Stinkweed

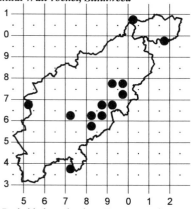

5 6 7 8 9 0 1 2

Probable introduction. Dry waste places. Fairly common on waste ground, railway lines and similar situations, mainly in the eastern half of the county.
First record: Druce 1876
Druce: An increasing species.

34 BRASSICA L.
1 B. oleracea L.
Cabbage
Introduction. Waste tips etc.
Usually occurring as an escape from cultivation.
Druce: Not permanently established.

2 B. napus L.
Rape
a subsp. **oleifera** (DC.) Metzger
Oil-seed Rape
Introduction. Roadsides and riverbanks etc.
Much grown as a crop and very common in all areas as an escape or a relic of cultivation on roadsides, riverbanks etc.
First record: Pitt 1813
Druce: Not permanently established.

b subsp. **rapifera** Metzger.
Swede
Introduction. Field borders etc.
No recent records but possibly overlooked.
First record: Druce 1876
Druce: (B napo-brassica) Not permanently established.

3 B. rapa L.
b subsp. **campestris** (L.) Clapham
Wild Turnip
Probable introduction. Beside streams and rivers.
Occasional. Sometimes established on river banks, waste places etc.
First record: Druce 1874
Druce: Local.

4 B. juncea (L.) Czernj.
Chinese Mustard
Adventive. Waste tips etc.
Two records from the Soke, from a car park in Peterborough in 1988 by T.C.E.Rich and earlier by John Chandler at Ailsworth.

5 B. nigra (L.) Koch   (8)
Black Mustard
Probably native. Rough ground.
Occasional. Found at a few sites, mainly in old quarries and tips, and on recently seeded verges. In 1994 it appeared in profusion at Summer Leys Country Park near Wollaston.
First record: Morton 1712
Druce: Local.

134

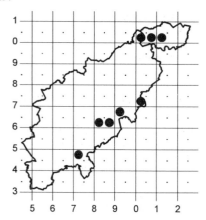

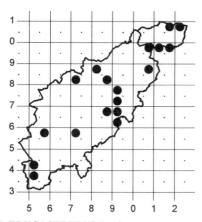

35 SINAPIS L.
1 S. arvensis L. (102)
Charlock, Wild Mustard

Probably native. Arable and wasteland, roadsides etc.
Very common on cultivated ground where it escapes the herbicide sprays.
First record: Pitt 1813
Druce: (Brassica arvensis) Too abundant in cultivated fields throughout the county.

2 S. alba L. (18)
White Mustard
Introduction. Arable or waste land.
Occasional. A weed of arable ground.
First record: Notcutt 1843
Druce: (Brassica alba) Rather rare.

36 ERUCASTRUM C.Presl
1 E. gallicum (Willd.) O.Schulz
Hairy Rocket
Introduction. On arable or waste land.
Only recorded from Newton Quarry in 1976.
First record:1976

38 HIRSCHFELDIA Moench
1 H. incana (L.) Lagr.-Fossat
Hoary Mustard
Introduction. Waste places.
Only two records of it established on rubbish tips - Wood Lane Tip at Kettering in 1974 and on waste ground at Draughton in 1986.
First record: 1974

40 RAPISTRUM Crantz
1 R. rugosum (L.) Bergeret (6)
Bastard Cabbage
Introduction. An occasional inhabitant of waste ground, tips etc.
The first record in this area is from Fengate, Peterborough, in 1949 by J.H.Gilbert. It is well established on the old airfield at Harrington, around the Grendon and Ecton areas, Whitworths Mill, Wellingborough, and at Helpston in the Soke of Peterborough where a colony has existed for twenty years.

42 RAPHANUS L.
1 R. raphanistrum L.
Wild Radish
a subsp. **raphanistrum** (35)
Probably introduced. Cultivated and rough ground.
Locally distributed on disturbed ground, railway sidings, rubbish tips etc.

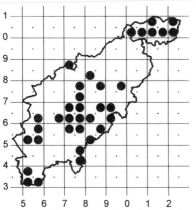

5 6 7 8 9 0 1 2

Most examples are the yellow-flowered form.
First record: Pitt 1813
Druce: Locally abundant but absent from large areas.

ERUCA Miller
E. vesicaria (L.) Cav.
(*E. sativa* Miller)
Garden Rocket
Introduction.
No recent records.
Druce: (E. eruca) [Only one record, but no status given].

NESLIA Desv.
N. paniculata (L.) Desv.
Ball Mustard
Introduction. Tips and waste places.
No recent records.
First record: French 1868
Druce: (Vogelia paniculata) [No status given].

CONRINGIA Heister ex Fabr.
C. orientalis (L.) Dumort.
Hare's-ear Mustard
Adventive. Waste ground etc.
No recent records.
First record: possibly Foord Kelcey 1906
Druce: Rare.

MYAGRUM L.
M. perfoliatum L
Adventive.
No recent records.
First record: Druce 1925
Druce: [No status given].

63 RESEDACEAE
1 RESEDA L.
1 R. luteola L. (86)
Weld

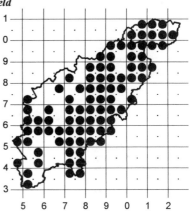

5 6 7 8 9 0 1 2

Native. Waste and disturbed ground, old quarries and disused railway lines.
Widely distributed and can be common in suitable habitats, especially in the east. It is very common on gravel diggings.
First record: Morton 1712
Druce: Not rare and widely distributed.

2 R. alba L.
White Mignonette
Introduction. Waste places.
No recent records.
First record: Duston 1876
Druce: Rare.

3 R. lutea L. (56)
Wild Mignonette

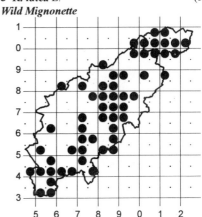

5 6 7 8 9 0 1 2

Native. Waste grassland, disturbed ground. Fairly frequent in waste places, old quarries and on railway lines on calcareous soils.
First record: Morton 1712
Druce: Local

65 ERICACEAE
2 RHODODENDRON L.
1 R. ponticum L. (27)
Rhododendron

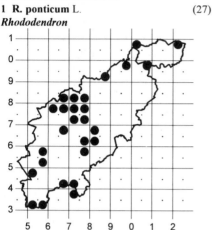

Introduction. Sandy and peaty soils. Established at a few sites in the south and west away from the areas of limestone or basic soils. Always a result of planting. Druce does not record this species but it must have been planted in his day.

11 CALLUNA Salisb.
1 C. vulgaris (L.) Hull (13)
Heather, Ling

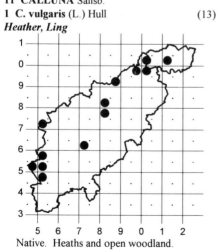

Native. Heaths and open woodland.

Rare. Generally confined to sandy, acidic soils and often on railway banks as at Kilsby, Gretton and Charwelton. At Harlestone Firs it regenerates on felled and cleared areas and it was present at Overstone in the 1940s. In the north it is still present in Wakerley Wood, Bedford Purlieus and at Ailsworth Heath.
First record: Morton 1712
Druce: Local and rare.

12 ERICA L.
3 E. tetralix L.
Cross-leaved Heath
Native. Bogs and wet heathland.
Extremely rare. It was believed to be extinct in the county, but one unconfirmed record was made from Harlestone Firs in the 1980s.
First record: Morton 1712
Druce: Very rare.

5 E. cinerea L.
Bell Heather
Native. Dry heaths.
Very rare. Currently only recorded at Harlestone Heath, near Northampton, the only heathland left in the county, in a recently felled area.
First record: Baker 1822
Druce: Very rare.

67 MONOTROPACEAE
1 MONOTROPA L.
1 M. hypopitys L.
Yellow Bird's-nest
a subsp. hypopitys
Native. Beech and pine woodland.
Extremely rare. Known only from Apethorpe and Wakerley Woods in the extreme north. In the latter it has recently appeared in large numbers in a conifer plantation.
First record: Rev. M.J. Berkeley c1860
Druce: (Hypopitys hypopitys) Very rare.

69 PRIMULACEAE
1 PRIMULA L.
1 P. vulgaris Hudson (90)
Primrose
Native. Woods, coppices, scrub, grassy banks, ditches, hedgebanks.
Frequent in suitable habitats, it is usually abundant during the open phase of coppicing. Generally found throughout the county

although it is absent from some central and western areas.

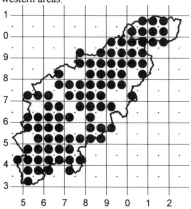

5 6 7 8 9 0 1 2

First record: Clare 1820
Druce: Locally abundant and widely distributed.

1 x 3 P. vulgaris x P. veris = P. x polyantha
Miller (17)
(*P x tommasinii* Gren. & Godron)
False Oxlip

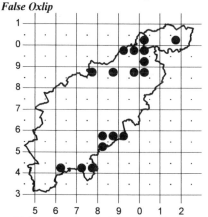

5 6 7 8 9 0 1 2

Native. Grassland and open woodland. Rare. A natural hybrid between *P. veris* and *P. vulgaris* which occurs where the two plants grow in close proximity. Known at a number of scattered sites throughout the north, south and east of the county.
First record: Recorded incorrectly as P. elatior by Baker 1822
Druce: No status given.

3 P. veris L. (90)
Cowslip

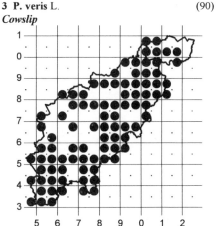

5 6 7 8 9 0 1 2

Native. Grassy habitats. Meadows, scrub, open woodland, banks and roadside verges. Occasional but sometimes common in suitable habitats on calcareous soils. Farming practices mean that only isolated pockets now remain in meadows, but it is establishing itself on roadside verges, notably in the Corby - Stamford area. It can still be common in more open parts of woodland throughout the county and also at Barnack Hills and Holes and Collyweston quarry. Some planting has recently been carried out by various local authorities which will undoubtedly lead to cowslips being more common along our newer roadways.
First record: Morton 1712
Druce: Abundant on calcareous soils.

2 HOTTONIA L.
1 H. palustris L.
Water-violet
Native. Still water. Extremely rare. Formerly this was locally common in the fen ditches in the Soke of Peterborough, and it was recorded in 1965 from the Tansor area. Recently it has been recorded along the ditches in the Nene Washes and it is present around Borough Fen Duck Decoy. It is also present as an introduction in ponds in Irchester Country Park.
First record: Morton 1712
Druce: Locally abundant.

4 LYSIMACHIA L.

1 L. nemorum L. (33)
Yellow Pimpernel

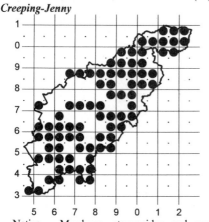

Native. Damp, shaded places.

Occasional in woods throughout the county but it is more commonly found in the south, only being present in a few woodlands in the north or the Soke of Peterborough.

First record: Morton 1712

Druce: Local.

2 L. nummularia L. (80)
Creeping-Jenny

Native. Meadows, streamsides and wet woods.

Occasional. Widely distributed in suitable habitats but not occurring anywhere in large numbers.

First record: Baker 1822

Druce: Widely distributed and not uncommon.

3 L. vulgaris L. (10)
Yellow Loosestrife

Native. Ditches and marshes.

Rare as a native plant. Occurs mainly along the Rivers Nene and Welland in the north of the county and in the Soke of Peterborough.

First record: Morton 1712

Druce: Local.

5 L. punctata L. (12)
Dotted Loosestrife

Introduction. Waste places and roadsides

A garden escape found at a few localities scattered throughout the county except in the extreme north. Slowly increasing in numbers.

6 ANAGALLIS L.

1 A. tenella (L.) L.
Bog Pimpernel

Native. Damp turf, bogs, marshy ground etc.

Extremely rare. It was present in the Soke at Bonemills Hollow up to the 1960s, when a pig farm destroyed the site. It still occurs at Sutton Heath and has recently been discovered near Wansford.

First record: Morton 1712

Druce: Very local.

2 A. arvensis L.
a subsp. arvensis (102)
Scarlet Pimpernel

Native. Cultivated fields, waysides and waste places.

Occasional, rarely found in large numbers and almost entirely absent from some areas in the west. Decreasing due to current farming practice. Pink flowered plants are not uncommon.

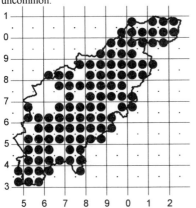

First record: Baker 1822
Druce: Common and widely distributed.

b subsp. **caerulea** Hartman
(*A. arvensis* L. subsp. *foemina* (Miller) Schinz & Thell.)
Blue Pimpernel
Adventive. Arable fields and gardens. Extremely rare. Only three records, from Southey Wood and Ailsworth in the Soke of Peterborough in the early 1960s and from Sywell Country Park in 1984.
First record: Parkinson 1640
Druce: (A. foemina) Very local.

8 SAMOLUS L.
1 S. valerandi L.   (10)
Brookweed

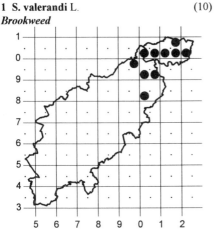

Native. Shaded wet grass, streams and pool margins on calcareous soils. Rare, being known at only a few scattered localities in the north of the county.
First record: Irvine 1838
Druce: Local.

71 HYDRANGEACEAE
1 PHILADELPHUS L.
1 P. coronarius L.
Mock-orange
Introduction. Hedgerows and copses. A common garden plant that survives in the wild, but usually as a relic of planting. Only known at Castle Ashby and at Woodford.

72 GROSSULARIACEAE
2 RIBES L.
1 R. rubrum L.   (51)
Red Currant
Introduction. Wet woods and hedgerows, streamsides etc.
Occasional. Scattered in suitable localities, including the crowns of pollarded willows near to Newton Field Centre.

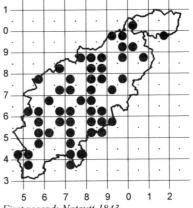

First record: Notcutt 1843
Druce: Local.

3 R. nigrum L.
Black Currant
Introduction. Wet woodland, hedgerows and stream banks.
Only recently recorded at five very scattered sites.
First record: Morton 1712
Druce: Rare

140

4 R. sanguineum Pursh
Flowering Currant
Introduction. Woodland.
A North American alien, that is a common garden plant, it has been recorded at a single site in Thoroughsale Wood, Corby.
First record: Druce 1927
Druce: Very rare.

7 R. uva-crispa L. (50)
Gooseberry
Introduction. Woodland, scrub, stream-sides and waste ground.
Scattered throughout the county, but less common in the west; may be well established.
First record: Notcutt 1843
Druce: Scattered throughout the county.

73 CRASSULACEAE
1 CRASSULA L.
3 C. helmsii (Kirk) Cockayne (3)
New Zealand Pigmyweed
Adventive. Marshes and ponds.
Extremely rare. Only recorded at three sites in the county, but likely to spread. This is a very aggressive species and poses a threat to native populations of plants where it occurs.

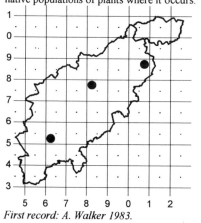

First record: A. Walker 1983.

2 UMBILICUS DC.
1 U. rupestris (Salisb.) Dandy (3)
Navelwort, Pennywort
Native. Old walls.
Extremely rare. Occurs only in a small area in the south-west of the county, growing on old stone walls at Canons Ashby, Eydon

churchyard, and at its most easterly location in England at Litchborough church.

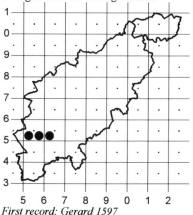

First record: Gerard 1597
Druce: (Cotyledon umbilicusveneris) Very local.

3 SEMPERVIVUM L.
1 S. tectorum L.
House-leek
Introduction. Walls and roofs.
Occasional on suitable walls, as at Castle Ashby.
First record: Pitt 1813
Druce: Scattered throughout the county, but always planted.

5 SEDUM L.
5 S. telephium L. (6)
Orpine

Native. Walls, rocks, woods.

Extremely rare. Recorded recently only from Badby Wood and Everdon Stubbs in the west and from four woods in the northern half of the county including Grafton Park Wood where Druce recorded it.
First record: Morton 1712
Druce: (S. purpureum) Rare.

10 S. rupestre L.   (32)
(*S. reflexum* L.)
Reflexed Stonecrop

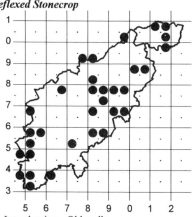

5 6 7 8 9 0 1 2

Introduction. Old walls.
Occasional in the county on suitable walls.
First record: Dickson 1792
Druce: (S. reflexum) Local.

11 S. forsterianum Smith
Rock Stonecrop
Druce: Recorded in error for S. reflexum.

12 S. acre L.   (95)
Biting Stonecrop

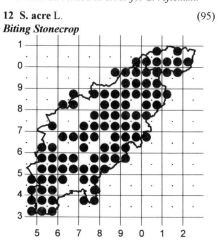

5 6 7 8 9 0 1 2

Native. Walls and on basic soils.
Frequent. Scattered throughout the county on suitable walls and in quarries.
First record: Clare 1821
Druce: (S. Drucei) Not unfrequent and widely distributed. Too common to need localities.

14 S. album L.   (40)
White Stonecrop

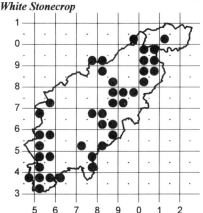

5 6 7 8 9 0 1 2

Probable introduction. Walls and dry places.
Occasional. Scattered throughout but more common in the eastern and southern areas.
First record: Stokes 1787
Druce: Local.

17 S. dasyphyllum L.
Thick-leaved Stonecrop
Introduction. Naturalised on walls.
Occurs in the south east, as a garden escape.
First record. W. Lewin, c. 1870
Druce: Rare.

S. stellatum L.
Starry Stonecrop
Introduction.
No recent records.
Druce: [A single record, no status given].

S. hybridum L.
Introduction. On walls
No recent records.
Druce: [Only two records, no status given].

74 SAXIFRAGACEAE
5 SAXIFRAGA L.
15 S. granulata L.   (36)
Meadow Saxifrage

142

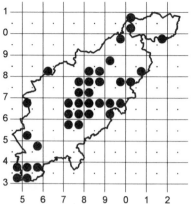

5 6 7 8 9 0 1 2

Native. Old meadows and particularly churchyards.
Uncommon but less so than formerly. Found at scattered localities, rarely in large numbers and usually in the central portion of the county. It was reduced due to the ploughing of meadows in river valleys, but it has increased in the last year or so. Numerous new sites have been recorded including some in set-aside farmland.
First record: Ray 1662
Druce: Locally common.

19 S. tridactylites L. (55)
Rue-leaved Saxifrage

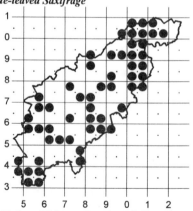

5 6 7 8 9 0 1 2

Native. Walls, roofs and on shallow dry soil.
Occasional. Scattered throughout the county, especially on walls and roofs and can sometimes occur in quantity.
First record: Baker 1822

Druce: Locally common and generally distributed, but lessening in frequency owing to the cement pointing of village walls.

9 CHRYSOSPLENIUM L.
1 C. oppositifolium L. (5)
Opposite-leaved Golden-saxifrage

5 6 7 8 9 0 1 2

Native. In boggy places in woods.
Very rare. Found at one locality in Whittlewood Forest in the extreme south; and at High Wood, Hen Wood, Mantles Heath and Ramsden Corner in the south-west. There is one isolated site in the north, Rockingham Park; it still grows where Druce recorded it..
First record: Morton 1712
Druce: Very rare.

10 PARNASSIA L.
1 P. palustris L.
Grass-of-Parnassus
Native. Bogs and marshy places.
Probably extinct. It has disappeared from all of the localities recorded by Druce.
First record: Johnson 1633
Druce: Very local.

75 ROSACEAE
3 SPIRAEA L.
Introduction. Hedges and rough ground.
There are two or three records of plants from this genera, mainly surviving as garden throw-outs in hedgerows.
First record: 1896
Druce. (S. salicifolia) No status given, only one record of a planted specimen in Newbottle Spinney.

6 FILIPENDULA Miller
1 F. vulgaris Moench (31)
Dropwort

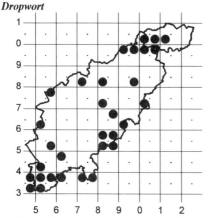

Native. Dry pasture on calcareous soil.
Rare. Found only on scattered sites in unimproved pasture predominantly in the south and north of the county on highly calcareous soils. It is very common at Barnack Hills and Holes national nature reserve and Collyweston Deeps nature reserve.
First record: Pitt 1813
Druce. (Spirea filipendula) No status given.

2 F. ulmaria (L.) Maxim. (129)
Meadowsweet

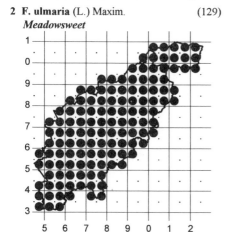

Native. Damp meadows, streamsides, ditches, damp woodland rides etc.
Very common, but more frequent in damp areas.
First record: Morton 1712

Druce: (S. ulmaria) Common and generally distributed.

8 RUBUS L.
7 R. idaeus L. (54)
Raspberry

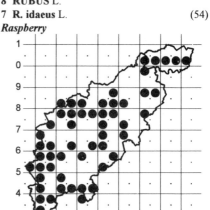

Occasional. Found mainly in the west, on lighter acid soils, and scattered elsewhere.
First record: Morton c1720
Druce: Local.

The following account of *Rubus* has been written by A.Newton. It is based primarily on field and herbarium records compiled for 'Brambles of the British Isles' (Edees and Newton 1988), published by the Ray Society. These have been augmented by observations made by the author between 1986 and 1994, during which several new discoveries have been made.

Most of the herbarium material was collected by L.Cumming and G.C.Druce and can be seen at Oxford. In addition a few gatherings were made chiefly by J.T.Powell (Daventry), A.Ley (Wadenhoe), W.H.Mills (Bedford Purlieus), H.J.Riddelsdell (Badby), and A.B.Jackson (Harleston) and can be inspected at the British Museum or Cambridge.

Much of Northamptonshire is unfavourable to the development of diverse bramble communities on account of the incidence of calcareous soils in many places and (in the north of the county) the prevalance of uplands exposed to cold winter winds from the north or north-east with few sheltered valleys.

Acid soil exposures are rare and ancient heathland non-existent. It is not surprising that those brambles that can best tolerate dry neutral - calcareous soils are the most frequent and widespread: these include in addition to *R.ulmifolius, R.vestitus, R.radula, R.echinatus,* and *R.leightonii. R. anglocandicans* and *R. winteri* favouring Jurassic derived soils are particularly well displayed in contrast to their scarcity or absence from many parts of Britain. The most rewarding areas for the batologist are the surviving patches of woods on ancient sites underlain by neutral-acid loams or clays e.g. Badby Wood, Plumpton Wood, Bucknell Wood and Southey Wood where many species, including representatives of the 'North Sea florula' group *R.raduloides, R.pedemontanus, R. macrophyllus* and the rare *R.drejeri* can be seen. Perhaps the choicest locality is Harlestone Firs, now managed woodland but formerly heathland on a sandy substrate, which exhibits a diverse bramble population and is the sole locality for several species.

All specimens and field records have been verified by the author unless otherwise indicated.

sect. **Rubus**
subsect. **Rubus**

15 R. bertramii G. Braun
Recorded by Druce at Whiston. No recent records.

23 R. nessensis Hall
Recorded at Badby in 1921 by L. Cumming. No recent records.

sect. **Hiemales** E.H.L.Krause
ser. **Sylvatici** (P.J.Mueller) Focke

34 R. albionis W.C.R. Watson
Recorded at Barby by L.Cumming prior to 1930. No recent records.
Druce: recorded as R. schlechtendahlii.

60 R. lindleianus Lees
Widespread and frequent, chiefly in hedges. It has been recorded mainly from the north of the county.

62 R. macrophyllus Weihe & Nees
Still present in many older woods: Everdon Stubbs, Easton Hornstock, Bedford Purlieus and Southey Wood. It has also been recorded in the area of Badby and Newnham.

69 R. platyacanthus P.J.Mueller & Lef.

No recent records. It was formerly recorded from Badby by H.J.Riddlesdell in 1921 and from near Harlestone by Druce.
Druce: recorded as R. carpinifolius.

72 R. poliodes W.C.R.Watson
Recorded in Southey Wood in 1976.

76 R. pyramidalis Kaltenb.
Recorded in Badby Wood since 1987.

ser. **Rhamnifolii** (Bab.) Focke

90 R. amplificatus Lees
Recently only seen at Badby and Wakerley Formerly recorded from Daventry by J.T.Powell.
Druce: recorded as R. schlectendahlii.

93 R. cardiophyllus Lef. & P.J.Mueller
Only recorded in the areas to the south of Daventry and near Brackley.
Druce:recorded as R. rhamnifolius.

109 R. lindebergii P.J.Mueller
Recorded at Badby from 1987 onwards.

112 R. nemoralis P.J.Mueller
Rare. Formerly recorded from Daventry by J.T.Powell in 1895. It has recently been discovered at Harlestone where it has been recorded since 1989.

117 R. polyanthemus Lindeb.
Remarkably scarce, it has been recorded to the south of Brackley and Daventry, and in the Soke of Peterborough.

120 R. rhombifolius Weihe ex Boenn.
No recent records. Recorded from Harlestone in 1905 by A.B.Jackson.
Druce: recorded as R. argenteus.

125 R. subinermoides Druce
An outlier of this common south-eastern species has been conspicuous at Harlestone since 1989.

ser. **Sprengeliani** Focke

132 R. sprengelii Weihe
No recent records. It was recorded from Badby by L. Cumming. It is a characteristic species of sessile oak-birch woodland or sandy soils.

ser. Discolores **(P.J.Mueller)** Focke

133 R. anglocandicans Newton

Well distributed particularly along the marlstone escarpment, mostly as single bushes in hedges.
Druce: recorded as R. thyrsoideus.

134 R. armeniacus Focke
Himalayan Giant
Introduction.
Much grown for its fruit and increasingly bird sown from gardens and allotments. It has been recorded from the area south of Daventry, in the general area of Corby and in the Soke of Peterborough; but it is no doubt in other suburban districts also.

135 R. armipotens W.C.Barton ex Newton
Present in some quantity in Plumpton Wood and Bucknell Wood since 1987. It is more or less at its northern limit .

142 R. ulmifolius Schott
The most prevalent bramble in hedges and banks; scarce in the windswept northern plateau. In virtually all 10km squares.

143 R. winteri P. J. Mueller ex Focke
Many good colonies of this robust pink flowered bramble are visible in hedges and wood borders especially on the marlstone. Collected by L.Cumming at Badby, Staverton and Preston Capes (where it still flourishes). It is also found at Newbottle, Plumpton Wood and Bucknell Wood.

ser. **Vestiti** (Focke) Focke

144 R. adscitus Genev.
A thriving population of this mainly westerly bramble was found at Mantles Heath in 1987. The nearest known sites are near Watford, Hertfordshire and near Coventry.

146 R. bartonii Newton
A flourishing colony of this handsome pink flowered species was discovered at Harlestone in 1993. This is the most easterly record for this plant.

163 R. vestitus Weihe
Common and widespread in woods, hedges and banks. Recorded from the south of the county.

ser. **Mucronati** (Focke) H.E.Weber

173 R. mucronulatus Boreau

No recent records. Found by Druce at Redhill and L.Cumming at Badby.
Druce: recorded as R. mucronifer.

ser. **Micantes** Sudre ex Bouvet

181 R. erythrops Edees & Newton
It has been recorded since 1987 at Plumpton Wood. It was formerly found at Weekley Hall Woods but it has not been refound there.
Druce: recorded as R. rosaceus

190 R. leightonii Lees ex Leighton
Widespread and common at least in the western half of the county.

199 R. raduloides (Rogers) Sudre
There are good colonies of this 'North Sea florula' member at Wothorpe in the Soke of Peterborough.

ser. **Anisacanthi** H.E.Weber

211 R.drejeri Jensen ex Lange
Several bushes of this scarce northerly bramble were found at Plumpton Wood in 1989; also at Whistley Wood in 1994.

217 R. infestus Weihe ex Boenn.
Only seen at Southey Wood in 1976.

ser. **Radula** (Focke) Focke

223 R. bloxamianus Coleman ex Purchas
Still present in quantity in the area where first found by A. Ley in 1910, in the woods near Wadenhoe and at Barnwell. In 1988, it was seen in one hedgerow near Little Preston, a link with the main Warwickshire population.

231 R. echinatoides (Rogers) Dallman
Still at Harleston where it was recorded by Druce, but it has not been seen elsewhere.

232 R. echinatus Lindley
This characteristic Midland species is widespread and common at least in the west of the county and no doubt occurs elsewhere.
Druce: recorded as R. discerptus

233 R. euryanthemus W.C.R.Watson
Recorded by W.H.Mills near Easton Hornstocks in 1949.

249 R. radula Weihe ex Boenn.
Widespread and common, often abundant, sometimes the only bramble present on the Oolite. Recorded at suitable sites scattered

throughout the county and the Soke of Peterborough.

253 R. rudis Weihe
At the north-west edge of its range. It was recorded from Badby by W.H.Mills. It is presently widespread around Wadenhoe where it was first found by A.Ley in 1910. It is present in some quantity at Harlestone and no doubt it is still present in other east Northants localities.

254 R. rufescens Lef. & P.J.Mueller
A large colony of this indicator of ancient forest was found at Whistley Wood in 1994. Oddly, this is the only recently observed occurrence.

ser. **Hystrices** Focke

268 R. dasyphyllus (Rogers) E. Marshall
Occasional, but frequent in the east. Much less prolific than in England as a whole.

270 R. hylocharis W.C.R.Watson
Found in some quantity at Bucknell Wood and Everdon Stubbs.
Druce: recorded as R. hystrix.

276 R. murrayi Sudre
Several bushes were seen at Harlestone in 1993 but it has not been detected elsewhere. It is frequent in the Warwickshire Arden.

ser. **Glandulosi** (Wimmer & Grab.) Focke

281 R. proiectus A. Beek
(*R. anglohirtus* Edees)
Specimens seen from Weekley and Wadenhoe but not seen in the field recently.

299 R. pedemontanus Pinkw.
A major ingredient of the ancient woodland ground flora (also in the Chilterns) this member of the 'North Sea florula' flourishes in several places: Badby, Plumpton, Everdon Stubbs, Harlestone, Wakerley and Wothorpe.
Druce: recorded as R. bellardii

sect. **Corylifolii** Lindley

304 R. bagnallianus Edees
Found in hedges in the Staverton area and to the east of Kettering; and on the bank of an abandoned railway in the extreme south of the county.

307 R. conjungens (Bab.) Rogers

Surprisingly scarce. It was recorded from Chalcombe by H.J.Riddlesdell. Recently it has been recorded in hedges at a few localities scattered across the county.

308 R. eboracensis W.C.R.Watson
It has been recorded at Braunston by Y.Heslop-Harrison and near Harlestone. It appears to have reached the Midlands along the Great Central Railway.

313 R. nemorosus Hayne & Willd.
Found in hedges near Plumpton and Everdon but not seen elsewhere
Druce: recorded as R. balfourianus.

315 R. pruinosus Arrh.
Recorded from Croughton, Badby and Harlestone.
Druce: recorded as R. sublustris

319 R. tuberculatus Bab.
Frequent on railway banks, roadsides and waste ground. It has been recorded from the general area to the south of Daventry.

320 R. warrenii Sudre
One colony recorded at Aston-le-walls in 1987, but this furzy hillside was cleared in 1993: hopefully it is still surviving in this area along old railway banks.

sect. **Caesii** Lej. & Courtois

321 R. caesius L.   (90)
Dewberry
Native. Damp open woodland and rough grassland.

Fairly common. Widespread on calcareous soils in woods and banks. Sites not localised.
First record: Parkinson 1640
Druce: Common and generally distributed.

9 POTENTILLA L.

2 P. palustris (L.) Scop.
Marsh Cinquefoil
Native. Bogs and marshes.
Extinct. It was recorded from Southorpe Marsh up to the Second World War and possibly into the 1950s, but the area was subsequently drained.
First record: Rev. M. J. Berkeley c1860
Druce: Very rare.

3 P. anserina L. (130)
Silverweed
Native. Waste ground, roadsides, grassland and open woodland, often in wet areas.
Common throughout the county on all types of soil, although it is often seen in leaf only.

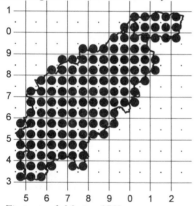

First record: Morton 1712
Druce: Common and generally distributed.

5 P. argentea L.
Hoary Cinquefoil
British. Waste ground.
This species was first recorded by Guy Messenger in 1965, together with *Trifolium scabrum* and *Trifolium striatum*, on dumped soil at Bonemills Hollow. It persisted for several years, at least into the 1970s.

7 P. recta L.
Sulphur Cinquefoil
Introduction. Waste ground.

Recorded from a single site below the rubbish tip in St. James, Northampton in the 1970s, where it was certainly a garden escape.
Druce: [No status given but recorded at a single site at Cranford].

8 P. intermedia L.
Russian Cinquefoil
Introduction.
No recent records.
First record: Goode 1917
Druce: [No status given, only recorded at one site, Northampton Racecourse].

9 P. norvegica L.
Ternate-leaved Cinquefoil
Introduction. Waste places.
Seen by Nick Turland in the centre of Harlestone Firs in 1987, where it persisted for a year or two. The area is now destroyed. The plant was probably a garden relic.
First record: Goode 1916
Druce: [No status given but recorded at only one site, Northampton Racecourse].

13 P. erecta (L.) Räusch. (54)
Tormentil

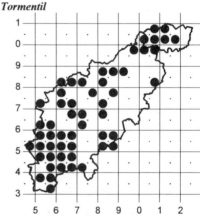

Native. Open, grassy areas and woodland rides.
Occasional in woodland and relict heathland. It is commoner in the south and west of the county and in woodland in the Soke of Peterborough.
First record: Baker 1822
Druce: Local.

14 P. anglica Laich. (12)
Trailing Tormentil

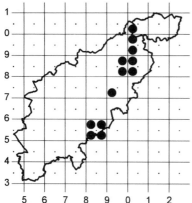

5 6 7 8 9 0 1 2

Native. Hedgerows rides and grassy areas. Rare. It is recorded at very few sites in the county. It is common in Yardley Chase and other woodlands in the area and at Bedford Purlieus. It is also recorded from Finedon Pits where it may have been introduced with tree planting.

First record: Druce 1878
Druce: (P. procumbens) Locally abundant.

14 x 15 P. anglica x P. reptans = P. x mixta Nolte ex Reichb.
Hybrid Cinquefoil
Native. Wood borders and dry banks.
Extremely rare, being recorded at only one site in the extreme south, although the ranges of the parent plants do overlap, and it may be overlooked in other areas.

15 P. reptans L.   (130)
Creeping Cinquefoil

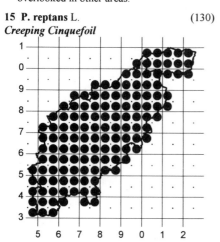

5 6 7 8 9 0 1 2

Native. Waste ground, grassy and bare areas. Common. Found throughout the county on virtually all types of soil.
First record: Gulliver 1841
Druce: Common and widely distributed.

16 P. sterilis (L.) Garcke   (52)
Barren Strawberry
Native. Open woodland and dry grassy areas. Fairly common in suitable habitats throughout the county but largely absent from the area between Northampton and Market Harborough.
First record: Notcutt 1844
Druce: Common and generally distributed.

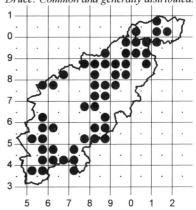

5 6 7 8 9 0 1 2

11 FRAGARIA L.
1 F. vesca L.   (82)
Wild Strawberry

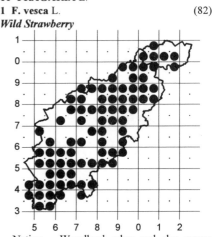

5 6 7 8 9 0 1 2

Native. Woodland edge and dry grassy habitats.

Occasional. Recorded throughout the county in old ironstone quarries and beside railway lines, and in woodlands. It generally occurs on calcareous soils.
First record: Clare 1821
Druce: Not uncommon and widely distributed throughout the county.

2 F. moschata Duchesne (Duchesne)
(*F. muricata* sensu D.H.Kent, non L.)
Hautbois Strawberry
Introduction. Shaded places.
No recent records.
First record: Druce 1902
Druce: (F. moschata) Very rare.

3 F. ananassa (Duchesne) Duchesne
Garden Strawberry
Introduction. Waste places and waste banks.
Occasional. Present at a few scattered localities throughout the county, always as an escape from cultivation, but it can become well established and it may survive for many years.
Druce: (F. chiloensis) No status given but he lists four localities.

12 DUCHESNEA Smith
1 D. indica (Andrews) Focke
Yellow-flowered Strawberry
Introduction. Rough grassland.
A single record as a garden escape in Badby churchyard by P. Rawlinson.

13 GEUM L.
1 G. rivale L.
Water Avens
Native. Damp woodlands and marshes.
Extremely rare. In 1993 two plants were found by Jenny Bourne, growing beside a small stream within a green area in Desborough. Whether these plants are wild in origin, or are garden escapes is unknown. The number of plants had increased in 1994. Prior to this it had only been recorded from Wakerley Woods in the 1950s by John Gilbert and from Bearshank Woods about 1960.
First record: H.N.Dixon 1907
Druce: Very local. Present in Wakerley Wood together with the hybrid G. x intermedium.

1 x 2 G. rivale x G. urbanum = G. x intermedium Ehrh.
Hybrid Avens
Native. Where both parents meet.
No recent records.
Druce: [No status given. Only two records, one of which is unconfirmed].

2 G. urbanum L. (127)
Wood Avens, Herb Bennet
Native. Woods and shaded habitats.
Common. Found throughout the county, and extremely common in favourable habitats.

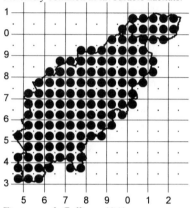

First record: Gulliver 1841
Druce: Common and generally distributed.

G. chiloense Balbis
(*G. Coccineum* auct. Non Sibth. & Smith)
Introduction.
A large patch of this plant was recorded in Wakerley Woods in 1993.

G. quellyon Sweet
Introduction.
A single record as an escape.

15 AGRIMONIA L.
1 A. eupatoria L. (113)
Agrimony
Native. Dry grassland on calcareous or mildly acid soils.
Fairly common in most areas throughout the county.
First record: Baker 1822
Druce: Locally abundant on dry soils.

150

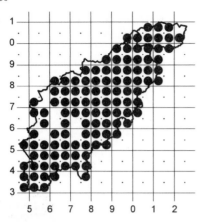

2 A. procera Wallr.
(*A. odorata* auct., non (L.) Miller
Fragrant Agrimony
Native. Woodland margins and rough grassland on heavier damp soils.
Extremely rare. Present at two widely separate locations in the extreme north and south; Wakerley Woods and Bucknell Wood.
First record: Druce 1891
Druce: (A. odorata) Rare.

17 SANGUISORBA L.
1 S. officinalis L. (67)
Great Burnet

First record: Parkinson 1640
Druce: (Poterium officinale) Locally abundant.

3 S. minor Scop.
a subsp. **minor** (64)
(*Poterium sanguisorba* L.)
Salad Burnet

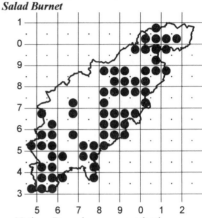

Native. Dry calcareous grassland.
Occasional, but can be locally common in the correct habitat; nevertheless, it is to be found on sites throughout much of the county especially in some of our churchyards.
First record: Clare 1821
Druce: (Poterium sanguisorba) Locally abundant.

b subsp. **muricata** (Gremli) Briq.
Fodder Burnet
Introduction. Field borders, railway banks.
Originally introduced as fodder and subsequently naturalised, but presently known only from one or two sites.
First record: Druce 1880
Druce: (Poterium polygamum) Local.

19 ALCHEMILLA L.
A. vulgaris L. agg.
Lady's-mantle
Native. Woodland rides and pastures.
The aggregate was regarded as a single species in Druce
First record: Morton 1712
Druce: Local

9 A. xanthochlora Rothm.
Lady's-mantle
Native. Grassland and woodland.

Native. Traditional hay meadows.
Occasional. Scattered on isolated sites throughout the county. It is decreasing due to the increased destruction of hay meadows by ploughing.

Probably extinct. Only recorded with certainty at Castle Ashby, but the glade where it grew is now over-run with common nettle (*Urtica dioica*) and it has disappeared.
First record: George Crawford (Castle Ashby) 1984

10 A. filicaulis Buser
Hairy Lady's-mantle
a subsp. vestita (Buser) Bradshaw (31)
Native. Woodland rides and pasture.
Occasional in most of our ancient woodlands: Rockingham, Whittlebury and Salcey Forests, Bedford Purlieus, Yardley and Geddington Chase. It is rare elsewhere in the county.

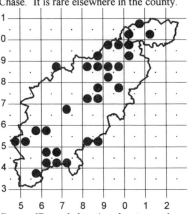

Druce: [Recorded as A. vulgaris agg.].

20 APHANES L.
1 A. arvensis L. (63)
Parsley-piert

Native. Bare ground especially at field edges.

Frequent. Found throughout the county on well drained, light soils.
First record: Notcutt 1843
Druce: (Alchemilla arvensis) Widely distributed and rather common.

2 A. inexspectata Lippert
(*A. microcarpa* auct., non (Boiss. & Reuter) Rothm.)
Slender Parsley-piert
Native. Open grassland and fields.
Extremely rare. Recorded at one site near Canons Ashby, in the south of the county.

21 ROSA L.
4 R. arvensis Hudson (96)
Field-rose

Native. Woodland and hedgerows.
Frequent. Generally distributed but less common than *R. canina* and absent from some areas in the eastern and central area of the county.
First record: Morton 1712
Druce: Common and generally distributed.

With the exception of *R. arvensis* the roses have not generally been recorded in detail. Apart from this species other entries should be taken as evidence of their existence within the Vice-county and not as a complete record.

4 x 12   R. arvensis x R. canina = R. x verticillicantha Mérat
Native. Hedgerows and woodland.
Occasionally recorded since 1950, but probably under-recorded.
First record: Druce 1900
Druce: (R. deseglisei) Rare.

152

5 **R. pimpinellifolia** L.
Burnet Rose
Native. Heathy places.
Very rare. Formerly recorded from Harlestone Firs, Kingsthorpe Bushes and Borough Hill by Druce, it had not been seen since until it was recorded in Cranford Quarry in 1993 by Jeff Best and Linda Moore. This plant may be of garden origin, but it was growing in large quantities..
First record: Morton 1712
Druce: (R. spinosissima) Very rare

5 x 16 **R. pimpinellifolia x R. sherardii = R. x involuta** Sm.
Native.
No recent records.
Druce: [No status given, only recorded twice and one record thought to be doubtful by Druce].

6 **R. rugosa** Thunb. ex Murray
Japanese Rose
Introduction. Waste ground.
An escape from cultivation that may be found more frequently as it is increasingly used on roadside plantings in towns and other areas.
First record: (on the railway betwen Harringworth and Seaton) 1965

8 **R. glauca** Pourret
Red-leaved Rose
Introduction.
Used in civic planting and sometimes escaping. Seen at Hall Lane quarry, near Kettering, in 1983.
First record: Druce 1880
Druce: Rare.

11 **R. stylosa** Desv.
Short-styled Field-rose
Native. Hedges on stiff soil.
This species may be under-recorded but it is present in King's Wood, Corby.
First record: Druce 1878
Druce: (R. stylosa var. systyla) Very local.

11 x 4 **R. stylosa x R. arvensis = R. x pseudorusticana** Crépin ex Rogers
Native.
No recent records but may be under-recorded.

11 x 12 **R. stylosa x R. canina = R. x andegavensis** Bast.

Native. Hedgerows etc.
Occasionally recorded since 1950, but may be under-recorded.
First record: Druce 1880
Druce: Local.

12 **R. canina** agg. L.   (134)
Dog-rose
Native. Hedgerows and woodland edge.
Common. Found throughout the county on all types of soil.
First record: Morton 1712 - recorded in 1706

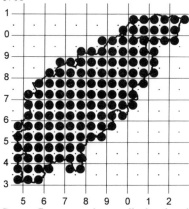

5   6   7   8   9   0   1   2

Druce: Common and generally distributed.
[Druce also records R. dumetorum and R. squarrosa as separate species, with a common distribution. These are now regarded as forms of R. canina].

12 x 13 **R. canina x R. caesia = R. x dumalis** Bechst.
Native.
No recent records.
First record: Druce 1880
Druce: Local.

12 x 16 **R. canina x R. sherardii = R. x rothschildii** Druce
Native. Hedges.
No recent records. First recorded by Druce at Ashton Wold. There are post 1930 records from the Barnack area by Mr Bishop.
First record: Druce 1911
Druce: Local.

12 x 18 **R. canina x R. rubiginosa = R. x nitidula** Besser
Native.

No recent records.
First record: Druce 1876
Druce: (R. Drucei) No status given.

13 R. caesia Smith
a subsp. **caesia**
(*R. coriifolia* Fries)
Hairy Dog-rose
Native. Hedges, scrub and wood borders. Extremely rare. Recorded at Old Sulehay Forest in the extreme north and Charlton in the extreme south.

b subsp. **glauca** (Nyman) G.Graham & Primavesi
(*R. afzeliana* Fries)
Glaucous Dog-rose
Native. Hedges, wood borders etc. Extremely rare, with only one record from Charlton in the south of the county. Most probably under-recorded.
First record: Druce 1880
Druce:(R. glauca) Rare

14 R. obtusifolia Desv.
Round-leaved Dog-rose
Native. Scrub banks and rough grass. Extremely rare. Recorded from an isolated site in the centre of the county. Most probably under-recorded.
First record: Druce 1880
Druce: Local.

14 x 18 R. obtusifolia x R. rubiginosa = R. x tomentelliformis W.-Dod
Native. Scrub banks and rough grass. No recent records but may be under-recorded.

15 R. tomentosa Smith
Harsh Downy-rose
Native. Hedges and open woods. Occasionally recorded since 1950, but probably under-recorded.
First record: Baker 1822
Druce: Local, rather rare.

16 R. sherardii Davies
Sherard's Downy-rose
Native. Hedgerows and open scrub. Very rare. Occurs at isolated sites in the north of the county including Rothwell Gullet nature reserve. In some cases, it may be a naturalised escape from cultivation.

First record: Druce 1878
Druce: Rare.

17 R. mollis Smith
(*R. villosa* auct., non L.)
Soft Downy-rose
Native. Hedges and open woodland. Extinct.
First record: Druce 1897
Druce: Very rare

18 R. rubiginosa L.
Sweet-briar
Native. Rough grassland and scrub. Rare. Found at an isolated site on calcareous soil in the extreme north of the county.
First record: Morton 1712
Druce: (R. eglanteria) Local.

19 R. micrantha Borrer ex Smith
Small-flowered Sweet-briar
Native. Hedges. No recent records but may be under-recorded. The last known record was prior to 1950.
First record: Druce 1884
Druce: Local.

19 x 4 R. micrantha x R. arvensis = R. x inelegans W.-Dod.
Native. Hedges. No recent records but may be under-recorded.
First record: Druce 1922 (as a new hybrid)
Druce: [No status given, only one record].

22 PRUNUS L.
3 P. cerasifera Ehrh. (13)
Cherry Plum
Introduction. Hedgerows. Occasional. Used in some areas as a plant for hedgerows, it is also recorded from Northampton Golf Links. There are some very fine hedgerow trees south of Nassington. Occasionally cv. *pissardii*, with dark red leaves and pink flowers is planted.
First record: 1922
Druce: Extensively planted for hedges.

4 P. spinosa L. (134)
Blackthorn
Native. Woodland and hedgerows.

Common. Occurs as large scrub patches or in hedgerows, occasionally replacing *Crataegus monogyna* as the dominant hedgerow plant.

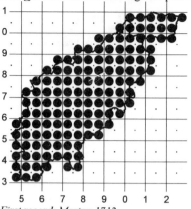

First record: Morton 1712
Druce: Abundant and widely distributed.

5 P. domestica L. (37)
Wild Plum
a subsp. **domestica**

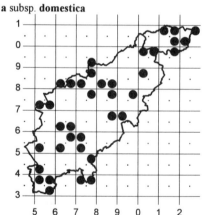

Introduction. Hedgerows and woodland margins, especially close to habitation. Infrequent, but found at widely scattered sites throughout the county.
First record: Clare 1827
Druce: Rather common and widely distributed.

b subsp. **insititia** (L.) Bonnier & Layens
Damson, Bullace
Native. Hedges and woodland margins.

Rare. It is recorded at a few sites within the county, but it is probably under-recorded.
First record: Druce 1875.
Druce: Scattered throughout the county.

6 P. avium (L.) L. (69)
Wild Cherry

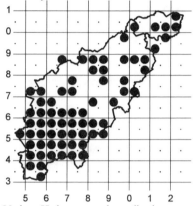

Native. Hedgerows and woodlands.
Occasional. It is present in woods either as a result of deliberate planting or natural generation. Under favourable circumstances it can become dominant making these woods a magnificent sight in the spring when they are in bloom, as at High Wood. Very occasionally found in hedgerows.
First record: Baker 1822
Druce: Local.

7 P. cerasus L.
Dwarf Cherry
Native. Hedgerows and small woodlands.
Extinct. The only known records are those listed by Druce, all but one of which can be dated to 1877 or earlier.
First record: Morton 1716
Druce: Very rare.

11 P. padus L.
Bird Cherry
Native. Woods and scrub.
A few records of planted trees at Barton Seagrave and other localities.
Druce: No status given

13 P. lusitanica L.
Portugal Laurel
Introduction. Parkland and shrubberies.

Planted and occasionally naturalised in shrubberies and parkland.

14 P. laurocerasus L.
Cherry Laurel
Introduction. Parkland and shrubberies.
Only present as a planted shrub, generally in parkland.
Druce: A planted shrub in many places.

26 PYRUS L.
P. pyraster (L.) Burgsd.
Wild Pear
Native.. Hedgerows.
Extremely rare.   A few trees have been recorded just to the east of Stamford.

P. communis L.   (11)
Pear

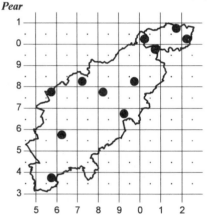

Introduced. Hedgerows and woodland edge.
Very rare, with a few isolated trees scattered along the length of the county.
First record: Beesley 1842
Druce: (P. communis) Rare.

27 MALUS Miller

1 M. sylvestris (L.) Miller   (125)
Crab Apple
Native. Woods and hedgerows.
Frequent or occasional. Occurs sporadically and often as an isolated example in areas of woodland or very occasionally in hedgerows.
First record: Morton 1712
Druce: (Pyrus malus) Not infrequent.

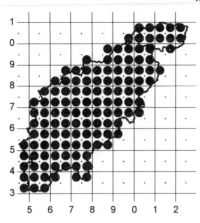

2 M. domestica Borkh.
(*M. sylvestris* subsp. *mitis* (Wallr.) Mansf.)
Apple
Introduction. Woods and hedgerows.
Uncommon. Only a few scattered naturalised specimens have been recorded.

28 SORBUS L.
1 S. aucuparia L.
Rowan, Mountain Ash
British. Hedges, thickets and plantations.
Almost certainly planted or surviving as a relic of cultivation, except perhaps in the woodlands of the south-west.
First record: Gulliver 1841
Druce: (Pyrus aucuparia) Rare, and usually, if not always, planted.

7 S. intermedia (Ehrh.) Pers.
Swedish Whitebeam
Introduction. Plantations.
Occasionally planted in managed woodland, as at Wakerley Great Wood.

9 S. aria (L.) Crantz
Common Whitebeam
British. Parks and plantations
There are a few records of this from Staverton, Gayton, a disused railway near Stanion, Bedford Purlieus and near Middleton.
First record: Druce 1877
Druce: (Pyrus aria) Probably planted.

24 S. torminalis (L.) Crantz   (13)
Wild Service-tree

156

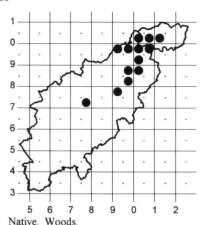

5 6 7 8 9 0 1 2

Native. Woods.
Very rare. Only a few scattered records in the northern calcareous areas, where the tree is a rare constituent of ancient woodland. Mainly confined to Rockingham Forest. An isolated example can be seen in the grounds of the Snooty Fox public house, Lowick.
First record: Morton 1712
Druce: (Pyrus torminalis) Very rare.

32 COTONEASTER Medikus
9 x 10 C. x watereri Exell
(*C. frigidus x C. salicifolius*)
Waterer's Cotoneaster
Introduction.
A single example recorded from the old railway line at Wakerley.

10 C. salicifolius Franchet
Willow-leaved Cotoneaster
Introduction. Damp scrub.
Only a single example of a naturalised plant recorded, on the Rothwell Gullet nature reserve.

15 C. congestus Baker
Congested Cotoneaster
Introduction. Naturalised on limestone.
An isolated record from the extreme north at Collyweston Deeps nature reserve.

16 C. integrifolius (Klotz) Klotz
Small-leaved Cotoneaster
Introduction.
Two records from the Soke of Peterborough.

21 C. horizontalis Decne.
Wall Cotoneaster

Introduction. Waste ground, railway embankments etc.
Isolated examples of naturalised plants from Irchester Country Park and other areas..

33 C. simonsii Baker
Himalayan Cotoneaster
Introduction. Waste ground.
A single record from the old site of Kettering Furnaces.

34 MESPILUS L.
1 M. germanica L.
Medlar
Introduction.
No recent records.
Druce: (Pyrus germanica) A single record of a tree, a relic of cultivation, now destroyed.

35 CRATAEGUS L.
7 C. monogyna Jacq.   (134)
Hawthorn

1
0
9
8
7
6
5
4
3

5 6 7 8 9 0 1 2

Native. Woodlands, hedgerows and waste land.
Common. It occurs throughout the county, being by far the most common constituent of hedgerows and a very invasive species of waste land.
First record: Morton 1712
Druce: Abundant throughout the county.

7 x 8 C. monogyna x C. laevigata = C. x macrocarpa Hegetschw.
Native. Woodlands and hedgerows.
Occasional, occurring naturally in the presence of both parents, in a variety of intermediate forms.

8 C. laevigata (Poiret) DC. (101)
(*C. oxyacanthoides* Thuill.)
Midland Hawthorn

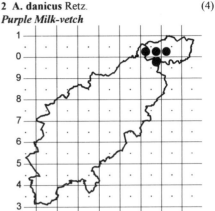

Native. Ancient woodlands and hedgerows.
Fairly common. Found in old woodlands, generally as isolated examples or in small numbers, and in old hedgerows.
First record: Druce 1908
Druce: (C. oxyacanthoides) Locally Common.

77 FABACEAE
(LEGUMINOSAE)

1 ROBINIA L.
1 R. pseudoacacia L.
False-acacia
Introduction. Scrub, parks and woodland. Usually occurring as a tree planted as ornamentation in parks etc. and sometimes naturalising itself, suckering freely.

2 GALEGA L.
1 G. officinalis L.
Goat's-rue
Introduction. Tips and waste places.
Sometimes abundant in rubbish tips and other places where garden refuse is dumped, as around Northampton tip in the early 1980s, and in Tiffield quarry.

3 COLUTEA L.
1 C. arborescens L.
Bladder-senna
Introduction. Waste and grassy places.
A escape from cultivation and naturalising in hedgerows, on railway banks etc.
First record: Druce 1930

Druce: [No status given].

4 ASTRAGALUS L.
2 A. danicus Retz. (4)
Purple Milk-vetch

Native. Short grass on calcareous soils.
Very rare and only known now from a few areas in the north, including Collyweston Deeps and Barnack Hills and Holes.
First record: Druce 1876.
Druce: Locally abundant.

4 A. glycyphyllos L. (35)
Wild Liquorice
Native. Mainly calcareous grassland.
Uncommon. Confined mainly to calcareous soils. It can be quite widespread in old quarries and sometimes on roadsides.
First record: Parkinson 1640
Druce: Local.

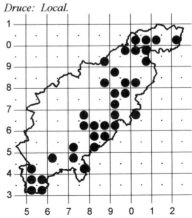

158

6 ONOBRYCHIS Miller
1 O. viciifolia Scop.   (16)
Sainfoin

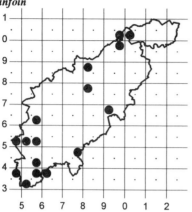

5   6   7   8   9   0   1   2

Possibly native.   Grassland, especially on limestone.
Occasional.   Scattered through the county, mainly as a relic of cultivation; the result of previous years when it was extensively grown as a fodder crop.
First record: Notcutt 1843
Druce: (O. onobrychis) Usually......occurs as the result of agricultural operations.

7 ANTHYLLIS L.
1 A. vulneraria L.   (43)
Kidney Vetch
a subsp. **vulneraria**

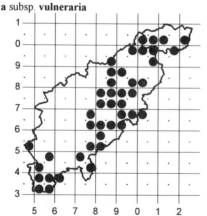

5   6   7   8   9   0   1   2

Native.   Grassland.
Fairly common in quarries, on railway banks and other places on calcareous soils. It has recently been introduced in seed mixtures for

roadside planting - particularly on the new A14.
First record: Morton 1712
Druce: Local.

d subsp. **carpatica** (Pant.) Nyman
Introduction. Marginal and waste land.
Found by Tim Rich in Peterborough, in 1988.

8 LOTUS L.
1 L. glaber Miller   (8)
(*L. tenuis* Waldst. & Kit. ex Willd.)
Narrow-leaved Bird's-foot-trefoil

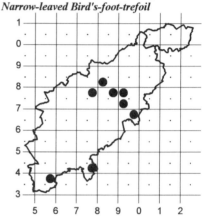

5   6   7   8   9   0   1   2

Introduction. Dry grassy places.
Uncommon and mostly occurring in old ironstone quarries and similar areas.
First record: Watson 1874
Druce: Often introduced with grass seeds.

2 L. corniculatus L.   (123)
Common Bird's-foot-trefoil

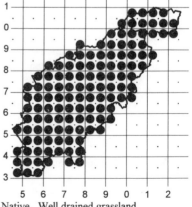

5   6   7   8   9   0   1   2

Native.   Well drained grassland.

Very common throughout the county in grassy areas. Recently, patches of upright, robust plants have been recorded beside the new A14 and other trunk roads throughout the county. This is an introduced alien, probably *var. sativus* which is increasingly being sown on new road verges.
First record: Pitt 1813
Druce: Common and generally distributed.

3 L. pedunculatus Cav. (88)
(L. uliginosus Schk.)
Greater Bird's-foot-trefoil

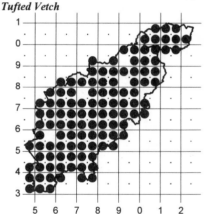

Native. Damp grassland and marshes. Fairly common throughout the county in suitable habitats; in marshes, damp woodland ridings etc.
First record: Morton 1712
Druce: Local.

10 ORNITHOPUS L.
3 O. perpusillus L.
Bird's-foot
Native. Dry, sandy ground.
A very rare plant, only occurring with any regularity on disturbed areas in Harlestone Firs although it has been recorded from areas as wide apart as a quarry at Yarwell in the north, and the Wildlife Trust reserve at Ramsden Corner in the west of the county.
First record: Morton 1712
Druce: Very local and rare.

12 HIPPOCREPIS L.
2 H. comosa L. (4)
Horseshoe Vetch
Native. Dry calcareous grassland.

Very rare and occurring mainly on the highly calcareous soils in the north of the county as at Collyweston, Easton on the Hill and Barnack Hills and Holes. There is just one record from as far south as Charlton stone pits.
First record: Druce 1878
Druce: Very rare.

13 SECURIGERA DC.
S. varia (L.) Lassen
(Coronilla varia L.)
Crown Vetch
Introduction. Grassy and rough ground. Occurs in a couple of sites at Northampton and Wollaston.
First record: Miss Duntsberry 1907
Druce: (Coronilla varia) Rare.

14 VICIA L.
2 V. cracca L. (113)
Tufted Vetch

Native. Grass and scrub. Fairly common on hedgebanks, woodland ridings and other grassy places.
First record: Pitt 1813
Druce: Common and generally distributed.

4 V. sylvatica L. (9)
Wood Vetch
Native. Woodland ridings and borders. Rare. Mostly occurring in woodland at Badby, Mantles Heath, in the Whittlebury area and at Bucknell Woods. It is also present at Gaultney Wood, near Desborough, and Wakerley Woods in the north of the county.

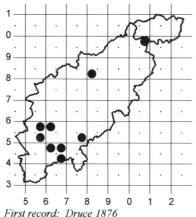

First record; Druce 1876
Druce: Very local and rare.

5 V. villosa Roth
Fodder Vetch
Introduction. Grassy places, waste tips etc.
Recorded in Wellingborough as a casual during the 1970s by Seán Karley.

6 V. hirsuta (L.) Gray (91)
Hairy Tare

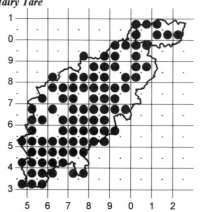

Native. Rough ground and grassy places.
Occasional in old quarries, waste ground, old railway tracks etc.
First record: Gulliver 1841
Druce: Local.

8 V. tetrasperma (L.) Schreber (65)
Smooth Tare
Native. Grassy places.
Occasional in similar habitats to *V. hirsuta*. It also occurs in some woodlands.

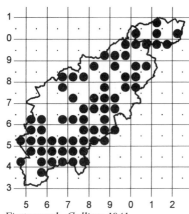

First record: Gulliver 1841
Druce: Local.

9 V. sepium L. (90)
Bush Vetch
Native. Grassy places, scrub and woodland.
Fairly common in woodland throughout the county.

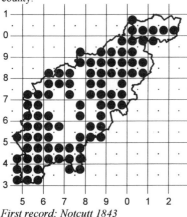

First record: Notcutt 1843
Druce: Widely distributed and not rare.

10 V. pannonica Crantz.
Hungarian Vetch
Introduction.
A single record from Kettering in 1945.

11 V. sativa L. (114)
Common Vetch
Native or introduced as a fodder plant. Roadside verges, waste ground etc. The map shows the distribution of the aggregate species.

First record: Gulliver 1841
Druce: Relic of cultivation.

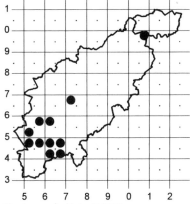

a subsp. nigra (L.) Ehrh.
(*V. angustifolia* L.)
Native. Sandy grassland.
Rare. It has been found in only a few localities, mainly in the west of the county.
Druce: (V. angustifolia) Not uncommon and widely distributed.

b subsp. segetalis (Thuill.) Gaudin
(*V. angustifolia* subsp. *segetalis* (Thuill.) Arcang.)
Probably introduced. This is the commonest sub-species and is found throughout the area.

c subsp. sativa
Introduction. Waste ground.
Occasional. Survives as a relic of cultivation.

13 V. lutea L.
(*V. laevigata* Smith)
Yellow-vetch
Native. Waste ground.
Extremely rare. This plant was noted on waste ground near to the Cock Hotel in Kingsthorpe in 1979, but the site has now been developed.

14 V. bithynica (L.) L.
Bithynian Vetch
Probably native. Scrub and rough grassland.
Probably extinct. Several plants were recorded from old ironstone pits at Finedon in 1968, the first record for the county. They have since disappeared.
First record: Mrs E.Cooke (Finedon) 1968

V. faba L.
Broad Bean
Introduction. Verges and field margins.
Sometimes establishing itself on grass verges, field margins and waste places as a relic of cultivation.

LENS Miller
L. culinaris Medikus
Lentil
Introduction. Waste tips etc.
Very occasionally turning up as a casual as at East Haddon in 1988.

15 LATHYRUS L.
3 L. linifolius (Reichard) Bässler   (11)
(*L. montanus* Bernh.)
Bitter-vetch
Native. Wood borders, hedgerows etc. on acid soils.
Rare. Mainly restricted to woodland in the south and west of the county around Badby and the Hazelborough area. There is one record from a dismantled railway near Boughton and it was also found at Bedford Purlieus.

First record: Notcutt 1843
Druce: (L. montanus) Woods, preferring acidulous soils.

4 L. pratensis L.   (125)
Meadow Vetchling
Native. Grassy places and rough ground.
Very common in grassy places throughout the county.

162

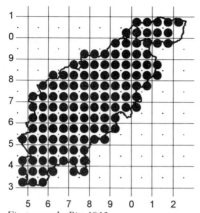

First record: Pitt 1813
Druce: Common and generally distributed.

6 L. tuberosus L.
Tuberous Pea
Introduction. Hedgerows and field margins.
A large number of plants came up on waste
ground off the Bedford Road, Northampton
in 1984 as a result of tipping.

8 L. sylvestris L. (12)
Narrow-leaved Everlasting-pea

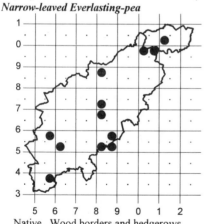

Native. Wood borders and hedgerows.
Rare. Occurring mainly in ancient woodland
at scattered localities throughout the county.
First record: Morton 1712
Druce: Very local.

9 L. latifolius L. (17)
Broad-leaved Everlasting-pea
Introduction. Hedges and roadside verges.

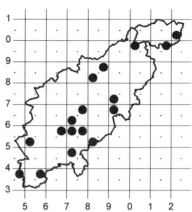

A showy cultivated species often escaping
and occasionally established on old railway
banks, roadsides etc.
First record: Druce 1876
Druce: Very rare.

11 L. hirsutus L.
Hairy Vetchling
Introduction. Rough, grassy ground.
This species occurred as a casual at
Kingsthorpe along with *Lathyrus nissolia* and
Vicia lutea and other species on waste
ground in 1979.
*First record: H.G.Allen 1946, Kettering
area.*

12 L. nissolia L. (15)
Grass Vetchling

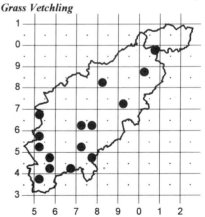

Native. Grassy places.
Rare. Locally scattered throughout the

county on railway banks, old quarries and similar habitats, especially in the west of the county. It is especially common in The Plens Wildlife Trust reserve at Desborough and it was discovered growing in quantity in a set-aside field near Kettering in 1993.
First record: Morton 1712
Druce: Very local.

13 L. aphaca L.
Yellow Vetchling
Adventive. Rough dry, grassy ground. No recent records, but recorded near Kettering in 1945.
First record: Druce 1900
Druce: Very rare.

PISUM L.
P. sativum L.
Garden Pea
Introduction. Roadsides and field margins. A rare casual, occurring as a result of cultivation.

16 ONONIS L.
3 O. spinosa L.   (28)
Spiny Restharrow

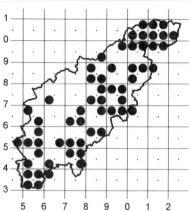

Native. Grassy places on rough ground. Occasional. Scattered throughout the county, mainly in the same areas as *O. repens*, but much less common than in the past owing to the destruction of suitable habitats.
First record: Morton 1712
Druce: Local.

4 O. repens L.
Common Restharrow
a subsp. **repens**   (58)

Native. Rough grassland on well drained soils.
Occasional. Scattered throughout the county on roadsides, old quarries and railway banks, tending to be more common than *O. spinosa*.
First record: Pitt 1813
Druce: Locally common.

6 O. baetica Clemente
Salzmann's Restharrow
Introduced with bird seed in Kettering in the 1970s.

17 MELILOTUS Miller
1 M. altissimus Thuill.   (49)
Tall Melilot

Introduction. Rough grassland.
Frequent. Widely distributed on waste ground, rubbish tips, railway lines etc.
First record: Pitt 1813
Druce: Local.

164

2 M. albus Medikus
White Melilot
Introduction. Rough grassland.
Well established in several places usually near rubbish tips and newly disturbed ground.
First record: Druce 1876.
Druce: Rare.

3 M. officinalis (L.) Pallas   (53)
Ribbed Melilot

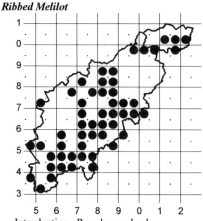

5 6 7 8 9 0 1 2

Introduction. Rough grassland.
Not quite so common as *M. altissimus* but growing in the same areas and often occurring together.
First record: Possibly Druce 1899
Druce: (M. arvensis) Rare.

4 M. indicus (L.) All.
Small Melilot
Introduction.   Rough ground and waste places.
An alien plant which establishes itself for a short time on newly disturbed ground, but never seems to survive very long. It has been recorded in a few scattered areas: Northampton and Wellingborough on dredgings, beside the River Ise and from one or two places around Peterborough.
First record: 1899
Druce: Rare.

18 MEDICAGO L.
1 M. lupulina L.   (126)
Black Medick
Native. Grassy places and rough ground.
Very common and well established all over the county.

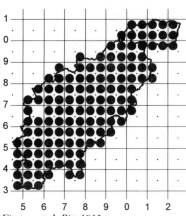

5 6 7 8 9 0 1 2
First record: Pitt 1813
Druce: Now abundantly spread through the county

2 M. sativa L.
a subsp. **falcata** (L.) Arcang.
Sickle Medick
Native. Grassland, rough or waste places.
Extremely rare. It was recorded on a disused railway near Sutton for many years up to the 1970s and at Grendon lakes in 1994.
First record: T.Brayne 1820
Druce: (M. falcata) Very rare.

c subsp. **sativa**   (45)
Lucerne

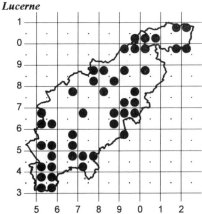

5 6 7 8 9 0 1 2
Native. Grassy places and waste ground.
Frequent. Often quite well established in many areas as a relic of cultivation as a fodder crop. A yellow flowered form occurs on the roadside near Weekley.

First record: Beesley 1842
Druce: Now established in many places throughout the county.

3 M. minima (L.) Bartal.
Bur Medick
Adventive. Sandy ground.
No recent records. It was last recorded in 1951, on a railway line near Peterborough by Dr John Dony.
First record: 1951

4 M. polymorpha L.
Toothed Medick
Adventive. Sandy ground.
No recent records.
First record: Druce 1878
Druce: (M. hispida var denticulata) Rare.

5 M. arabica (L.) Hudson   (10)
Spotted Medick

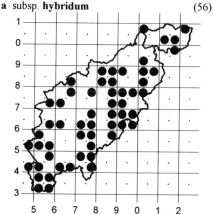

Adventive. Bare grassland.
Very rare. Established in a few places in the county: by the canal at Rothersthorpe, in the Wildlife Trust reserve at Farthinghoe and a few other places. In 1993 several hundred plants were discovered around new flats in Wellingborough, introduced, no doubt, with grass seed.
First record: Druce 1879
Druce: Very rare.

19 TRIFOLIUM L.
2 T. repens L.   (133)
White Clover
Native. Grass and rough ground.

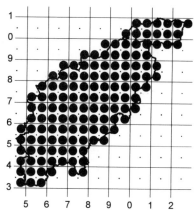

Very common throughout the county in grassy places.
First record: Pitt 1813
Druce: Plentiful.

4 T. hybridum L.
Alsike Clover
a subsp. **hybridum**   (56)

Introduction. Grass and rough ground.
Occasional. Occurring commonly throughout on roadsides and disturbed ground.
First record: Druce 1877
Druce: Completely naturalised.

8 T. fragiferum L.
Strawberry Clover
a subsp. **fragiferum**   (26)
Native. Grassy places on heavy soils.
Occasional on clay soils and often a feature of old green lanes and roadsides in the eastern half of the county.

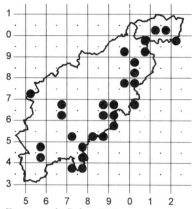

First record: Baker 1822
Druce: Local.

9 T. resupinatum L.
Reversed Clover
Introduction. Damp grassland.
Recorded as a casual on the roadside near
Helmdon in 1992, after being unrecorded for
many years. It only lasted a single season.
First record: 1878
Druce: Very rare.

10 T. aureum Pollich
Large Trefoil
Introduction. Rough and grassy ground.
No recent records.
First record: Druce 1878-79
Druce: (T. agrarium) Very rare.

11 T. campestre Schreber   (99)
Hop Trefoil

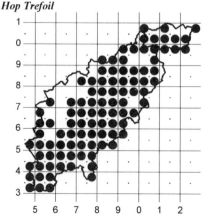

Native. Grassed and bare places.
Frequent. Scattered throughout the county
and growing in areas such as disused railway
lines, waste ground, quarries etc.
First record: Pitt 1813
Druce: (T. procumbens) Not uncommon.

12 T. dubium Sibth.   (120)
Lesser Trefoil

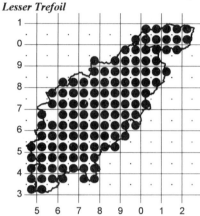

Native. Grassy and open ground.
Very common and well distributed.
First record: Druce 1877
Druce: Common and widely distributed.

13 T. micranthum Viv.   (6)
Slender Trefoil
Native. Short turf, lawns etc.
Very rare but possibly overlooked. It occurs
on well established lawns as at Courteenhall,
Wellingborough Bowling Greens and on open
sandy areas at Harlestone Firs and Billing
Lings. Also recorded for Castor Hanglands
national nature reserve in the 1960s.
First record: Druce 1901
Druce: (T. filiforme) Very rare.

14 T. pratense L.   (129)
Red Clover
Native. Grassy places, rough and waste
ground.
Very common throughout the county.
First record: Pitt 1913
Druce: Common and generally distributed.

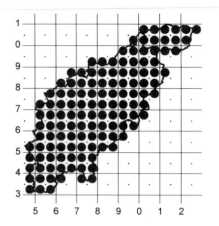

15 T. medium L. (35)
Zigzag Clover

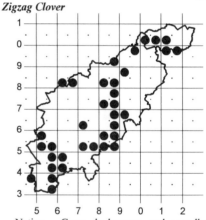

Native. Grass, hedgerows and woodland borders.
An occasional plant of woodland ridings and roadsides.
First record: Pitt 1813
Druce: Rare.

16 T. ochroleucon Hudson
Sulphur Clover
Native. Grassy places on heavy soils.
Extremely rare. Thought to be extinct for many years having disappeared completely from its former sites, due no doubt to the destruction of habitats, but it was found in Sudborough Meadow in 1994 by Adrian Colston, Rosemary Parslow and Mark July.
First record: Hudson 1778
Druce: Very local.

19 T. incarnatum L.
a subsp. **incarnatum**
Crimson Clover
Introduction.
No recent records.
First record: Druce 1878
Druce: Occurring as an escape from cultivation but not permanently established.

20 T. striatum L.
Knotted Clover
Native. Short grassland on sandy soil.
A very rare plant only being recorded from four places on sandy soil: in Tiffield quarry, Harlestone Firs, Bonemills Hollow near Wittering and on a disused railway line near Wellingborough.
First record: Morton 1712
Druce: Very local.

22 T. scabrum L.
Rough Clover
Native. Short grassland.
Probably extinct. Recorded by Guy Messenger in 1965, growing on dumped rubble at Bonemills Hollow, growing with *Potentilla argentea* and *Trifolium striatum*.
First record: Alfred French 1874
Druce: Very rare.

23 T. arvense L. (17)
Hare's-foot Clover

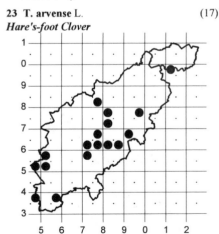

Native. Grassland on sandy soils.
Occasional. Scattered, but mainly in sandy areas and on disused railway lines.
First record: Druce 1877
Druce: Very local.

168

20 THERMOPSIS R.Br.
1 T. montana Nutt. ex Torrey & A.Gray
False Lupin
Introduction.
An established garden escape that was present for many years at Oundle gravel pits, now disappeared.

21 LUPINUS L.
1 L. arboreus Sims
Tree Lupin
Introduction. Naturalised in waste places. Usually found as a garden outcast as on the old rubbish tip at Milton Malsor.

L. polyphyllus group
Lupin
Introduction. Naturalised on rough ground. Well established on roadsides and railway banks in a few places. It is thought that all records are for *L. polyphyllus* Lindley x *L. arboreus = L. x regalis* Bergmans as *L. polyphyllus* is now rarely grown.

22 LABURNUM Fabr.
1 L. anagyroides Medikus
Laburnum
Introduction. Self sown in rough ground. Occasional. Introduced as an ornamental tree and often escaping. Established in Salcey Forest and other areas.

23 CYTISUS Desf.
4 C. scoparius (L.) Link
(Saromanthus scoparius (L.) Wimmer)
Broom
a subsp. **scoparius** (25)

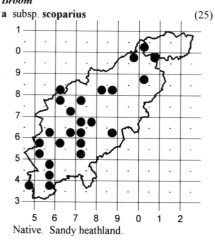

5 6 7 8 9 0 1 2
Native. Sandy heathland.

Occasional and scattered. A local plant and usually restricted to the sandy soils associated with areas on the Northampton sands around Duston, Hunsbury Hill, Harlestone Firs and Billing Lings. It also occurs in the west of the county at Badby Woods, Ramsden Corner and other sites and again on the lighter patches of soil in Bedford Purlieus.
First record: Morton 1712
Druce: Rare.

25 GENISTA L.
2 G. tinctoria L.
Dyer's Greenweed
a subsp. **tinctoria** (6)

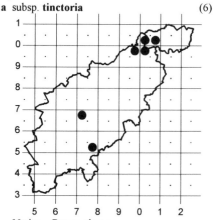

5 6 7 8 9 0 1 2
Native. Grassy places.
Very rare, although it occurs in quantity in Collyweston Deeps and in Wakerley and Fineshade Woods. Otherwise extremely rare with one site in the south of the county.
First record: Dickson 1792
Druce: Very local.

4 G. anglica L.
Petty Whin
Native. Sandy or peat heathland.
Extremely rare. Thought to be extinct in the county until it was re-discovered by John Barker in Harlestone Firs in 1969 confirming the record by Morton in 1712.
First record: Morton 1712
Druce: Very rare, almost extinct.

5 G. hispanica L.
Spanish Gorse
a subsp. **occidentalis** Rouy
Introduction.

Naturalised on the side of A5 near Weedon.
First record: Andrew Robinson 1987

26 ULEX L.

1 U. europaeus L. (80)
Gorse
Native. Grassy places, open woodland and heathy areas, railway banks and old quarries. Common in suitable habitats on lighter soils but absent from some parts of the county. It is often a feature of some of our more western hilltops where the ground is not cultivated.

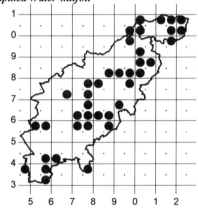

First record: Morton 1712
Druce: Local.

3 U. minor Roth
Dwarf Gorse
Native. Heaths
Extinct. Druce considered this species very local and cites two areas; Badby Woods and Harlestone Firs, dating from 1877. These are the last known records.
First record: Druce 1877
Druce: Very local.

78 ELAEAGNACEAE
1 HIPPOPHAE L.
1 H. rhamnoides L.
Sea-buckthorn
British. Road verges, often planted.
Occasionally planted along roadsides and on development sites and sometimes escaping.

79 HALORAGACEAE
2 MYRIOPHYLLUM L.
1 M. verticillatum L.
Whorled Water-milfoil

Native. Slow streams, canals, ponds and ditches.
Extremely rare. Recently recorded from a fen ditch near Peakirk. It is also recorded from Peter's Pond and in the nearby backwater of the River Welland, where it is abundant.
First record: Morton 1712
Druce: Local.

2 M. aquaticum (Vell. Conc.) Verdc.
(*M. brasiliense* Cambess.)
Parrot's Feather
Adventive. Still waters and wet places.
Found in abundance in 1994 near to Cat's Water in Flag Fen. A marsh plant from South America, it is sold as an oxygenator.
First record: Brian Adams 1994

3 M. spicatum L. (39)
Spiked Water-milfoil

Native. Rivers and the larger water bodies.
Fairly common in streams, the River Welland between Duddington and Tinwell, the Rivers Nene and Ise and in most of the larger reservoirs. It often fails to flower in very fast water. Also occasionally found in ponds.
First record: Notcutt 1843
Druce: Local.

4 M. alterniflorum DC.
Alternate Water-milfoil
Native. Dykes and pools.
Recorded from Deanshanger Gravel Pits.
First record: Druce 1911
Druce: Very local.

81 LYTHRACEAE
1 LYTHRUM L.
1 L. salicaria L. (60)
Purple-loosestrife

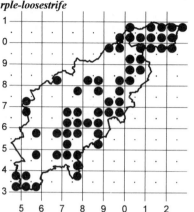

5 6 7 8 9 0 1 2

Native. Beside rivers, lakes and canals.
Frequent beside water in the east of the
county and in the Soke of Peterborough. It is
also fairly abundant along the canals.
First record: Pitt 1813
Druce: Locally abundant.

2 L. hyssopifolia L.
Grass-poly
Adventive. Wet bare ground.
No recent records. It was last known from
the Welland valley near Barrowden.
First record: Morton 1716
Druce: Very rare.

3 L. portula (L.) D.Webb
Water-purslane
Native. Marshy places and pond sides.
Extinct. Only recorded pre-1930, in Badby
Woods and from Farthingstone Castle Dykes.
First record: Druce 1877
Druce: Rare.

L. junceum Banks & Sol
Adventive.
No recent records.
*Druce: (L. meonanthum) Rare, only one
record.*

82 THYMELAEACEAE
1 DAPHNE L.
1 D. mezereum L.
Mezereon
Probably native. Woods and shrubberies.

Extinct. The last example, in a copse near
Evenley, was dug up in 1909.
First record: Druce 1898
Druce: Very rare.

2 D. laureola L. (35)
Spurge-laurel

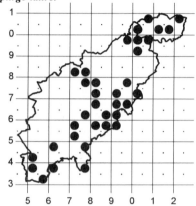

5 6 7 8 9 0 1 2

Native. Woodland, mainly on calcareous soil.
Occasional. Found in woodlands in some
parts of the county but strangely absent from
others. It is more common in the centre of
the county, woods in the north and the Soke.
First record: Morton 1712
Druce: Locally scattered throughout.

84 ONAGRACEAE
1 EPILOBIUM L.
1 E. hirsutum L. (133)
Great Willowherb

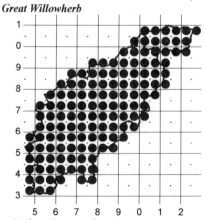

5 6 7 8 9 0 1 2

Native. Damp and wet areas.

Common in all areas, especially within its preferred habitat in roadside ditches.
First record: Pitt 1813
Druce: Locally abundant and generally distributed in all districts.

2 E. parviflorum Schreber (102)
Hoary Willowherb

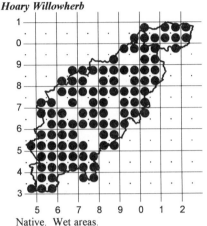

Native. Wet areas.
It can be locally abundant in suitable wet areas such as marshes, gravel quarries, damp woodland etc.
First record: Notcutt 1843
Druce: Rather frequent and widely distributed.

2 x 6 E. parviflorum x E. obscurum = E. x dacicum Borbas
Native. Damp Woodland.
Very rare. Only found once by John Gilbert at Yarwell in 1951 but may be overlooked.
Druce: A probable record at Althorpe.

3 E. montanum L. (116)
Broad-leaved Willowherb
Native. Walls, cultivated ground in shade. Very common and well distributed throughout the county in waste places and as a garden weed. Also common in woodlands and many other habitats.
First record: Morton 1712
Druce: Common and generally distributed in all the districts.

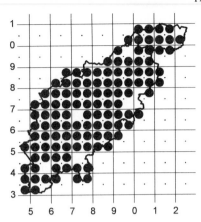

4 E. lanceolatum Sebast. & Mauri
Spear-leaved Willowherb
Native. Waste ground.
Extremely rare. It was found at Canon's Ashby in 1979 and again at Corby in 1992 by Rob Wilson on the site of former ironstone workings. These are the only records for the county but it may be overlooked.

5 E. tetragonum L. (38)
Square-stalked Willowherb

Occasional but can be common in its habitat, particularly where water stands in the winter, in quarries, on canal banks, beside gravel pits etc.
First record: Baker 1822
Druce: Local.

172

6 E. obscurum Schreber (20)
Short-fruited Willowherb

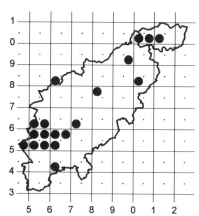

5 6 7 8 9 0 1 2

Native. Open woodland, hedges etc.
Rare. Only recorded in a very few areas in
damp woodland and churchyards. It also
occurs as a garden weed. Possibly overlooked.
First record: Druce 1875
Druce: Local.

6 x 8 E. obscurum x E. ciliatum
Native. Open Woodland.
This was found by John Gilbert at Yarwell in
1951 but there is no subsequent record. It
could re-occur where both parents are present.
First record: Gilbert 1951

7 E. roseum Schreber
Pale Willowherb
Native. Shady, damp and waste areas.
Extremely rare. Only recorded from Ash
Coppice, from near Badby Woods in 1978, and
from the garden of Guilsborough Court in
1994 by Rob Wilson .
First record: Druce 1911
Druce: Very local. [only one certain locality].

8 E. ciliatum Raf. (79)
(*E. adenocaulon* Hausskn.)
American Willowherb
Introduction. Waste and cultivated land.
Becoming fairly common in all types of
habitats; waste areas, railway lines and
woodland especially if recently cleared.
First record:J.L.Gilbert (Yarwell) 1948

9 E. palustre L. (19)
Marsh Willowherb

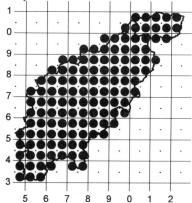

5 6 7 8 9 0 1 2

Native. Marshes and ditches.
Very rare and only occurring in very marshy
places at Bulwick, Badby Marsh, Naseby
reservoir and one or two other places, mainly
in the west and at White Water, Castor
Hanglands and Sutton in the Soke.
First record: Druce 1884
Druce: Rare.

2 CHAMERION (Raf.) Raf.
1 C. angustifolium (L.) Holub (127)
Rosebay Willowherb

5 6 7 8 9 0 1 2

Native. Verges, waste ground, woodland
clearings etc. Native. Open woodland, hedges,
beside water, etc.
It has become common and widely distributed
in all areas since Druce's day; in woodland and
waste areas, and as a common weed around
towns, railways etc.
First record: Baker 1822

Druce: (Epilobium angustifolium) Local but rapidly extending its area.

4 OENOTHERA L.
1 O. glazioviana Micheli ex C.Martius
Large-flowered Evening-primrose
Introduction. Waste ground, verges etc.
Scattered throughout the county, an escape - mainly near railways and in derelict areas.
First record: Druce 1910
Druce: (O. grandiflora) Casual.
3 O. biennis L.
Common Evening-primrose
Introduction. Waste ground and verges.
Naturalised near the railway at Wellingborough and Kettering.
First record: Druce 1930
Druce: Rare.

4 O. cambrica Rostánski
(*O. novae-scotiae* auct., non Gates)
Small-flowered Evening-primrose
Introduction. Field margins, road verges and beside water.
Recorded at two sites in 1992, at Wakerley, as solitary plants, and near Kettering, where it was abundant in the margins of a large field. There is also a record from the south-west and it may have occurred elsewhere. Hybrid swarms have been reported from the new road developments around Kettering and Corby.

6 CIRCAEA L.
1 C. lutetiana L. (97)
Enchanter's-nightshade

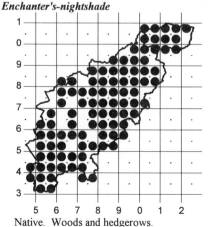

Native. Woods and hedgerows.

Frequent in all areas; in woodland, churchyards and often as a garden weed in shady gardens.
First record: Notcutt 1843
Druce: Locally abundant, and widely distributed in all the districts.

CLARKIA Pursh
(*Godetia* Spach)
C. unguiculata Lindley
Clarkia
Introduction. Casual on rubbish tips.
Sometimes occurring as a garden escape on rubbish tips and other waste areas.

85 CORNACEAE
1 CORNUS L.
(*Thelycrania* (Dumort.) Fourr., *Swida* Opiz)
1 C. sanguinea L. (102)
(*Thelycrania sanguinea* (L.) Fourr., *Swida sanguinea* (L.) Opiz.)
Dogwood

Native. Woods and hedgerows.
Frequent. Scattered across the county, but less common in the centre. Usually occurring as single examples unless planted in hedgerows.
First record: Berkeley 1836
Druce: Locally common and widely distributed in all districts.

87 VISCACEAE
(LORANTHACEAE PRO PARTE)
1 VISCUM L.
1 V. album L. (13)
Mistletoe
Native. Parasitic on deciduous trees.
Rare. Scattered through the county and sometimes introduced onto apple trees,

although it is recorded on various host trees. There are isolated examples in Salcey Forest, Horton and Fermyn Woods but the best example is possibly in the grounds of Burghley House, Stamford, where it hangs on nearly every lime tree in the avenue.

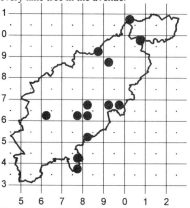

First record: Morton 1712
Druce: Very local.

88 CELASTRACEAE
1 EUONYMUS L.
1 E. europaeus L. (71)
Spindle

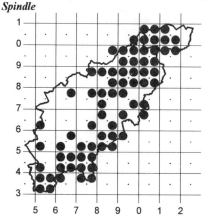

Native. Woodland, scrub and hedgerows. Occasional. Its preference for calcareous soils means that it is largely absent from the west. It is quite a feature of woodland in the area of Salcey, Whittlebury and Yardley Chase and in the Lincolnshire limestone areas in the north.
First record: Baker 1822

Druce: Locally common, chiefly in calcareous areas.

89 AQUIFOLIACEAE
1 ILEX L.
1 I. aquifolium L. (100)
Holly

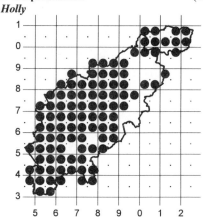

Possibly native. Woodland, hedgerows and parkland.
Found throughout the county, but usually as a planted tree. Where regeneration occurs, as at High Wood, it forms a component of the shrub layer.
First record: Beesley 1842
Druce: Rare.

I. aquifolium x I. perado Aiton = **I. altaclerensis** (hort ex Loudon) Dallimore
Highclere Holly
Introduction. Woodland, hedgerows and parkland.
Occasionally found in parks, but can occur in woodland and hedges as garden escapes.

90 BUXACEAE
1 BUXUS L.
1 B. sempervirens L. (30)
Box
British. Plantations and hedgerows.
Occasional, but more common in the centre of the county. It is always a planted species and can sometimes be abundant where it has been planted as cover for game, as on the Lilford Estate.
Druce: In plantations etc., but not as native species.

91 EUPHORBIACEAE
1 MERCURIALIS L.
1 M. perennis L. (93)
Dog's Mercury

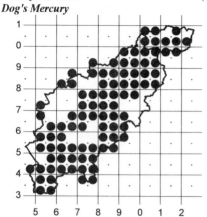

Native. Woods, especially on calcareous soils. Common throughout the county and can sometimes totally dominate the herb layer in older woodland.
First record: Morton 1712
Druce: Abundant and an increasing species.

2 M. annua L. (8)
Annual Mercury

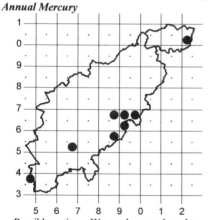

Possibly native. Waste places and gardens. Rare. It has only been recorded from Yardley Hastings, Burton Latimer, Rushden, Northampton, Wollaston and Wellingborough and from one site in the Soke of Peterborough.
First record: Lewis c1870
Druce: Very rare.

2 EUPHORBIA L.
6 E. platyphyllos L.
Broad-leaved Spurge
Native. Cultivated fields. Extremely rare. A solitary record in a beanfield near Raunds in 1991.
First record: Morton 1712
Druce: Very rare. A decreasing species.

8 E. helioscopia L. (99)
Sun Spurge

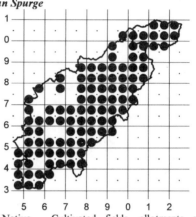

Native. Cultivated fields, allotments and gardens. Common. Generally scattered across the county; can be locally dominant in the right environment, such as recently tilled land.
First record: Gulliver 1841
Druce: Abundant and widely spread.

9 E. lathyris L. (6)
Caper Spurge

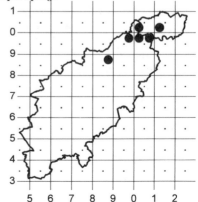

Possibly native. Waste places and gardens. Extremely rare as a native plant. It occurs within Bedford Purlieus and Wakerley Woods in the north of the county, where it is reputedly native. Otherwise it can be frequent as a garden escape in some areas.
First record: Irvine 1838
Druce: Very local.

10 E. exigua L. (50)
Dwarf Spurge

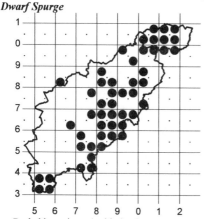

5 6 7 8 9 0 1 2

Probably native. Arable land. Frequent but a declining species due to sprays. Found in the eastern half and the south-west of the county. Largely absent from the non calcareous areas in the west.
First record: Gulliver 1841
Druce: Common.....and widely distributed.

11 E. peplus L. (116)
Petty Spurge

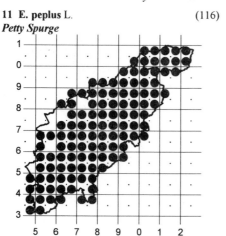

5 6 7 8 9 0 1 2

Native. Cultivated and waste land. Common. The most widely distributed member of this family within the county.
First record: Gulliver 1841
Druce: Common throughout the county.

E. escula x E. waldsteinii = E. x pseudovirgata (Schur) Soo
Twiggy Spurge
Introduction. Hedgerows and grassy waste places.
Known only at a single site in the east of the county and on a disused railway embankment in the west.
First record: Chester 1911
Druce: (E. virgata) Rare.

15 E. cyparissias L.
Cypress Spurge
Possibly British. Rough grassland and waste places.
There is a single old record from the Soke of Peterborough.
Druce: [No status given. Only two records listed].

16 E. amygdaloides L.
Wood Spurge
a subsp. **amygdaloides** (11)

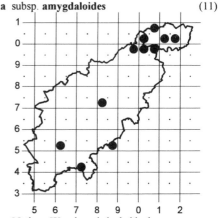

5 6 7 8 9 0 1 2

Native. Woods and shaded hedgerows. Rare. Generally in the northern, limestone, area with a few scattered records in the extreme south. Discovered in Yardley Chase in 1990, the first record from the woods around Northampton where it was stated to be absent by Druce.
First record: Morton 1712

Druce: Locally common, but absent from large tracts, even of woodland areas.

92 RHAMNACEAE
1 RHAMNUS L.
1 R. cathartica L. (97)
Buckthorn

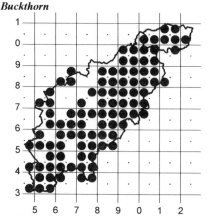

Native. Woodland, scrub and hedgerows. Frequent. A small shrub or tree preferring calcareous soil and found in woodland and along hedgerows in these areas throughout the county.
First record: Dickson in Mastin 1792
Druce: Common, especially in calcareous areas.

2 FRANGULA Miller
1 F. alnus Miller
Alder Buckthorn
Native. Damp woods and hedgerows. Extremely rare. Recorded by Mark July in 1979 near the River Tove in the south-east of the county. It still grows at Castor Hanglands where it has been recorded for many years.
First record: Rev. M.J.Berkeley c1850
Druce: Very rare.

93 VITACEAE
1 VITIS L.
1 V. vinifera L.
Grape-vine
Introduction. Hedges and scrub beside tips. Only three records during this survey, at Kettering Tip, Wansford Quarry and in a hedge near the railway embankment at Barford Bridge. Probably not persisting.
First record: c1979

94 LINACEAE
1 LINUM L.
1 L. bienne Miller
Pale Flax
Possibly British. Dry grassy places. Found on waste ground in two places, in Wellingborough in 1975 and at East Carlton in 1988.
Druce: (L. angustifolium) No corroborative evidence of its occurrence in the county exists. [Druce's flora includes only two doubtful records].

2 L. usitatissimum L. (8)
Flax
Introduction. Casual beside fields.
This species was noted in 1979 in the Kings Sutton area and will probably become more common as a relic of cultivation with the introduction of alternative farm crops. It also occurs as a bird-seed alien.
Druce: Only of casual occurrence.

3 L. perenne L.
Perennial Flax
a subsp. **anglicum** (Miller) Ockendon
Native. Dry limestone fields.
Extinct. For many years it occurred beside the A1 at Wansford prior to road works in the 1950s.
First record: Morton 1712
Druce: (L. anglicum) Very rare, probably extinct.

4 L. catharticum L. (72)
Fairy Flax, Purging Flax

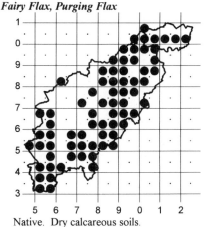

Native. Dry calcareous soils.

Frequent in grass, on railway banks, in old quarries and in unimproved pastures.
First record: Notcutt 1843
Druce: Locally common.

95 POLYGALACEAE
1 POLYGALA L.
1 P. vulgaris L.
Common Milkwort
a subsp. **vulgaris** (24)

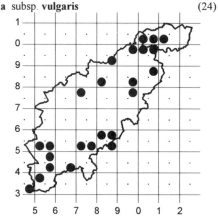

5 6 7 8 9 0 1 2

Native. Generally calcareous grassland.
Occasional. Much less common than formerly, owing to destruction of permanent pastures etc.
First record: Druce 1876
Druce: (P. vulgare) Local.

b subsp. **collina** (Reichb.) Borbas
Native. Generally calcareous grassland.
Extinct. The only record was by George Chester at Sutton Heath in 1917.
First record: Chester 1917
Druce: (P. dubium) Very local.

2 P. serpyllifolia Hose
Heath Milkwort
Native. Acid grassland and heathland.
Rare. Recorded from a few well scattered areas such as Harlestone Firs, Hardwick Wood Field, Wakerley Woods and the old railway cutting at Roade.
First record: (P. serpyllifolium) Druce 1865
Druce: Local.

98 HIPPOCASTANACEAE
1 AESCULUS L.
1 A. hippocastanum L. (118)
Horse-chestnut

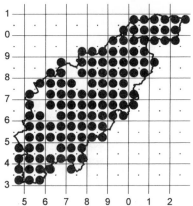

5 6 7 8 9 0 1 2

Introduction. Parks, hedgerows and woodland.
Common. Usually present as a result of earlier, sometimes formal, planting.
Druce: Planted in many localities.

99 ACERACEAE
1 ACER L.
1 A. platanoides L.
Norway Maple
Introduction. Woods and hedgerows.
Established in the northern half of the county as a result of occasional planting in hedgerows, shelter belts and plantations.

3 A. campestre L. (130)
Field Maple

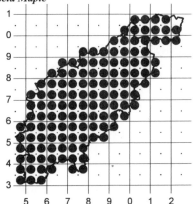

5 6 7 8 9 0 1 2

Native. Woodland and hedgerows.
Common. Found throughout the county, mainly as a component of hedges, but is also

found as a tree within a hedge or, more commonly, as a constituent of woodland.
First record: Morton 1712
Druce: Common in calcareous areas of the county.

4 A. pseudoplatanus L. (127)
Sycamore

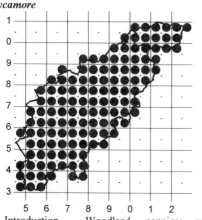

Introduction. Woodland, coppices and hedgerows.
Common. Naturalised throughout the county, it seeds freely, and is a threat to the native flora in some places.
First record: Morton 1712
Druce: Found throughout the county.

102 OXALIDACEAE
1 OXALIS L.
3 O. corniculata L.
Procumbent Yellow-sorrel
Introduction. Dry, cultivated and waste places. Mainly found in the south of the county. Often a persistent weed in gardens and on pathways.
First record: probably 1940s, but may be earlier.

4 O. exilis Cunn.
(*O. corniculata var. microphylla* Hook. f.)
Least Yellow-sorrel
Introduction. Cultivated land and waste places.
It has been recorded from a single location in the extreme south of the county.

6 O. stricta L.
(*O. europaea* Jordan)
Upright Yellow-sorrel

Introduction. Cultivated land and waste places.
Occasionally seen throughout the county.

8 O. articulata Savigny
(*O. floribunda* auct. non Lehm.)
Pink-sorrel
Introduction. Waste ground.
A garden escape.

9 O. acetosella L. (50)
Wood-sorrel

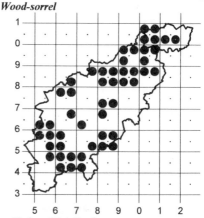

Native. Woodland.
Occasional. Found in lightly shaded areas in most ancient woodland areas but less common in the limestone belt in the extreme north.
First record: Notcutt 1843
Druce: Locally common.

10 O. debilis Kunth
(*O. corymbosa* DC.)
Large-flowered Pink-sorrel
Introduction. Waste ground.
Present in the county only as a garden escape.

103 GERANIACEAE
1 GERANIUM L.
1 G. endressii Gay
French Crane's-bill
Introduction. Grassy places and waste ground.
Present in the county only as a garden escape.

2 G. versicolor L.
Pencilled Crane's-bill
Introduction.
Present in the county only as a garden escape.

4 G. rotundifolium L. (15)
Round-leaved Crane's-bill

180

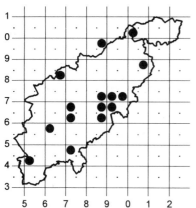

5 6 7 8 9 0 1 2

Native. Banks, walls and stony ground.
Occasional but well established in a few areas,
such as Irchester Country Park. It still grows
near Harlestone, where Druce noted it.
First record: E. Forster 1793
Druce: Very local.

7 G. pratense L. (93)
Meadow Crane's-bill

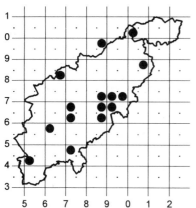

5 6 7 8 9 0 1 2

Native. Roadside verges, meadows and field
margins.
Common in most areas. This species is
especially a feature of the roadsides north of
Kettering, and south from Brackley to the
Oxfordshire border.
First record: Morton 1712
*Druce: Widely distributed and locally
common.*

9 G. sanguineum L.
Bloody Crane's-bill
British. Calcareous grassland.
Present only as a garden escape.
*Druce: Rare. [Recorded in Steane Park and
Peterborough].*

10 G. columbinum L. (5)
Long-stalked Crane's-bill
Native. Grassy places and scrub.
Rare. Only recorded from a few localities - on
disused railway lines at Thrapston and King's
Cliffe, as a cornfield weed in the Soke of
Peterborough, in Bedford Purlieus and
Wakerley Woods.
First record: T Beesley, c.1842
Druce: Very local.

11 G. dissectum L. (122)
Cut-leaved Crane's-bill

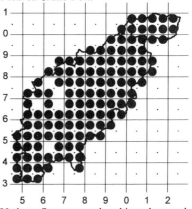

5 6 7 8 9 0 1 2

Native. Stony ground, cultivated ground and
waste places.
Common. Found almost everywhere where the
ground is disturbed.
First record: J. Dickson 1792
Druce: Common and widely distributed.

14 G. pyrenaicum Burman f. (57)
Hedgerow Crane's-bill
Possibly native. Hedgerows and grass verges.
Occasional but may be abundant in suitable
habitats. It has become more common on
roadside verges over the past twenty to thirty
years.
First record: Druce 1874
Druce: Local.

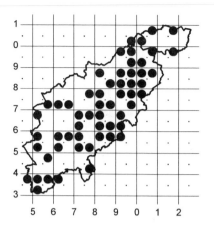

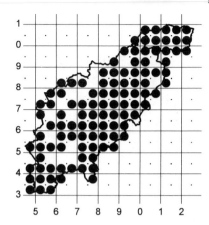

15 G. pusillum L.   (42)
Small-flowered Crane's-bill

18 G. lucidum L.   (29)
Shining Crane's-bill

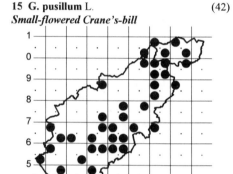

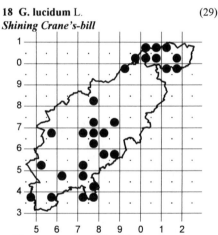

Native. Fields and waste land.
Occasional. Found in similar places to *G. molle*, but very much less common. Often the two species grow together.
First record: Paley 1860
Druce: Local.

16 G. molle L.   (107)
Dove's-foot Crane's-bill
Native. Fields and waste land.
Very common in all areas, occurring mainly where soil is disturbed and on wall-tops, road verges, etc.
First record: Gulliver 1841
Druce: Common and generally distributed.

Native. Bare ground, walls etc.
Very occasional. Occurs on old stone walls in the Collyweston and Duddington areas, in Harringworth churchyard, on walls and waste ground within the Soke of Peterborough and in the south of the county, including sites at Potterspury, Wicken, Eydon and Castle Ashby where it is common on an old boundary wall between the church and the park. It is also recorded as a garden weed in Northampton, Boughton and Lamport, where Druce recorded it.
First record: Morton 1712
Druce: Very local.

19 G. robertianum L.   (128)
Herb-Robert

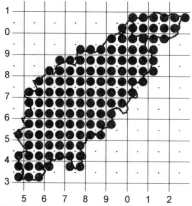

Native. Woodland and hedgerows.
Very common throughout the county. White flowered plants occur in Wellingborough.
First record: Pitt 1813
Druce: Common and generally distributed.

23 G. phaeum L.
Dusky Crane's-bill
Introduction. Shaded places such as hedgerows.
A garden escape but well established in two or three places in the county, notably in Abington Park and in Potterspury churchyard.
First record: Druce 1930
Druce: Rare.

2 ERODIUM L'Her.
2 E. moschatum (L.) L'Hér.
Musk Stork's-bill
Native. Bare ground and rough grassland.
Probably extinct. There is only one record from the roadside near Geddington during the 1940s.
First record: Druce 1876
Druce: Very rare.

3 E. cicutarium (L) L'Her. (31)
Common Stork's-bill
Native. Bare ground and rough grassland.
Occasional, but can be abundant especially on sandy soils, as at Harlestone Firs. It also occurs where cinders and slag from the old iron workings have been utilised for ballast, and it is particularly common on the old railway tracks in the M.O.D. area of Yardley Chase.
First record: Beesley 1842
Druce: Local.

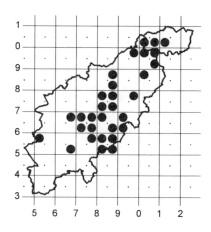

105 BALSAMINACEAE
1 IMPATIENS L.
1 I. noli-tangere L.
Touch-me-not Balsam
Introduction. Damp places in woods.
Extinct. The last records are prior to 1930, from Castle Ashby, where it may have been planted, and also from Woodnewton.
First record: Gulliver 1841
Druce: Very rare.

2 I. capensis Meerb. (31)
Orange Balsam

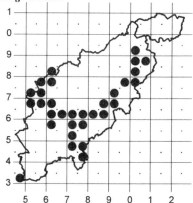

Adventive. Shaded watersides.
Occasional, but becoming more common, particularly beside the River Nene and the Grand Union Canal. It has spread to the county from the southern parts of the Grand Union and consequently it is found less frequently along the Oxford Canal.

183

First record: H. G. Allen (Blisworth) 1946

3 I. parviflora DC.
Small Balsam
Introduction. Disturbed ground and roadsides.
Rare. It had been found at five localities including a woodyard in Northampton, where it has been known since the 1950s, in the grounds of Thornby Hall, at Kettering, in a disused garden centre in Wellingborough, and in Laundimer Wood.
First Record: V.G.Crawley 1930
Druce: Rare.

4 I. glandulifera Royle   (25)
Indian Balsam, Policeman's Helmet

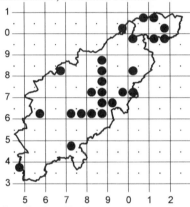

Introduction. Beside water.
Occasional, but common beside the River Nene between Northampton and Thrapston. Also to be found occasionally beside water and in damp areas on waste ground in the north.
First record: F.D.Payne (Corby) 1966

106 ARALIACEAE

1 HEDERA L.
2 H. helix L.
Common Ivy
a subsp.**helix**   (132)
Native. Climbing over hedges, walls and trees. Very common. To be found growing in almost any situation where established hedges, trees, walls etc. offer a foothold, and on the woodland floor.
First record: Clare 1827
Druce: Abundant throughout the county.

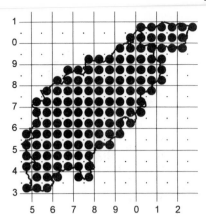

107 APIACEAE
(UMBELLIFERAE)
1 HYDROCOTYLE L.
1 H. vulgaris L.   (7)
Marsh Pennywort, White-rot

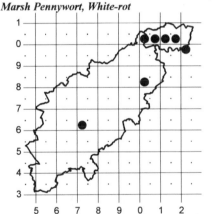

Native. Bogs, fens and marshes, usually on acid soils.
Rare. Very scattered, with half of the sites in the Soke of Peterborough. It is found at Harlestone Heath nature reserve and Aldwincle Marsh. It is plentiful at Sutton Heath and in the White Water valley.
First record: Druce 1874
Druce: Local.

2 SANICULA L.
1 S. europaea L.   (60)
Sanicle
Native. Woods.

Occasional, but can be common in ancient woodlands.

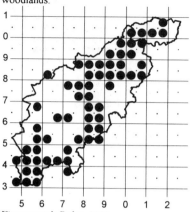

First record: Baker 1822
Druce: Common.

4 ERYNGIUM L.
4 E. campestre L.
Field Eryngo, Watling Street Thistle
Introduction. Dry grassy places.
No recent records.
First record: Ray 1670
Druce: Extinct.

5 CHAEROPHYLLUM L.
3 C. temulum L.   (120)
(*C.temulentum* L.)
Rough Chervil

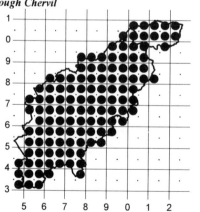

Native. Hedgebanks, roadsides and grassy places.
Common and widely distributed.

First record: Gulliver 1841
Druce: Too common to need localities.

6 ANTHRISCUS Pers.
1 A. sylvestris (L.) Hoffm.   (132)
Cow Parsley, Keck , Queen Anne's Lace

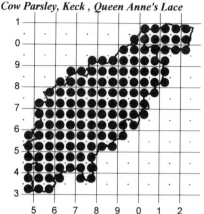

Native. Roadsides, hedgerows and waste places.
Very common. The commonest of the early flowering umbellifers.
First record: Pitt 1813
Druce: (Chaerefolium sylvestre) Very common and widely distributed.

2 A. caucalis M.Bieb
Bur Parsley
Native. Dry hedgebanks and waste places, especially on sandy soils.
Extremely rare. It grows at Collyweston on a field wall adjoining the churchyard but was once more widespread, and prior to the 1970s was recorded from Yarwell and Helpston in the Soke and at Oundle and Irthlingborough.
First record: Notcutt 1843
Druce: (Chaerofolium anthriscus) Local.

7 SCANDIX L.
1 S. pecten-veneris L.
Shepherd's-needle
Native. A weed of arable land.
Very rare, but found in arable fields at Glendon and Raunds, and at other scattered sites. Formerly quite common, it has become rarer because of herbicides and more efficient seed cleaning equipment.
First record: Pitt 1813

Druce: Common but locally distributed throughout the county.

8 MYRRHIS Miller
1 M. odorata (L.) Scop.
Sweet Cicely
British. Grassy places and hedgerows. It may occasionally be found as a garden escape.
First record: Wildgose. Baker 1822
Druce: Very rare and only of garden origin, now extinct.

9 CORIANDRUM L.
1 C. sativum L.
Coriander
Introduction. Waste places and rubbish dumps. When found it is always a garden escape.
First record: Leach 1910
Druce: Very rare.

10 SMYRNIUM L.
1 S. olusatrum L.
Alexanders
Adventive. Roadside verges.
A few plants have been found at Mears Ashby, Moulton, Northampton and Barnack in recent years and it still grows at St Andrew's Hospital, Northampton where it has been established for many years. In 1994 it was recorded on the verge of the A47 near Wansford.
First record: H.G.Allen. Present at St Andrew's Hospital, Northampton many years prior to publication of the record in 1963.

12 CONOPODIUM Koch
1 C. majus (Gouan) Loret   (81)
Pignut

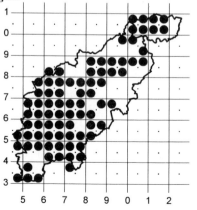

Native. Grassy places, meadows, hedgebanks and woods.
Occasional, can be common when found especially in unimproved pasture.
First record: Gulliver 1841
Druce: Common in all the districts.

13 PIMPINELLA L.
1 P. major (L.) Hudson   (58)
Greater Burnet-saxifrage

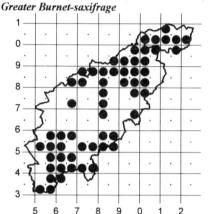

Native. Grassy places, woods, hedgebanks and roadsides.
Frequent throughout the county but can be common in suitable habitats. Replaces *P. saxifraga* in damper habitats.
First record: Beesley 1842
Druce: Locally common.

2 P. saxifraga L.   (97)
Burnet-saxifrage

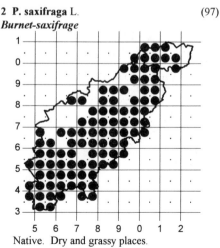

Native. Dry and grassy places.

Occasional throughout the county but can be common in suitable habitats. Frequent in many churchyards throughout the county.
First record: Notcutt 1843
Druce: Locally abundant.

14 AEGOPODIUM L.
1 A. podagraria L. (120)
Ground-elder, Goutweed

Adventive. Naturalised in waste places, roadsides and gardens, where it is a persistent weed.
Common throughout the county. Often found near abandoned or derelict buildings.
First record: Baker 1822
Druce: Common and widely distributed.

15 SIUM L.
1 S. latifolium L. (3)
Greater Water-parsnip
Native. Wet places, dyke sides and rivers.
Very rare. Recorded only from a very few locations; on the rivers Welland and Nene near Wadenhoe and Perio Mill.
First record: Baker 1822
Druce: Local.

16 BERULA Besser ex Koch
1 B. erecta (Hudson) Cov. (39)
Lesser Water-parsnip
Native. Ditches, ponds and wet places.
Occasional. Found in a few areas throughout the county. It is fairly common in drainage ditches near Duddington and fishponds near Collyweston and around the lakes at Castle Ashby.
First record: Baker 1822

Druce: (Sium erectum) Locally common.

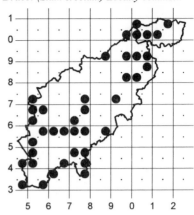

19 OENANTHE L.
1 O. fistulosa L. (21)
Tubular Water-dropwort

Native. Marshy places and shallow water.
Very rare. Found in suitable habitats at scattered sites across the county. It is present at Great Doddington Marsh, Harringworth Meadow and in the Welland Valley. It is also recorded from Castor Hanglands national nature reserve in the Soke of Peterborough and near Aynho in the south.
First record: Druce 1875
Druce: Local.

2 O. silaifolia M.Bieb.
Narrow-leaved Water-dropwort
Native. Damp, rich meadows, usually near rivers.

Extremely rare within the county. The best site was in the meadows beside the River Cherwell to the west of Aynho which were recently ploughed up. Francis Rose recorded it from Kingsthorpe meadows in 1944 and it is still reputed to be at Ailsworth Heath in the Soke.
First record: Druce 1920
Druce: Very local.

4 O. lachenalii C.Gmelin
Parsley Water-dropwort
Native. Marshes and fens.
Extinct. Recorded at King's Sutton Bog, Evenley Camp, and bogs near Wansford, Ailsworth and Wittering prior to 1930.
First record: Irvine 1838
Druce: Very local.

5 O. crocata L.
Hemlock Water-dropwort
Native. Wet places.
Possibly extinct. This plant became established by the River Nene in Northampton between 1960 and 1963. Subsequent disturbance of the riverbank eradicated it and there has been no further sign of the plant. There is one other record, for the Soke of Peterborough, which also dates from the 1960s.
First record: Goodyer c.1660
Druce: Very rare or extinct.

6 O. fluviatilis (Bab.) Coleman   (10)
River Water-dropwort

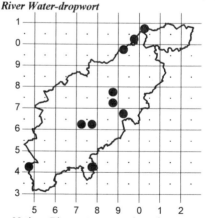

Native. Rivers, streams and ponds
Very rare. Found along the River Nene at Northampton, and along the River Welland in the Collyweston area. It is also reported from the River Ise between Warkton and Kettering and downstream almost to Wellingborough. It also occurs in the River Tove.
First record: Watson 1851
Druce: Locally common and widely distributed.

7 O. aquatica (L.) Poiret   (4)
Fine-leaved Water-dropwort
Native. Slow flowing or stagnant water.
Very rare, mostly in the north of the county.
Found in the River Ise south of Warkton in large quantities in 1991.
First record: Baker 1822
Druce: Local.

20 AETHUSA L.
1 A. cynapium L.
Fool's Parsley
a subsp. **cynapium**   (107)

Native. A weed of cultivation.
Common and widely distributed throughout the county.
First record: Gulliver 1841
Druce: Common and generally distributed.

21 FOENICULUM Miller
1 F. vulgare Miller
Fennel
Introduction. Naturalised in waste places.
Usually a garden escape.
Druce: (F.Foeniculum) Rare.

FERULA L.
F. communis L.
Giant Fennel
Adventive. Waste ground.

188

This plant, which is widespread throughout the Mediterranean, was recorded in a builders' yard at Oundle between 1956 and 1988, possibly introduced with marble imported from Italy. The site was built over and the plant disappeared, but in 1994 a single plant forced its way through the tarmac to make a dramatic reappearance!

ANETHUM L.
A. graveolens L.
Dill
Introduction. Rubbish tips, gardens.
Recorded only from the Pipewell Road Rubbish Tip, Desborough in 1984.

22 SILAUM Miller
1 S. silaus (L.) Schinz & Thell.   (45)
Pepper-saxifrage

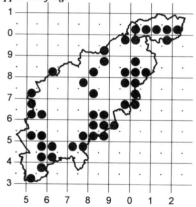

Native. Meadows and grassy places.
Occasional but can be common in un-improved grassland as at Alder Wood Meadow, Rushton; Tailby's Meadow local nature reserve, Desborough and Great Oakley Meadow nature reserve and other areas in the county.
First record: Gulliver 1841
Druce: Locally common.

25 CONIUM L.
1 C. maculatum L.   (114)
Hemlock
Native. Damp places, roadsides and near water.
Common throughout the county in suitable habitats. It can sometimes form very large

stands, as beside the new A14 road to the east of Kettering in 1994.

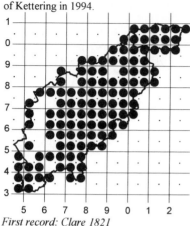

First record: Clare 1821

26 BUPLEURUM L.
3 B. tenuissimum L.
Slender Hare's-ear
Native. Grassy, usually saline habitats.
Probably extinct. Most of the records given by Druce date from the 19th century. A few are undated, the most recent being from Thornhaugh and Southorpe where it was described as abundant in 1920.
First record: T.Beesley 1842
Druce: Very rare.

B. rotundifolium L.
Thorow-wax
Introduction. Arable land, cornfields.
Occasionally found as a bird-seed alien, but no recent records.
First record: Beesley 1842
Druce: Very rare.

28 APIUM L.
1 A. graveolens L.
Wild Celery
Introduction. Damp places beside rivers and ditches, usually brackish.
No recent records.
First record: Baker 1822
Druce: Garden outcast.

2 A. nodiflorum (L.) Lagasca   (122)
Fool's Water-cress
Native. Ditches and shallow ponds.
Frequent throughout the county, abundant in suitable habitats.

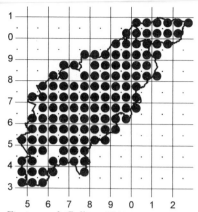

First record: Gulliver 1841
Druce: Common and generally distributed.

2 x 4 A. nodiflorum x A. inundatum = A. x moorei (Syme) Druce
Native. Ditches and shallow ponds.
No recent records.
First record: Druce 1911
Druce: [No status given. One record from the Welland near Deeping and Peakirk].

4 A. inundatum (L.) Reichb.f.
Lesser Marshwort
Native. Lakes, ponds and ditches.
Extremely rare. It has been recorded during this survey in a few locations, Short Wood Pond, near Draughton, Naseby reservoir and at Peakirk and near Castor in the Soke of Peterborough.
First record: Druce 1878
Druce: Local.

29 PETROSELINUM Hill
1 P. crispum (Miller) Nyman ex A.W.Hill
Garden Parsley
Introduction. Grassy and waste places.
When found, an escape from cultivation.
First record: Druce 1876
Druce: (Carum petroselinum) Scarcely established.

2 P. segetum (L.) Koch
Corn Parsley
Native. Hedgerows and grassy places.
Extremely rare. A Red Data Book species which is found on the roadside at Great Oxendon, Kingsthorpe Scrub Field and King's Cliffe, on the edge of a set-aside field.

First record: Morton 1712
Druce: (Carum segetum) Very rare.

30 SISON L.
1 S. amomum L.   (31)
Stone Parsley

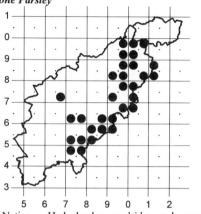

Native. Hedgebanks, roadsides and grassy places.
Occasional, but can be common in suitable habitats. Mostly confined to the eastern edge of the county.
First record: Notcutt 1843
Druce: Rather common and widely distributed.

32 AMMI L.
1 A. majus L.
Bullwort
Introduction. Waste places and gardens.
Rare casual. Regularly grows in a garden in Desborough, where it was not planted.
First record: Druce (Railway at Roade) 1930?
Druce: Rare.

33 FALCARIA Fabr.
1 F. vulgaris Bernh.
Longleaf
Introduction. Hedgerows.
Locally naturalised on the roadside north of Ailsworth.
First record: J.H.Chandler (Ailsworth) 1959

34 CARUM L.
1 C. carvi L.
Caraway
Introduction. Waste places.
If found, it will be of garden origin.
First record: French 1878
Druce: Very rare.

190

37 ANGELICA L.
1 A. sylvestris L.   (119)
Wild Angelica

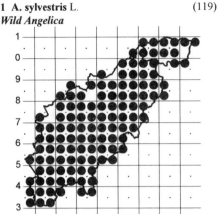

5 6 7 8 9 0 1 2
Native. Damp meadows, woods and roadsides.
Common throughout the county in suitable
habitats.
First record: Clare 1827
*Druce: Locally common and widely
distributed.*

40 PASTINACA L.
1 P. sativa L.   (65)
Wild Parsnip

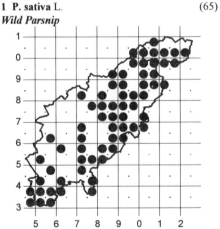

5 6 7 8 9 0 1 2
Native. Dry roadside verges and waste grassy
places.
Occasional throughout the county, especially
on calcareous grassland and scrub.
First record: Pitt 1813
*Druce: (Peucedanum sativum) Locally
abundant.*

41 HERACLEUM L.
1 H. sphondylium L.
Hogweed
a subsp. **sphondylium**   (132)

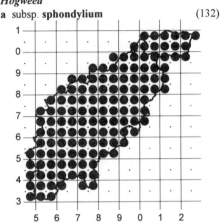

5 6 7 8 9 0 1 2
Native. Grassy places beside roads, hedges
and woods.
Common and widely distributed throughout the
county.
First record: Pitt 1813
Druce: Common throughout the county.

2 H. mantegazzianum Sommier & Levier   (15)
Giant Hogweed

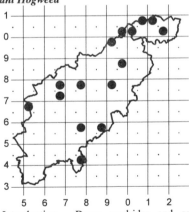

5 6 7 8 9 0 1 2
Introduction. Damp roadsides and grassy
places.
Growing in large quantities on the towpath of
the northern Oxford Canal near Braunston, just
inside the county border, and occasionally
found in other places, such as the grounds of
Kelmarsh Hall and Castle Ashby. On the
outskirts of Bainton, in the Soke of

Peterborough, there is a dense forest of this plant covering a small area of land between the road to Ufford and a small stream. It grew at Rushmere, near Northampton for several years.

43 TORILIS Adans.
1 T. japonica (Houtt.) DC. (128)
Upright Hedge-parsley

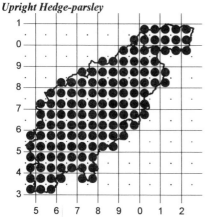

Native. In hedges and grassy places.
Common and widely distributed, the last of the common wayside umbellifers to flower.
First record: Gulliver 1841
Druce: (Caucalis anthriscus) Very common and widely distributed.

2 T. arvensis (Hudson) Link
Spreading Hedge-parsley
Probable introduction. Arable fields and disturbed ground.
The only recent record is at Irchester in 1974.
First record: Druce 1874
Druce: (Caucalis arvensis) Locally common.

3 T. nodosa (L.) Gaertner (16)
Knotted Hedge-parsley
Native. On dry bare banks and arable fields.
Rare. It has recently been found in the Wittering and Ailsworth area growing as a weed of cultivation and also in Wakerley Woods. Otherwise it has a liking for canal bridges and river embankments. It has been established in Wellingborough by the River Nene since the early 1960s.
First record: Notcutt 1843
Druce: (Caucalis nodosa) Local.

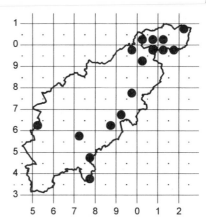

44 DAUCUS L.
1 D. carota L.
Wild Carrot
a subsp. **carota** (89)

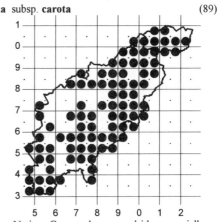

Native. Grassy places, roadsides especially on dry soils.
Common throughout the county in suitable habitats.
First record: Pitt 1813
Druce: Common and widely distributed.

CAUCALIS L.
C. platycarpos L.
Small Bur-parsley
Adventive. Arable fields and waste places.
No recent records.
First record: Merrett 1666
Druce: (C. daucoides) Very rare.

TURGENIA Hoffm.
T. latifolia (L.) Hoffm.
Greater Bur-parsley
Introduction. Arable fields and waste places.
No recent records.
First record: Druce 1896
Druce: (Caucalis latifolia) Very rare.

108 GENTIANACEAE
3 CENTAURIUM Hill
2 C. erythraea Rafn   (66)
Common Centaury

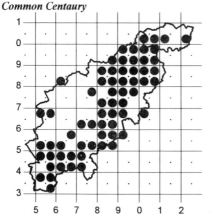

5   6   7   8   9   0   1   2

Native. Grassland, open ground and wood margins.
Occasional but can be common and quite a feature of disused quarries. It is largely absent from the west of the county. White flowered plants occur in Wakerley Woods.
First record: Coles 1657
Druce: (C. centaurium) Locally common and widely distributed.

4 C. pulchellum (Sw.) Druce
Lesser Centaury
Native. Dry, calcareous ground.
Extremely rare. It was thought to be extinct within the county until 1991 when three sites were discovered in the Wansford area - Ringhaw, near Old Sulehay and Great Morton Sale, all in abandoned quarries. It was also reported in the same year from a sandy riding in Bedford Purlieus.
First record: Paley 1860
Druce: Very rare.

4 BLACKSTONIA Hudson
1 B. perfoliata (L.) Hudson   (20)

Yellow-wort

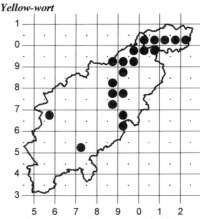

5   6   7   8   9   0   1   2

Native. Open calcareous grassland.
Rare. Established on scattered sites - often old quarries - mainly in the north of the county, but also at Irchester Country Park in the East.
First record: Morton 1712
Druce: Not common.

5 GENTIANELLA Moench
2 G. campestris (L.) Boerner
Field Gentian
Native. Grassland.
Probably extinct. All records date from prior to 1930.
First record: Wallis c1710
Druce: (Gentiana campestris) Very rare.

4 G. amarella (L.) Boerner
Autumn Gentian, Felwort
a subsp. **amarella**
Native. Calcareous pastures.
Rare. Only found growing at a series of sites across the north - Collyweston Deeps, Barnack Hills and Holes, Southorpe Roughs and Castor Hanglands national nature reserves, Easton Hornstocks, Bonemills Hollow, Wakerley Spinney and at Cosgrove Pits in the south of the county.
First record: Morton 1712
Druce: (Gentiana amarella) Local.

5 G. anglica (Pugsley) E.Warb.
Early Gentian
Native. Limestone grassland
Possibly extinct. There are records from Wittering in 1959 by J.H.Chandler and by F.H.Perring in the 1960s, but nothing since.

First record: J.H.Chandler 1959

109 APOCYNACEAE
1 VINCA L.
1 V. minor L.
Lesser Periwinkle
Probable introduction. Woods, copses and hedgebanks. Almost certainly only present as a relic of cultivation. Can occasionally be abundant in its habitat, as at Woodford Spinney and in a spinney at Broughton, although sometimes only a few plants will flower. A roadside colony in Wellingborough was isolated from any buildings from at least 1959, and still persists
First record: Baker 1822
Druce: Rare and probably always a relic of cultivation in the county.

3 V. major L.
Greater Periwinkle
Introduction. Hedges and banks. Possibly less common than *V. minor*, but will sometimes establish itself in the wild. Always present as a relic of cultivation or as a result of the dumping of garden waste. White flowered plants occur at Castle Ashby.
First record: Morton 1712
Druce: A relic of cultivation. Naturalised here and there.

110 SOLANACEAE
1 NICANDRA Adans.
1 N. physalodes (L.) Gaertner
Apple-of-Peru, Shoo-fly Plant
Introduction. Occurs very occasionally on waste ground. Found in an area of derelict ground in Kettering in 1975, in Peterborough in 1982 and in Wellingborough School Grounds in 1992.
First Record: Andrew Robinson 1970s

2 LYCIUM L.
1 L. barbarum L.
(*L. halimifolium* Miller)
Duke of Argyll's Teaplant
Introduction. Occurs sporadically in hedgerows and on old walls etc. Occasional. Found at scattered localities, especially in villages.
Druce: [No status given].

3 ATROPA L.
1 A. belladonna L. (17)
Deadly Nightshade

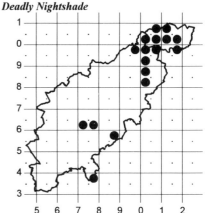

Native. In woods and thickets mostly on calcareous soils. Occasional. With a few exceptions it is confined to the calcareous soil in the extreme north where it is not only quite a feature of the woodland ridings, as in Bedford Purlieus and other woods in that area, but also old quarries and open areas. It has been present in the car-park of Northampton Hospital for many years!
First record: Morton 1712
Druce: Rare.

4 HYOSCYAMUS L.
1 H. niger L. (17)
Henbane

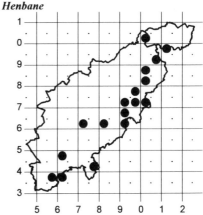

Native. Waste and newly disturbed ground.

Rare. Occurs sporadically on scattered sites across Northamptonshire, the seeds often lying dormant for many years.
First record: Pitt 1813
Druce: A rare and decreasing species.

7 LYCOPERSICON Miller
1 L. esculentum Miller
Tomato
Introduction. Waste ground and tips. Occasionally found as a throw-out on rubbish tips and waste ground, especially where nitrate rich. It does not survive long.
Druce (L. lycopersicon) Soon dies out.

8 SOLANUM L.
1 S. nigrum L.
Black Nightshade
a subsp. **nigrum**   (67)

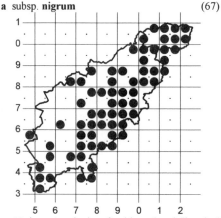

5   6   7   8   9   0   1   2

Native. A colonist of cultivated and disturbed ground, especially if nitrate rich.
Occasional, but is generally distributed across the centre, south and east of the county.
First record: Baker 1822
Druce: Rare.

4 S. sarachoides Sendtner
Leafy-fruited Nightshade
Adventive. Waste ground.
A solitary plant recorded from dumped soil beside the A47 near Easton Hornstocks.

6 S. dulcamara L.   (130)
Bittersweet, Woody Nightshade
Native. Hedges, woods and beside rivers and streams.

Common and often abundant in its habitat. A common feature of hedgerows in every part of the county.

First record: Clare 1821
Druce: Generally distributed and locally common.

S. rostratum Dunal
Buffalo-bur
Adventive. Waste ground.
Found at one site, Upton Mill Lane, by Tom Barrett in 1969. Subsequently it was recorded in the draw-down zone at Sywell reservoir in 1994.
First record: Goode 1917
Druce: Recorded but no status given.

9 DATURA L.
1 D. stramonium L.
Thorn-apple
Adventive. Waste and cultivated ground.
Sporadic in appearance but generally confined to the centre of the county.
First record: Marchioness of Huntley c.1870?
Druce: Sporadic.

D. metel L.
Adventive. Waste and cultivated ground.
This species was discovered in 1986, on a site destined to become an industrial area in Wellingborough. It never regenerated.

111 CONVOLVULACEAE
2 CONVOLVULUS L.
1 C. arvensis L.   (130)
Field Bindweed
Native. Roadsides, cultivated and waste ground.

Common. Invasive and abundant in suitable habitats throughout the county.

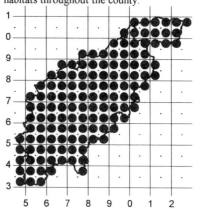

5 6 7 8 9 0 1 2

First record: Pitt 1813
Druce: Abundant in all the districts.

3 CALYSTEGIA R.Br.
2 C. sepium (L.) R.Br.
Hedge Bindweed
a subsp. **sepium**   (123)

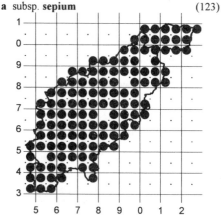

5 6 7 8 9 0 1 2

Native. Hedges, thickets, gardens, wasteland and roadside verges.
Common. It can be found throughout the area, often becoming a dominant feature of hedgerows.
First record: Clare 1827
Druce: (Volvulus sepium) [No status given].

3 C. pulchra Brummitt & Heywood
(*C. sepium* (L.) R.Br. subsp. *pulchra* (Brummitt & Heyw.) Tutin nom. inval.)
Hairy Bindweed

Origin uncertain. Hedgerows near buildings and waste areas.
Rare. Recorded only a few times within the county, on isolated sites, where it has become naturalised since escaping from gardens.

4 C. silvatica (Kit) Griseb.   (66)
(*C. sepium* (L.) R.Br. subsp. *silvatica* (Kit.) Battand)
Large Bindweed

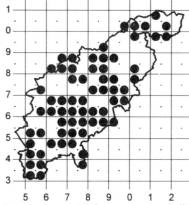

5 6 7 8 9 0 1 2

Introduction. Hedgerows, near buildings, roadside verges and waste areas.
Occasional. Found throughout in similar habitats to *C. sepium*, but usually near habitation. It often grows with *C. sepium* and it may be sometimes overlooked.

112 CUSCUTACEAE
1 CUSCUTA L.
1 C. campestris Yuncker
Yellow Dodder, Field Dodder
Introduction. Parasitic on cultivated *Trifolium* sp.
No recent records.
First record: French 1870
Druce (C. trifolii) Now becoming scarce when cleaner seed is sown.

2 C. europaea L.
Greater Dodder
Native. Grassland. Parasitic mainly on *Urtica dioica* in this county.
Very rare. It was recorded at four sites in the county, mainly during the 1970s and early 1980s: Glapthorn Cow Pasture, near Apethorpe and Bozenham Mill. A colony near Maxey was parasitic on wild Hops.

196

First record: Morton 1712
Druce: Very rare.

3 C. epithymum (L.) L.
Dodder
Native. Grasslands. Parasitic mainly on leguminous plants.
Very rare, and found at four localities, mainly in the Soke; the prime site of which is Collyweston Deeps nature reserve, where the host plants are *Genista tinctoria* subsp. *tinctoria* and *Helianthemum chamaecistus*. There is one southern record from the disused railway near Woodford Halse.
First record: Druce 1878
Druce: Very rare.

C. epilinum Weihe
Flax Dodder
Adventive. Parasitic on flax.
No recent records - it no longer occurs in the British Isles.
First record: Druce 1883
Druce: Very rare.

113 MENYANTHACEAE
1 MENYANTHES L.
1 M. trifoliata L.
Bogbean
Native. Bogs, marshes and shallow standing water.
Very rare. It is recorded from a very few sites, now mainly in the north including Aldwincle, White Water valley and Wadenhoe. It is also in the grounds of the former Samuel Lloyd School at Corby and at Thornby Hall. In the latter two cases it has definitely been introduced and has become established.
First record: Baker 1822
Druce: Very local.

2 NYMPHOIDES Séguier
1 N. peltata Kuntze (9)
Fringed Water-lily
Native. Slow streams, ponds.
This was found in three localities on the River Welland during a recent survey, confirming Mark July's records from the 1970s. It is also naturalised at Drayton reservoir, in ponds near Sulby, Brigstock and Sywell Country Parks and Astwell Castle.
First record: Morton 1712
Druce: (N. Nymphoides) Very rare.

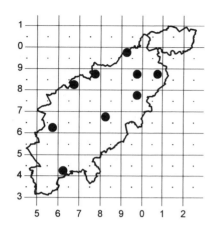

114 POLEMONIACEAE
1 POLEMONIUM L.
1 P. caeruleum L.
Jacob's-ladder
British. Open grassland.
Recorded as a garden escape on the roadside near Stanwick in 1994.
First record: W.H.Jones c1878

115 HYDROPHYLLACEAE
1 PHACELIA Juss.
1 P. tanacetifolia Benth..
Phacelia
Introduction. One recent record as an escape.
First record: Andrew Robinson 1987

116 BORAGINACEAE
1 LITHOSPERMUM L.
2 L. officinale L. (25)
Common Gromwell, Grummel

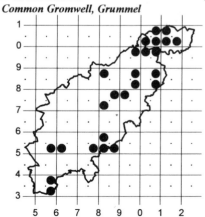

Native. Grass, hedgerows, wood borders etc.
Occasional. Occurs mainly in woodland ridings in calcareous areas of the county, and generally occurs in small numbers.
First record: Morton 1712
Druce: Local.

3 L. arvense L.   (12)
(Buglossoides arvensis (L.) I.M.Johnston)
Field Gromwell, Corn Gromwell

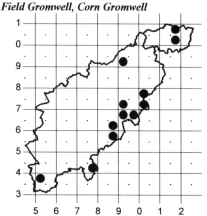

Native. Grassy places, rough ground at field margins.
Rare, but occasionally found in arable field borders where herbicide sprays have not reached.
First record: Banbury Cat. 1841
Druce: Local.

2 ECHIUM L.
1 E. vulgare L.   (20)
Viper's-bugloss

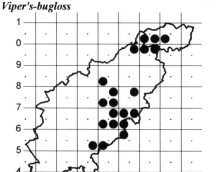

Native. Rough, calcareous ground.
Rare. Very local on disturbed soils, mainly in the north and east of county. It appeared in quantity beside the new A14 road between Kettering and Rothwell and near the Twywell junction in 1993.
First record: Morton 1712
Druce: Local.

3 PULMONARIA L.
1 P. officinalis L.
Lungwort
Introduction. Waste ground.
Only found as garden outcast on rubbish tips etc.and in King's Wood, Corby.
First record: Druce 1930?
Druce: Garden escape.

4 SYMPHYTUM L.
1 S. officinale L.   (97)
Common Comfrey

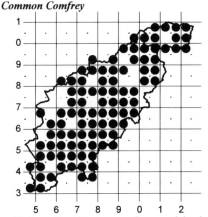

Native. Beside streams, rivers and in damp grassland.
Common. Regularly found near water and on some roadsides throughout the county.
First record: Pitt 1813
Druce: Rather Common.

1 x 2 S. officinale x S. asperum = S. x uplandicum Nyman   (35)
Russian Comfrey
Introduction. Woodland edge, rough grassland etc. especially near roadsides.
Once grown as a fodder plant, it is now established in many places throughout the county.
Druce: (S. peregrinum) No status given.

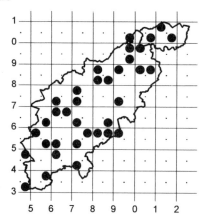

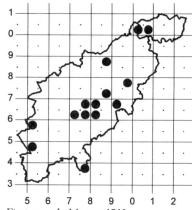

First record: Morton 1712
Druce: (Lycopsis arvensis) Locally common.

2 S. asperum Lepechin
Rough Comfrey
Introduction. Rough and waste ground.
Naturalised only near Crick and in North-
ampton. It is often confused with *S. x
uplandicum*.
Druce: (S. asperrimum) No status given.

3 S. tuberosum L.
Tuberous Comfrey
British. Damp woods, river banks etc.
No recent records.

6 S. orientale L. (7)
White Comfrey
Introduction. Shaded hedgerows etc.
Naturalised on roadsides, and on rubbish tips.
*First record: F.D.Payne (Barton Seagrave)
c1965*

6 ANCHUSA L.
(Lycopsis L.)
2 A. officinalis L.
Alkanet
Introduction. Rough and waste ground.
No recent records.
First record: Chester1906
Druce: No status given.

4 A. arvensis (L.) M.Bieb. (14)
(Lycopsis arvensis L.)
Bugloss
Native. Arable weed on light soils.
Rare and decreasing owing to the decline of
cornfield weeds. It is usually found on the
lighter sandy soils of the county.

8 PENTAGLOTTIS Tausch
1 P. sempervirens (L.) Tausch ex L.Bailey (49)
(Anchusa sempervirens L.)
Green Alkanet

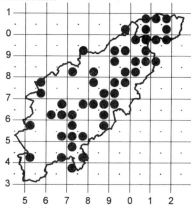

Introduction. Waste ground, rough grassland
and gardens.
Naturalised throughout the county, mainly as a
garden throw-out, but established and
persisting.
First record: Druce 1876?
Druce: (Anchusa sempervirens) Rare.

9 BORAGO L.
1 B. officinalis L.
Borage
Introduction. Verges and waste tips.
Sometimes occurring as an escape on roadsides
and rubbish tips etc. Could become more

common if the recent tendency to grow this as an alternative crop continues.
First record: Paley 1870
Druce: Sporadic.

10 TRACHYSTEMON D.Don
1 T. orientalis (L.) Don
Abraham-Isaac-Jacob
Introduction. Shady woodland. Naturalised in two areas at Castle Ashby.

12 AMSINCKIA Lehm.
1 A. lycopsoides (Lehm.) Lehm.
Scarce Fiddleneck
Introduction. Sandy soils.
No recent records.
Druce: (Benthamia lycopsioides) [No status given].

2 A. micrantha Suksd.
Common Fiddleneck
Introduction. Arable land.
A considerable number of plants were found in a field near Fotheringhay in 1993. There are also a couple of recent records from gardens in Tansor.
Druce: (Benthamia menziesii) [No status given].

14 ASPERUGO L.
1 A. procumbens L.
Madwort
Introduction. Fields, waste and rough ground. Only one recent record, by George Crawford, is from the edge of an arable field on the Bedfordshire-Northamptonshire border near Bozeat in the 1982.
First record: J.L.Gilbert (Wansford)1933

15 MYOSOTIS L.
1 M. scorpioides L. (97)
Water Forget-me-not
Native. Beside or in streams, ditches, ponds etc.
Very common and well distributed by rivers, canals, gravel pits and reservoirs etc.
First record: Clare 1835
Druce: (M. palustris) Very common and well distributed.

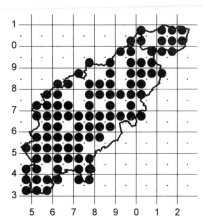

4 M. laxa Lehm.
Tufted Forget-me-not
a   subsp. **caespitosa** (Schultz) N.Hylander ex Nordh.   (58)

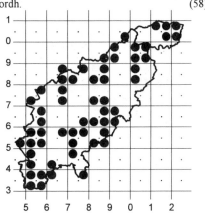

Native.   In or beside streams, ponds, ditches etc.
Occasional.   Less common than *M. scorpioides* but distributed in similar places.
First record: Druce 1875
Druce: (M. caespitosa)Local.

7 M. sylvatica Hoffm.   (9)
Wood Forget-me-not
British. Woods.
Scattered throughout the county, mainly as a garden escape.
First record: Druce 1925
Druce: [No status given].

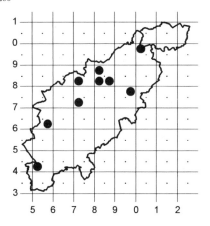

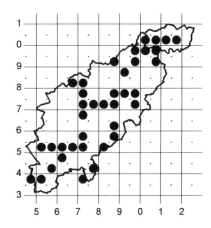

8 M. arvensis (L.) Hill   (129)
Field Forget-me-not

10 M. discolor Pers.   (21)
Changing Forget-me-not

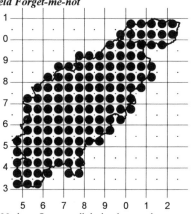

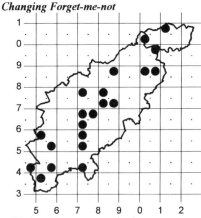

Native. Open, well drained ground.
Very common in woodland, on disturbed ground and other open habitats.
First record: Gulliver 1841
Druce: Common.

9 M. ramosissima Rochel   (38)
Early Forget-me-not
Native. Dry places and open grassland.
Occasional on old walls and quarries. There is a fine display at Collyweston Deeps nature reserve and on churchyard walls at Brixworth, Newbottle and Walgrave.
First record: Druce1879
Druce: (M. collina) Local.

Native. Dry open grassland.
Occasional and confined to disturbed sandy soils, where it may be common for a time.
First record: (M. versicolor) Notcott 1843
Druce: Local.

LAPPULA Gilib.
L. squarrosa (Retz.) Dumort.
Bur Forget-me-not
Introduction. Waste and rough ground, tips etc.
No recent records.
First record: French 1870
Druce: (Thought to be Lappula lappula in Druce) Rare.

16 OMPHALODES Miller
1 O. verna Moench
Blue-eyed-Mary
Introduction. Rough grassland.
Well established at Castle Ashby near the engine pond.

17 CYNOGLOSSUM L.
1 C. officinale L.　　　　　　(16)
Hound's-tongue

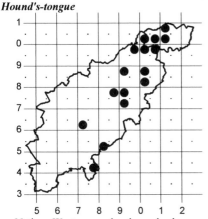

Native. Waste ground and grassland.
Rare. Occurs mainly in the more calcareous areas in the north of the county and in some disused ironstone quarries, but is much less common than hitherto.
First record: Druce 1880
Druce: Local.

2 C. germanicum Jacq.
Green Hound's-tongue
Native. Woods, hedgerows etc.
Extinct. Druce considered it very rare and it appears not to have been seen since 1883, when it was recorded at Apethorpe.
First record: Morton 1712
Druce: Very rare.

HELIOTROPIUM (Tourn.) L.
H. europaeum L.
No recent records.
First record: Leach 1911
Druce: [No status given].

117 VERBENACEAE
1 VERBENA L.
1 V. officinalis L.　　　　　　(8)
Vervain

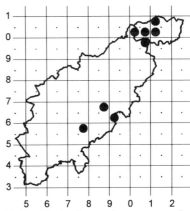

Native. Dry banks on calcareous ground.
Rare. Mostly confined to more calcareous soils in the Soke of Peterborough, in the Barnack, Helpston and Wittering area. There are three other well established sites which have been noted since the 1940s at Wilby, Northampton and near Bozeat.
First record: Baker 1822
Druce: Local.

118 LAMIACEAE
(LABIATAE)
1 STACHYS L.
1 S. officinalis (L.) Trev.St.Léon　　(57)
(Betonica officinalis L.)
Betony

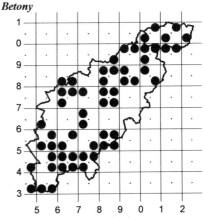

Native. Ancient grassland.
Occasional, but can be locally plentiful in old meadows, woodland ridings etc. Less common in grassland due to the changes in agricultural practices over the last 50 years.

First record: Clare 1821
Druce: Local.

2 S. byzantina K.Koch
Lamb's-ear
Introduction. Waste ground.
A single record from the edge of a field of barley near Racecourse Road, between Easton on the Hill and the A1.
First record: Rob Wilson 1994

3 S. germanica L.
Downy Woundwort
Native. Rough grassland.
Extinct. Recorded from near Wakerley in 1870. The site has since been destroyed. This is the only record.
First record: Lewin c1870
Druce: Extinct?

5 S. sylvatica L.   (130)
Hedge Woundwort

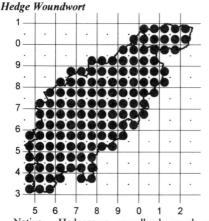

5 6 7 8 9 0 1 2
Native. Hedgerows, woodland, rough and waste ground.
Very common in all areas, often as a weed of cultivation.
First record: Gulliver 1841
Druce: Common and widely distributed.

5 x 6 S. sylvatica x S. palustris = S. x ambigua Smith
Hybrid Woundwort
Native. Hedgerows, rough or waste ground or beside water.
It has been recorded at Towcester but it may be overlooked elsewhere. It could occur where both parents grow together.

First record: Beesley 1842
Druce: Rare.

6 S. palustris L.   (78)
Marsh Woundwort
Native. Damp places on rough ground and beside rivers, ponds, canals and gravel workings etc.
Common in its habitat and common throughout most of the county.

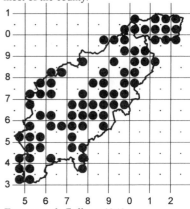

5 6 7 8 9 0 1 2
First record: Gulliver 1841
Druce: Common and widely distributed.

8 S. arvensis (L.) L.
Field Woundwort
Native. Arable ground on non-calcareous soils.
Rare. Recorded twice in the late 1970s from cultivated areas in the Glapthorn and Easton Hornstocks areas, in 1993 from Wittering and in 1994 from Peakirk.
First record: Morton 1712
Druce: Very local.

S. annua (L.) L.
Annual Yellow-woundwort
Introduction. Waste ground.
No recent records.
First record: Leach 1911
Druce: [No status given].

2 BALLOTA L.
1 B. nigra L.
Black Horehound
a subsp. **foetida** (Vis.) Hayek   (111)
Native. Hedgerows, rough and waste ground.
Very common on roadsides, waste areas and as a garden weed.

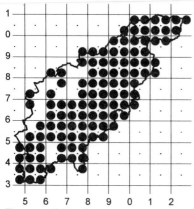

5 6 7 8 9 0 1 2

First record: Beesley 1842

Druce: Common throughout the county, but rarer in the clay areas.

4 LAMIASTRUM Heister ex Fabr.
1 L. galeobdolon (L.) Ehrend. & Polatschek
Yellow Archangel
b subsp. **montanum** (Pers.) Ehrend.& Polatshek

(53)

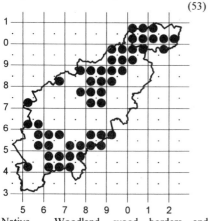

5 6 7 8 9 0 1 2

Native. Woodland, wood borders and hedgerows.

Occasional. Found throughout as an ancient woodland indicator in Rockingham Forest, Bedford Purlieus, Wakerley and Fineshade Woods in the northern half of the county; and in Salcey Forest, Yardley Chase, Whittlebury, Hazelborough, Bucknell and Badby Woods in the southern district.

First record: Baker 1822

Druce: (Lamium galeobdolon) Local but widely distributed.

c subsp. **argentatum** (Smejkal) Stace
Introduction. Rough and waste ground.
Often grown in gardens and occasionally found established in the wild, as at Barnack Hills and Holes.

5 LAMIUM L.
1 L. album L.   (131)
White Dead-nettle

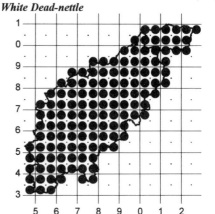

5 6 7 8 9 0 1 2

Native. Hedge-banks, waysides and waste ground.

Very common and widespread throughout the county.

First record: Morton 1712

Druce: Locally common and widely spread.

2 L. maculatum (L.) L.
Spotted Dead-nettle
Introduction. Rough ground and tips.
An escape from cultivation that establishes itself on roadsides, rubbish tips etc. At present under-recorded, but it is established in Pipewell Woods.

First record: Rugby School Report 1905

Druce: Rare.

3 L. purpureum L.   (120)
Red Dead-nettle
Native. Cultivated and waste ground.
Very common throughout the county. White flowered plants have been recorded at Wollaston and Rothwell.

First record: Gulliver 1841

Druce: Abundant and generally distributed.

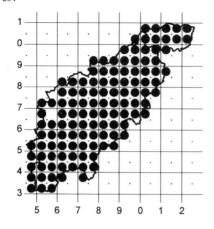

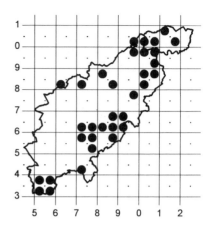

4 L. hybridum Villars (24)
Cut-leaved Dead-nettle

Native. Cultivated and waste ground.
Rare. A plant of cultivated areas which seems to be more common than Druce thought - he only gave two sites. Most of the known sites are scattered through the eastern half of the county and the Soke of Peterborough.
First record: W. Lewin 1860
Druce: Very rare.

6 L. amplexicaule L. (33)
Henbit Dead-nettle

Native. Open, cultivated and waste ground.
Occasional, but scattered throughout the county.
First record: Gulliver 1841
Druce: Locally common.

6 GALEOPSIS L.
2 G. angustifolia Ehrh. ex Hoffm.
Red Hemp-nettle

Native. Arable ground, mostly on calcareous soils.
May now be extinct as there have been no records since the 1960s of this plant, once a fairly common arable weed in the Soke of Peterborough and other areas. The last record appears to be from Gray's Pit, near Burton Latimer, in 1965.
First record: Druce 1874
Druce: (G. ladanum) Locally common and widely distributed.

3 G. speciosa Miller (8)
Large-flowered Hemp-nettle

Native. Arable land often with root crops.
Rare in the county although it may still be seen in fields around Peakirk, Newborough and Maxey. It has also been recorded from Ecton sewage farm in abundance in 1975 and in 1993 it appeared as a solitary plant in a field boundary hedge near Maidwell.
First record: Notcutt 1843
Druce: Very local.

4 G. tetrahit L. (70)
Common Hemp-nettle

Native. Arable ground, waste land, damp places.
Common, especially on cultivated ground and in hedgerows. Often a feature of recently cleared woodlands.

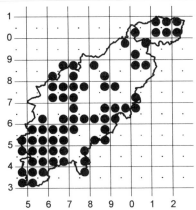

First record: Morton 1712
Druce: Locally common and widely spread.

5 G. bifida Boenn. (6)
Bifid Hemp-nettle

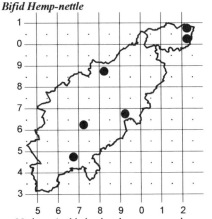

Native. Arable land and waste ground.
Rare. Only known from six localities in the county and the Soke of Peterborough. Possibly overlooked.
Druce: (G. tetrahit var. bifida) [Recorded from seven localities but no status given].

9 MARRUBIUM L.
1 M. vulgare L.
White Horehound
Native. Short grass, open or rough ground.
Probably extinct. Last recorded near Wakerley and around the old gas works in Tanner Street, Northampton in the 1970s. Prior to this it was recorded from several sites in the Soke of Peterborough.

First record: Morton 1712
Druce: Very local.

10 SCUTELLARIA L.
2 S. galericulata L. (71)
Skullcap

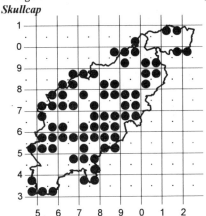

Native. Beside ponds, rivers, streams, gravel workings and canals.
Common throughout the county.
First record: Gulliver 1841
Druce: Rather common and widely distributed.

11 TEUCRIUM L.
1 T. scorodonia L.
Wood Sage
Native. Woods and hedgerows on well drained soils.
Extremely rare. This plant has recently been recorded from Harlestone Firs, where it came up in a recently cleared area, and along a ride that had been newly opened up in Bedford Purlieus. Although the first area is noted by Druce, the second is a new locality.
First record: Druce 1877
Druce: Very rare.

3 T. scordium L.
Water Germander
Native. Fen ditches.
Almost certainly extinct, having not been seen for many years. All the records are prior to 1930.
First record: Morton 1712
Druce: Very rare if not extinct.

12 AJUGA L.
1 A. reptans L. (100)
Bugle

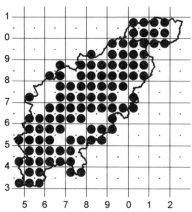

5 6 7 8 9 0 1 2

Native. Woods, shaded places.
Very common in woodland ridings and sometimes in unimproved pastures.
First record: Clare 1821
Druce: Common and widely distributed in all the districts.

3 A. chamaepitys (L.) Schreber
Ground-pine
Native. Bare chalk and chalky calcareous fields.
Extinct. Druce thought it had possibly been destroyed by the enclosures of the early 19th century.
First record: Morton 1712
Druce: Very rare, probably extinct.

13 NEPETA L.
1 N. cataria L.   (11)
Cat-mint

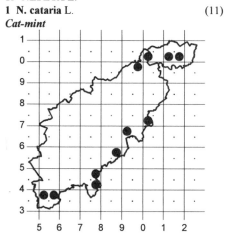

5 6 7 8 9 0 1 2

Native. Grassland on calcareous soils. Rare and very scattered. Locations for this species seem to have dwindled drastically over the last twenty years largely due to the 'tidying up' of hedgerows etc.
First record: Morton 1712
Druce: Local.

N. racemosa Lam. **x N. nepetella** L. = **x faassenii** Bergmans ex Stearn
Garden Cat-mint
Introduction. Tips and rough ground.
Occasionally established as a garden escape.

14 GLECHOMA L.
1 G. hederacea L.   (131)
Ground-ivy

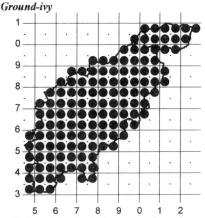

5 6 7 8 9 0 1 2

Native. Woods, hedgerows and rough ground on heavier soils.
Very common throughout the county.
First record: Morton 1712
Druce: (Nepeta hederacea) Common and generally distributed.

15 PRUNELLA L.
1 P. vulgaris L.   (125)
Selfheal
Native. Rough grassland, open woodland rides and clearings.
Very common throughout the county, on lawns and roadside verges, in churchyards etc.
First record: Morton 1712
Druce: Common throughout the county.

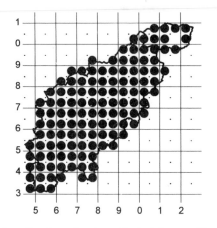

5 6 7 8 9 0 1 2

1 x 2 P. vulgaris x P. laciniata = P. x intermedia Link
Native. Grassland.
Recorded by John Chandler at Ailsworth in 1975.

16 MELISSA L.
1 M. officinalis L.
Balm
Introduction. Waste ground.
Occasionally established as a garden throw-out.
First record: Druce 1878
Druce: Rare.

18 CLINOPODIUM L.
(*Calamintha* Miller)
2 C. ascendens (Jordan) Samp.   (11)
(*Calamintha sylvatica* Bromf. subsp. *ascendens* (Jordan) P. Ball)
Common Calamint

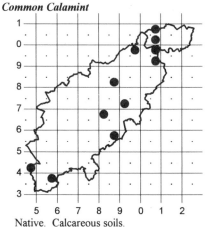

5 6 7 8 9 0 1 2

Native. Calcareous soils.

Rare. Only recorded from a very few localities in the county. It still occurs at Easton Maudit where it was recorded by Druce; near Bainton and in Mears Asby where it has occured on the same wall for fifty years.
First record: Ray 1662
Druce: (Satureia ascendens) Local.

3 C. calamintha (L.) Stace
(*Calamintha nepeta (L.) Savi*)
Lesser Calamint
Native. Calcareous, dry grassland.
Possibly extinct; last recorded in the area of Sulehay Forest, in 1957, by John Gilbert.

4 C. vulgare L.   (73)
Wild Basil

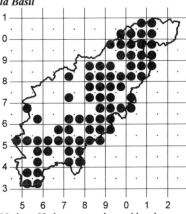

5 6 7 8 9 0 1 2

Native. Hedgerows and wood borders.
Common, especially in dry, mainly calcareous areas, roadsides and railway banks etc. throughout most of the county.
First record: Morton 1712
Druce: Rather common and widely distributed.

5 C. acinos (L.) Kuntze   (8)
(*Acinos arvensis* (Lam.) Dandy)
Basil Thyme
Native. Dry, calcareous disturbed areas.
Rare. A very local plant of old quarries and railway lines occurring mainly in the north of the county, with a couple of localities around the Brackley area.
First record: Clare 1821
Druce: (Satureja acinos) Local.

208

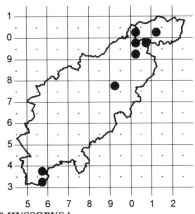

5 6 7 8 9 0 1 2

19 HYSSOPUS L.
1 H. officinalis L.
Hyssop
Introduction. Old walls.
No recent records.
First record: Ellis (Sibbertoft) 1930
Druce: [No status given, only one record].

20 ORIGANUM L.
1 O. vulgare L.   (22)
Wild Marjoram
Native. Dry grassland, hedgebanks and scrub.
Common on calcareous soils, especially in the
north of the county and the Soke of
Peterborough, occasional elsewhere in
scattered localities throughout the county.
First record: Morton 1712
Druce: Local.

21 THYMUS L.
2 T. pulegioides L.
Large Thyme
Native. Short turf.
Extremely rare. Only recorded with any
certainty from two places in the county, a
railway cutting near Gayton and near
Wadenhoe. Both records are from the early
1970s.
First record: Druce 1873?
Druce: Rare.

3 T. polytrichus A.Kerner ex Borbas
Wild Thyme
a subsp. **britannicus** (Ronn.) Kerguélen   (16)
(*T. drucei* Ronn., *T. praecox* Opiz subsp. *arcticus*
(E. Durand) Jalas, *T. Praecox* Opiz subsp.
britannicus (Ronn.) Holub)

Native. Short turf.
Frequent in the limestone areas in the north of
the county, occasional elsewhere. It is
confined to the undisturbed grasslands of old
quarries and railway banks where it occurs in
the south of the county.

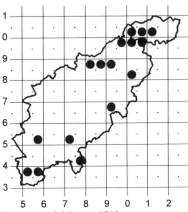

5 6 7 8 9 0 1 2
First record: Morton 1712
*Druce: (T. serpyllum) Locally common and
widely distributed.*

22 LYCOPUS L.
1 L. europaeus L.   (91)
Gypsywort
Native. Damp ground, often beside lakes,
rivers and canals.
Common near water throughout the county
and very often an early coloniser of bare mud
around new gravel pits.

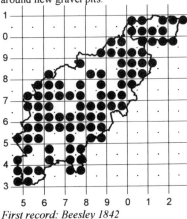

5 6 7 8 9 0 1 2
First record: Beesley 1842
Druce: Widely distributed and not uncommon.

23 MENTHA L.

1 M. arvensis L. (81)
Corn Mint

Native. Arable fields and woodland ridings. Common within its habitat. A local species now growing mainly in damp woodland ridings and not often as an arable weed as formerly.

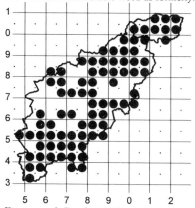

First record: Beesley 1842
Druce: Widely distributed.

1 x 2 M. arvensis x M. aquatica = M. x verticillata L.
Whorled Mint

Native. Damp places, woodland ridings. Rare. Probably under-recorded; there are records from Pitsford reservoir, Yardley Chase and from a couple of places in the Peakirk area.
First record: Druce 1877
Druce: Rather common and widely distributed.

1 x 2 x 3 M. arvensis x M. aquatica x M. spicata = M. x smithiana R.A.Graham
Tall Mint

Probable introduction. Damp places and waste ground.
No recent records.
First record: Druce 1877
Druce: (M .rubra) Very rare.

2 M. aquatica L. (118)
Water Mint

Native. Marshes, ditches, damp woodland rides and beside ponds .
Common throughout the county in suitable habitats.
First record: Clare 1827
Druce: Common throughout the county.

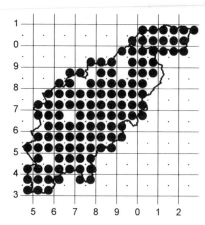

2 x 3 M. aquatica x M. spicata = M. x piperita L.
Peppermint

Native. Damp ground and waste places.
Extremely rare. Found by Grand Union Canal at Grafton Regis in 1981.
First record: Druce 1878
Druce: Rare.

3 M. spicata L.
(*M. longifolia* auct., non (L.) Hudson)
Spear Mint

Introduction. Rough and waste ground.
Scattered throughout the county as a garden escape on rubbish tips, waste ground etc.
First record: Morton 1712
Druce: Rare.

3 x 4 M. spicata x M. suaveolens = M. x villosa Hudson
Apple-mint

Introduction. Rough and waste ground.
Well established on railway banks at Roade, its only known location.. Var. *alopecuroides* (Hull) Briq. - the usual garden variety - was recorded in Fineshade Woods in 1980. It is still established there.
First record: Loydell 1904

4 M. suaveolens Ehrh.
(*M. rotundifolia* sensu S. Robson et auct., non (L.) Hudson)
Round-leaved Mint

Native. Ditches and damp places.
Extinct.
First record: Morton 1712

Druce: (M. rotundifolia) Very rare.

M. suaveolens x **M. longifolia** = **M. x rotundifolia** (L.) Hudson
False Apple-mint
Introduction. Damp places.
No recent records.
First record: Druce 1904
Druce: Rare.

5 M. pulegium L.
Pennyroyal
Native. Damp grassland near ponds.
Probably extinct.
First record: Morton 1712
Druce: Very rare.

M. longifolia (L.) Hudson
Horse Mint
The records in Druce are apparently incorrect, as this mint does not occur in the British Isles.

25 SALVIA L.
1 S. sclarea L.
Clary
Introduction. Waste tips and rough ground. Sometimes naturalised on rubbish tips etc. and one record from the roadside at Ailsworth.

3 S. pratensis L.
Meadow Clary
Native. Calcareous grassland, wood borders. Extinct. The only known record is the first record, from Yardley Gobion, in 1884.
First record: Druce 1884
Druce: Very rare.

4 S. verbenaca L. (7)
Wild Clary

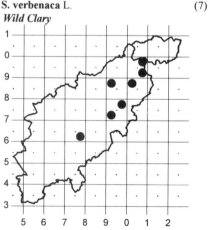

Native. Dry, grassy or bare ground.
Very rare. Now only known from a very few sites in the county. Recorded from Weldon, Oundle and Warmington and from Irthlingborough churchyard where it seems able to withstand constant mowing.
First record: Morton 1712
Druce: Local.

5 S. viridis L.
Annual Clary
Introduction. Tips and waste ground. Occasionally recorded as a garden escape or throw-out. It made a surprising appearance in the middle of Yardley Chase in 1990.
First record: Chester 1916
Druce: (S. horminum) [No status given].

6 S. verticillata L.
Whorled Clary
Introduction. Rough ground and beside roads and railway lines.
No recent records.
First record: Foord Kelcey 1906-7
Druce: Appears likely to spread.

S. reflexa Hornem.
Mintweed
Introduction. Waste and rough ground.
A casual species recorded from the site of demolished buildings in Wellingborough in the 1980s, and previously at Sibbertoft about 1939.

119 HIPPURIDACEAE
1 HIPPURIS L.
1 H. vulgaris L. (34)
Mare's-tail

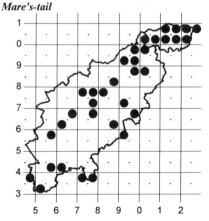

Native. Shallow water.
Occasionally common in streams, dykes and the larger water bodies. There are particularly large colonies in Cransley reservoir and at Lyveden New Bield, in the Elizabethan water gardens.
First record: Irvine 1838
Druce: Local.

120 CALLITRICHACEAE
1 CALLITRICHE L.
3 C. stagnalis Scop. (107)
Common Water-starwort

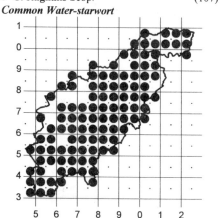

Native. All wet places, including wheel ruts in woods.
Common in all areas of the county.
First record: Druce 1874
Druce: Common, generally distributed.

4 C. platycarpa Kütz. (24)
Various-leaved Water-starwort

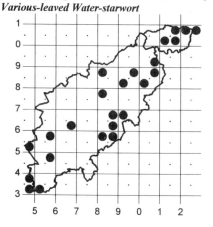

Native. Ponds, ditches, streams etc.
Occasional in scattered localities throughout the county.
First record: Crick 1880
Druce: (C. stagnalis var. platycarpa) [No status given].

5 C. obtusangula Le Gall (13)
Blunt-fruited Water-starwort

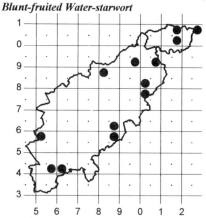

Native. Ponds, ditches, streams etc.
Occasional in scattered localities throughout the county.
First record: Druce 1885
Druce: Locally common.

7 C. hamulata Kütz. ex Koch (9)
(C. intermedia Hoffm.)
Intermediate Water-starwort

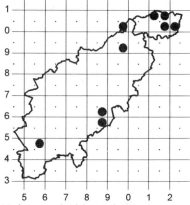

Native. Ponds, dykes and still water.

Rare. Recorded in a few locations but probably overlooked as it often grows with other species of the same genus.
First record: Druce 1874
Druce: (Callatriche intermedia) Local.

C. palustris L.
This record in Druce is almost certainly an error.

121 PLANTAGINACEAE
1 PLANTAGO L.
1 P. coronopus L.
Buck's-horn Plantain
Native. Dry sandy heath ground.
Extinct. The last known record is from Great Billing, recorded in The History and Antiquities of the County of Northampton, by George Baker, in 1822.
First record: Morton 1712
Druce: Very rare.

3 P. major L.
Greater Plantain
a subsp. **major** (132)
Native. Grass and waste land.
Very common. Found throughout the county on almost all open, uncultivated land, particularly in well-trodden areas.
First record: Pitt 1813
Druce: Common and generally distributed.

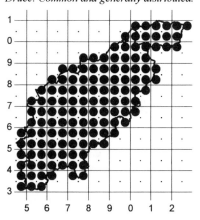

4 P. media L. (99)
Hoary Plantain
Native. Dry grassland on calcareous soils.
Occasional. Found wherever soil conditions are suitable. It occurs throughout the county,

especially in old churchyards, but it is largely absent from an area in the north-west.

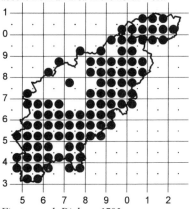

First record: Dickson 1792
Druce: Locally common on calcareous soils.

5 P. lanceolata L. (132)
Ribwort Plantain

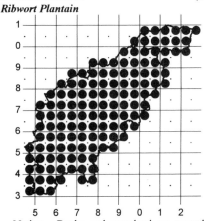

Native. Banks and grassland on neutral or basic soils.
Common throughout the county.
First record: Pitt 1813
Druce: Abundant throughout the county and a polymorphic species.

6 P. arenaria Waldst. & Kit.
Branched Plantain
Introduction. Rough ground on sandy soil.
No recent records.
First record: French 1868
Druce: (P. indica) [No status given].

2 LITTORELLA P.Bergius
1 L. uniflora (L.) Asch.
Shoreweed
Native. Muddy margins of brackish water bodies.
Extremely rare. Recorded only at Pitsford and Daventry reservoirs.
First record: Sir George Chester 1910
Druce: Very local.

122 BUDDLEJACEAE
1 BUDDLEJA L.
2 B. davidii Franchet
Butterfly-bush
Introduction. Waste land, railway embankments etc.
Occasional. Naturalised at a few sites within the county and generally spreading.

123 OLEACEAE
2 FRAXINUS L.
1 F. excelsior L. (134)
Ash
Native. Hedgerows and woodland.
Frequent. Generally distributed throughout the county.
First record: Morton 1712

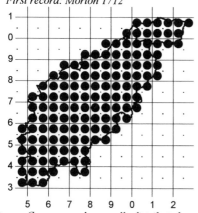

Druce: Common and generally distributed.

F. ornus L.
Manna Ash
Introduction. Hedgerows.
A single record from near Castor.

3 SYRINGA L.
1 S. vulgaris L.
Lilac

Introduction. Hedgerows, waste land and railway embankments.
A common garden shrub that will occasionally establish itself in the wild, as a colourful constituent of hedges as at Corby and Glendon, or exist as a relic of planting, as at some of the old level crossings on what is now the Brampton Valley Way.

4 LIGUSTRUM L.
1 L. vulgare L. (112)
Wild Privet

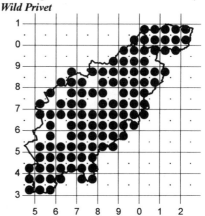

Native. Woodland edge, hedgerows and waste land.
Occasional. Commonly found on the limestone areas of the county but missing from a few areas of more acid soils.
First record: Clare 1821
Druce: Local.

2 L. ovalifolium Hassk.
Garden Privet
Introduction. Waste land and hedgerows.
Occasionally found naturalised.

124 SCROPHULARIACEAE
1 VERBASCUM L.
1 V. blattaria L.
Moth Mullein
Introduction. Waste ground.
There are two records for this plant, one for Wilby in the 1960s, and the other from the Delapre Abbey area in 1992.
First record: Rev. W. Wood 1805
Druce: Very rare.

2 V. virgatum Stokes
Twiggy Mullein

Introduction. Waste places.
The only recent record is in a quarry near Bedford Purlieus in 1988.
First record: Druce 1877
Druce: Very rare.

6 V. densiflorum Bertol.
Dense-flowered Mullein
Introduction. Waste and rough ground.
Recorded from Milton Malsor tip in 1991 and subsequently from a garden.
First record: Andrew Robinson 1991.

7 V. thapsus L. (82)
Great Mullein, Aaron's Rod

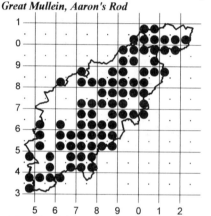

Occasional, but can be common in old quarries, abandoned railway tracks etc. Found throughout most of the county except the north-western area.
First record: Clare 1821
Druce: Thinly scattered through the county, but in many places probably only a garden escape.

9 V. nigrum L. (16)
Dark Mullein
Native. Waste and rough ground, especially on limestone.
Rare. Occurs at scattered sites, mainly in the limestone areas in the north and in the Soke of Peterborough, but it also occurs along the Brampton Valley Way and in some quantity in Mears Ashby.
First record: Morton 1712
Druce: Very local.

12 V. lychnitis L.
White Mullein

British. Waste and bare ground.
A single record of this British native as a casual at Collingtree golf course.

2 SCROPHULARIA L.

1 S. nodosa L. (86)
Common Figwort

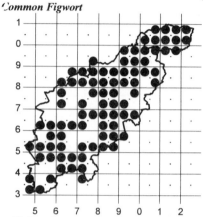

Native. Damp, open and shaded places.
Occasional. Occurs in wooded areas and other shaded habitats throughout the county.
First record: Baker 1822
Druce: Scattered through the woodlands of the county.

2 S. auriculata L. (122)
(*S. aquatica* L.)
Water Figwort

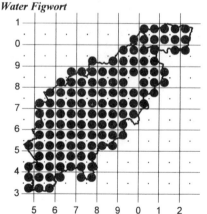

Native. Similar habitats to *S. nodosa*, but generally preferring wetter places.

Common beside water and other damp areas throughout most of the county, but it is absent from some central areas.
First record: Gulliver 1841
Druce: (S. aquatica) Common and widely distributed.

5 S. vernalis L.
Yellow Figwort
Introduction. Waste and rough ground. It is only recorded from three sites, Ferry Meadows near Peterborough, Thorpe Malsor and at Castle Ashby where Druce recorded it.
First record: G.Adams 1892-93
Druce: Very rare.

4 MIMULUS L.
1 M. moschatus Douglas ex Lindley
Musk
Introduction. Wet places or shallow water. Only very rarely present as a garden escape, but not persisting in any one location.
First record: Gill Gent (Harlestone Firs)1967

2 M. guttatus Fischer ex DC.
Monkeyflower
Introduction. Damp or wet places. Occurs only as a garden escape, never surviving long in any one locality.
Druce: Now naturalised by stream sides and likely to spread.

5 LIMOSELLA L.
1 L. aquatica L.
Mudwort
Native. Disturbed mud beside water. Very rare and not seen in the county for many years until 1987, when it was recorded at Pitsford reservoir. Subsequently it has been found on dry mud in old gravel workings near Grendon, beside Daventry reservoir and at Titchmarsh Wildlife Trust reserve.
First record: Morton 1712
Druce: Very rare.

7 ANTIRRHINUM L.
1 A. majus L.
Snapdragon
Introduction. Rough ground and walls. Found at sites scattered throughout the county but generally close to domestic dwellings.
First record: Paley 1860
Druce: Rather Rare.

8 CHAENORHINUM (DC. ex Duby) Reichb.
2 C. minus (L.) Lange   (61)
Small Toadflax

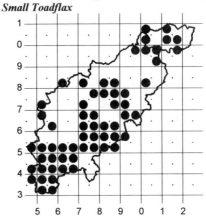

Native. Arable and waste land. Occasional, but can be frequent in its habitat. Predominantly found in the south of the county, but is quite common on the ballast of old railways, such as the Brampton Valley Way (the former Northampton to Market Harborough railway line) and stretches of the old Northampton to Wellingborough line near Grendon. It is also found in quantity on old railway ballast near Bozeat and in the M.O.D. area of Yardley Chase.
First record: Morton 1712
Druce: (Linaria minor) Local.

9 MISOPATES Raf.
1 M. orontium (L.) Raf.
Weasel's-snout
Possibly native. Weed of cultivated ground. Extinct. Last recorded in 1951 near Sulehay.
First record: Morton 1712
Druce: (Antirhinum orontium) Very rare.

11 CYMBALARIA Hill
1 C. muralis P.Gaertner, Meyer & Scherb.
Ivy-leaved Toadflax
a subsp. **muralis**   (101)
Introduction. Walls. Common. Found throughout most of the county, especially on old stone or brick walls. White flowered plants occur at Kingsthorpe and Barnack.
First record: Woodward 1787
Druce: (Linaria cymbalaria) Common and widely distributed.

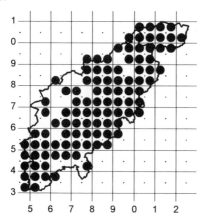

12 KICKXIA Dumort.
1 K. elatine (L.) Dumort.   (23)
Sharp-leaved Fluellen

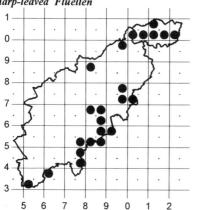

Probably native. Field margins on light soil.
Rare. Occurs less frequently than *K. spuria,*
but in similar habitats and often in similar
locations.
First record: Morton 1712
Druce: (Linaria elatine) Local.

2 K. spuria (L.) Dumort.   (31)
Round-leaved Fluellen
Probably native.   Field margins on light
cultivated soil.
Rare. Found mainly along the Nene valley and
the eastern and southern borders in the stubble
of cereal and other crops. This, and *K. elatine*
were once a feature of recently cut cornfields in
the late summer but with changes in
agricultural practices this is no longer the case.

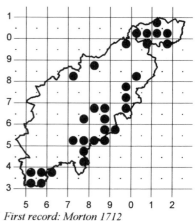

First record: Morton 1712
Druce: (Linaria spuria) Local.

13 LINARIA Miller
1 L. vulgaris Miller   (83)
Common Toadflax, Yellow Toadflax

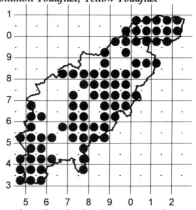

Native. Grassland and waste ground.
Occasional. Found throughout the county, but
it is more common in the east. Often found
growing in the ballast of old railway lines and
other stony places where there is little
competition.
First record: Notcutt 1843
Druce: (L. linaria) Locally common.

1 x 4 L. vulgaris x L. repens = L. x sepium
Allman
Native. Rough grassland.
Extremely rare, with only two known records
at isolated sites within the localities of the

parents, at Finedon Old Furnaces and at Braunston.

3 L. purpurea (L.) Miller (41)
Purple Toadflax
Introduction. Rough grassland or walls. Occasional. Found at scattered locations throughout the area but seems to be more common in the central northern part of the county.
First record: Druce 1874
Druce: Rare.

4 L. repens (L.) Miller
Pale Toadflax
British. Stony ground and rough grassland. Rare. This was found both at Braunston old station and at Finedon old sidings in 1968, both sites have been developed and lost. Subsequently it has been found in some quantity on the disused railway at Charwelton in 1988.
First record: A plant was found in 1883, near Aynhoe, beside the railway. The seeds were brought by passing trains from South Oxford, where it is abundant.
Druce: [No status given].

14 DIGITALIS L.
1 D. purpurea L. (33)
Foxglove

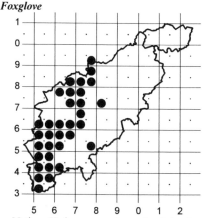

Native. Hedgerows and woodland clearings. Rare. Predominantly southern and western in distribution, avoiding the basic soils. Often present as a garden escape.
First record: Morton 1712
Druce: Very local.

15 ERINUS L.
1 E. alpinus L.
Fairy Foxglove
Introduction. Walls.
Found occasionally growing at the base, or in the mortar of walls as in Charlton village .

16 VERONICA L.
1 V. serpyllifolia L.
Thyme-leaved Speedwell
a subsp. serpyllifolia (106)

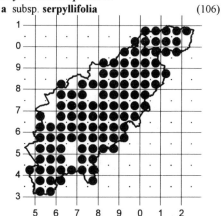

Native. Woodland rides, grass and damp lawns. Frequent, and found in suitable habitats in virtually the whole county.
First record: Gulliver 1841
Druce: Abundant and generally distributed.

6 V. officinalis L. (31)
Heath Speedwell

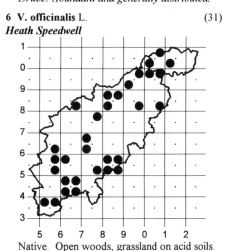

Native. Open woods, grassland on acid soils.

Occasional. Scattered through the county. It is recorded from Borough Hill and the Daventry area, Harlestone Firs and around Northampton, grasslands in Corby, Cowthick Plantation near Stanion and Yardley Chase. It is fairly common in Bedford Purlieus and Wakerley Woods and in the Brackley area in the south.
First record: Rev. M.J. Berkeley 1837
Druce: Local.

7 V. chamaedrys L. (127)
Germander Speedwell

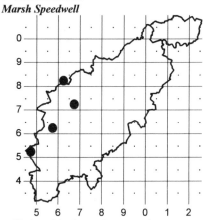

Native. Hedgerows and grassland.
Very common. It is recorded in almost all areas of the county.
First record: Gulliver 1841
Druce: Common and generally distributed.

8 V. montana L. (16)
Wood Speedwell

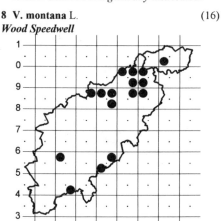

Native. Damp woodlands.
Rare. Found mainly in the north of the county within the Rockingham Forest area, but it also occurs at Finedon Cally Banks Wildlife Trust reserve and at a few localities in the extreme south, which may reflect the predominantly northern distribution of accessible woodlands. It is an indicator of ancient woodland.
First record: Baker 1822
Druce: Very rare. The occurrence of the plant within the county needs verification.

9 V. scutellata L.
Marsh Speedwell

Native. Marshes and wet meadows.
Very rare. Recorded only in the west of the county where it is known at only five sites, Drayton, Boddington, Stanford and Hollowell reservoirs, and in a marshy area on Borough Hill near Daventry.
First record: Littleton Brown 1726
Druce: Local and rare.

10 V. beccabunga L. (124)
Brooklime
Native. Streams, ditches and shallow standing water.
Common throughout the county in suitable habitats where it can become the dominant plant. White flowered varieties have been found at Crick and in Castle Ashby ponds.
First record: Gulliver 1841
Druce: Common in all districts.

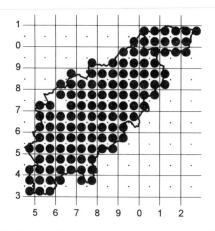

11 V. anagallis-aquatica L.   (36)
Blue Water-speedwell

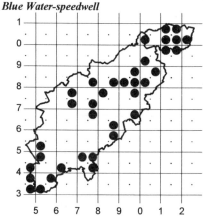

Native. Wet areas, particularly shallow, still water.
Very occasional. Recorded from a number of localities, predominantly in the north-eastern half of the county, but also on the southern and eastern boundaries.
First record: Baker 1822
Druce: Common in all low-lying tracts of the county.

12 V. catenata Pennell   (50)
Pink Water-speedwell
Native. Wet areas, particularly shallow, still water.
Occasional, mainly in the eastern half of the county and at isolated sites along the western boundary. It can be common in all suitable habitats.

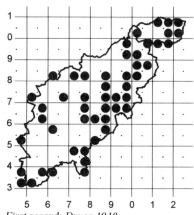

First record: Druce 1910
Druce: (V. aquatica) Common.

16 V. arvensis L.   (116)
Wall Speedwell

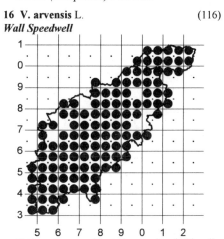

Native. Open, cultivated ground and old walls.
Common throughout the county.
First record: Gulliver 1841
Druce: Common and widely distributed.

19 V. agrestis L.   (39)
Green Field-speedwell
Native. Cultivated ground.
Occasional in the county, and found only at widely separated sites. A decreasing species due to modern farming practices.
First record: Gulliver 1841
Druce: Rather common and generally distributed but a diminishing species.

220

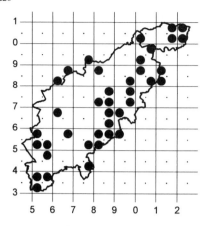

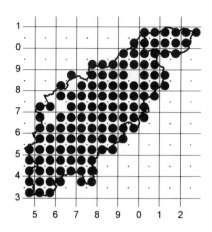

5 6 7 8 9 0 1 2

20 V. polita Fries (18)
Grey Field-speedwell
Native. Cultivated ground.
Fairly rare. Recorded at about eighteen
localities. It is becoming increasingly
uncommon due to modern farming practices.

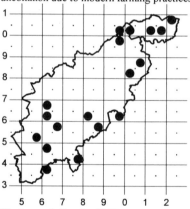

5 6 7 8 9 0 1 2
First record: Beesley 1842
*Druce: (V. didyma) Common and widely
distributed.*

21 V. persica Poiret (124)
Common Field-speedwell
Introduction. Grassland and waste ground.
Common throughout the county, it can become
a locally dominant plant on disturbed ground.
It is apparently more resistant than other
veronica species to weedkillers.
First record: G.C. Druce 1874
*Druce: (V. tournefortii) Generally distributed
and very common.*

23 V. filiformis Smith (74)
Slender Speedwell

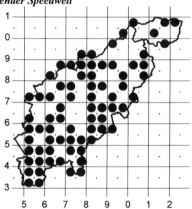

5 6 7 8 9 0 1 2
Introduction. Grassland and streamsides.
Common, found at scattered sites throughout
the county, especially recreation grounds and
churchyards. This species has become more
common over the past twenty-five years being
spread by vegetative means and not by seed,
which it only rarely sets.
First record: 1959?

24 V. hederifolia L. (115)
Ivy-leaved Speedwell
Native. Cultivated ground, woodland rides etc.
Occasional throughout most of the county.
This has been recorded as an aggregate species
but there are a few records for *V. hederifolia
subsp. lucorum* from shady habitats in four
churchyards.

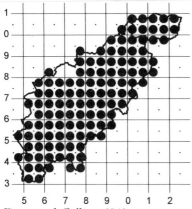

First record: Gulliver 1841
Druce: Abundant and generally distributed.

9 MELAMPYRUM L.
1 M. cristatum L.
Crested Cow-wheat
Native. Woods.
Extremely rare and possibly extinct. It occurred on Ailsworth Heath, probably up to the 1960s and may still occur on one roadside in the Soke of Peterborough although searches in 1993 and 1994 failed to reveal it.
First record: Morton 1712
Druce: Very local and rare.

3 M. pratense L.
Common Cow-wheat
a subsp. **pratense** (2)

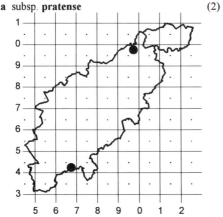

Native. Woodland.
Extremely rare. Found only at Wakerley in the extreme north of the county and at Bucknell

Wood in the south. It has also been recorded from Bedford Purlieus and Marholm in the Soke of Peterborough, but not in recent years.
First record: Notcutt 1843
Druce: Local.

20 EUPHRASIA L.
7 E. nemorosa (Pers.) Wallr. (38)
Eyebright

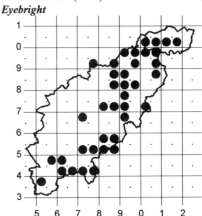

Native. Grassy places, woodland rides etc. Occasional. Mainly restricted to woodland ridings and old ironstone workings in the north and east of the county.
Druce 1876
Druce: Locally common.

8 E. pseudokerneri Pugsley
Eyebright
Native. Grassy places, woodland rides etc. Two records from the Soke of Peterborough on the Lincolnshire limestone.

10 E. stricta D.Wolff ex J.Lehm.
Eyebright
Introduction. Grassy places and old quarries. No recent records.
First record: Druce 1913
Druce: Local.

21 ODONTITES Ludwig
2 O. vernus (Bellardi) Dumort.
Red Bartsia
b subsp. **serotinus** (Syme) Corbière (95)
Native. Waste ground and arable land.
Common throughout the north east and the south of the county but absent from the west.

222

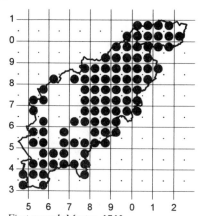

First record: Morton 1712
Druce: (Bartsia odontites) Locally abundant and widely distributed.

24 RHINANTHUS L.
2 R. minor L.
Yellow-rattle
a subsp. **minor** (55)

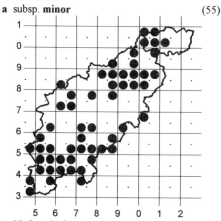

Native. Unimproved grassland.
A diminishing species as its natural habitats disappear, but it can still be found in areas in the north and south of the county.
First record: Pitt 1813
Druce: (R. Crista-Galli) Too abundant and widely distributed.

25 PEDICULARIS L.
1 P. palustris L.
Marsh Lousewort, Red Rattle
Native. Marshes and wet grassland.

Extremely rare. It is recorded from Aldwincle marsh, which was one of the few localities recorded by Druce, and is the only recent record in Northamptonshire. It also occurs at one site in the Soke of Peterborough.
First record: Notcutt 1843
Druce: Local and rare.

2 P. sylvatica L.
Lousewort
a subsp. **sylvatica**
Native. Damp heaths, bogs and pastures. Presumed extinct as there are no recent records. It was present in the Soke of Peterborough during the 1950s.
First record: Notcutt 1843
Druce: Local.

125 OROBANCHACEAE
1 LATHRAEA L.
1 L. squamaria L. (6)
Toothwort

Native. Woods and coppices.
Very rare and only known from Fermyn Wood, Bedford Purlieus, Old Sulehay Forest, Castor Hanglands and Wakerley Wood in the north of the county where it is parasitic on hazel and occurs in old hazel coppices.
First record: Rev. H.J. Berkley 1860
Druce: Very rare.

2 OROBANCHE L.
4 O. elatior Sutton (13)
Knapweed Broomrape, Tall Broomrape
Native. On *Centaurea scabiosa* on limestone.
Rare but can be frequent in its habitat, as at Barnack Hills and Holes national nature

reserve. There are several other records from calcareous areas in the north of the county, notably Collyweston Deeps nature reserve and the roadside near Wakerley. It has also been found on Northampton Golf Links and at Evenley, Croughton and Whitfield in the extreme south of the county. It appears to be more widespread than Druce originally thought.

First record: Rev. M.J. Berkley 1860
Druce: (O. major) Very local and rare.

7 O. crenata Forsskål
Bean Broomrape
Adventive. On herbaceous Fabaceae.
This very unlikely species, parasitic on beans etc., was discovered in a container of Pelargoniums at Woodend in 1983.
First record: Andrew Robinson 1983

8 O. hederae Duby
Ivy Broomrape
British. On Ivy.
No recent records. The first record, by H.N.Dixon in 1909, is the only one.
Druce: [No status given but one record listed].

10 O. minor Smith (6)
Common Broomrape. Lesser Broomrape, Clover Broomrape
Native. Roadsides and clover fields.
Very rare. There are scattered records from near Brackley on *Medicago lupulina*, and from Duddington by-pass on *Trifolium* species. It is also very prolific in Irchester

Country Park as a result of being introduced in a clover field about fifty years ago!

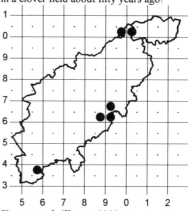

First record: Chester 1919
Druce: Very rare.

O. ramosa L.
Hemp Broomrape
Adventive. Formerly naturalised.
An unusual species and introduced accidentally to a garden near Finedon in 1986 from the Mediterranean area.

128 LENTIBULARIACEAE
1 PINGUICULA L.
3 P. vulgaris L.
Common Butterwort
Native. Bogs.
Now extremely rare, and found only at one site in the Soke of Peterborough. Until the 1980s it was also present in the south of the county near Croughton.
First record: How 1650
Druce: Very local.

2 UTRICULARIA L.
1 U. vulgaris L.
Greater Bladderwort
Native. Ditches, dykes and pools of stagnant water.
Probably extinct. In recent years only seen at Cosgrove Pits, a former gravel quarry in the extreme south where it was recorded by Mike Wallis in 1968. Development of Milton Keynes in this area may have made this species extinct within the county. It was common in the Titchmarsh ox-bow in the 1950s.

224

First record: Gibson 1685
Druce: Very local.

6 U. minor L.
Lesser Bladderwort
Native. In dykes.
Probably extinct. Recorded by Druce in the
Soke and by P. Rixon in the ox-bow at
Wadenhoe in the late 1960s, but there are no
recent records.
First record: Hill 1756
Druce: Very rare.

129 CAMPANULACEAE
1 CAMPANULA L.
5 C. medium L.
Canterbury-bells
Introduction. Waste ground
Present only as a casual or garden escape.

7 C. glomerata L.   (11)
Clustered Bellflower

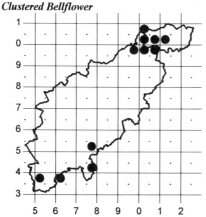

Native. Pastures and old quarries.
Very rare and recorded only on calcareous
sites in the north plus a few old quarries and
railway lines in the extreme south. It can also
occur intermittently as a garden relic or
escape.
First record: Morton 1712
Druce: Local.

11 C. latifolia L.   (24)
Giant Bellflower
Native. Woodland rides and hedgerows.
Occasional. Found on scattered sites across
the county, in ancient woodlands and
plantations and in light shade beside
hedgerows. It is generally supposed that this

plant, being a mainly northern species, is on
its southern limit in Northants. Some plants
may be relics of earlier planting.

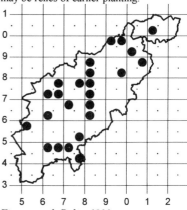

First record: Baker 1822
Druce: Very local.

12 C. trachelium L.   (41)
Nettle-leaved Bellflower

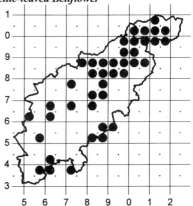

Native. Woodland rides and hedgerows.
Occasional. Scattered across the county in
similar locations to *C. latifolia*, and
sometimes in the same places, but more
common than that species. It is particularly
common in the ancient woodland in the north
of the county.
First record: Morton 1712
Druce: Local.

13 C. rapunculoides L.
Creeping Bellflower
Alien. Waste ground.

This plant has been found on only three sites in the north of the county, at all of which it probably exists as a garden escape.
First record: Irvine 1838
Druce: Very Rare.

15 C. rotundifolia L. (57)
Harebell

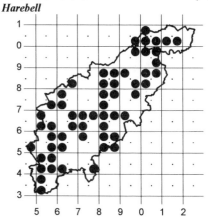

5 6 7 8 9 0 1 2

Native. Dry pasture and old quarries. Occasional. Scattered across the county, often on isolated sites and it can be frequent within its habitat. It has been reduced in numbers by the ploughing of grassland in recent years.
First record: Morton 1712
Druce: Locally common.

2 LEGOUSIA Durande
1 L. hybrida (L.) Delarbre (18)
Venus's-looking-glass

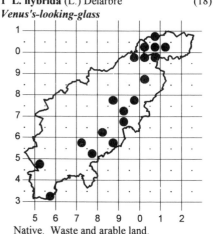

5 6 7 8 9 0 1 2

Native. Waste and arable land.

Rare. Occasionally found on scattered sites in the eastern half of the county, but is more frequent in the limestone areas of the north, in and around the Soke of Peterborough.
First record: J. Adkins 1822
Druce: Locally plentiful.

L. speculum-veneris (L.) Chaix
Large Venus's-looking-glass
Introduction. Cultivated land.
No recent records.
Druce: Rare.

6 JASIONE L.
1 J. montana L.
Sheeps-bit
Native. Dry, sandy heathland.
Probably extinct. This species made a surprising appearance on decaying brickwork at the deserted station at Braunston in 1964, where it was recorded by M.E.L.Nobles. It persisted for a couple of years only, the site having now been developed. Earlier records from Borough Hill and Newnham Hill, in the 1800s, were from the same general area.
First record: Notcutt 1843
Druce: Very rare.

130 RUBIACEAE
3 SHERARDIA L.
1 S. arvensis L. (42)
Field Madder

5 6 7 8 9 0 1 2

Native. Arable fields, unimproved pasture and waste places.
Occasional. Present at scattered locations throughout the county but decreasing owing to the reduction of suitable habitats.

First record: Morton 1712
Druce: Common and generally distributed in all districts.

4 PHUOPSIS (Griseb.) J.D.Hook
1 P. stylosa (Trin.) Benth. & J.D.Hook. ex B.D.Jackson
Caucasian Crosswort
Introduction. Waste ground.
Recorded from Irchester Country park as a garden escape between 1965 and 1969.

5 ASPERULA L.
1 A. cynanchica L.
Squinancywort
a subsp. **cynanchica** (5)

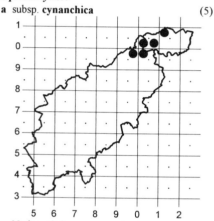

5 6 7 8 9 0 1 2

Native. Calcareous grassland.
Very rare. Known at only five sites, including Barnack Hills and Holes, within the limestone belt that crosses the northern end of the county and the Soke of Peterborough.
First record: Morton 1712
Druce: Very local.

A. arvensis L.
Blue Woodruff
Introduction. Waste tips.
Recorded at a single location, probably as a result of the germination of discarded bird seed.
First record: Morton 1712
Druce: Very rare.

6 GALIUM L.
2 G. odoratum (L.) Scop. (25)
Woodruff, Sweet Woodruff

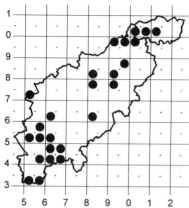

5 6 7 8 9 0 1 2

Native. Damp woodlands and hedgerows.
Occasional. Found predominantly in ancient woodlands in the north and the south of the county, where it can be abundant.
First record: Morton 1712
Druce: (Asperula odorata) Local.

3 G. uliginosum L. (20)
Fen Bedstraw

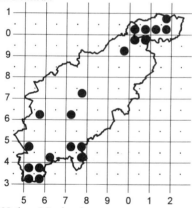

5 6 7 8 9 0 1 2

Native. Marshy places.
Occasional. With rare exceptions confined to base-rich marshy areas in the north of the county and the Soke of Peterborough, and also towards the south.
First record: Notcutt 1843
Druce: Very local.

5 G. palustre L. (100)
Common Marsh-bedstraw
Native. Damp meadows, ditches, dry pond beds etc.

Common. Although absent from some areas it can be locally common and even dominant in the right habitat. It is found at sites spread throughout the county. This has been recorded as an aggregate species, with just a single record for *G. palustre subsp. elongatum* in the south-west, but it is probably much under-recorded

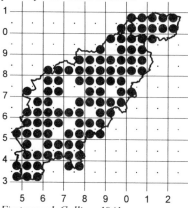

First record: Gulliver 1841
Druce: Common and generally distributed.

6 G. verum L. (122)
Lady's Bedstraw

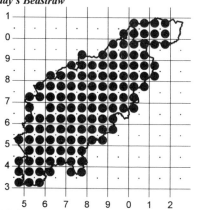

Native. Dry grassland especially, but not solely, on calcareous soils.

Common. Found throughout the county in suitable habitats, particularly on unimproved grasslands.

First record: Gulliver 1841
Druce: Common and widely distributed.

6 x 7 G. verum x G. mollugo = G. x pomeranicum Retz. (6)
Hybrid Yellow Bedstraw

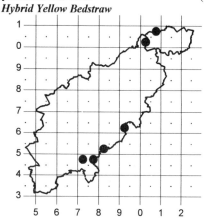

Native. Dry grassy places.

Very rare. Known at half a dozen sites on the eastern boundary and in the Soke of Peterborough, mainly on old bridleways, where both parents occur.

7 G. mollugo L.
Hedge Bedstraw
a subsp. **mollugo** (92)

Native. Hedgerows on calcareous soils.

Common. Can be a locally dominant species in the correct environment, occurring predominantly through the north and east of the county on calcareous soils.

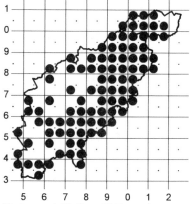

First record: Gulliver 1841
Druce: (G. mollugo) Common and widely distributed.

b subsp. erectum Syme
(G. album Miller*)*
Native. Hedgerows and grassy places.
Scattered. At present under-recorded.
First record: Anderson 1835
Druce: (G. erectum) Rare.

8 G. pumilum Murray
Slender Bedstraw
British. Dry chalk and limestone grassland.
No recent records. This species was last
recorded at Bearshank Wood in 1965-66.
This wood has now been felled and replanted.
First record: Chester 1914
Druce: Very rare.

10 G. saxatile L.   (23)
Heath Bedstraw

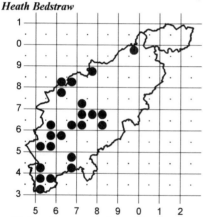

Native. Dry grassland on acid soils.
Very occasional with a scattered distribution.
Recorded from Harlestone Firs and some of
the woodlands in the south-west: Badby,
High Wood, Mantles Heath etc. It is also
recorded from Borough Hill and Honey Hill.
First record: Baker 1822
Druce: (G. hercynicum) Local.

11 G. aparine L.   (134)
Cleavers, Goosegrass
Native. Hedgerows, scrub, grassland,
woodland and cultivated land.
Extremely common throughout the county.
It can be a dominant species in any of its
habitats, given the right circumstances.
First record: Gulliver 1841
Druce: Abundant and generally distributed.

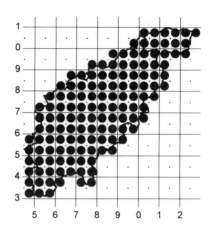

13 G. tricornutum Dandy
Corn Cleavers
Probable introduction.   Arable and waste
places.
No recent records.
First record: Hudson 1778
Druce: Locally common.

14 G. parisiense L.
Wall Bedstraw
Native. Walls and sandy banks.
Extremely rare.   A solitary specimen was
found near Helpston in 1992.
First record: Gilmour 1926
Druce: (G. anglicum) Very rare.

7 CRUCIATA Miller
1 C. laevipes Opiz   (34)
(G. cruciata (L.) Scop.)
Crosswort

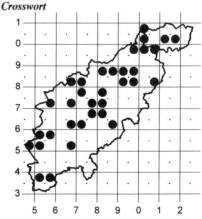

Native. Grassy places, rough ground and hedgerows.
Occasional. Scattered throughout the county; often in churchyards and on road verges.
First record: Gulliver 1841
Druce: Locally common.

131 CAPRIFOLIACEAE
1 SAMBUCUS L.
1 S. racemosa L.
Red-berried Elder, Alpine Elder
Introduction. Woodland.
Present as a garden escape in Lings Wood, a Wildlife Trust reserve within the Northampton boundary.

2 S. nigra L. (133)
Elder
Native. Hedges and thickets.
Very common. Well established throughout the county. In some places it can be the dominant plant in hedgerows.

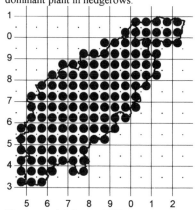

First record: Morton 1712
Druce: Common and generally distributed.

4 S. ebulus L.
Dwarf Elder, Danewort
Possibly native. Hedges and verges.
Rare but well established where it does occur. It is recorded near Stanion, Thrapston, Easton Maudit and Wansford and at a couple of sites in the Soke of Peterborough.
First record: Defoe c1710
Druce: Very local.

2 VIBURNUM L.
1 V. opulus L. (93)
Guelder-rose

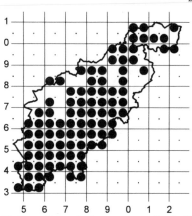

Native. Damp hedgerows, woodland rides etc.
Fairly frequent. Scattered in most areas of the county but totally absent from two or three small areas in the west and the east. It prefers damper sites than *V. lantana.*
First record: Gulliver 1842
Druce: Local. Not common.

2 V. lantana L. (85)
Wayfaring-tree

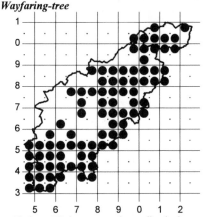

Native. Hedgerows and woodland edges.
Fairly frequent. Scattered across the county, especially in the limestone areas in the north.
First record: Baker 1822
Druce: No status given.

3 SYMPHORICARPOS Duhamel
1 S. albus (L.) S.F.Blake (90)
(S. rivularis Suksd.)
Snowberry

230

Introduction. Hedges and plantations.
Frequent. It was planted in the past as game
cover and is often locally naturalised.
*Druce: (S. Symphoricarpos) Rare, only
present as planted shrub.*

6 LONICERA L.
4 L. xylosteum L.
Fly Honeysuckle
British. Woods and hedgerows.
No recent records.
Druce: Very rare.

7 L. periclymenum L. (100)
Honeysuckle

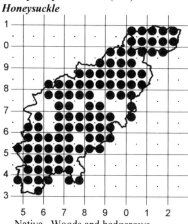

5 6 7 8 9 0 1 2
Native. Woods and hedgerows.
Common within its habitat. Found in the
main areas of deciduous woodland
throughout the county.
First record: Clare 1821
*Druce: Not uncommon and widely
distributed.*

8 L. caprifolium L.
Perfoliate Honeysuckle
Introduction. Hedges.
A solitary record, on the eastern border,
where it probably exists as a garden escape.
First record: Beesley 1842
Druce: Very rare.

132 ADOXACEAE
1 ADOXA L.
1 A. moschatellina L. (19)
Moschatel, Townhall Clock
Native. Shaded habitats on damp sandy soils.
Rare. Found in three fairly distinct areas
within the county; centred upon High Wood

Whittlebury and Mantles Heath in the south-
west, Salcey Forest in the south-east,
Desborough and Pipewell woods in the north
and at a solitary site in the Soke of
Peterborough. In most of these areas it is
quite prolific in a small number of woodlands
in close proximity to one another.

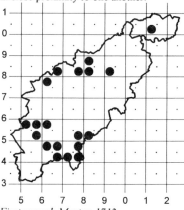

5 6 7 8 9 0 1 2
First record: Morton 1712
Druce: Local.

133 VALERIANACEAE
1 VALERIANELLA Miller
1 V. locusta (L.) Laterr. (37)
Common Cornsalad, Lamb's Lettuce

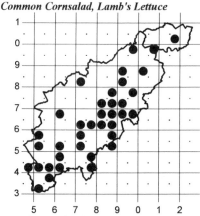

5 6 7 8 9 0 1 2
Native. Arable lands, banks and walls.
Occasional, but can be locally frequent in
suitable habitats such as old railway tracks,
quarries etc.
First record: Morton 1712
Druce: (V. olitaria) Local.

2 V. carinata Lois.
Keeled-fruited Cornsalad
Native. Arable land, banks and walls.
Extinct. The only record is at Dallington prior to 1930.
Druce: Rare. [A single record].

3 V. rimosa Touss. Bast.
Broad-fruited Cornsalad
Native. Arable land.
Extinct. The only record is from Burton Latimer in 1882.
First record: Lewin 1882
Druce: Very rare. [A single record].

4 V. dentata (L.) Pollich
Narrow-fruited Cornsalad
Possibly native. Cornfields.
Very rare and probably decreasing as suitable habitats disappear. Known only from one site in Northamptonshire and three in the Soke of Peterborough where it was fairly common in cornfields around the Wittering and Barnack areas up to the 1980s.
First record: French 1864
Druce: Local.

5 V. eriocarpa Desv.
Hairy-fruited Cornsalad
Introduction. Rough ground.
One record from a cornfield near Barnack in 1964.

2 VALERIANA L.
1 V. officinalis L.   (64)
Common Valerian

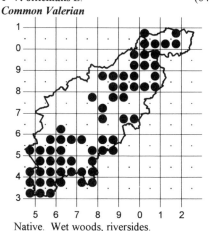

Native. Wet woods, riversides.

Frequent and widely distributed throughout the county.
First record: Druce 1876
Druce: (V. mikanii & V. sambucifolia) Local, rather frequent.

3 V. dioica L.   (17)
Marsh Valerian

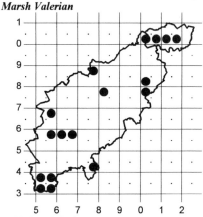

Native. Marshy areas.
Very occasional, and a decreasing species due to drainage of its natural habitats over the past decade. It is still present near Badby, in several areas around Brackley and at a few sites in the Soke of Peterborough - Castor Hanglands, White Water valley and Wittering. It is also present at Aldwincle marsh.
First record: Notcutt 1843
Druce: Local.

3 CENTRANTHUS Necker ex Lam. & DC
1 C. ruber (L.) DC.
Red Valerian
Adventive.   Naturalized   on   old   walls, especially if limestone.
Occasional but can be abundant on railway embankments, in old quarries etc. - it is a prominent feature on the bank beside the railway bridge in Rushton. It is only present as a garden escape.
Druce: (Kentranthus ruber) [No status given].

134 DIPSACACEAE
1 DIPSACUS L.
1 D. fullonum L.   (117)
Wild Teasel, Teasel

232

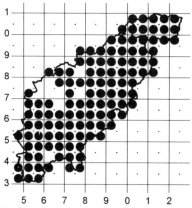

5 6 7 8 9 0 1 2

Native. Rough ground, especially beside streams, new road verges.
Common throughout the county except in a small area in the west. Can occur in large numbers on new road verges.
First record: Pitt 1813
Druce: (D. sylvestris) Locally common.

3 D. pilosus L.   (7)
Small Teasel

1
0
9
8
7
6
5
4
3

5 6 7 8 9 0 1 2

Native. Damp places in open woods, hedgerows etc.
Rare. Recorded from seven scattered localities. It is particularly common at Wakerley and Fineshade Woods and well established along the canal near Norton. Also recorded from Bowd Lane Wood, Brockhall, Whilton and Bozenham Mill.
First record: Baker 1822
Druce: Very local. Inconstant in its occurrence.

D. laciniatus L.
Cut-leaved Teasel
Introduction.
Two plants recorded from a garden in Wellingborough in 1994. This is the first record from the county, the only other records being from sites at Charlbury in Oxfordshire in 1989 and 1990 and at the Finsbury Park extension of Parkland Walk, in London in 1992.

3 KNAUTIA L.
1 K. arvensis (L.) Coulter   (92)
Field Scabious

1
0
9
8
7
6
5
4
3

5 6 7 8 9 0 1 2

Native. Dry grassland on lighter soils.
Frequent. Found throughout, but absent from the acid soils of the central western region. Can be abundant on roadsides, in old quarries and other disturbed soils.
First record: Gulliver 1841
Druce: (Scabiosa arvensis) Common and generally distributed.

4 SUCCISA Haller
1 S. pratensis Moench   (42)
Devil's-bit Scabious
Native. Grassy places and damp woodland rides, unimproved meadow land and marshes.
Occasional. Mainly southern in distribution and decreasing with loss of former habitats through drainage.
First record: Pitt 1813
Druce: (Scabiosa succisa) Locally common and widely distributed.

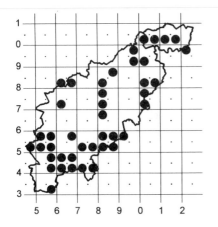

5 SCABIOSA L.
1 S. columbaria L.   (26)
Small Scabious

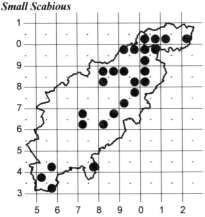

Native. Dry grassland on limestone soils.
Rare. Found on un-improved grassland, mainly in the north at Barnack Hills and Holes and Collyweston Deeps. It also occurs at Weldon, Cosgrove Pits and several other scattered localities through the county.
First record: Morton 1712
Druce: Locally common.

135 ASTERACEAE
(COMPOSITAE)

1 ECHINOPS L.
1 E. sphaerocephalus L.
Glandular Globe-thistle
Introduction. Waste places.
Rare. Grown in gardens and escaping or being thrown out.

2 CARLINA L.
1 C. vulgaris L.
Carline Thistle   (15)

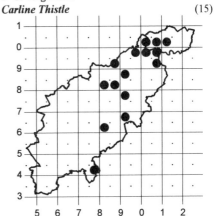

Native. Dry calcareous grassland.
Rare. Appears to be mainly restricted to limestone quarries and grasslands in the northeast of the county. It is singularly plentiful at Cranford Quarry and Irchester Country Park and on limestone grassland areas at Collyweston and Barnack. Distribution reduced due to ploughing etc.
First record: Druce 1862
Druce: Local.

3 ARCTIUM L.
1 A. lappa L.   (53)
Greater Burdock

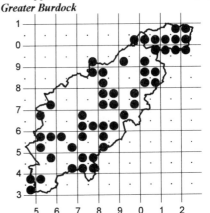

Native. Verges, hedgerows, woodland clearings.
Occasional. Widely scattered but preferring the wetter sites, often in woodland rides.

First record: possibly Gulliver 1841 but
definitely Druce 1880
Druce: Local.

2 A. minus (Hill) Bernh.   (128)
Lesser Burdock

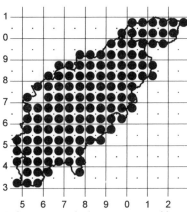

5   6   7   8   9   0   1   2
Native.   Verges,   hedgerows,   woodland
clearings.
Common, almost everywhere. The short list
of localities given by Druce may mean that it
has extended its range. The majority of the
records during this survey are of *subsp.
minus*, but *subsp. nemorosum* is almost
certainly overlooked.
*First record: (A.minus) Druce 1876;
(A.nemorosum) 1909
Druce:(A.minus) Not common; (A.
nemorosum) Very local.*

5 CARDUUS L.
1 C. tenuiflorus Curtis
Slender Thistle
Native.
Extinct. The only record is in The History
and Antiquities of the County of
Northampton by George Baker, published in
1822.
*First record: Baker 1822
Druce: (C. pycnocephalus var. tenuiflorus)
Very rare, perhaps now lost.*

3 C. crispus L.
Welted Thistle
a subsp. **multiflorus** (Gaudin) Gremli   (126)
(*C. acanthoides* auct., non L.)

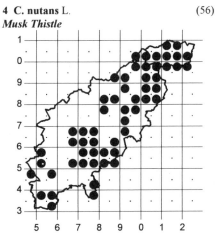

5   6   7   8   9   0   1   2
Native. Verges, hedgerows, streamsides.
Frequent.   Well distributed and common
where conditions are suitable.
*First record: Wildgose 1822
Druce: Common and widely distributed in all
districts.*

3 x 4 C. crispus x C. nutans = C. x dubius
Balbis
Native. Calcareous grasslands, quarries.
Occasional.   Found with the parents.
Confined to the calcareous soils along the
southern boundary and in the north-east, but
can be quite common where both parents
occur.
*First record: Huntly 1886
Druce: (C. x newbouldii) [No status given].*

4 C. nutans L.   (56)
Musk Thistle

5   6   7   8   9   0   1   2
Native. Calcareous grasslands, quarries.

Occasional. Confined to the calcareous soils in the southern and eastern half of the county and in the Soke of Peterborough.
First record: Morton 1712
Druce: Local.

6 CIRSIUM Miller

1 C. eriophorum (L.) Scop. (41)
Woolly Thistle

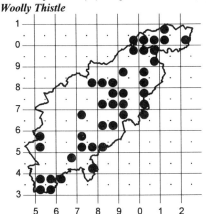

Native. Limestone soils.
Occasional. Similar habitats to *Carduus nutans* but less frequent - probably requiring soils with a higher calcium content.
First record: Pulteney 1760
Druce: (C. eriophorum var. britannicum) Local.

2 C. vulgare (Savi) Ten. (133)
Spear Thistle

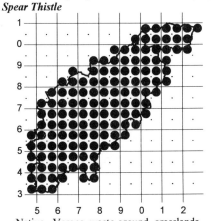

Native. Verges, waste ground, grasslands.

Very common. Grows almost anywhere - a good advertisement for its efficient method of dispersal.
First record: Pitt 1813
Druce: (C. lanceolatum) Common and generally distributed.

3 C. dissectum (L.) Hill
Meadow Thistle

Native. Fens, wet meadows.
Probably extinct. There are records from Southorpe Bog in 1950, both by Ian Hepburn and John Gilbert, there is also a record from Perio dykes, dating from the early 1960s, by Oundle School.
First record: Baker 1822
Druce: (C. pratense) Local and rather rare.
[Seven localities are named].

8 C. acaule (L.) Scop. (69)
Dwarf Thistle

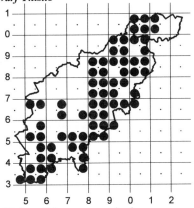

Native. Calcareous grassland.
Occasional. In unimproved grassland and old quarries through most of the county except the west. Not as common as previously due to destruction of habitats by modern farming methods.
First record: Baker 1822
Druce: Locally abundant and widely distributed.

9 C. palustre (L.) Scop. (112)
Marsh Thistle

Native. Damp woods, marshes.
Frequent in suitable habitats. Probably our tallest thistle, with some examples over two

metres tall, especially in woodlands. White flowered plants do commonly occur.

First record: Clare 1835
Druce: Common and generally distributed.

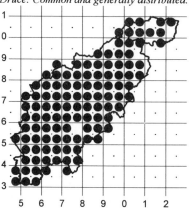

10 C. arvense (L.) Scop.   (133)
Creeping Thistle

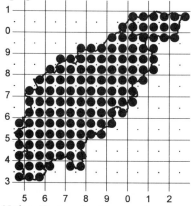

Native. Waste and arable ground. Frequent. Especially so in hedgerows and ditches but not such an agricultural pest as in the first half of the century due to the extensive use of herbicides.

First record: Morton 1712
Druce: A great agricultural pest.

7 ONOPORDUM L.

1 O. acanthium L.

Cotton Thistle, Queen Mary Thistle

Introduction. Waste ground, calcareous soils. An uncommon plant, usually on calcareous soils hence found chiefly along the southern and eastern parts of the county. Not usually persistent and probably always a garden escape. It still grows on the earthworks of Fotheringhay Castle, where Queen Mary was kept prisoner prior to her execution.

First record: Baker 1822
Druce: (Onopordon acanthium) Very rare.

8 SILYBUM Adans.

1 S. marianum (L.) Gaertner

Milk Thistle

Adventive. Waste ground. A possible a bird-seed alien found near Geddington in the 1980s by Claire Williams

First record: Paley 1860
Druce: (Mariana marianum) Waste places, rare.

9 SERRATULA L.

1 S. tinctoria L.   (11)
Saw-wort

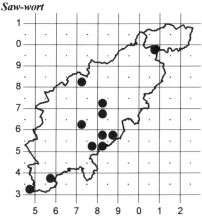

Native. Grassland, open woodland. Very rare. Scattered through the county in unimproved pasture and woodland. It is particularly well established in the Yardley Chase area and on some of the old railway lines. It also occurs in Old Sulehay Forest.

First record: Notcutt 1843
Druce: Rare.

11 CENTAUREA L.

1 C. scabiosa L.   (85)
Greater Knapweed

Native. Calcareous grassland. Occasional. Now mainly on roadsides, embankments and woodlands due to destruction of grasslands by ploughing. It is very common at Barnack Hills and Holes national nature reserve and Kingsthorpe Scrub Field where it is the host plant of *Orobanche major*. It is also plentiful in some old quarries in the eastern half of the county.

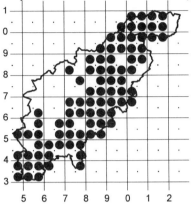

First record: Morton 1712
Druce: Locally common.

2 C. montana L.
Perennial Cornflower
Introduction. Waste areas.
A few records of this species, which is often grown in gardens, naturalised beside roads.

3 C. cyanus L.
Cornflower, Blue Cap
Formerly native, now an introduction.
Extinct as a native plant, it is occasionally found as a garden escape which can become well established. Formerly common as a cornfield weed it has gradually decreased and finally disappeared during the 1940s, due to changed farming practices.
First record: Morton 1712
Druce: Local and decreasing.

4 C. calcitrapa L.
Red Star-thistle
Introduction. Well drained waste places.
No recent records but never common. It was recorded in a cornfield near Cotterstock in 1950, by Ian Hepburn.
First record: Morton 1712
Druce: Very rare and almost extinct.

6 C. solstitialis L.
Yellow Star-thistle, St. Barnaby's Thistle
Adventive. Dry waste places.

Occuring as a casual from bird-seed etc. It was found on the old railway near Southey Wood in 1962 and in a car park in Northampton in 1966. The most recent example was found in a carrot bed in Wollaston in 1978.
First record: Druce 1882
Druce: Rare. Sporadic.

7 C. nigra L.   (127)
Common Knapweed, Hardheads

Native. Grassland, waste places.
Common especially on calcareous soils throughout the county.
First record: Pitt 1797
Druce: Common and generally distributed in all districts.

C. diluta Aiton
Lesser Star-thistle
Adventive. Waste places.
A single record from 1961 in the Wellingborough area is the only record of this Western Mediterranean plant as a garden escape in the county.
First record: 1961

C. melitensis L.
Maltese Star-thistle
Adventive. Waste places.
Found mainly on tips as a residue from bird-seed. No recent records.
First record: Chester 1910
Druce: Rare.

12 CICHORIUM L.
1 C. intybus L.   (12)
Chicory

Probably native. Verges, waste places. Rare, but it often occurs in short-lived abundance especially where the soil has been disturbed during road building and development, especially around the north of Northampton in the 1970s and 80s. A solitary plant appeared beside the new A14 at Rothwell in 1994.
First record: Morton 1712
Druce: Locally common.

13 ARNOSERIS Gaertner
1 A. minima (L.) Schweigger & Koerte
Lamb's Succory, Small Swine's Succory
Probably native. Sandy cornfields.
Extinct. Formerly very local in sandy fields with cereal crops. All the local records date from before 1879, and it has been extinct in Britain since 1971.
First record: Morton 1712
Druce: Very rare if not extinct.

14 LAPSANA L.
1 L. communis L.
Nipplewort
a subsp. **communis** (127)

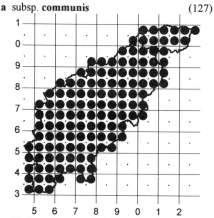

Native. Open ground, in gardens etc.
Common. Widespread especially in arable ground, roadside verges and rough ground.
First record: Gulliver 1841
Druce: Common and generally distributed.

15 HYPOCHAERIS L.
1 H. radicata L. (113)
Cat's-ear, Long-rooted Cat's-ear
Native. Grassland.

Common. An abundant yellow composite on roadside verges, in old quarries and old unimproved meadows.

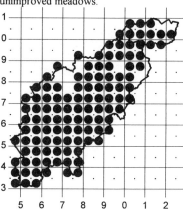

First record: Gulliver 1841
Druce: Common and generally distributed.

2 H. glabra L.
Smooth Cat's-ear
Native. Open ground on sandy soils.
Extinct. Druce records it at Blisworth in 1878 and it has not been recorded since.
First record: Druce 1878
Druce: Very rare, possibly extinct.

3 H. maculata L.
Spotted Cat's-ear
Native. Calcareous grassland.
Extremely rare. Formerly only recorded at two localities in the Soke of Peterborough, but in 1980 a single plant was found in the old limestone quarry at Collyweston Deeps where it has since become established. A nationally rare British Red Data Book species.
First record: Ray 1696
Druce: Very rare, if not extinct. [Southorp Quarries and Barnack are the only localities named].

16 LEONTODON L.
1 L. autumnalis L. (123)
Autumn Hawkbit
Native. Grassy places, roadside verges etc.
Common, and occurring in all types of grassland.

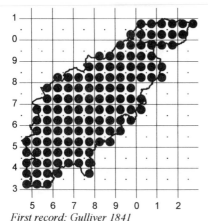

First record: Gulliver 1841
Druce: Very common and generally distributed.

2 L. hispidus L. (103)
Rough Hawkbit

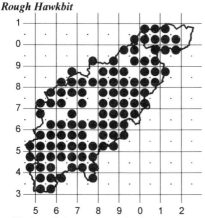

Native. Calcareous grassland.
Common. An abundant plant of grassland, but is now becoming less common due to ploughing up of old grassland etc.
First record: Baker 1822
Druce: Rather common and widely distributed.

3 L. saxatilis Lam. (19)
(*L. taraxacoides* (Villars) Mérat, *L. leysseri* (Wallr.) G.Beck)
Lesser Hawkbit, Smooth Hawkbit
Native. Dry grasslands.
Very occasional. It is found both on sandy and calcareous soils. It is probably under-

recorded. It is particularly common around the bunkers in the M.O.D. area of Yardley Chase.

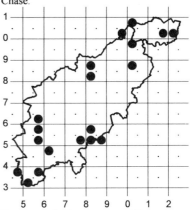

First record: Watson circa 1870
Druce: (L. nudicaulis) Local.

17 PICRIS L.
1 P. echioides L. (78)
Bristly Oxtongue

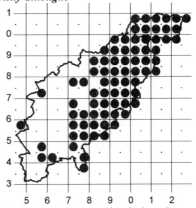

Probably native. Disturbed and rough ground.
Frequent. An aggressive coloniser of recently disturbed ground especially of roadsides, common on the clay soils of the north and east.
First record: Baker 1822
Druce: Local.

2 P. hieracioides L. (17)
Hawkweed Oxtongue
Native. Calcareous grasslands.

240

Occasional on railway banks and in quarries.

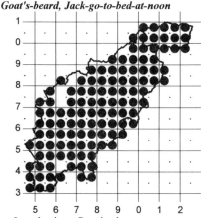

First record: Druce 1878
Druce: Locally common.

19 TRAGOPOGON L.
1 T. pratensis L. (118)
Goat's-beard, Jack-go-to-bed-at-noon

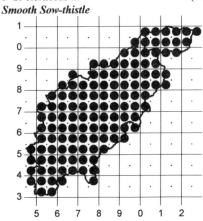

Introduction. Grasslands.
Frequent on roadside verges. Recorded as an aggregate species. Both *subsp. pratensis* and *subsp. minor* have been recorded but the latter is by far the more common.
First record: Gulliver 1841
Druce: Not uncommon.

2 T. porrifolius L.
Salsify
Introduction. Tips, waste ground etc.
Probably introduced with bird-seed, it can survive in the wild for a number of years. Few records.

Druce: Garden relic.

21 SONCHUS L.
1 S. palustris L.
Marsh Sow-thistle
Native. Marshy ground and damp woodland. Extremely rare. Although naturalised on Ashton Wold estate for many years, it was not until 1986 that it was recorded by Alan Newton at Cranford Wood, where it is becoming well established.
First record: Probably Wildgose 1822

2 S. arvensis L. (122)
Perennial Sow-thistle, Corn Sow-thistle

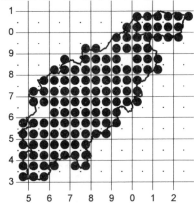

Native. Arable and waste land, verges etc.
Very common in all parts of the county.
First record: Notcutt 1844
Druce: Common and generally distributed.

3 S. oleraceus L. (124)
Smooth Sow-thistle

Native. Waste land, cultivated ground, roadside verges.

Very common on cultivated ground throughout the county.

First record: Pitt 1813

Druce: Abundant and generally distributed.

4 S. asper (L.) Hill (128)

Prickly Sow-thistle, Spiny Sow-thistle, Rough Sow-thistle.

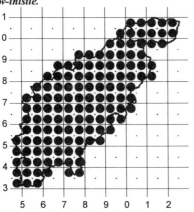

Native. Waste land, cultivated ground and roadside verges.

Very common on cultivated ground throughout the county.

First record: Notcutt 1843

Druce: Common and generally distributed.

22 LACTUCA L.

1 L. serriola L. (82)

Prickly Lettuce

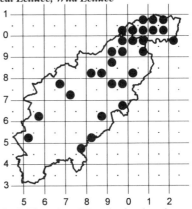

Probably native. Waste and rough ground.

Occasional. More common in the east and north of the county. Seems to have a liking for the ballast of old railway tracks and disturbed roadside verges. It is often common around operational gravel pits.

First record: J. Gilbert 1947

2 L. virosa L. (29)

Great Lettuce, Wild Lettuce

Probably native. Waste land and road verges. Becoming much more common in the north-east of the county and the Soke of Peterborough, as it takes advantage of the bare ground alongside abandoned railway tracks and new roads and in old quarries.

First record: J.Morton 1712

Druce: Rare and decreasing. [Five localities are named].

23 CICERBITA Wallr.

2 C. macrophylla (Willd.) Wallr.

Common Blue-sow-thistle

a subsp. *uralensis* (Rouy) Sell

Introduction. Rough grassland, verges etc. Established in a few places in the county, e.g. Badby, Desborough and Kelmarsh.

24 MYCELIS Cass.

1 M. muralis (L.) Dumort. (17)

Wall Lettuce

Native. Shaded areas.

Occasional. Mainly found in shady churchyards and on brickwork, with one record from woodland at Newbottle. It occurs in churchyards at East Haddon, Irthlingborough, Isham, Loddington, Harpole and Towcester and is very well established in the Northampton Racecourse area and also in Wellingborough. In both the latter cases it is possible that it was introduced with timber.

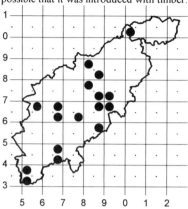

First record: J.Morton 1712
Druce: (Lactuca muralis) Rare.   [Eleven localities are named].

25 TARAXACUM Wigg.
Taraxacum agg.   (132)
Dandelion

Native.   Pastures, meadows, waste land, cultivated ground and roadside verges.
Very common. This has generally been recorded as an aggregate species but there are a few records for *T. palustre*, *T. lacistophyllum*, and *T. faroense* listed below.
First record: J.Morton 1712
Druce: Abundantly and generally distributed.

15 T. lacistophyllum (Dahlst.) Raunk.

A single recent record.
Druce: [Fourteen localities].

32 T. palustre (Lyons) Symons
Recent records from two or three localities by R.C. Palmer and Dr Franklyn Perring.
Druce: (T. paludosum) [Four localities].

sect. **Spectabilia** (Dahlst.) Dahlst.
A single recent record from between Warkton and Weekley by Dr Franklyn Perring.

Below are listed the microspecies recorded by Druce. The names have generally been updated to conform with the latest taxonomic thought but synonyms are not given. Names in a lighter type have not been traced to currently recognised micro-species

4	**T. brachyglossum** (Dahlst.) Dahlst.
12	**T. fulvum** Raunk.
22	**T. rubicundum** (Dahlst.) Dahlst.
42	**T. naevosum** Dahlst.
72	**T. nordstedtii** Dahlst.
89	**T. hamatum** Raunk.
108	**T. alatum** Lindb. f.
121	**T. cordatum** Palmgren
125	**T. cyanolepis** Dahlst.
130	**T. dilatatum** Lindb. f.
148	**T. laciniosum** Dahlst.
149	**T. laeticolor** Dahlst.
158	**T. longisquameum** Lindb. f.
166	**T. mimulum** Dahlst.
178	**T. pallescens** Dahlst.
204	**T. subexpallidum** Dahlst.
213	**T. tenebricans** (Dahlst.) Dahlst.
	T. orcadense Dahlst
	T. privum Dahlst.

26 CREPIS L.
3 C. biennis L.
Rough Hawk's-beard
Native. Rough grassy places.
Rare. Only known from two or three sites on railway lines in the county. A glabrous form was found in quantity in a set-aside field near Nene Bridge in the Soke of Peterborough in 1993.
First record: H.C. Watson 1851
Druce: Local.

4 C. capillaris (L.) Wallr.   (124)
Smooth Hawk's-beard

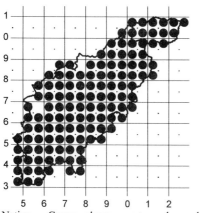

5 6 7 8 9 0 1 2

Native. Grassy places, waste and rough ground.
Very common in all areas.
First record: Gulliver 1841
Druce: Abundant and generally distributed.

5 C. vesicaria L.
Beaked Hawk's-beard
a subsp. **taraxacifolia** (Thuill.) Thell. ex Schinz
& Keller   (99)
(*C. taraxacifolia* Thuill.)

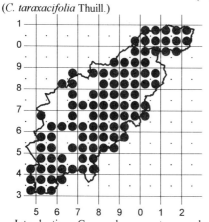

5 6 7 8 9 0 1 2

Introduction. Grassy places, waste ground.
Very common throughout beside roads, waste ground, especially where soil is bare or newly broken, and other suitable places.
First record: Druce 1877
Druce: (C. taraxifolia) Now abundant and widely distributed.

6 C. foetida L.
Stinking Hawk's-beard

Native. Rough ground.
Extinct, if ever present.
First record: 1712, Mr Bobart
Druce: "This [record of Mr Bobart] has never been rediscovered. One wonders if the plant was not taraxacifolia [i.e. C. vesicaria subsp. taraxicifolia])."

C. setosa Haller f.
Introduction. Casual with crops.
No recent record.
First record: A. French, 1875
Druce: Rare.

27 PILOSELLA Hill
2   P. officinarum F.Schultz & Schultz-Bip.
                                                  (106)
(*Hieracium pilosella* L.)
Mouse-ear-hawkweed

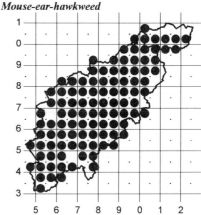

5 6 7 8 9 0 1 2

Native. Short grassland on well drained soils.
Fairly common throughout the county on railway banks, old quarries and in churchyards and similar dry pasture areas.
First record: Notcutt 1843
Druce: (Hieracium pilosella) Locally abundant in dry sunny situations on sandy or calcareous soils.

2 x 6 P. officinarum x P. aurantiaca = P. x stolonifera (Waldst. & Kit.) F.Schultz & Schultz-Bip
Native. Short grassland on well drained soils..
No recent records.
First record: Druce 1899
Druce: [No status given, only one record].

3 P. flagellaris (Willd.) Sell & C.West
Shetland Mouse-ear-hawkweed
a subsp. flagellaris
Introduction. Grassy roadsides and railway banks as a garden escape.
Extremely rare. It was first found by Druce on the railway between Roade and Hanslope in 1899. Subsequently it was discovered on the mineral railway from the ironstone quarry at Irthlingborough in 1967 by F.D.Payne. In 1978 Seán Karley recorded it from the banks of the River Ise and Finedon Pits where it was very well established. There is also a colony at Raunds on the old railway.
First record: Druce 1899
Druce: (Hieracium stoloniflorum) [No status given].

4 P. praealta (Villars ex Gochnat) F.Schultz & Schultz-Bip.
Tall Mouse-ear-hawkweed
a subsp. praealta
(subsp. *brunneocrocea* (Pugsley) Sell & C. West)
Introduction. Rough ground and railway banks.
Recorded on the old railway line between Chacombe and Thorpe Mandeville by R.C.Palmer in 1964, confirmed by Sell and West.
First record: G.C.Druce 1899
Druce: (Hieracium praealtum) [No status given. The first record is the only one named. It was still there in 1929].

6 P. aurantiaca (L.) F.Schultz & Schultz-Bip.
(Hieracium aurantiacum L.)
Fox-and-cubs
a subsp. aurantiaca   (18)
Introduction. Rough ground, railway banks.
Occasionally found as an escape from cottage gardens.

b subsp. carpathicola (Naeg. & Peter) Sojak
(Hieracium aurantiacum L. subsp. *carpathicola* Naeg. & Peter)   (9)
Introduction. Rough grassland.
Established in many places on railway banks, roadsides and waste places.
First record: (Hieracium aurantiacum?) possibly Canons Ashby 1916
Druce: [No status given].

28 HIERACIUM L.
The species recorded during the collection of data for this flora have all been verified by authorites, unless otherwise stated. It is certain that further work could usefully be carried out and that the species here are very much under-recorded.

1 H. sabaudum L.
(H. perpropinquum (Zahn) Druce)
Native. Railway banks and woodland.
It has been recorded from Bucknell Wood in 1965, by R.C.Palmer, Southey Wood and Wothorpe Grove in 1971, by J.H.Chandler and from the old railway line at Thrapston in 1986, by Dr F.H.Perring.
First record: Morton 1712
Druce: Local and rather rare.

4 H. salticola (Sudre) Sell & C.West
Native. Disused railway banks.
Recorded in Wellingborough between 1971 and 1981, determined by Claude Andrews.

5 H. vagum Jordan
Native. Railway banks.
Found on the railway between Eydon and Moreton Pinkney, determined by Claude Andrews.

6 H. umbellatum L.
a subsp. umbellatum
Native. Dry banks.
Extremely rare. Well established on a disused railway line and bridge in Wellingborough since 1964, when it was first recorded by F.D.Payne. The only other record is from the Braunston railway area, by M.D.Jones in the 1960s.
First record: Morton 1712
Druce: Very local.

21 H. trichocaulon (Dahlst.) Johansson
Native. Heathy Woods
No recent records
First record: Notcutt 1843
Druce: (H. tridentatum) Very rare.

62 H. vulgatum Fries
Common Hawkweed
Native. Railway banks and dry places.
There are at present several unconfirmed records of this species, mainly from railway banks and associated areas at

Wellingborough, Irchester and Irthlingborough and on the railway near Charwelton.
First record: Probably J.Morton 1712
First certain record: G.C.Druce 1910
Druce: (H. lachenalii) Very local. [Eight localities are named].

68 H. cheriense Jordan ex Boreau
Native. Old Quarries.
Recorded from the quarry at Helpston in 1976 by B.N.K.Davis, confirmed by P.D.Sell.

69 H. acuminatum Jordan
Native. Wooded banks.
No recent records.
First certain record: Druce 1910
Druce: Very local.

72 H. diaphanum Fries
Native. Old quarries.
Recorded in the quarry at Newton-in-the-Willows in 1971, confirmed by Claude Andrews.
First record:Druce 1910
Druce: (H. cacuminatum) Very local.

74 H. maculatum Smith
Spotted Hawkweed
Native. Roadside verges.
Extremely rare. Recorded on a roadside verge at an old quarry near Newton-in-the-Willows and in a nearby quarry in 1971, and in Wellingborough in 1984, confirmed by Claude Andrews.
First record: Notcutt 1843
Druce: Very local. [Borough Hill and between Roade and Castlethorpe (1906) are the only localities named].

137 H. severiceps Wiinst.
Native. Old quarries.
Recorded by J.N.Mills in the ironstone pits at Finedon in 1971, and confirmed by P.D.Sell.

140 H. exotericum Jordan ex Boreau
Native. Rough ground.
A single record on the railway.

30 FILAGO L.
1 F. vulgaris Lam. (9)
(*F. germanica* L., non Hudson)
Common Cudweed

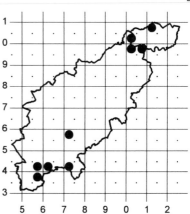

Native. Dry sandy places.
Very rare. Now probably only in woodlands with a sandy acid soil. It occurs plentifully at Ring Haw and in other quarries near Yarwell in the north of the county and also from Wicken and Whistley Woods in the south. It was formerly on the old mineral railway line at Hunsbury Hill.
First record: Notcutt 1843
Druce: (F. germanica) Local.

4 F. minima (Smith) Pers.
Small Cudweed
Native. Neutral to mildly acid grassland.
Probably extinct. Not seen during the present survey, but it was recorded in a sandpit in the area to the south of Northamptonon a BSBI outing in the 1950s, and from a garden path in Kettering in 1953.
First record: Morton 1712
Druce: Very rare.

5 F. gallica L.
Narrow-leaved Cudweed
Introduction. Arable weed.
Not seen since 1838, when it was recorded at Kings Cliffe. Now confined to Sark in the Channel Isles.
First record: Irvine 1838
Druce: Very rare, not recently observed.

31 ANTENNARIA Gaertner
1 A. dioica (L.) Gaertner
Mountain Everlasting, Cat's Foot
Native. Heathland.

Extremely rare. Recorded from Barnack Hills and Holes in the Soke of Peterborough, one of the most southerly localities in Britain.
First record: Dr Bowles 1650
Druce: Very rare.

33 GNAPHALIUM L.
2 G. sylvaticum L.
Heath Cudweed

Native. Open ground and heaths. Extremely rare. Only previously known from Harlestone Firs and Bedford Purlieus where it was very unpredictable in its appearance. A single plant was recorded in Wakerley Woods in 1993 by Peggy Tuffs.
First record: Morton 1712
Druce: Very rare.

5 G. uliginosum L. (57)
Marsh Cudweed

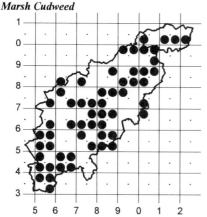

Native. Damp places in fields, arable land and woodland rides.
Occasional. Scattered through the county and the Soke of Peterborough. It is very common around reservoirs, in the draw down zone.
First record: Notcutt 1843
Druce: Locally abundant and widely distributed.

35 INULA L.
1 I. helenium L.
Elecampane

Introduction. Verges, hedgerows etc.
Formerly grown as a medicinal herb and very occasionally occurring as a remnant of cultivation.

First record: Morton 1712
Druce: Very rare.

3 I. conyzae (Griess.) Meikle (34)
(*I. conyza* DC.)
Ploughman's-spikenard

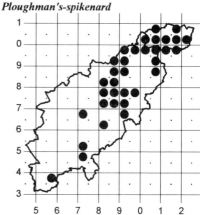

Native. Calcareous quarries, grassland.
Occasional. Found in dry, fairly open calcareous habitats but does not appear to the west of the Watling Street (A5) with one exception near Brackley on a disused railway embankment.
First record: Morton 1712
Druce: (I. squarrosa) Local.

37 PULICARIA Gaertner
1 P. dysenterica (L.) Bernh. (79)
Common Fleabane

Native. Wet grassland, ditches.
Occasional. Decreasing due to drainage and improvement of grassland but still occurs in

suitable wet habitats e.g. woodland rides, rough meadows, verges.
First record: G.Baker, 1822
Druce: Locally abundant and widely distributed in clayey areas.

40 SOLIDAGO L.
1 S. virgaurea L.
Goldenrod
Native. Open woodland and grassland. Probably extinct. It no longer occurs in Druce's localities in Harlestone, Borough Hill, Brigstock and Badby Woods, where it was last recorded in 1876, although there is a record from the 1960s in Laundimer Woods by Oundle School.
First record: Morton 1712
Druce: Very Local.

3 S. canadensis L.
Canadian Goldenrod
Introduction. Waste land, verges, banks etc. Scattered throughout the county but at present probably under-recorded. Well established just beyond the county border near Market Harborough, on the Brampton Valley Way.
First record: Shaw 1907
Druce: [No status given].

4 S. gigantea Aiton
(*S. serotina* Aiton)
Early Goldenrod
a subsp. **serotina** (Kuntze) McNeill
Introduction. Waste land.
Occasional.
First record: 1929
Druce: (S. serotina) [No status given].

41 ASTER L.
4 A. novi-belgii L.
Confused Michaelmas-daisy
Introduction. Waste and rough ground. Occasional as an established plant in the wild.
First record: J.L. Gilbert (Peterborough) 1951 (believed to be this species)

5 A. lanceolatus Willd.
Narrow-leaved Michaelmas-daisy
Introduction. Hedgerows and waste ground. Occasional as an established plant in the wild, although at present it is probably under-recorded.

6 A. tripolium L.
Sea Aster
British. Road verges. Introduction, possibly with salt spray, to the verges of the A 45 Northampton Ring Road in the 1980s.
First record: Nick Scott 1980s

7 A. linosyris (L.) Bernh.
Goldilocks Aster
British. Waste places. No recent record.
First record: J. Leach, 1910
Druce: Very rare.

43 ERIGERON L.
6 E. acer L.   (54)
Blue Fleabane

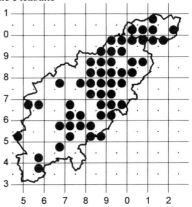

Native. Bare, sandy or limestone soils. Occasional. Scattered throughout the eastern half of the county where it has benefitted from new areas of bare land both as a consequence of gravel working and ironstone quarrying.
First record: Morton 1712
Druce: Local and rather rare.

44 CONYZA Less.
1 C. canadensis (L.) Cronq.   (48)
(*Erigeron canadensis* L.)
Canadian Fleabane
Introduction. Waste or rough ground. Occasional, but becoming more common in the built-up parts of the county, having a liking for waste ground in towns and disused railway lines etc.

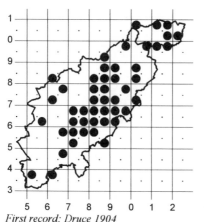

First record: Druce 1904
Druce:(Erigeron canadensis) Casual, likely to spread.

47 BELLIS L.
1 B. perennis L. (132)
Daisy

Native. Short grass, especially lawns. Very common. It is found in every square within the county and the Soke of Peterborough.
First record: Morton 1712
Druce: Abundant and generally distributed.

48 TANACETUM L.
1 T. parthenium (L.) Schultz-Bip. (56)
(*Chrysanthemum parthenium* (L.) Bernh.)
Feverfew
Introduction. Walls, waste ground and waysides.

Occasional. Possibly under-recorded as a cottage garden escape within villages. A rayless, and a double form occur occasionally.
First record: Gulliver 1841
Druce: (Chrysanthemum parthenium) Rare.

3 T. vulgare L. (32)
(*Chrysanthemum vulgare* (L.) Bernh., non (Lam.) Gaterau)
Tansy

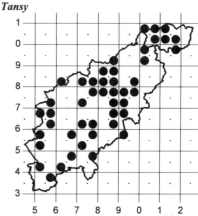

Native. Grassy places and waysides.
Well scattered through the county and usually quite common on railway banks, particularly at Northampton and Wellingborough. It grows in profusion beside the railway at Barford Bridge.
First record: Morton 1712
Druce: Rare.

T. balsamita L.
(*B. major* Desf., *Chrysanthemum balsamita* (L.) Baillon non L.)
Costmary
Introduction. Garden relic.
No recent records.
First record: H.N.Dixon, 1906
Druce: (C. balsamita) Very rare.
[Collyweston is the only locality named].

50 ARTEMISIA L.
1 A. vulgaris L. (121)
Mugwort
Native. Rough grassland and waste ground. Very common. Occurs in suitable localities throughout the county.

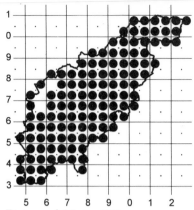

First record: Morton 1712
Druce: Rather common and widely distributed.

3 A. absinthium L. (18)
Wormwood

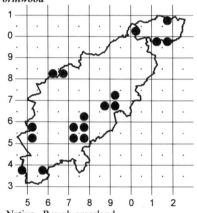

Native. Rough grassland.
Uncommon. Occuring mainly on rubbish tips and other waste areas throughout the county, particularly near railways. It has been present near the main London railway line at Wellingborough for over 45 years.
First record: Baker 1822
Druce: Rare.

7 A. biennis Willd.
Slender Mugwort
Introduction. Waste ground and reservoirs
No recent records.
First record: J. Leach, 1911
Druce: Rare.

A. dracunculus L.
Tarragon
Introduction. Tips and waste ground.
One recent record from dumped soil in a field at Rushton near the railway.

A. scoparia Waldst. & Kit.
Introduction. Waste places.
No recent records.
First record: J. Leach 1911, Northampton
Druce: [No status given. Northampton is the only locality given].

53 ACHILLEA L.
1 A. ptarmica L. (41)
Sneezewort

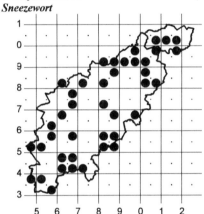

Native. Damp fields and marshy places.
Uncommon and decreasing, confined to scarce marshy ground. It occurs at three places on the River Welland, at Middle Bridge, near Drayton and on a river shoal near Caldecot, in grasslands at Corby, at Yardley Chase, Salcey Forest and Barnwell Wold plus several other localities.
First record: Baker 1822
Druce: Scattered throughout the county.

3 A. millefolium L. (131)
Yarrow
Native. Short grassland.
Very common. Found throughout in verges, hedgerows, field margins, lawns etc.
First record: Gulliver 1841
Druce: Common and generally distributed.

250

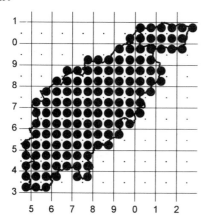

54 CHAMAEMELUM Miller
1 C. nobile (L.) All.
Chamomile
British. Short grassy places.
No recent records.
First record: 1880
Druce: (Anthemis nobile) Very rare.

55 ANTHEMIS L.
2 A. arvensis L. (6)
Corn Chamomile

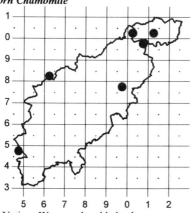

Native. Waste and arable land.
Very rare and only occurring in scattered areas, near Chipping Warden, Welford and Woodford; and from the areas of Castor Hanglands, Easton on the Hill and Wittering areas of the Soke of Peterborough.
First record: Pitt 1813
Druce: Local.

3 A. cotula L. (41)
Stinking Chamomile, Stinking Mayweed

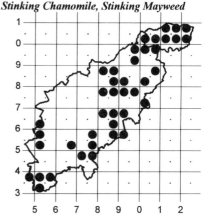

Native. Rough or marginal ground.
Fairly frequent as a weed in arable fields, but generally confined to the eastern areas, mainly on limestone soils.
First record: Morton 1712
Druce: Abundant and generally distributed.

4 A. tinctoria L.
Yellow Chamomile
Introduction. Waste and marginal land.
Extremely rare. Present at three isolated sites, at one of which, near Irthlingborough, it has been present for at least thirty years.
First record: Druce 1899
Druce: Locally abundant.

56 CHRYSANTHEMUM L.
1 C. segetum L. (45)
Corn Marigold

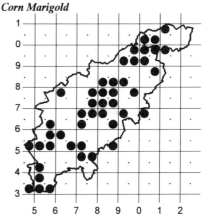

Introduction. Arable field margins. A victim of modern farming practices, it still exists in a few of the localities cited by Druce, including Rothwell, which is the locality of the first county record. It can also be found on disturbed ground along new road verges.
First record: Pitt 1813
Druce: Local.

58 LEUCANTHEMUM Miller
1 L. vulgare Lam. (122)
(*Chrysanthemum leucanthemum* L.)
Oxeye Daisy, Moon Daisy, Dog Daisy

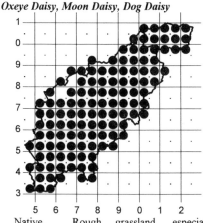

Native. Rough grassland, especially calcareous.
Frequent. Found on a wide variety of suitable sites: old hay meadows, railway banks etc. and especially new road verges where it may sometimes be introduced in seed mixes.
First record: Gulliver 1841
Druce: (Chrysanthemum leucanthemum) Abundant and generally distributed.

L. x superbum (Bergmans ex J.Ingram) D.H.Kent
(*Chrysanthemum x maximum* hort., non Ramond)
Shasta Daisy
Introduction. Waste ground and rough grass. Often escaping and becoming established on rubbish tips, quarry banks and roadsides.

59 MATRICARIA L.
1 M. recutita L. (45)
Scented Chamomile, Wild Chamomile, Scented Mayweed
Introduction. Weed of bare ground.

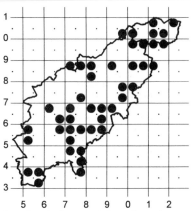

Occasional. Scattered throughout the county on the lighter soils.
First record: Gulliver 1841
Druce: (M. chamomilla) Common and widely distributed.

2 M. discoidea DC. (128)
(*M. matricarioides* (Less.) Porter, pro parte, non. illegit.)
Pineappleweed, Pineapple Mayweed

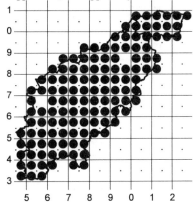

Introduction. Weed of bare ground.
Common. Found throughout the county in field edges, on roadsides and especially in gateways etc. where it withstands trampling.
First record: H. N. Dixon 1909
Druce: (M. suaveolens) Rapidly spreading.

60 TRIPLEUROSPERMUM Schultz-Bip.
2 T. inodorum (L.) Schultz-Bip. (126)
(*T. maritima* L. subsp. *inodorum*)
Scentless Mayweed

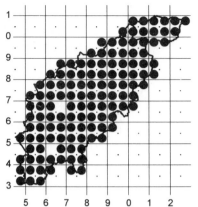

5 6 7 8 9 0 1 2

Native. Waste land and field margins. Common. Found throughout the county in all suitable habitats.

First record: Gulliver 1841

Druce: *(Matricaria inodora) Common and generally distributed.*

62 SENECIO L.

4 S. fluviatilis Wallr.

Broad-leaved Ragwort

Introduction. Streamsides and ditches. Naturalised in a roadside ditch between Cranford and Woodford, now cut off by recent road-building. It is spreading at this site.

First record: Cook 1971

10 S. jacobaea L. (127)

Common Ragwort

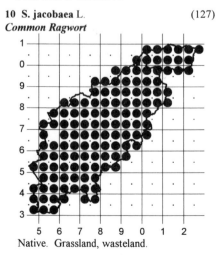

5 6 7 8 9 0 1 2

Native. Grassland, wasteland.

Common. Found on all but the poorest soils, but usually not on grazed land where it has been eradicated because it is poisonous to cattle. Rare in some calcareous areas where it is replaced by *S. erucifolius.*

First record: Pitt 1813

Druce: *Common and generally distributed.*

11 S. aquaticus Hill (29)

Marsh Ragwort

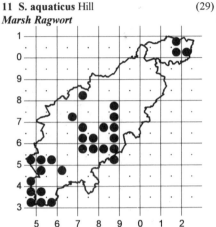

5 6 7 8 9 0 1 2

Native. Marshes, river banks.

Occasional. Mostly found on the banks of streams, in the west and centre of the county, and again in the Soke of Peterborough.

First record: Dickson 1792

Druce: *Locally common and widely distributed over the clay areas.*

12 S. erucifolius L. (95)

Hoary Ragwort

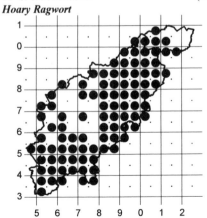

5 6 7 8 9 0 1 2

Native. Grasslands, verges, especially on calcareous soils.
Occasional. Sometimes replacing *S. jacobaea* in limestone areas, especially on roadside verges, woodland rides and grassy banks.
First record: Dickson 1792
Druce: [No status given. More than 40 localities are named].

13 S. squalidus L. (83)
Oxford Ragwort

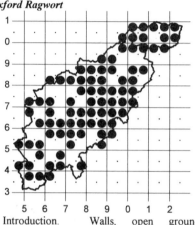

Introduction. Walls, open ground, occasionally railways.
Occasional. Originally on the ballast of railways radiating from Oxford; rarely in these habitats now, and it is more common on waste areas and roadsides, especially where there has been recent disturbance.
First record: Druce 1916
Druce: Rare. [Only two localities named].

13 x 18   S. squalidus x S. viscosus = S. x subnebrodensis Simonkai
(*S. x londinensis* Lousley)
Native. Railway ballast, gravels etc.
Rare. Found on disused sidings at Wellingborough and in Peterborough.
First record: J.H.Chandler 1965

15 S. vulgaris L. (131)
Groundsel
Native. Arable ground, gardens and waste places.
Extremely common. Possibly the commonest garden weed. Rayed forms of the plant (*var. hibernicus* Syme), first recorded in 1956, at

Milton, by A.S.Harris and D.E.Allen, are occasionally found and are well established on the Holcot causeway at Pitsford reservoir. A colony in a garden at Wollaston in the early 1980s ousted the common form in about three years, and then vanished.

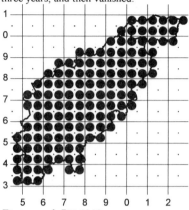

First record: Pitt 1813
Druce: Ubiquitous.

16 S. vernalis Waldst. & Kit.
Eastern Groundsel
Adventive. Arable and waste ground.
Introduced accidentally with grass seed. It appeared on a re-sown verge near to Market Harborough, most of the plants were in Leicestershire and only a few in Northants, but were very short-lived.
First record: Guy Messenger 1968

17 S. sylvaticus L. (9)
Heath Groundsel, Wood Groundsel

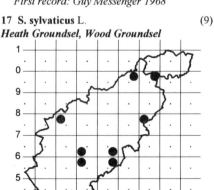

Native. Non-calcareous sands and in woods. Rare. Less common than in Druce's day because of ploughing and improvement of marginal grasslands; now principally in woodlands. Hundreds of plants came up in 1992, in a recently cleared area of Old Pastures, near Yardley Hastings.
First record: Baker 1822
Druce: Local.

18 S. viscosus L.   (70)
Sticky Groundsel

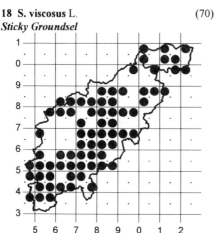

Adventive. Railway ballast, gravel. Occasional. Often with *S. squalidus* on bare ground, especially gravel and sand, particularly in man-made habitats. It is increasing, probably due to new habitats being created.
First record: Druce 1919
Druce: A recent introduction [Recorded in only two localities].

64 TEPHROSERIS (Reichb.) Reichb.
1 T. integrifolia (L.) Holub.
Field Fleawort
(*Senecio integrifolius* (L.) Clairv.)
a subsp. *integrifolia*
Native. Calcareous grasslands. Extinct. The only records are from near Southorpe, prior to 1712, and Wittering prior to 1930.
First record: J.Morton 1712
Druce: (Senecio integrifolius) Very rare.

69 DORONICUM L.
1 D. pardalianches L.
Leopard's-bane, Greater Leopard's-bane

Introduction. Spinneys, plantations. Established in a few small areas of woodland, mainly near habitation, and usually long-lived.
Druce: Very rare.   [Five localities are named].

1 x 2 D. pardalianches x D. plantagineum = D. x willdenowii (Rouy) A.W.Hill
Willdenow's Leopard's-bane
Introduction. Shaded places. One record from a roadside between West Haddon and Long Buckby in 1981.
First record: Ian Cameron 1981

2 D. plantagineum L.
Plantain-leaved   Leopard's-bane,   Common Leopard's-bane
Introduction. Spinneys, plantations. A garden escape in the same habitats as *D. pardalianches*.
Druce: Very rare. [Four localities named].

70 TUSSILAGO L.
1 T. farfara L.   (126)
Colt's-foot

Native. Verges and waste places. Common on clay soils, especially cuttings and embankments, spoil heaps of old ironstone quarries and verges. The first yellow composite to flower in the spring.
First record: Morton 1712
Druce: Frequent, especially common on railway-banks.

71 PETASITES Miller
1 P. hybridus (L.) P.Gaertner, Meyer & Scherb.   (49)
Butterbur

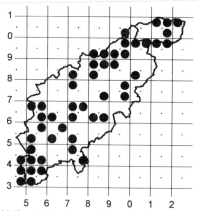

5 6 7 8 9 0 1 2

Native. Wet places and stream sides. Occasional. More common in the western areas of the county, often in large patches of the usually 'male' plants. 'Female' plants are known to occur at Apethorpe in the north-east and at Boughton, near Northampton.
First record: Baker 1822
Druce: (P. petasites) Locally common, but absent from large areas.

2 P. japonicus (Siebold & Zucc.) Maxim.
Giant Butterbur
Introduction. Damp places.
This early flowering species is naturalised in the wild garden at Rockingham Castle.

3 P. albus (L.) Gaertner
White Butterbur
Introduction. Waste places.
An escape from the gardens of large country estates, it is found in Castle Ashby and Maidwell churchyards.
First record: Rogers
Druce: [No status given. Castle Ashby is the only locality named].

4 P. fragrans (Villars) C.Presl
Winter Heliotrope
Introduction. Verges, waste places.
Rare. Naturalised as an escape from gardens. Scattered throughout the county, mainly in or near villages.
Druce: Rare. [Only two localities].

73 CALENDULA L.
1 C. officinalis L.
Pot Marigold
Introduction. Waste ground, tips.

A frequent, but short-lived garden escape.
Druce: [No status given. Five well distributed localities are named].

74 AMBROSIA L.
1 A. artemisiifolia L.
Ragweed, Common Ragweed
Adventive. Waste ground, tips etc.
There is only one record from a fowl-run in Yarwell in 1953.
First record: Leach 1910
Druce: Rare. [Only a single locality].

76 XANTHIUM L.
2 X. spinosum L.
Spiny Cocklebur
Adventive. Arable weed.
No recent records. The spines of the fruit often became fastened in wool and consequently discarded in shoddy, which was formerly used as manure on light sandy soils.
First record: Goode 1917
Druce: [No status given, but only recorded from the site of the first record].

79 HELIANTHUS L.
1 H. annuus L.
Sunflower
Introduction. Waste ground especially rubbish tips.
A few records on rubbish tips etc., probably derived from bird seed, lasting for a short time only. Sometimes grown as a farm crop for its oily seeds.

80 GALINSOGA Ruiz Lopez & Pavón
1 G. parviflora Cav. (8)
Gallant-soldier

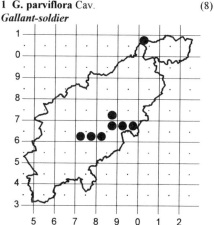

5 6 7 8 9 0 1 2

Adventive. Gardens and waste places. Uncommon. A fairly recent addition to our county flora, it also occurs in window-boxes and cracks in pavements.
First record: J. Chandler, Wothorpe 1966

2 G. quadriradiata Ruiz Lopez & Pavón (5)
(*G. ciliata* (Raf.) S.F.Blake)
Shaggy-soldier

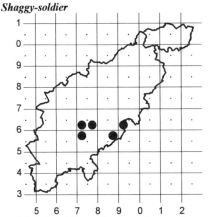

Adventive. Waste places, gardens etc. Rare. First recorded in England in 1909, it has spread rapidly as a weed of cultivation. Only known from five areas in Northants, but it could become more common in the future.
First record: S.L.M.Karley, Wollaston, 1968
Druce: [Not known in Northamptonshire in Druce's day].

81 BIDENS L.
1 Bidens cernua L. (10)
Nodding Bur-marigold

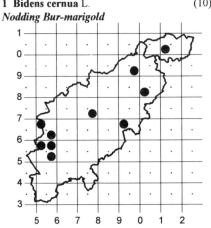

Native. Streamsides and ponds, especially where water stands during the winter. Rare. Found mainly in the Fawsley area. It is also quite common around Pitsford and Daventry reservoirs, Titchmarsh nature reserve and the canal near Welton.
First record: Baker 1822
Druce: Very local [six localities named].

1 x 2 B. cernua x B. tripartita = B. x peacockii Druce
This hybrid is recorded by Druce from Sibbertoft. Recent research by Tutin (Stace 1975) has cast doubts on its authenticity.

2 Bidens tripartita L. (40)
Trifid Bur-marigold

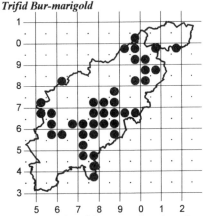

Native. Sides of rivers, canals and ponds. Occasional. Widely distributed throughout the county in suitable habitats but never common.
First record: Gulliver 1841
Druce: Rather local.

3 B. connata Mühlenb. ex Willd.
London Bur-marigold
Introduction. Canals.
This fairly recent introduction, although known for some years from Buckinghamshire, was recorded in Northamptonshire close to the county boundary in 1994.
First record: Roy Maycock and Aaron Woods, 1994.

86 EUPATORIUM L.
1 E. cannabinum L. (39)
Hemp-agrimony

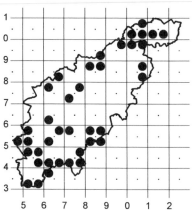

5 6 7 8 9 0 1 2

Native. Damp places and beside water.
Occasional. Found mainly in the south and north-east of the county. It is very common in some damp woodlands.
First record: Morton 1712
Druce: Locally common and widely distributed.

LILIIDAE
Monocotyledons

136 BUTOMACEAE
1 BUTOMUS L.
1 B. umbellatus L. (35)
Flowering-rush

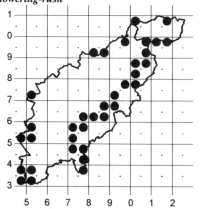

5 6 7 8 9 0 1 2

Native. Rivers and canals.
Occasional. Found on canal sides and in most stretches of the Nene, less frequently in the Welland, (although it is abundant in the old meanders near Bringhurst and Caldecot).
First record: Pitt 1813

Druce: Locally common.

137 ALISMATACEA
1 SAGITTARIA L.
1 S. sagittifolia L. (60)
Arrowhead

5 6 7 8 9 0 1 2

Native. In all sorts of shallow water.
Common throughout the county in rivers, streams and canals.
First record: Baker 1822
Druce: Locally common.

2 BALDELLIA Parl. (3)
1 B. ranunculoides (L.) Parl.
Lesser Water-plantain
Native. Still water.
Very rare. It still occurs in the Soke of Peterborough in a few fen ditches, but seems to have disappeared from Castor Hanglands where it formerly occurred.
First record: Paley 1860
Druce: (Echinodorus ranunculoides) Very local.

3 LURONIUM Raf.
1 L. natans (L.) Raf.
Floating Water-plantain
Native. Still waters.
Extremely rare. There is one record for the county from old gravel workings near Castle Ashby in 1986 but it has not been seen subsequently.
First record: George Crawford 1986

4 ALISMA L.
1 A. plantago-aquatica L. (104)
Water Plantain

258

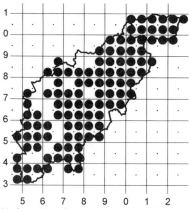

5   6   7   8   9   0   1   2

Native. Wet places, particularly still waters.
Common and widespread in ponds, canals,
rivers and other suitable habitats.
First record: Gulliver 1841
Druce: Common and widely distributed.

2 A. lanceolatum With.   (10)
Narrow-leaved Water-plantain
Native. Wet places, particularly small, still
water bodies.
Rare, but probably under-recorded. Found in
scattered localities throughout the county; in
ponds near Onley, Horton and Grendon and
in the canal near Grafton Regis. It is also
present in some of the fen ditches in the Soke.

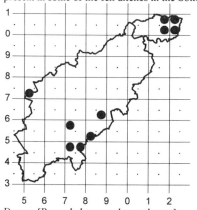

5   6   7   8   9   0   1   2

Druce: [Recorded as var. lanceolatum].

138 HYDROCHARITACEAE
1 HYDROCHARIS L.
1 H. morsus-ranae L.
Frogbit

Native. Still waters.
Thought to be extinct as it has not been seen
since 1957, although in 1993 it was recorded
at Sywell Country Park as an introduction. It
is also known to be in the Nene Washes.
First record: Morton 1712
Druce: Local and rare.

2 STRATIOTES L.
1 S. aloides L.
Water-soldier
Native. Still waters.
Only three locations in the county. Certainly
an introduction at one site, a pond near
Draughton, and probably introduced at the
other two - Drayton House fish ponds and
ponds at Ailsworth Heath.
First record: Morton 1712
Druce: Very rare if not extinct.

4 ELODEA Michaux
1 E. canadensis Michaux   (71)
Canadian Waterweed, Canadian Pondweed
Adventive. All water bodies.
Less common than previously, although still
widespread throughout the county.

5   6   7   8   9   0   1   2

First record: T. Kirk 1850
Druce: Common and widely distributed.

2 E. nuttallii (Planchon) H.St.John   (22)
Nuttall's Waterweed
Adventive. All water bodies.
Becoming more common particularly in the
Nene and Welland, often overlooked owing
to difficulty in identification.

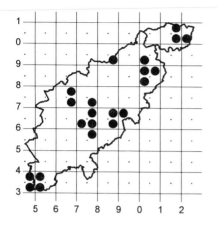

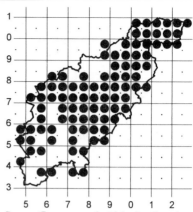

5 6 7 8 9 0 1 2

Druce: Common and widely distributed.

6 LAGAROSIPHON Harvey
1 L. major (Ridley) Moss
(*Elodea crispa* Hort)
Adventive. Still waters.
Two records only from ponds near Brigstock and Maidwell. It is sold in aquarist centres as *Elodea crispa* and sometimes introduced by pond-keepers.
First record: Brian Adams 1993

141 JUNCAGINACEAE
1 TRIGLOCHIN L.
1 T. palustre L.
Marsh Arrowgrass
Native. Marshy places and wet fields.
Very rare. Although never a common plant it is still found in the county where there are suitable habitats such as in Mawsley and Badby Marshes, the old fish ponds near Titchmarsh, Castor Hanglands, Sutton Bog and White Water.
First record: Dickson 1792
Druce: Local and rather rare.

142 POTAMOGETONACEAE
1 POTAMOGETON L.
1 P. natans L.   (93)
Broad-leaved Pondweed, Floating Pondweed
Native. Mostly established in still waters, but occasionally will grow in running water. It will tolerate some pollution.
Fairly common in all parts of the county, particularly in small ponds.
First record: Morton 1712

1 x 5 P. natans x P. lucens = P. x fluitans
Roth
Native. Large water bodies.
Probably extinct. There is one record by Chester from Peakirk but it has not been recorded since.
First record: G. Chester 1914

2 P. polygonifolius Pourret
Bog Pondweed
British. Acid bogs and ponds.
Doubtful county status - Dandy doubts if it ever existed in the county.
First record: Druce 1912
Druce: (P. oblongus) Rare.

3 P. coloratus Hornem.
Fen Pondweed
Native. Still water.
Extremely rare, with only one location in the county; at an old ironstone pit near Corby. It was previously found in the Soke by Druce.
First record: Druce 1910
Druce: Very local.

5 P. lucens L.   (45)
Shining Pondweed
Native. Still and slow flowing waters.
Not uncommon in the Nene and Welland and the Grand Union Canal, some reservoirs, large lakes and gravel pits, often growing abundantly.
First record: Morton 1712
Druce: Common and widely distributed.

260

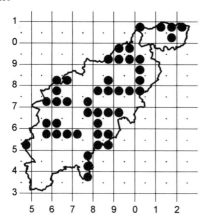

5 6 7 8 9 0 1 2

5 x 6 P. lucens x P. gramineus = P. x zizii
Koch ex Roth
Long-leaved Pondweed
Native. Fen dykes.
Probably extinct, recorded by Druce in Car
Dyke but not recorded since.
First record: Druce 1910
Druce: (P. angustifolius) Very rare.

**5 x 9 P. lucens x P. perfoliatus = P. x
salicifolius** Wolfg.
Willow-leaved Pondweed
Native. Still waters.
Extremely rare. It has been recorded for
many years in the canal at Market
Harborough and Foxton so it may be in other
parts of the canal system within the county.
Dandy records it from the canal at Aynho but
it has not been seen there for some years.
First record: Druce 1878
Druce: (x P. decipiens) Very rare.

6 P. gramineus L.
Various-leaved Pondweed
Native. Fen ditches.
Probably extinct. Druce records it from four
localities in the Soke of Peterborough, but it
has not been seen for many years.
First record: Druce 1910
Druce: Very rare.

**6 x 9 P. gramineus x P. perfoliatus = P. x
nitens** G.Weber
Bright-leaved Pondweed
Native. Fen ditches.

Possibly extinct. Recorded only from the
Soke of Peterborough by both Dandy and
Druce, but no recent records.
First record: Druce 1910
Druce: Very rare.

7 P. alpinus Balbis
Red Pondweed
Native. Acid lakes, ditches and streams.
Probably extinct. Recorded from a few
places by Druce, but not seen for many years.
First record: Beesley 1842
Druce: Very rare.

8 P. praelongus Wulfen
Long-stalked Pondweed
Native. Rivers and streams.
Extremely rare and possibly extinct, it was
recorded many years ago from the Nene at
Northampton by Druce, and by Chester from
the Nene near Thrapston.
First record: Druce 1874
Druce: Rare.

9 P. perfoliatus L.   (45)
Perfoliate Pondweed
Native. Rivers, streams and canals.
Common in all suitable habitats throughout
the county and particularly common in the
Nene and Welland. Not common in still
waters other than canals, but it has been
recorded from the bunker ponds within the
M.O.D. area at Yardley Chase, and in a
former gravel pit near Cogenhoe.

1
0
9
8
7
6
5
4
3

5 6 7 8 9 0 1 2

First record: Morton 1712
*Druce: Rather common and widely
distributed.*

11 P. friesii Rupr.
Flat-stalked Pondweed
Native. Still waters.
Probably extinct. Recorded from a few localities by Druce, but not seen for many years.
First record: Druce 1877
Druce: (P. mucronatus) Local.

13 P. pusillus L.   (12)
Lesser Pondweed

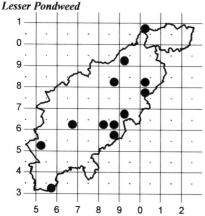

Native. Still and slow running water.
Very occasional, possibly overlooked, found in various locations throughout the county, mostly in lakes and gravel pits.
First record: Druce 1902
Druce: (P. panormitanus) Local.

14 P. obtusifolius Mert. & Koch
Blunt-leaved Pondweed, Grassy Pondweed
Native. Ponds.
Extremely rare, only four locations known in the county, one of which, at Foxhall quarry, has been filled in recently.
First record: Druce 1877
Druce: Very rare.

15 P. berchtoldii Fieber   (21)
Small Pondweed
Native. Slow flowing and still waters.
Occasional. Parts of the Nene; the Welland, where it is found in a backwater near Easton on the Hill, the Grand Union Canal and gravel pits. Also found in lakes and some of the older reservoirs.
First record: Morton 1712
Druce: (P. pusillus) Local.

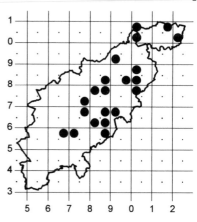

16 P. trichoides Cham. & Schldl.
Hairlike Pondweed
Native. Still waters.
Extremely rare and possibly extinct. An old record collected by Druce from Oxney Lode and cited as *P. interuptus var. diffusus* was determined by Dandy as *P. trichoides.*
First record: Druce [date unknown].

17 P. compressus L.   (14)
Grass-wrack Pondweed
Native. Rivers and streams.
Occasional, found so far only in the Nene, including the old oxbow at Cogenhoe, and the Grand Union Canal.

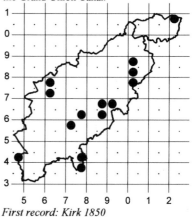

First record: Kirk 1850
Druce: Local.

18 P. acutifolius Link
Sharp-leaved Pondweed
Native. Fens and water meadows.

Probably extinct, the only certain record is from Borough Fen, by Dandy, some years ago and possibly by Druce from High Drove.
First record: Druce 1910 or Dandy (date unknown)
Druce: Very rare.

19 P. crispus L. (60)
Curled Pondweed

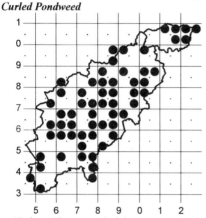

Native. Rivers, ponds, lakes etc. Fairly common. There are plenty of locations throughout ; it is most common in the Ise and Welland and less plentiful in the Nene.
First record: Morton 1712
Druce: Rather local.

21 P. pectinatus L. (69)
Fennel Pondweed, Fennel-leaved Pondweed

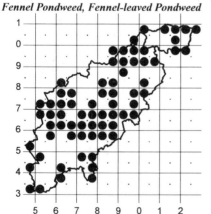

Native. Lakes, reservoirs, rivers and canals. Common and widespread in all suitable localities. Often abundant and the dominant

aquatic plant in gravel pits and reservoirs.
First record: Morton 1712
Druce: (P. pectinatus and P. interuptus) Locally abundant.

2 GROENLANDIA Gay
1 G. densa (L.) Fourr. (17)
Opposite-leaved Pondweed

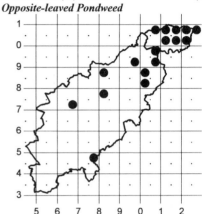

Native. Running water, rarely in still water. Occasional and mainly found in the Soke. It is often plentiful where it does occur.
First record: Morton 1712
Druce: (Potamogeton densus) Locally common.

145 ZANNICHELLIACEAE
1 ZANNICHELLIA L.
1 Z. palustris L. (43)
(Z. gibberosa Reichb.)
Horned Pondweed

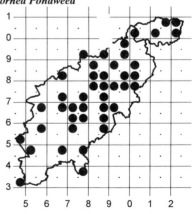

Native. In all types of water bodies. Not uncommon in many areas of the county, but it is easily overlooked due to its superficial resemblance to *Potamogeton pectinatus*. It is found in the River Welland between Market Harborough and Weston by Welland.

First record: Morton 1712
Druce: Local.

147 ARACEAE
1 ACORUS L.
1 A. calamus L. (13)
Sweet-flag
Introduction. River and canal margins. Local, by the River Nene, and by the Grand Union Canal between Yelvertoft and Watford. It was used for strewing on floors during the Middle Ages.

First record: Rev. Berkeley c 1860
Druce: Very local.

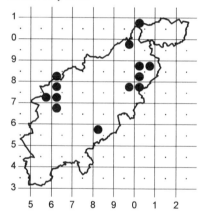

5 ARUM L.
1 A. maculatum L. (126)
Lords-and-Ladies
Native. Woodland and hedgerows. Common and distributed through the county, beneath hedgerows, in woodlands, spinneys, abandoned and overgrown mineral workings and other shaded places. A variant with a yellow spadix occurs rarely. The form with unspotted leaves is the commoner in the county, in spite of the systematic name.

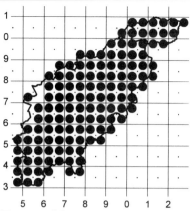

First record: Morton 1712
Druce: Locally common and widely distributed.

148 LEMNACEAE
1 SPIRODELA Schleiden
1 S. polyrhiza (L.) Schleiden
(*Lemna polyrhiza* L.)
Greater Duckweed
Native. Slow and still waters. Extremely rare and decreasing. Only recorded at two localities, near Mallows Cotton and the Grand Union canal near Cosgrove.

First record: Watson 1874
Druce: (Lemna polyrhiza) Not uncommon.

2 LEMNA L.
1 L. gibba L. (16)
Fat Duckweed, Gibbous Duckweed

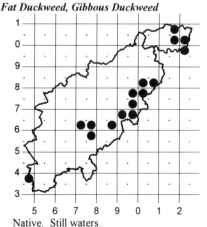

Native. Still waters.

Occasional. Most frequent in the middle reaches of the River Nene but usually among other *Lemna* species and easily overlooked.
First record: Beesley 1842
Druce: Local.

2 L. minor L. (111)
Common Duckweed, Lesser Duckweed

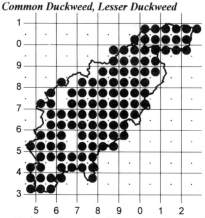

5 6 7 8 9 0 1 2

Native. Slow and still water, cattle troughs, wheel ruts etc.
Common and widespread in all suitable habitats. It is sometimes found in slow running rivers and streams.
First record: Gulliver 1841
Druce: Common and widely distributed.

3 L. trisulca L. (46)
Ivy-leaved Duckweed

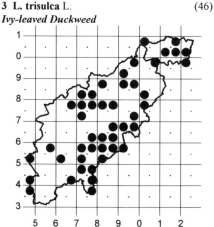

5 6 7 8 9 0 1 2

Native. Slow and still water in ponds, ditches and canals.

Common and widespread in suitable habitats, but often submerged beneath *Lemna minor* and therefore often overlooked.
First record: Goodyear 1660
Druce: Locally common.

4 L. minuta Kunth
(*Lemna minuscula* Herter nom. illegit.; *L. valdiviana* auct., non Philippi)
Least Duckweed
Native. Ponds, ditches and canals.
This new county record was reported from a pond at Ufford in 1991 (confirmed by A.C.Leslie).
First record: C.D.Preston et al (Ufford) 1991

151 JUNCACEAE
1 JUNCUS L.
1 J. squarrosus L.
Heath Rush
Native. Bogs on acid heaths.
Extinct. Last recorded at Harlestone Firs prior to 1930.
First record: Morton 1712
Druce: Very rare.

3 J. compressus Jacq. (8)
Round-fruited Rush

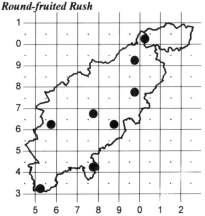

5 6 7 8 9 0 1 2

Native. Marshes and wet meadows.
Rare and only known with any certainty from localities in marshy meadows. There are eight localities including Bulwick marsh, Daventry reservoir, meadows at Denford and Croughton and very strong colonies around Pitsford reservoir.
First record: Druce 1877
Druce: Local.

4 J. gerardii Loisel.
Saltmarsh Rush
British. Saline areas.
Quite large patches of this saltmarsh rush were discovered growing along the margin of Pitsford reservoir in 1993.
First record: (Pitsford) 1993

7 J. bufonius L.   (81)
Toad Rush

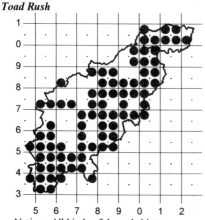

5 6 7 8 9 0 1 2
Native. All kinds of damp habitats.
Fairly common in damp places, woodland rides, pond margins and on bare mud where it will often be one of the early colonisers.
First record: 1842
Druce: Locally common.

11 J. subnodulosus Schrank   (33)
Blunt-flowered Rush

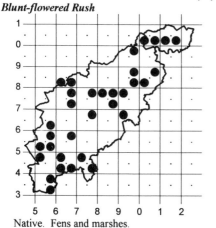

5 6 7 8 9 0 1 2
Native. Fens and marshes.
Occasional.   A local species of base-rich

marshes, and scattered through the county in suitable areas.   It has been recorded at St Luke's meadow, near Wakerley, where it grows with *Eriophorum angustifolium* and *J. inflexus* and has recently been discovered in a marshy field near Wellingborough.
First record: Mr Stockdale 1788
Druce: Locally abundant, chiefly in basic soils, and absent from considerable areas.

13 J. articulatus L.   (107)
Jointed Rush

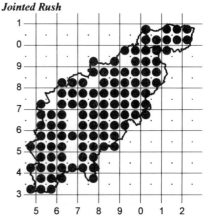

5 6 7 8 9 0 1 2
Native.   Damp grassland, woodland rides, marshes etc.
Very common throughout the county in suitable habitats.
First record: Notcutt 1843
Druce: Rather common.

14 J. acutiflorus Ehrh. ex Hoffm.   (43)
Sharp-flowered Rush

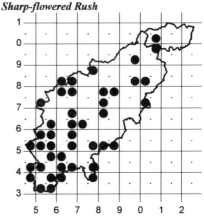

5 6 7 8 9 0 1 2

Native. Marshes, damp grassland and river margins.
Occasional. A very local species of marshes and swamps and scattered in a few localities through the county.
First record: 1842
Druce: Local.

15 J. bulbosus L.
Bulbous Rush
Native. Wet and damp places.
Extremely rare. Recorded at Kilsby landfill site and Mawsley Marsh SSSI, the only two records during the period of this survey.
First record: Morton 1712
Druce: Very local.

25 J. inflexus L.   (127)
Hard Rush

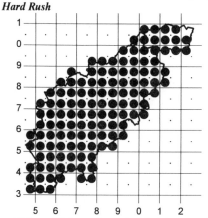

Native. Wet meadows, beside lakes, ponds etc.
Very common in damp situations throughout the county.
First record: Clare 1820
Druce: Common on clayey soils in all districts.

26 J. effusus L.   (118)
Soft-rush
Native. Marshes, ditches, damp meadows etc.
Common in marshes, beside water and in wet woodland throughout the county.
First record: Gulliver 1841
Druce: Rather common and widely distributed, although absent from large areas of well drained cultivated country.

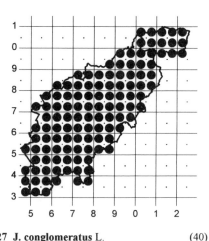

27 J. conglomeratus L.   (40)
Compact Rush, Compact Conglomerate-rush

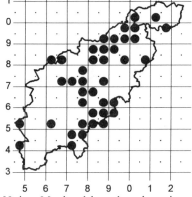

Native. Marshes, lake and pond margins, wet meadows etc.
Very occasional, and generally found on more acid soils in badly drained areas, but also in wet woodland.
First record: Clare 1820
Druce: Locally common.

2 LUZULA DC.
1 L. forsteri (Smith) DC.
Southern Wood-rush
Native. Woods and hedgerows.
Extremely rare. It appears in one ride in Bedford Purlieus fairly constantly.
First record: P. Rixon 1960s

2 L. pilosa (L.) Willd.   (21)
Hairy Wood-rush

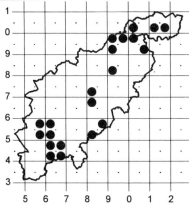

Native. Woods and hedgerows.
Rare. Very local and scattered in woodland on the lighter soils throughout the county.
First record: Notcutt 1843
Druce: (Juncoides pilosum) Rather common and widely spread.

3 L. sylvatica (Hudson) Gaudin (9)
Great Wood-rush

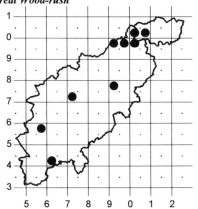

Native. Woods and shaded streamsides.
Very rare. A very local plant restricted to the Soke of Peterborough, Easton Hornstocks and Wakerley in the north of county and to Badby and Whittlebury in the south.
First record: Morton 1712
Druce: (Juncoides sylvaticum) Very local.

5 L. campestris (L.) DC. (102)
Field Wood-rush, Good Friday Grass
Native. Short grassland.

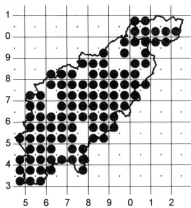

An occasional plant in unimproved pastures, churchyards and other grassy areas. It has decreased due to agricultural improvements.
First record: Beesley 1842
Druce: (Juncoides campestre) Common.

6 L. multiflora (Ehrh.) Lej. (19)
Heath Wood-rush, Many-headed Wood-rush

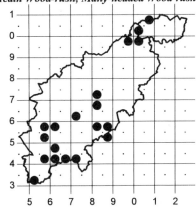

Native. Grassland on acid soil.
Very occasional in damp heathy areas and woodland rides in areas such as Harlestone Firs, Yardley Chase, Badby Woods and Whittlebury Forest.
First record: Notcutt 1843
Druce: (Juncoides multiflorum) Local and rather rare.

152 CYPERACEAE
1 ERIOPHORUM L.
1 E. angustifolium Honck.
Common Cottongrass

Native. Acid marshes.
Extremely rare. Known only from four widely scattered sites, including Aldwincle Marsh, Sutton Bog, Bugbrooke Meadows and St. Luke's Meadow, near Wakerley.
First record: Baker 1822
Druce: Very local and, owing to drainage, a decreasing species.

2 E. latifolium Hoppe
Broad-leaved Cottongrass
Native. Bogs.
Probably extinct. The only former locality was at Bonemills Hollow in the former Soke of Peterborough. This site has altered in character however, probably due to the lowering of the water table, and the species has not been seen there in recent years.
First record: J. Dickson 1792
Druce: (E. paniculatum) Rare.

3 E. gracile Koch ex Roth
Slender Cottongrass
Native. Wet acid bogs
Extinct if ever present. The only site, near Easton Hornstocks where it was recorded prior to 1930, has been searched in recent years but no possible habitats remain.
Druce: Needs further study before we can claim it for the county.

3 ELEOCHARIS R.Br.
1 E. palustris (L.) Roemer & Schultes
Common Spike-rush
a subsp. **vulgaris** Walters   (93)

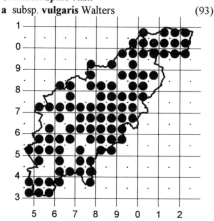

Native. Old quarries, reservoir and pond edges etc.
Frequent. Common within its habitat, and often abundant.
First record: Gulliver 1841
Druce: Common and widely distributed.

3 E. uniglumis (Link) Schultes.
(Scirpus uniglumis Link)
Slender Spike-rush
Native. Marshes.
Presumed extinct. The last known record is by John Gilbert, who recorded it at Sutton Bog in 1955.

4 E. multicaulis (Smith) Desv.
(Scirpus multicaulis Smith)
Many-stalked Spike-rush
Native.
Presumed extinct. Last recorded from a few localities in the north of the county prior to 1930.
First record: H.N.Dixon 1906
Druce: Very rare.

5 E. quinqueflora (F.Hartmann) O.Schwarz
Few-flowered Spike-rush
Native. Bogs and marshes.
Possibly extinct. Southorpe Bog, where it was recorded by Druce, was drained after the Second World War.
First record: Druce 1886
Druce: (Scirpus pauciflorus) Very rare.

6 E. acicularis (L.) Roemer & Schultes
Needle Spike-rush
Native. Edges of reservoirs.
Extremely rare. The only recent records are from Ravensthorpe reservoir, by L.Moore, Sutton Bog and Flag Fen in the Soke of Peterborough, and very recently a colony was discovered in a marshy field near Burton Latimer.
First record: J.Dickson 1792
Druce: Local.

5 SCIRPUS L.
1 S. sylvaticus L.   (6)
Wood Club-rush
Native. Streamsides, wet woodland and grassland flushes.
Rare. Found mainly in the south-west, around the Fawsley - High Wood area. A

single stand was found at Grendon in 1980 but has not been seen since.

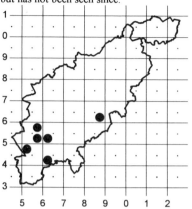

First record: Morton 1712
Druce: Local.

7 SCHOENOPLECTUS (Reichb.) Palla
1 S. lacustris (L.) Palla (85)
Common Club-rush

Native. Ponds, lakes, old gravel workings etc.
Frequent. Absent in parts of the north-central, south and west of the county, especially where the streams are not wide or deep, common elsewhere.
First record: Clare 1821
Druce: (Scirpus lacustris) Locally abundant and widely distributed.

2 S. tabernaemontani (C.Gmelin) Palla
Grey Club-rush
British. Ponds in old quarries.

Extremely rare. It has been recorded from Irchester Country Park, since about 1968 and it is present at Sane Copse SSSI, Yardley Chase. It also occurred at Stanwick, in the middle of a derelict arable field which is now lost in gravel workings. Very recently two large stands have been recorded from near the River Nene in Wellingborough.
First record:. P.Rixon & Seán Karley c1968

8 ISOLEPIS R.Br.
1 I. setacea (L.) R. Br. (7)
Bristle Club-rush

Native. Damp grassland, woodland rides.
Rare and only found in a very few areas: Yardley Chase, Salcey Forest, old fish ponds near Titchmarsh, Hogs Hole at Moulton and Wansford.
First record: Druce. 1886
Druce: (Scirpus setaceus) Rare.

9 ELEOGITON Link
1 E. fluitans (L.) Link
Floating Club-rush
Native.
Extinct. Druce thought that at Morton's site at Badby it was already extinct and he records only one other site, near Peakirk. There are no recent records.
First record: Morton 1712
Druce: (Scirpis fluitans) Very rare.

10 BLYSMUS Panzer ex Schultes
1 B. compressus (L.) Panzer ex Link
Flat-sedge
Native. Marshy fields cut for hay and the aftermath grazed.

Extremely rare. There is an old record from Aldwincle, but it is only presently found at Bulwick and on the nature reserve at Wansford.
First record: J.Dickson 1792
Druce: (Scirpus compressus) Very rare.

11 CYPERUS L.
1 C. longus L.
Galingale
British. Pond sides.
Extremely rare. Recorded by A. Newton as from a pond at Upper Catesby in 1987.

12 SCHOENUS L.
1 S. nigricans L.
Black Bog-rush
Native. Marshes.
Extremely rare. Present only at Sutton Bog and in the White Water valley in the Soke of Peterborough. It was recorded at both of these sites in 1993.
First record: Druce 1877
Druce: Rare.

14 CLADIUM P.Browne
1 C. mariscus (L.) Pohl
Great Fen Sedge
Native. Base-rich areas beside streams or ponds.
Probably extinct. It has only been recorded once in the county.

16 CAREX L.
1 C. paniculata L. (19)
Greater Tussock-sedge

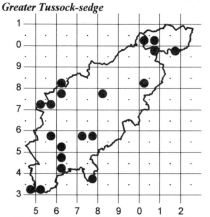

Native. Marshes, flushes in grassland, wet woods and canal-banks.

Occasional. Scattered throughout the county. There are particularly good stands at Mawsley Marsh and Birch Spinney and in the Soke of Peterborough, at Wittering.
First record: Baker 1822
Druce: Local.

1 x 15 C. paniculata x C. remota = C. x boenninghauseniana Weihe
Native. Where the parents occur.
Probably extinct. Formerly recorded from Mawsley, but recent searches have failed to reveal it.

4 C. vulpina L.
True Fox-sedge
British. Damp places and ditches.
No authentic records. Druce did not record *C. otrubae* as a different species (See note under this species.) His records, and any other records for this county prior to the publication of Clapham, Tutin and Warburg's Flora in 1952 are best taken to be *C. otrubae*.
First record: Gulliver 1841, but probably this is C. otrubae
Druce: Common and widely distributed [but probably this should refer to C. otrubae].

5 C. otrubae Podp. (103)
False Fox-sedge
Native. Marshes, wet grassland, river banks etc.
Occasional. It can be frequent in its habitat, except around Northampton. It is also occasionally to be found in woodland.

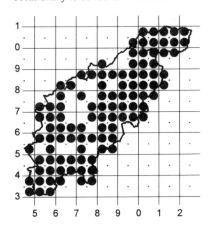

First record: Probably Gulliver 1841 (recorded in error as *C. vulpina*) Druce: Common and widely distributed. [as *C. vulpina q.v.*].

5 x 15   C. otrubae x C. remota = C. x pseudoaxillaris K.Richter
Native. Where the parents occur. Probably extinct.

7 C. spicata Hudson   (52)
Spiked Sedge

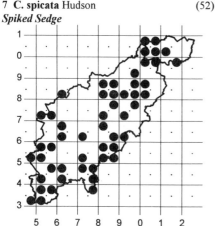

5   6   7   8   9   0   1   2

Native. Grassland.
Occasional, scattered throughout the county in grassy areas, particularly unimproved grassland, railway banks etc.
First record: Gulliver 1841
Druce: (C. muricata) Not uncommon.

8 C. muricata L.
Prickly Sedge
b subsp. *lamprocarpa* Celak.
Native. Dry grassy places.
Extremely rare. Known at Broughton and on a roadside at Clopton plus a few plants on the airfield at Draughton. Probably overlooked, but it is generally rare in the midlands.
First record: Druce 1914
Druce: (C. Pairaei) Local.

9 C. divulsa Stokes
Grey Sedge
a subsp. **divulsa**   (10)
Native. Grassland.
Rare. Occasional examples do appear, mainly in old woodland. It has been recorded from Yardley Chase, Badby Woods, Draughton, Wollaston and near Castor Hanglands.

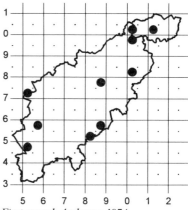

5   6   7   8   9   0   1   2
First record: Anderson 1874
Druce: (C. divulsa) Local.

b subsp. **leersii** (Kneucker) W.Koch
Native. Calcareous grassland.
Extremely rare. Recorded only at Bedford Purlieus in 1976 and near Wothorpe by R.C.Palmer in 1975. An earlier record from Old Sulehay by John Gilbert dates from 1960.

11 C. disticha Hudson   (47)
Brown Sedge

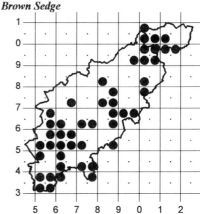

5   6   7   8   9   0   1   2
Native. Marshes, wet grassland etc.
Occasional, but well established in marshy areas throughout the county. There is quite a large stand in a wet area at the base of Easton Hillside, near the Welland.
First record: Notcutt 1843
Druce: Locally common.

15 C. remota L.   (52)
Remote Sedge

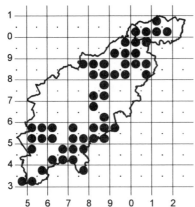

```
5   6   7   8   9   0   1   2
```

Native. Damp woodland, scrub etc.
Frequent. This plant is found in most woodlands throughout the county.
First record: Morton 1712
Druce: Local.

16 C. ovalis Gooden. (24)
Oval Sedge

```
5   6   7   8   9   0   1   2
```

Native. Grassland, grassy rides etc.
Occasional around Hollowell, Sywell and Byfield reservoirs, in Hardwick, Sywell and Whistley Woods, Salcey Forest, Harlestone Firs and, in the north, at Bedford Purlieus.
First record: Notcutt 1843
Druce: (C. leporina) Rather rare.

17 C. echinata Murray
Star Sedge
Native. Bogs.
Possibly extinct. There are records for Harlestone and Kingsthorpe, now devoid of

suitable habitats. It may still be present at Sutton Bog, but there are no recent records.
First record: Druce 1880
Druce: (C. stellulata) Local and rare.

18 C. dioica L.
Dioecious Sedge
Native.
Probably extinct. Last recorded by John Gilbert at Sutton Bog in 1965.
First record: J.Dickson 1792
Druce: Very rare.

23 C. hirta L. (111)
Hairy Sedge

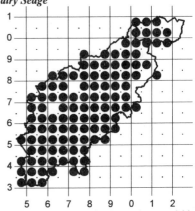

```
5   6   7   8   9   0   1   2
```

Native. Damp grassland, marshes, roadsides.
Common in suitable habitats throughout.
First record: Notcutt 1843
Druce: Common.

25 C. acutiformis Ehrh. (60)
Lesser Pond-sedge

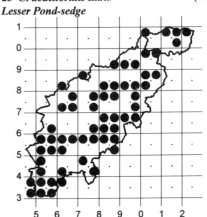

```
5   6   7   8   9   0   1   2
```

Native. Wet woodlands, grassland, riversides etc.
Frequent. Widespread, but absent from well-drained areas of intense arable farming.
First record: Beesley 1842
Druce: Locally abundant and widely distributed.

26 C. riparia Curtis   (91)
Greater Pond-sedge

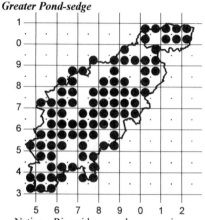

5   6   7   8   9   0   1   2

Native. Riversides, canals, reservoirs, gravel pits.
Frequent in habitat. May form extensive stands at the sides of ponds, in damp grassland and by rivers.
First record: Clare 1827
Druce: Common in all the districts.

27 C. pseudocyperus L.   (16)
Cyperus Sedge

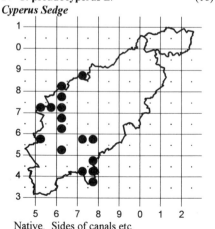

5   6   7   8   9   0   1   2

Native. Sides of canals etc.

Occasional. Found in the western half of the county, it can be particularly plentiful beside the canals.
First record: Druce 1877
Druce: (C. pseudo-cyperus) Local.

28 C. rostrata Stokes
Bottle Sedge
Native. Bogs.
Extremely rare. A site at Wollaston was lost to the plough, but it is still present at Wadenhoe and it was recorded at Sutton Bog and Bonemills Hollow in the 1970s.
First record: Morton 1712
Druce: (C. inflata) Rare and decreasing.

29 C. vesicaria L.
Bladder-sedge
Native.   Water's edge in emergent vegetation.
Extremely rare.   Found at Ravensthorpe reservoir and at Wadenhoe in 1981.
First record: Rev. M.J.Berkeley, c1860
Druce: (C. helodes) Very rare.

31 C. pendula Hudson   (40)
Pendulous Sedge

5   6   7   8   9   0   1   2

Native. Damp woodlands on heavy soils.
Occasional. Frequent within its habitat in the north-east and southern areas but absent from the extreme south-west; scattered elsewhere. Bedford Purlieus contains fine stands, and the flowering stems may exceed three metres.
First record: Rev. M.J.Berkeley 1851
Druce: Local.

32 C. sylvatica Hudson   (71)
Wood-sedge

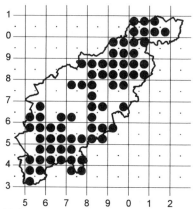

5 6 7 8 9 0 1 2

Native. Damp neutral and basic woodlands. Frequent. Present in most suitable woodlands, including secondary and recent plantations. Occasionally seen in urban sites.
First record: Notcutt 1843
Druce: Common.

34 C. strigosa Hudson
Thin-spiked Wood-sedge
Native. Damp woodland rides on heavy soils.
Very rare. In Salcey Forest it is virtually confined to the rides (past and present), but can be dominant there. It is also present in Horton Woods, where it is plentiful, Nobottle Wood and Bowd Lane Wood.
First record: Druce 1874
Druce: Very rare.

35 C. flacca Schreber   (96)
Glaucous Sedge

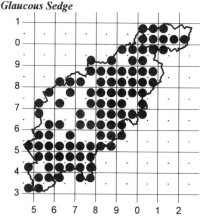

5 6 7 8 9 0 1 2

Native. Grassland, roadsides, old quarries etc.
Frequent. Widespread, but absent from some areas. Sometimes abundant on sites with a wet and disturbed clay soil.
First record: Baker 1822
Druce: (C. diversicolor) Common and widely distributed.

36 C. panicea L.   (24)
Carnation Sedge

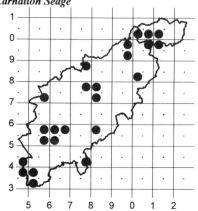

5 6 7 8 9 0 1 2

Native. Damp grassland, roadsides.
Rare. Scattered throughout the county in marshy places which have escaped drainage.
First record: Druce 1877
Druce: Local.

39 C. laevigata Smith
Smooth-stalked Sedge
Native Reservoir edges.
Extinct. Recorded at Ravensthorpe reservoir in 1905 by H.N.Dixon. There are no more recent records..
First record: H.N.Dixon 1905
Druce: (C. helodes) Very rare.

40 C. binervis Smith
Green-ribbed Sedge
Native. Acid grassland.
Extremely rare. Found only in the Wildlife Trust nature reserve at Harlestone Heath.
First record: Druce 1889
Druce: Very Rare.

41 C. distans L.   (5)
Distant Sedge
Native. Marshes.

Extremely rare. Always considered rare in the county, it may now have disappeared from its former habitats.
First record: Alfred French. c1876
Druce: Rare.

44 C. hostiana DC.
Tawny Sedge
Native. Marshy ground.
Extremely rare and found only in the centre of the county and in the Soke of Peterborough.
First record: Druce 1877
Druce: (C. fulva) Local.

46 C. viridula Michaux
Yellow-sedge, Long-stalked Yellow-sedge
a subsp. **brachyrrhyncha** (Celak.) B.Schmid
(9)
(*C. lepidocarpa* Tausch)

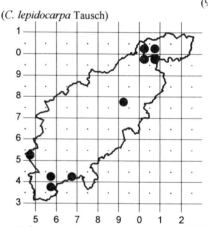

Native. Wet grassland, marshes and old quarries.
Very rare. Present in Hazelborough Woods , Cranford Quarry, Aldwincle, Bedford Purlieus, Sutton Bog and White Water.
First record: Druce. 1889
Druce: (C. lepidocarpa) Rare. [Druce also has records of C. flava agg. which would almost certainly be one of the sub-species of C. viridula].

b subsp. **oedocarpa** (Andersson) B. Schmid
(*C. demissa* Hornem.)
Native. Marshes.
Very rare and now only present in one area in the south-west of the county and at Bedford Purlieus in the Soke of Peterborough.

First record: Druce 1877
Druce: (C. oederi) Rare.

47 C. pallescens L. (18)
Pale Sedge

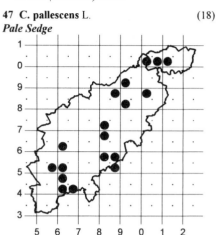

Native. Damp woodland rides.
Occasional but well established in a few woodland areas including Hazelborough, Plumpton, Sywell, Hardwick and Bucknell Woods and Yardley Chase; Bedford Purlieus and Southey Wood in the Soke of Peterborough. It is also found at High Wood nature reserve.
First record: J.Dickson 1792
Druce: Local.

51 C. caryophyllea Latour. (8)
Spring-sedge

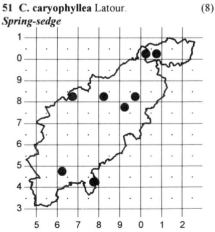

Native. Grassland.
Rare. Confined to a few sites, including Cranford and Barnack Hills and Holes, and

the former limestone quarry at Cosgrove in the south.
First record: Notcutt 1843
Druce: Locally common.

53 C. ericetorum Pollich
Rare Spring-sedge
Native. Short and dry calcareous grassland. Extremely rare. Only at Barnack Hills and Holes national nature reserve. It normally occurs in the Breckland.
First record: P.S.Lusby, M.E.Massey, and M.E.S.Rooney (Barnack) 1978

55 C. pilulifera L.
Pill Sedge
Native. Acid sandy woodland.
Very rare. It can occur abundantly when conifer plantations are felled and replanted. It has been recorded from Harlestone Firs, Overstone, Bedford Purlieus and High Wood.
First record: J. Dickson 1792
Druce: Very rare.

65 C. acuta L. (27)
Slender Tufted-sedge

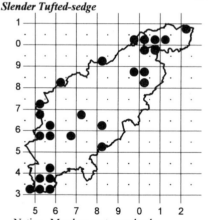

Native. Marshes, wet grassland.
Occasional, scattered in the county in marshy areas.
First record: Druce 1880
Druce: (C. gracilis) Locally common.

67 C. nigra (L.) Reichard (29)
Common Sedge
Native. Marshes, flushes in grassland.
Occasional, and scattered in marshy ground. Where it does occur it can form large stands, as at High Wood.

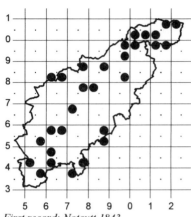

First record: Notcutt 1843
Druce: (C. Goodenowii) Local.

68 C. elata All.
Tufted-sedge
Native. Marshes and pool margins.
Extremely rare. Found in shaded areas at the west end of White Water, Wittering. It was recorded between Easton on the Hill and Wittering in 1975 by R. C. Palmer.
First record: Druce 1886
Druce: Local.

73 C. pulicaris L.
Flea Sedge
Native. Damp grassland.
Extremely rare. Found in neutral grassland at Hardwick and recorded in 1991 at Sutton Bog. No other recent records.
First record: J. Dickson 1792
Druce: Rare.

153 POACEAE
(GRAMINEAE)
8 NARDUS L.
1 N. stricta L.
Mat-grass
Native. Acid heathland.
Probably extinct. It is lost from Naseby and Harlestone Firs where it was last seen prior to 1930. It has not been seen during this survey.
First record: Dickson 1792
Druce: Very rare.

11 MILIUM L.
1 M. effusum L. (40)
Wood Millet

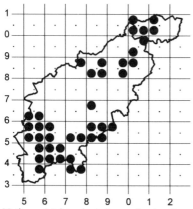

5 6 7 8 9 0 1 2

Native.   Moist, shaded woodland, often on humus rich soil.

Most frequent in woods in the north and west of the county, but locally scattered.

First record: Notcutt 1843

Druce: Local.

12 FESTUCA L.

1 F. pratensis Hudson (98)

Meadow Fescue

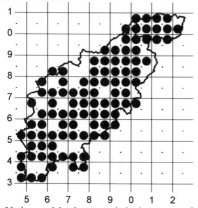

5 6 7 8 9 0 1 2

Native.   Meadows and hedgerows, often beside ditches, rivers etc.

Frequent in all areas.

First record: Gulliver 1841

Druce: (F. elatior) Common in all districts.

2 F. arundinacea Schreber (94)

Tall Fescue

Native. Rough grassland, roadside verges. Fairly common in suitable habitats.

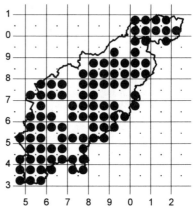

5 6 7 8 9 0 1 2

First record: Druce   1890   (first certain record)

Druce: Local.

3 F. gigantea (L.) Villars (97)

Giant Fescue

5 6 7 8 9 0 1 2

Native. Woods and hedgerows.

Common in many woodlands throughout the area. A good indicator of ancient woodland.

First record: Notcutt 1843

Druce: Common in all the districts.

7 F. rubra L.

Red Fescue

a subsp. **rubra** (122)

Native. Grassland and rough ground. Very common in all areas.

First record: Druce   1890   (First certain record)

Druce: Common and generally distributed in all districts.

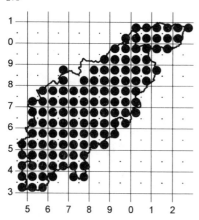

5 6 7 8 9 0 1 2

g subsp. **megastachys**
Probable introduction. Grassland.
A single record but it may be under-recorded.

8 F. ovina L.
Sheep's-fescue
a subsp. **ovina**   (25)

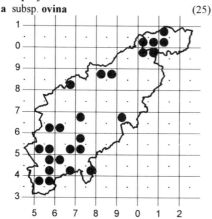

5 6 7 8 9 0 1 2

Native. Grassland.
Rare and only recorded in the calcareous
areas in the north and the south-west of the
county.
First record: Druce 1877
Druce: Local.

10 F. filiformis Pourret
(*F. ovina* L. subsp. *tenuifolia* (Sibth.) Dumort.)
Fine-leaved Sheep's-fescue
Native. Grassland on acid and sandy soils.
Probably extinct, the first and only record is
from Southorpe.

First record: Druce 1878
Druce: (F. capillata) Rare.

**12 x 13   FESTUCA x LOLIUM = X FES-
TULOLIUM** Asch. & Graebner
**1 x 1   F. pratensis x L. perenne = X F.
loliaceum** (Hudson) P.Fourn.
Hybrid Fescue
Native. Meadows and other grassland.
A not infrequent hybrid, turning up in any
area.

13 LOLIUM L.
1 L. perenne L.   (132)
Perennial Rye-grass

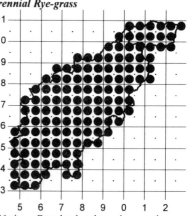

5 6 7 8 9 0 1 2

Native. Grassland and rough ground.
Very common and often sown as part of grass
mixtures on improved grassland. One of the
commonest grasses in the county.
First record: Pitt 1813
Druce: Abundant in all the districts.

2 L. multiflorum Lam.
Italian Rye-grass
Introduction. Grassland and waste ground.
Fairly common in suitable areas.
First record: Druce 1876
*Druce: (L. multiflorum var. italicum) Occurs
as a relic of cultivation on field borders, in
cultivated ground and waste places.*

L. temulentum L.
Darnel
Introduction. Tips and other waste ground.
No recent records.
First record: Druce 1878
Druce: Very rare.

14 VULPIA C.Gmelin
2 V. bromoides (L.) Gray (47)
Squirreltail Fescue

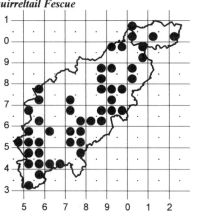

Native. Well drained grassland and waste places.
Occasional, but often abundant on old railway tracks.
First record: Druce 1880
Druce: (Festuca bromoides) Local.

3 V. myuros (L.) C.Gmelin (17)
Rat's-tail Fescue

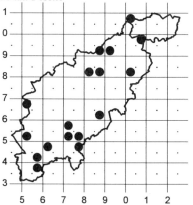

Native. Rough ground, walls and railways.
Common along railway tracks, on waste ground, etc. and especially on the tops of old stone walls.
First record: Morton 1712
Druce: (F. myuros) Local.

15 CYNOSURUS L.
1 C. cristatus L. (118)
Crested Dog's-tail

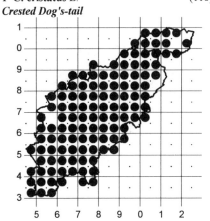

Native. Grassland.
Common on dry pastures etc.
First record: Pitt 1813
Druce: Locally abundant and widely spread in all the districts.

2 C. echinatus L.
Rough Dog's-tail
Adventive. Waste ground.
No recent records.
First record: Chester 1914
Druce: [No status given].

16 PUCCINELLIA Parl.
1 P. maritima (Hudson) Parl.
Common Saltmarsh-grass
British. Roadside verges.
Extremely rare. Found on a roadside near Salcey Forest in 1991, the result of salt spray.

2 P. distans (Jacq.) Parl.
Reflexed Saltmarsh-grass
British. Roadsides.
This saltmarsh species is becoming more common as a result of salt spray on main roads. The first recent records within the county were 1980 on the M1 motorway, and the A1 near Wansford, by Nick Scott. It is recorded by Druce as 'abundant about the Sewage works, Northampton, but apparently not elsewhere in the neighbourhood'.
First record: Druce 1876
Druce: (Glyceria distans) Rare.

17 BRIZA L.

1 B. media L. (73)

Quaking-grass, Totter-grass

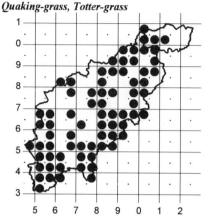

```
      5   6   7   8   9   0   1   2
```

Native. Grassland on a variety of base rich soils.
A once common species but now becoming scarce as a result of grassland improvement.

First record: Clare 1827
Druce: Locally common.

3 B. maxima L.

Great Quaking-grass

Introduction. Banks and field margins.
Sometimes turning up in tips and other areas, as a bird seed introduction. It has persisted as a tolerated garden weed for some years in Raunds.

18 POA L.

2 P. annua L. (132)

Annual Meadow-grass

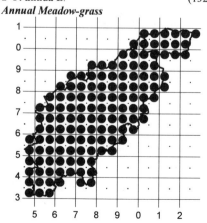

```
      5   6   7   8   9   0   1   2
```

Native. Rough ground, paths and lawns and garden-beds.
Very common in all areas.

First record: Pitt 1813
Druce: Ubiquitous. Our commonest species.

3 P. trivialis L. (122)

Rough Meadow-grass

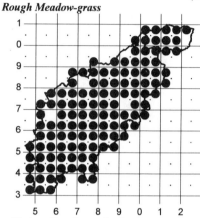

```
      5   6   7   8   9   0   1   2
```

Native. Rough grassland
Very common in all areas.

First record: Pitt 1813
Druce: Abundant in all the districts but usually found in damper and shadier situations than P. pratensis.

4 P. humilis Ehrh. ex Hoffm.

(*P. pratensis* L. subsp. *alpigena* sensu Tutin, non (Fries) Hiit.)

Spreading Meadow-grass

Native. Dry banks and old walls.
Extremely rare. Only recorded with any certainty at Litchborough Churchyard and at one site in the Soke of Peterborough, but probably under-recorded.

First record: Druce 1888
Druce: (P. subcaerulea) No status given.

5 P. pratensis L. (110)

Smooth Meadow-grass

Native. Meadows and pastures, road verges and waste land.
Very common in all areas.

First record: Pitt 1813
Druce: Abundant in every district.

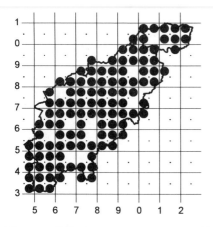

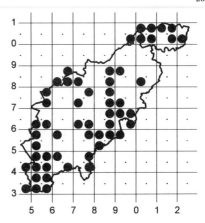

6 P. angustifolia L. (8)
(*P. pratensis* L. subsp. *angustifolia* (L.) Dumort.)
Narrow-leaved Meadow-grass

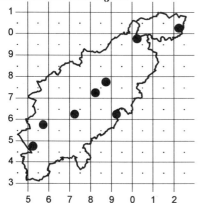

Native. Grassy places, hedgerows etc. on well drained soil.
Sometimes plentiful on wall tops and other dry places, and often the first meadow grass to flower. Possibly under-recorded.
First record: Chester (date unknown)

9 P. compressa L. (55)
Flattened Meadow-grass
Native. Walls, dry paths, railway ballast etc. Fairly common and often overlooked.
First record: Watson 1874
Druce: Local.

10 P. palustris L.
Swamp Meadow-grass
Adventive. Marshes and damp grassland. This species was found for the first time in the county in 1994 during a survey at Pitsford reservoir by Jeff Best and Adrian Colston. The nearest station for this species is at Woodwalton Fen in Huntingdonshire.

12 P. nemoralis L. (58)
Wood Meadow-grass

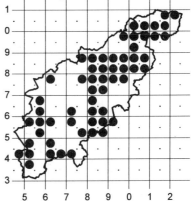

Native. Woods, hedgerows and other shaded habitats.
Occasional. Usually restricted to established woodland areas where it may be quite widespread. It also occurs in some church-yards such as at Stoke Albany.
First record: Druce 1879
Druce: Local and an uncommon species, shunning stiff clay soils.

19 DACTYLIS L.
1 D. glomerata L. (134)
Cock's-foot

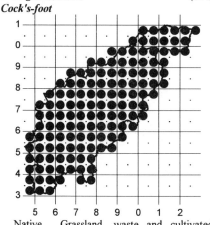

5 6 7 8 9 0 1 2

Native. Grassland, waste and cultivated ground.
A very common grass in all areas.
First record: Pitt 1813
Druce: Abundant in rich soils throughout the county.

20 CATABROSA P.Beauv.
1 C. aquatica (L.) P.Beauv. (19)
Whorl-grass

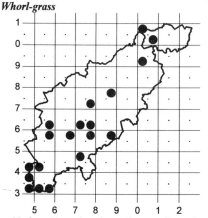

5 6 7 8 9 0 1 2

Native. Damp locations often on almost bare mud.
Uncommon. Only known from a few widely separated areas, but it is usually well established where it does occur.
First record: Pitt 1813
Druce: Local.

21 CATAPODIUM Link
1 C. rigidum (L.) C.E.Hubb. (67)
(*Desmazeria rigida* (L.) Tutin)
Fern-grass

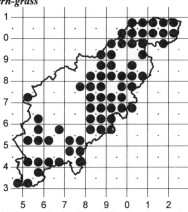

5 6 7 8 9 0 1 2

Native. Dry, often fairly bare ground, on banks, walls etc.
Fairly common in dry places, especially on limestone walls.
First record: H.C. Watson 1874
Druce: (Festuca rigida) Locally common.

24 GLYCERIA R.Br.
1 G. maxima (Hartman) O.Holmb. (109)
Reed Sweet-grass

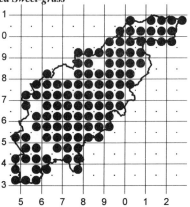

5 6 7 8 9 0 1 2

Native. Water body margins.
Common in water margins of lakes, rivers and streams and other wet areas.
First record: Clare 1827
Druce: (G. aquatica) Locally abundant in all the low lying districts.

2 G. fluitans (L.) R.Br. (82)
Floating Sweet-grass

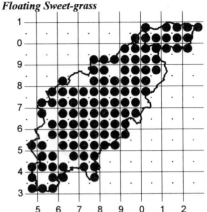

Native. Small water bodies.
Common, particularly in small ponds. Found at widely scattered sites throughout the county.
First record: Pitt 1813
Druce: Common and widely distributed in all the districts.

2 x 4   G. fluitans x G. notata = G. x pedicellata F.Towns.
Hybrid Sweet-grass
Native. In mud or shallow water.
Extremely rare. Known only from three widely scattered sites in the north-east.
Druce: (G. pedicillata) [No status given].

3 G. declinata Bréb. (36)
Small Sweet-grass
Native. In mud or shallow water.
Fairly common. Widely distributed but more common in the south of the county.
First record: Druce 1909
Druce: (G. plicata var. declinata) [No status, one record only].

4 G. notata Chevall. (43)
(*G. plicata* (Fries) Fries)
Plicate Sweet-grass
Native. Water body margins.
Uncommon but possibly overlooked.
First record: Druce 1880
Druce: (G. plicata) Rather common in the clay areas.

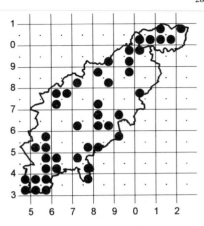

25 MELICA L.
1 M. nutans L.
Mountain Melick
Native. Woodlands.
Extremely rare. Only found in the Bedford Purlieus area, where it has been established for many years. An interesting species being on the southern limit of its range.
First record: Druce 1874
Druce: Very rare.

2 M. uniflora Retz. (32)
Wood Melick

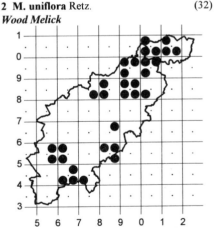

Native. Woods and shady hedgebanks.
Common in woodlands on light soils, both in the north and south of the county.
First record: Notcutt 1843
Druce: Local.

26 HELICTOTRICHON Besser ex Schultes & Schultes f.
1 H. pubescens (Hudson) Pilger (50)
(*Avena pubescens* Hudson)
Downy Oat-grass

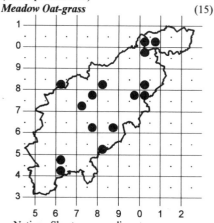

Native. Grassland on limestone.
Occasional. A decreasing species due to the improvement of much of our grasslands.
First record: Norton 1712
Druce: (Avena pubescens) Locally common.

2 H. pratense (L.) Besser
(*Avena pratensis* L.)
Meadow Oat-grass (15)

Native. Short grass on limestone.
Rare and like *H. pubescens* a decreasing species.
First certain record: Druce 1880
Druce: (Avena pratensis) Rare.

27 ARRHENATHERUM P.Beauv.
1 A. elatius (L.) P.Beauv. ex J.S.Presl & C. Presl (130)
False Oat-grass

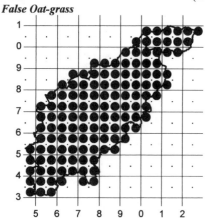

Native. Coarse grassland.
Common. One of the most common species of grass in most rough habitats.
First record: Pitt 1813
Druce: Abundant in all the districts.

28 AVENA L.
2 A. strigosa Schreber
Bristle Oat
Introduction. Casual cornfield weed.
No recent records.
First record: Druce 1878
Druce: Rare.

3 A. fatua L. (73)
Wild-oat, Slender-oat
Introduction. Rough and arable land.
Found in all districts on disturbed ground but gradually being eliminated by spraying.
First record: Gulliver 1841
Druce: Found in all districts but, owing to the rotation of crops, not permanently established.

4 A. sterilis L.
Winter Wild-oat
a subsp. **ludoviciana** (Durieu) Gillet & Magne
(*A. ludoviciana* Durieu)
Introduction. Arable land.
Weed of rough ground and arable land, usually on heavy soils.

5 A. sativa L.
Oat

Introduction. Waste ground and tips.
A relic of cultivation. It never establishes
itself for more than a year.
*Druce: Occurs as a relic of cultivation in all
districts, but is not permanently established.*

30 TRISETUM Pers.
1 T. flavescens (L.) P.Beauv. (107)
Yellow Oat-grass

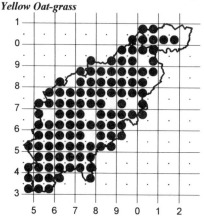

5 6 7 8 9 0 1 2

Native. Meadows, pastures etc.
Fairly common in most areas.
First record: Pitt 1813
Druce: Locally abundant on dry soils.

31 KOELERIA Pers.
2 K. macrantha (Ledeb.) Schultes. (15)
(*K. gracilis* Pers., nom. illegit)
Crested Hair-grass

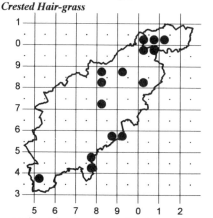

5 6 7 8 9 0 1 2

Native. Limestone or sandy soils.
An uncommon species of limestone grassland
which ocurs mainly in areas of unimproved
pasture and in old quarries. It is particularly
common in the Lincolnshire limestone areas
in the Soke of Peterborough, at Barnack,
Collyweston etc.
First record: Druce 1880
Druce: (K. gracilis & K. britannica) Local.

32 DESCHAMPSIA P.Beauv.
1 D. cespitosa (L.) P.Beauv
Tufted Hair-grass
a subsp. **cespitosa** (125)

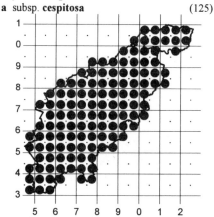

5 6 7 8 9 0 1 2

Native. Damp meadows, verges and ditches.
Common in suitable areas of damp grassland
and woodland.
First record: Pitt 1813
*Druce: (D. caespitosa) Occurs in all the
districts and locally common.*

3 D. flexuosa (L.) Trin. (6)
Wavy Hair-grass

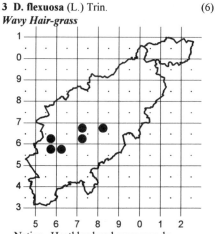

5 6 7 8 9 0 1 2

Native. Heathland and open woods.

A very uncommon species, occurring mainly in the west of the county on the lighter acid soils such as at Harlestone Firs and Badby Woods.
First record: Notcutt 1843
Druce: Local and rather rare.

33 HOLCUS L.
1 H. lanatus L. (128)
Yorkshire-fog

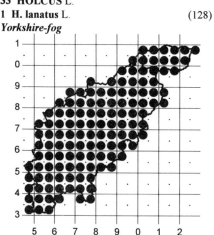

5 6 7 8 9 0 1 2

Native. Rough grassland and woodland ridings.
A very common species throughout the county.
First record: Pitt 1813
Druce: Too abundant and widely distributed to need localities.

2 H. mollis L. (69)
Creeping Soft-grass

5 6 7 8 9 0 1 2

Native. Woodland and hedgerows.

Very common in woodland on lighter, sandy soils, and often forming large patches.
First record: Gulliver 1841
Druce: Local.

35 AIRA L.
1 A. caryophyllea L. (15)
Silver Hair-grass

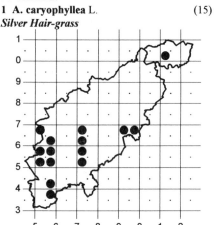

5 6 7 8 9 0 1 2

Native. Dry ground.
An uncommon species found at sites scattered through the the county, mainly on sandy soils and relict heathland, as in the Wellingborough and Rushden areas. It also shows a liking for railway ballast in some areas.
First record: J. Dickson 1792
Druce: Rare.

2 A. praecox L. (4)
Early Hair-grass

5 6 7 8 9 0 1 2

Native. Dry ground.

Very rare and only found in four localities on light, sandy soils in the Badby area, at High Wood, Brampton golf course and on Borough Hill.
First record: Druce 1877
Druce: Local.

37 ANTHOXANTHUM L.
1 A. odoratum L. (107)
Sweet Vernal-grass

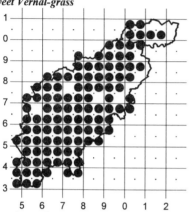

Native. All types of grassland.
Common throughout the county, especially in un-improved grassland, old churchyards etc.
First record: Pitt 1813
Druce: Abundant throughout the county except in cold damp meadows.

2 A. aristatum Boiss.
(*A. puelli* Lecoq & Lamotte)
Annual Vernal-grass
Introduction. Sandy cultivated land or waste ground.
Seen in both Weekley Hall Woods and Southorpe Paddock during the 1950s by Geoff Laundon. A Red Data Book species, it does not appear to have been since.
First record: H.N. Dixon 1885
Druce: Introduced with grass-seeds, not permanently established.

38 PHALARIS L.
1 P. arundinacea L. (123)
Reed Canary-grass
Native. Marshy and wet places around ditches, ponds and rivers.
Very common beside streams, ponds and reservoirs. Often a dominant species.

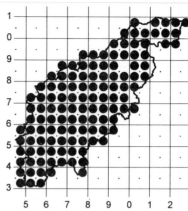

First record: Pitt 1813
Druce: Common and widely distributed.

2 P. aquatica L.
Bulbous Canary-grass
Introduction. Rough ground.
There are two records from the south of the county and one from Lyveden New Bield, where it appeared on disturbed soil in 1994.

3 P. canariensis L.
Canary-grass
Introduction. Tips and waste ground.
Occurs mainly as a casual or bird-seed introduction.
First record: A. French
Druce: Rare.

4 P. minor Retz.
Lesser Canary-grass
Introduction. Casual on sandy soils.
Only one record from the Litchborough area in 1973.
First record: 1973

39 AGROSTIS L.
1 A. capillaris L. (101)
(*A. tenuis* Sibth.)
Common Bent
Native. Dry grassy places and rough ground.
Common. The commonest species of *Agrostis* in dry grassy areas.
First record: Pitt 1813
Druce: Rather common and widely distributed.

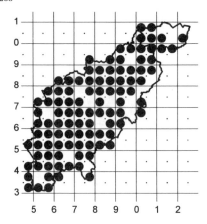

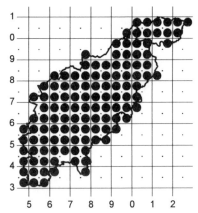

2 A. gigantea Roth   (27)
Black Bent

7 A. canina L.   (16)
Velvet Bent

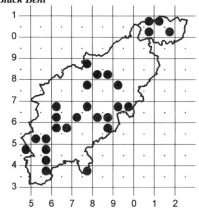

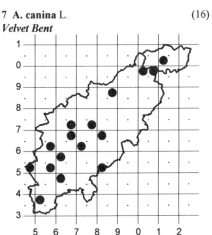

Native. Grassy places and rough ground.
Occasional.   An uncommon species of disturbed ground.
First record: Druce 1883
Druce: (A. nigra) Local.

4 A. stolonifera L.   (121)
Creeping Bent

Native. Damp grassland beside rivers, ponds, ditches and in woodland.

A very common grass in damp areas almost anywhere and well distributed across the county.

First record: Pitt 1813
Druce: (A. alba) Common in all the districts.

Native. Heaths, acidic grassland etc.
Rare, although it is quite plentiful in places such as Borough Hill, Harlestone Firs and in the Badby area.   It is also recorded from Hollowell reservoir and from Ailsworth Heath in the Soke of Peterborough.
First record: Druce 1878
Druce: Rare.

40 CALAMAGROSTIS Adans.
1 C. epigejos (L.) Roth   (92)
Wood Small-reed, Bush Grass

Native. Damp woods, woodland margins, ditches etc.

Very common in damp woodland around the county. It often forms large patches and can be the dominant species in newly cleared woodland.

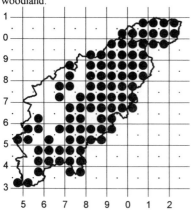

5 6 7 8 9 0 1 2

First record: Ray (Cat) 1670
Druce: Locally abundant.

2 C. canescens (Wigg.) Roth   (6)
Purple Small-reed, Wood Small-reed

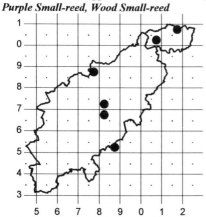

5 6 7 8 9 0 1 2

Native. Marshes and wet woodland.
Rare and only known from very few wooded areas including Sywell and Hardwick Woods, Bedford Purlieus, Yardley Chase, Borough Fen duck decoy and the Wittering area.
First record: Ray 1724
Druce: (C. calamagrostis) Locally abundant over small areas.

43 LAGURUS L.
1 L. ovatus L.
Hare's-tail
Introduction. Disturbed ground and rubbish tips.

Occurring very rarely as an outcast from gardens.
Druce: Casual.

44 APERA Adans.
2 A. interrupta (L.) P.Beauv.
Dense Silky-bent
Introduction. Dry sandy fields and rough land.
The first recent record was by John Manning in 1969, on the Kettering Town football ground. Subsequently it has been found near the site of Kettering Furnaces and a quarry site near Geddington in 1988. It was also recorded at three separate sites around Grendon in the late 1980s.
First record: H.N.Dixon 1908
Druce: Very rare.

46 POLYPOGON Desf.
1 P. monspeliensis (L.) Desf.
Annual Beard-grass
British. Waste places.
No recent records.
First record: Druce 1878
Druce: Rare.

47 ALOPECURUS L.
1 A. pratensis L.   (128)
Meadow Foxtail

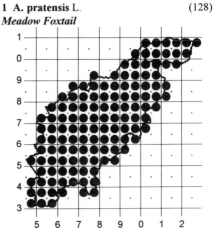

5 6 7 8 9 0 1 2

Native. Grassy places on damp soils.
A very common species throughout the county and the Soke of Peterborough.
First record: Pitt 1813
Druce: Common throughout the county.

1 x 2 A. pratensis x **A. geniculatus** = **A. x brachystylus** Peterm.

290

Native. With the parents.
Only one recent record but almost certainly overlooked.

2 A. geniculatus L.   (96)
Marsh Foxtail

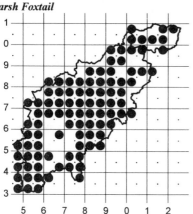

Native. Wet meadows, ditches etc.
Fairly common in wet places.
First record: Gulliver 1841
Druce: Common and widely distributed.

4 A. aequalis Sobol.   (9)
Orange Foxtail

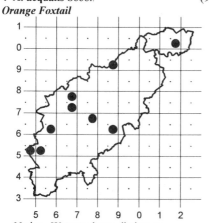

Native. Wet meadows, ditches etc.
A rare species, usually found around reservoirs and similar habitats on bare mud. It is very common around Pitsford, Daventry, Hollowell and Boddington reservoirs
First record: Notcutt 1843
Druce: Very local.

6 A. myosuroides Hudson   (97)
Black-grass

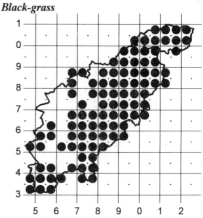

Native. Weed of arable and waste ground.
A very common weed of arable areas, especially cereal crops.
First record: J. Dickson 1792
Druce: Common. Occurs in all districts.

49 PHLEUM L.
1 P. pratense L.   (129)
Timothy

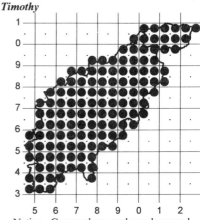

Native. Grassy places and rough ground.
A common meadow grass which is widely distributed in all areas.
First record: Beesley 1841
Druce: Common in all the districts.

2 P. bertolonii DC.   (99)
(*P. nodosum* auct., non L.)
Smaller Cat's-tail

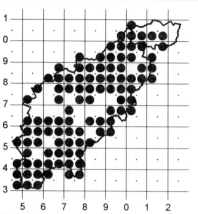

Native. Dry grassland.
Very common in most areas throughout the county.
Druce: (P, pratense var. nodosum) [No status given].

50 BROMUS L.
1 B. arvensis L.
Field Brome
Introduction. A weed of arable and waste ground.
No recent records.
First record: 1877
Druce: Rare.

2 B. commutatus Schrader   (18)
Meadow Brome
Native. Grassland and waste gound.

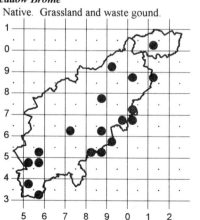

Very occasional in disturbed ground and along farm tracks.
First record: Miss Brent c.1865

Druce: (B. pratensis) Local.

3 B. racemosus L.   (4)
Smooth Brome
Native. Grassland and rough ground.
Extremely rare and only recorded recently from four widely separated sites. There are older records; by C.E.Hubbard in 1943 at Croughton and from Warmington in 1954.
First record: J.Dickson 1798
Druce: Local.

4 B. hordeaceus L.
Soft-brome
a subsp. **hordeaceus**   (115)
(*B. mollis* L.)

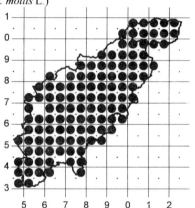

Native. Grassy and rough ground.
Very common throughout the whole county.
First record: Gulliver 1841
Druce: (B. hordeaceus) Abundant in all districts.

c subsp. **thominei** (Hardouin) Braun-Blanquet
(*B. thominei* Hardouin)
Native. Sandy places.
Extremely rare, but probably overlooked.
Only recorded from Ashby St. Ledgers in 1961, by Mary Jones.

4 x 5 B. hordaeceus x B. lepidus = B. x pseudothominei P.M.Smith.
(*B. hordaeceus* L. subsp. *pseudothomenei* (P.M.Smith) H.Scholz)
Lesser Soft-brome
Probably native. Grassland, rough ground and roadside verges, often without either parent.

This recently named hybrid may turn out to be quite common but at present very few localities have been found.
First record: c1983

5 B. lepidus O.Holmb. (15)
Slender Soft-brome

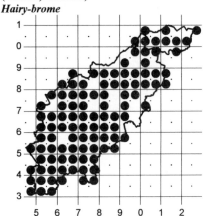

5 6 7 8 9 0 1 2

Probably Native. Grassland, and rough ground.
Rare. One record from Barnack in 1951, near Crick in 1961 by Mary Jones and at a few other localities across the county.

6 B. interruptus (Hackel) Druce
Interrupted Brome
Native. Arable land and waste ground. Probably extinct, not seen during this survey. The last dated record is from near Rainsborough Camp in 1907.
First record: Druce 1901
Druce: Local, now decreasing.

7 B. secalinus L.
Rye Brome
Introduction. Weed of crops and waste ground.
No recent records. It was recorded at Catesby in 1925.
First record: Druce 1870
Druce: Rather rare and not permanent.

B. alopecuros Poiret
(*B. Alopecuroides* Poiret)
Introduction. Waste places.
No recent records.
First record: Rogers 1886
Druce: (B. alopecuroides) Rare.

51 BROMOPSIS (Dumort.) Fourr.
(*Zerna* auct. non Panzer, *Bromus* sect. *Pnigma* Dumort.)

1 B. ramosa (Hudson) Holub (105)
(*Bromus ramosus* Hudson, *Zerna ramosa* (Hudson) Lindman)
Hairy-brome

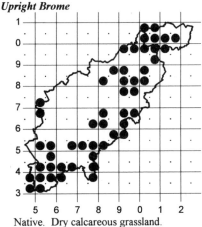

5 6 7 8 9 0 1 2

Native. Woods, woodland edge and hedgerows.
Common in most of our woodlands , and sometimes in hedgerows.
First record: Gulliver 1841
Druce: (Bromus ramosa) Rather common in the woodlands in all the districts.

3 B. erecta (Hudson) Fourr. (51)
(*Bromus erecta* Hudson, *Zerna erecta* (Hudson) Gray)
Upright Brome

5 6 7 8 9 0 1 2

Native. Dry calcareous grassland.

Fairly common in calcareous areas, mainly on the Jurassic limestones.
First certain record: Druce 1880
Druce: (Bromus erecta) Locally abundant.

4 B. inermis (Leysser) Holub
Hungarian Brome
Introduction. Rough grassland.
Recorded by R.C.Palmer in 1963 and 1967, both records from the Brackley area.

52 ANISANTHA K.Koch
(*Bromus* sect. *Genea* Dumort.)
3 A. sterilis (L.) Nevski   (112)
(*Bromus sterilis* L.)
Barren Brome

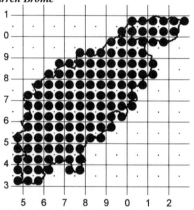

Native. Waste land, rough ground, grassland and arable land.
Very common in all areas.
First record: Gulliver 1841
Druce: (Bromus sterilis) Abundant and widely distributed in all the districts.

53 CERATOCHLOA DC & P.Beauv.
(*Bromus* sect. *Ceratochlea* (DC. & P.Beauv.) Griseb.)
3 C. cathartica (M.Vahl) Herter
(*Bromus willdenowii* Kunth)
Rescue Brome
Introduction. Rough ground, verges and field edges.
An introduced species from South Africa that was seen in the grounds of Northampton General Hospital in 1978 and as a garden weed in Wellingborough in 1980.
First record: Chester 1910
Druce: (Bromus unioloides) Rare.

54 BRACHYPODIUM P.Beauv.
1 B. pinnatum (L.) P.Beauv.   (50)
Tor-grass

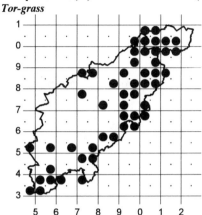

Native. Limestone grassland.
Fairly common in limestone areas; and an aggresive species often ousting the more sensitive vegetation.
First record: Rev. M.J.Berkeley 1836
Druce: Locally abundant and an aggressive species.

2 B. sylvaticum (Hudson) P.Beauv.   (114)
False Brome

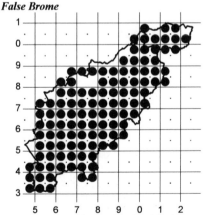

Native. Woods, woodland edges and hedgerows.
Very common throughout the county.
First record: Baker 1822
Druce: Locally common.

55 ELYMUS L.
(*Agropyron* auct. non Gaertner)

1 E. caninus (L.) L. (55)
(Agropyron caninum (L.) Beauv.)
Bearded Couch

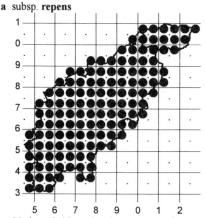

5 6 7 8 9 0 1 2

Native. Woodland edges, hedgerows and shaded river banks.
Occasional. An infrequent species of woodland in areas such as Salcey, Yardley Chase and Pipewell Woods. It can be quite common in some hedgerows, as around Yardley Gobion and some other areas. Probably much under-recorded.
First record: H.C.Watson 1874
Druce: (Agropyron caninum) Local.

56 ELYTRIGIA Desv.
(Agropyron auct. non Gaertner)
1 E. repens (L.) Desv. ex Nevski (131)
(Agropyron repens (L.) P.Beauv.)
Common Couch, Twitch
a subsp. **repens**

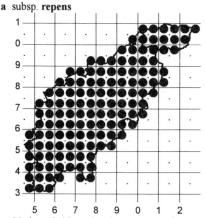

5 6 7 8 9 0 1 2

Native. Cultivated and waste ground.

Very common throughout the county.
First record: Pitt 1813
Druce: (Agropyron repens) Too abundant in all the districts and an aggressive pest to agriculturists.

58 HORDELYMUS (Jessen) Jessen
1 H. europaeus (L.) Jessen
Wood Barley
Native. Woods and copses.
Extremely rare. One record from Bedford Purlieus in 1970.
First record: Rev M.J. Berkeley c1860
Druce: (Elymus europaeus) Rare.

59 HORDEUM L.
1 H. distichon L.
Two-rowed Barley
Introduction. Waste ground.
No recent record. Although it is still grown as a crop it does not establish itself in the wild.

2 H. murinum L.
Wall Barley
a subsp. **murinum** (120)

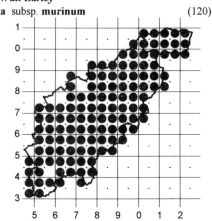

5 6 7 8 9 0 1 2

Native. Rough ground and waste land.
Very common in all areas.
First record: Pitt 1813
Druce: Locally common in all districts.

3 H. jubatum L.
Foxtail Barley
Introduction.
It is often introduced in grass mixtures. The first recent record is from the old gravel workings at Titchmarsh, where it was first noticed about 1976 and it has subsequently

been found on the verges of the A45 and other trunk roads throughout most of the county.
First record: Goode 1917

4 H. secalinum Schreber   (94)
Meadow Barley

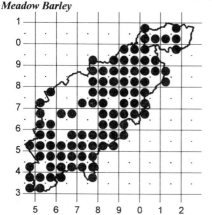

Native. Meadowland and pastures.
Fairly common in suitable habitats throughout most of the county.
First record: Pitt 1813
Druce: (H. nodosum) Locally abundant.

5 H. marinum Hudson
Sea Barley
British. Waste ground and verges.
No recent records, although in view of the appearance of other salt-marsh species along road verges in recent years, it may well be found again.
First record: G. Chester 1914
Druce: [No status given].

H. vulgare L.
Six-rowed Barley
Introduction. Waste ground.
No recent record. It is still grown as a crop, although not as frequently as *H. distichon*, but it does not establish itself in the wild.
Druce: This, H. hexastichon L., and H. distichon L., occur as relics of cultivation from time to time, but are not permanently established.

SECALE L.
S. cereale L.
Rye
Introduction. Waste places.

No recent records, but no longer grown in the county.
Druce: Occurs as a relic of cultivation on field-borders, in cultivated ground and waste places, but is not permanent.

60 TRITICUM L.
1 T. aestivum L.
Bread Wheat
Introduction. Cultivated fields and adjoining grassland.
Modern hexoploid bread wheats are bred with a dependence on fertilizers and so do not persist for long in the wild.
Druce: The wheat in several varieties - turgidum, anglicum etc. Occurs as a relic of cultivation in ground disturbed by man, but it is not permanently established.

61 DANTHONIA DC.
1 D. decumbens (L.) DC.
(*Sieglingia decumbens* L. Bernh.)
Heath-grass
Native. Sandy or peat soils, often in damp situations.
Very rare and only known from a very few sites including Hardwick Meadow, the Yardley Chase M.O.D. area and High Wood Meadow.
First record: J. Dickson 1792
Druce: (Sieglingia decumbens) Rare.

63 MOLINIA Schrank
1 M. caerulea (L.) Moench
Purple Moor-grass
b subsp. **arundinacea** (Schrank) K, Richter
Native. Heaths and fens.
Very rare. This is known to occur in about three sites in the county and the Soke of Peterborough. It used to be abundant in the Croughton valley but may well have succumbed to recent drainage. It is still abundant in the White Water valley and at Sutton in the Soke.
First record: Druce 1877
Druce: Rare.

64 PHRAGMITES Adans.
1 P. australis (Cav.) Trin. ex Steudel   (95)
(*P. communis* Trin.)
Common Reed
Native. Shallow water, river and stream sides, marshes etc.

Common in all suitable habitats in most parts of the county.
First record: Morton 1712
Druce: (P. Phragmites) Locally abundant, occurring in all the districts and, when unchecked by agriculture, an aggressive species.

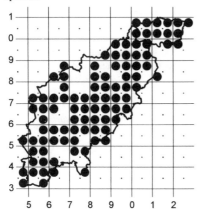

PANICUM L.
P. miliaceum L.
Common Millet
Introduction. Tips and waste ground.
One record of a bird-seed alien in a garden in Collingtree in 1994.
First record: Druce 1888
Druce: Rare.

68 ECHINOCHLOA P.Beauv.
1 E. crusgalli (L.) P.Beauv.
Cockspur
Introduction. Tips and waste ground.
One record of a bird-seed alien in a garden in Collingtree in 1994.
First record: Goode 1916
Druce: (Panicum Crus-galli) Rare.

70 SETARIA P.Beauv.
S. pumila (Poiret) Roemer & Schultes
(*Panicum viride* L.)
Yellow Bristle-grass
Introduction. Cultivated or waste ground, tips etc.
Occasional. Often occurring as a casual from wild bird-seed, but never persisting.
First record: H.N.Dixon 1885
Druce: (S.glauca) Rare.

1 S. viridis (L.) P.Beauv.
Green Bristle-grass
Introduction. Cultivated or waste ground.
Occasional. Casual status only, often from bird-seed.
First record: Beesley 1842
Druce: As a casual only.

71 DIGITARIA Haller
D. sanguinalis (L.) Scop.
Hairy Finger-grass
Introduction.
Recorded as a bird-seed alien in Wellingborough in 1985-6.

154 SPARGANIACEAE
1 SPARGANIUM L.
1 S. erectum L.   (113)
Branched Bur-reed

Native.   Borders of streams, rivers, canals etc.
Common and widespread throughout the county.   In the River Welland it is most common between Market Harborough and Welham.   Generally recorded within the county as an aggregate species, but both subsp. *oocarpum* and *neglectum* have been recorded as present.
First record: Druce 1886
Druce: (S. neglectum) Locally common.

2 S. emersum Rehmann   (41)
Unbranched Bur-reed
Native.   Streams, rivers and canals.
Occasional, but perhaps overlooked as it often fails to flower in deep water. This deep

water form occurs in parts of the Ise and Welland.

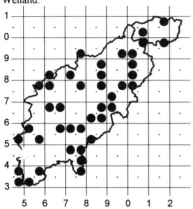

First record: Gulliver 1841
Druce: (S. simplex) Not uncommon.

4 S. natans L.
(*S. minimum* Wallr.)
Least Bur-reed, Small Bur-reed
Native. Lakes, pools and ditches, generally on peaty soils.
Probably extinct as there are no recent records. The first record is the only record.
First record: Druce 1910
Druce: (S. minimum) Abundant in drains at High Boro Fen near Peakirk.

155 TYPHACEAE
1 TYPHA L.
1 T. latifolia L. (110)
Bulrush, Reedmace

Native. Reed-swamp at pond, lake and canal margins.
Common and widespread, but mainly in still waters. The seedheads were formerly used for stuffing pillows.
First record: Baker 1822
Druce: Locally common and increasing.

1 x 2   T. latifolia x T. angustifolia = T. x glauca Godron
Native. Wet places.
Extremely rare. One record by Druce and one recent record from Finedon Pits.
First record: Druce (undated)
Druce: [No status given].

2 T. angustifolia L. (38)
Lesser Bulrush, Lesser Reedmace

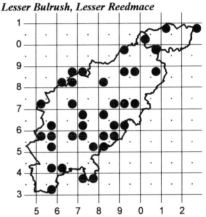

Native. Reed swamps at pond, lake and canal edges.
Occasional, but sometimes in large stands where it does occur.
First record: Goodyer 1660
Druce: Locally common.

158 LILIACEAE
7 COLCHICUM L.
1 C. autumnale L.
Meadow Saffron
Native. Rough pasture.
Recorded during the current survey at a single site in a meadow near Towcester, now developed as a housing estate. This may well have been an an escape from cultivation.
First record: Gerard 1597
Druce: Very local.

9 GAGEA Salisb.
1 G. lutea (L.) Ker Gawler (3)
Yellow Star-of-Bethlehem

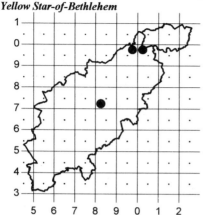

5 6 7 8 9 0 1 2

Native. Woodlands.
Very rare but may be abundant where found. Recorded in isolated areas in Bedford Purlieus, Fineshade Woods Wakerley Wood and Badsaddle Wood.
First record: Druce 1876
Druce: Very rare.

10 TULIPA L.
1 T. sylvestris L.
Wild Tulip
Introduction. Parks and woodland.
Established only within parkland, or former parkland, as relics of planting, at Castle Ashby, Courteenhall, Brockhall and near Greatworth.
First record: Sir Hereward Wake 1885
Druce: Very rare.

11 FRITILLARIA L.
1 F. meleagris L.
Fritillary
Native. Damp meadows.
A recent record from Delapre Abbey, Northampton, is probably planted or a garden escape. It appeared along a damp riding in Salcey Forest, on the Buckinghamshire side of the county boundary, for a couple of years in the 1960s, it was very short lived.
First record: Baker 1822
Druce: Very rare.

12 LILIUM L.
1 L. martagon L.

Martagon Lily
Introduction. Parks and plantations.
It is present at Castle Ashby, Brockhall, Newbottle and Finedon Spinneys, and at one site in the Soke of Peterborough. In all cases it is a relic of planting, generally in the grounds or former grounds of large houses.

13 CONVALLARIA L.
1 C. majalis L.
Lily-of-the-Valley
Native. Woodlands.
Extremely rare. Truly wild only in Bedford Purlieus and Easton Hornstocks. Two other records are of garden escapes. It was formerly more common as a wild plant in the north-east, with old records from several woods in this area.
First record: Morton 1712
Druce: Very local.

14 POLYGONATUM Miller
1 P. multiflorum (L.) All.
Solomon's-seal
Native. Woodlands.
Probably extinct as a native plant, with the last record dating from 1907, when it was seen at West Haddon. Recent records are of garden escapes at Harlestone Firs, Daventry Country Park and near Woodford.
First record: Miss Lightfoot 1860
Druce: Very rare.

17 PARIS L.
1 P. quadrifolia L. (25)
Herb Paris

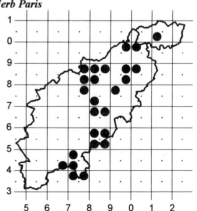

5 6 7 8 9 0 1 2

Native. Ancient woodlands. Rare, usually being seen as isolated plants within ancient woodland in the eastern half of the county but often overlooked.
First record: Morton 1712
Druce: Local.

18 ORNITHOGALUM L.

1 O. pyrenaicum L.
Spiked Star-of-Bethlehem, Bath Asparagus
British. Meadows, scrub and open woodland. Recorded on a former railway near Eydon.

2 O. angustifolium Boreau
(*O. umbellatum* auct., non L.)
Star-of-Bethlehem
Native in extreme north-east and in the south. Grassland and woodland. Extremely rare. Grows in considerable numbers on a grass verge near Helpston, where it may be native, but other recent records may well be garden escapes.
First record: Beesley 1842
Druce: (O. umbellatum) Very rare.

3 O. nutans L.
Drooping Star-of-Bethlehem
Introduction. Woodlands. Only recorded from Woodford Spinney where it is certainly a relic of earlier cultivation that has persisted for many years.
First record: Rev. T. Hitchens 1884
Druce: Very rare.

19 SCILLA L.

3 S. siberica Haw.
Siberian Squill
Introduction. Gardens etc. A single record, a relic of planting, at Castle Ashby.

20 HYACINTHOIDES Heister ex Fabr.
(*Endymion* Dumort.)

2 H. non-scripta (L.) Chouard ex Rothm.
(102)
(*Endymion non-scriptus* (L.) Garcke)
Bluebell
Native. Woodland. Very common in habitat. Generally found within ancient woodland throughout the county, but also found in smaller quantities in plantations or in shaded habitats, such as beneath hedgerows, on former woodland sites.

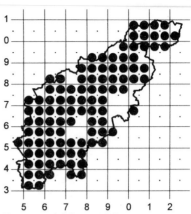

First record: Morton 1712
Druce: (Scilla non-scripta) Locally abundant and widely distributed.

3 H. hispanica (Miller) Rothm. (12)
(*Endymion hispanicus* (Mill.) Chouard)
Spanish Bluebell
Introduction. Woodlands. An occasional garden escape, or a relic of earlier cultivation.

22 CHIONODOXA Boiss.

1 C. forbesii Baker
Glory-of-the-snow
Introduction. Gardens etc. Two records, both relics of earlier planting at Castle Ashby and Burghley House.

23 MUSCARI Miller

1 M. neglectum Guss. ex Ten.
(*M. atlanticum* Boiss. ex Reuter)
Grape-hyacinth
British. Parkland. A relic of former planting in parkland where it is occasionally still to be found.
First record: C.E.Wright 1905
Druce: (M. racemosum) [Recorded at two locations. No status given].

2 M. armeniacum Leichtlin ex Baker
Garden Grape-hyacinth
Introduction. Waste ground. A relic of former planting in gardens, it has established itself on waste ground and roadside verges.

4 M. comosum (L.) Miller
Tassel Hyacinth

Introduction. Waste ground. A solitary record.

24 ALLIUM L.

9 A. paradoxum (M.Bieb.) Don

Few-flowered Garlic, Few-flowered Leek

Introduction. Waste places and cultivated ground.

Naturalised on isolated sites as an escape or a relic of planting, as in the wild garden at Cottesbrooke Hall. It is well established on the roadside between East Haddon and Guilsborough, probably as a throw-out.

First record: Northampton Natural History Society excursion (Flore) 1961-2

10 A. ursinum L.   (39)

Ramsons

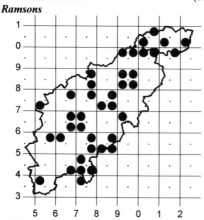

Native. Woodlands.

Occasional but may be abundant in habitat. Mainly confined to old woodlands but sometimes existing as relic populations in hedgerows and plantations.

First record: Morton 1712

Druce: Very local.

11 A. oleraceum L.

Field Garlic

Native. Rocky ground, walls and scrub. Extinct. The last record is from old walls at Thorp in 1873.

First record: Pitt 1813

Druce: Very rare.

16 A. vineale L.   (11)

Wild Onion, Crow Garlic

Native. Verges, cultivated and waste ground.

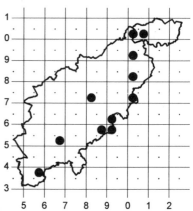

Rare. Much of its grassland habitat has now been destroyed by ploughing, and it is now found mainly on canal banks, roadside verges etc., where it can be well established.

First record: Morton 1712

Druce: Local.

31 LEUCOJUM L.

2 L. vernum L.

Spring Snowflake

Possibly British.   Woods copses and meadows.

Still present at Castle Ashby, and recorded from a couple of churchyards. In all instances it is present as a planted species.

Druce: In plantations at Castle Ashby. Obviously planted.

32 GALANTHUS L.

1 G. nivalis L.   (55)

Snowdrop

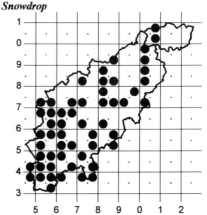

Introduction. Woodland and shaded sites. Occasional, but may be abundant, especially well established in parklands. It is always a result of planting or disposal of garden waste and can be abundant in some neglected churchyards.
Druce: [Only three records, but no status given].

33 NARCISSUS L.

1 x 3 N. tazetta x N. poeticus = N. x medioluteus Miller
Primrose-peerless
Introduction. Grassland.
No recent records.
Druce: (N. biflorus) Moat of Fotheringhay Castle. Extinct.

3 N. poeticus L.
Pheasant's-eye Daffodil, Poet's Narcissus
a subsp. *poeticus?*
Introduction. Meadows.
An isolated record of a garden escape or throw-out.
First record: John Roby 1850
Druce: [First and only record listed].

5 N. pseudonarcissus L.
Wild Daffodil
a subsp. **pseudonarcissus**   (4)
Daffodil

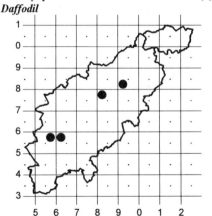

Native. Woodlands and open grassland. Extremely rare. Localised and isolated populations, generally within or close to ancient woodlands, as at Geddington Chase and Everdon Stubbs. Dumping of garden rubbish, escapes from cultivation and

deliberate, well-intentioned, plantings mean that a variety of cultivated species are now established in the countryside in roadside verges, churchyards and other localities.
First record: Baker 1822
Druce: Local and rare.

c subsp. **major** (Curtis) Baker
Spanish Daffodil, Large Daffodil
Introduction. Plantations.
No recent records.
First record: Druce 1875
Druce: (N. major) Rare.

34 ASPARAGUS L.

1 A. officinalis L.
b subsp. **officinalis**
Garden Asparagus
Introduction.   Scrub,   wasteland   and cultivated ground.
Probably under-recorded, usually a garden escape or distributed by birds.
Druce: Present as garden escape or garden outcast.

35 RUSCUS L.

1 R. aculeatus L.   (10)
Butcher's-broom

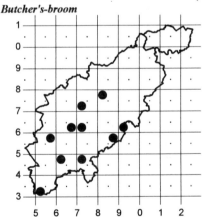

British. Hedges and plantations.
Rare, and in every case a relic of planting.
First record: Druce 1878
Druce: [Only three records but no status given].

159 IRIDACEAE

5 IRIS L.
3 I. pseudacorus L.   (103)
Yellow Iris, Yellow Flag

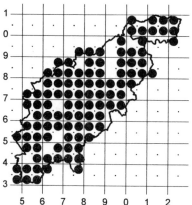

5 6 7 8 9 0 1 2

Native. Marshes, streams and watersides. Occasional in all wet habitats throughout the county, particularly by the Rivers Nene and Welland and Grand Union Canal.
First record: Clare 1821
Druce: Common.

8 I. foetidissima L.   (12)
Stinking Iris

5 6 7 8 9 0 1 2

Native. Open woodland.
Rare. Sometimes probably seeded from discarded plants, which may account for its presence in the churchyard at Stoke Doyle. It is naturalised in Castle Ashby Woods, where it may have been deliberately planted and there are also colonies in both Wicken and Fineshade woods and other scattered areas.
First record: Druce 1886
Druce: Very rare.

8 CROCUS L.
C. sativus L.
Saffron Crocus
Possible introduction - origin uncertain.
Probably present only as a garden escape or throw-out.

3 C. nudiflorus Smith
Autumn Crocus
Introduction. Parks and grassland.
Present as a relic of cultivation, as in the wild garden at Kelmarsh Hall.

13 CROCOSMIA Planchon
C. x crocosmiiflora (Lemoine)
Montbretia
Introduction. Waste ground.
Present as a garden escape.

161 DIOSCOREACEAE
1 TAMUS L.
1 T. communis L.   (122)
Black Bryony

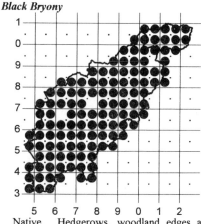

5 6 7 8 9 0 1 2

Native. Hedgerows, woodland edges and rides.
Common, only being absent from a very few isolated areas.
First record: Pitt 1813
Druce: Common and widely distributed.

162 ORCHIDACEAE
2 CEPHALANTHERA Rich.
1 C. damasonium (Miller) Druce
White Helleborine
Native. Woodlands on calcareous soil.
Present in small numbers in Woodford Shrubbery and reported at Ashton Wold. There are also unconfirmed reports from

places such as East Carlton Country Park, near Corby where it may be a wild plant or a relic of planting. None of these localities provide the correct habitat for this plant and in most cases there is evidence that it may have been introduced into these areas.
First record: Henderson 1873
Druce: Very rare.

2 C. longifolia (L.) Fritsch
Narrow-leaved Helleborine
Native. Woodlands on calcareous soil. Extremely rare. An unconfirmed record from Old Dry Hills, Brigstock in 1969.

3 EPIPACTIS Zinn
1 E. palustris (L.) Crantz
Marsh Helleborine
Native. Marshes and bogs.
Extremely rare and possibly extinct. It still existed in the Soke of Peterborough until recently, but a search in 1993 failed to reveal it.
First record: Goodyer 1660
Druce: (Helleborine palustris) Very local and rare.

3 E. purpurata Smith   (9)
Violet Helleborine
Native. Coppiced woodland and woodland rides.
Rare. Confined to ancient woodland in the far north and the south of the county such as Easton Hornstocks, Short Wood nature reserve, Geddington Chase, Salcey Forest and Yardley Chase.
First record: Berkeley c1850
Druce: (Helleborine purpurata) Local.

4 E. helleborine (L.) Crantz   (53)
Broad-leaved Helleborine
Native. Coppiced woodland and woodland rides.
Occasional. It shows a distinct preference for the ancient woodlands both in the north and south of the county, but sometimes establishes itself in old quarries.
First record: Baker 1822
Druce: (Helleborine Helleborine) Local.

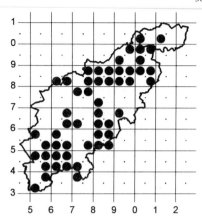

6 E. leptochila (Godfery) Godfery
Narrow-lipped Helleborine
Native. Woodland.
Extremely rare. There is a single record of a small colony in a privately owned woodland in the north-west of the county.

5 NEOTTIA Guett.
1 N. nidus-avis (L.) Rich.   (11)
Bird's-nest Orchid

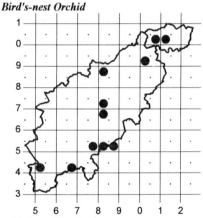

Native. Woodland.
Very rare. It is now known to be at only six sites, the ancient woodlands of Bedford Purlieus, Salcey Forest, Yardley Chase and Sywell Wood, where it was recorded by Druce. It has also been recorded in both Hardwick Wood, a plantation on the site of an ancient woodland where over 100 flower spikes were found in 1992, and Short Wood, both sites discovered since Druce published

his flora. In 1993 it was re-discovered in Stoke Wood, confirming a record by Sir George Chester, and in 1994 a second colony was discovered there. It has formerly been recorded in other ancient woodlands, including Bowd Lane Wood and some in the Soke of Peterborough, and it is possible that, because of its preference for deep shade, it may still be present but overlooked in other woodlands.

First record: Irvine 1838
Druce: Local and rather rare.

6 LISTERA R.Br.
1 L. ovata (L.) R.Br. (59)
Common Twayblade

Native. Woodland and thickets.
Occasional. One of the commoner of the orchid species within the county, being found in both ancient woodland and beneath the shrub layer of newly colonised ground such as in abandoned quarries, and in open grassland. It occasionally occurs in a three-leaved form.
First record: Baker 1822
Druce: Locally common.

7 SPIRANTHES Rich.
1 S. spiralis (L.) Chevall.
Autumn Lady's-tresses
Native. Calcareous pastures.
Extremely rare. Recorded by Druce from a few areas but there have been no recent records except for one during the 1950s, when it occurred on a road verge near Whittlebury. It was subsequently thought to be extinct, but there is a recent and currently

unconfirmed report of this orchid from the Farthingstone area.
First record: Morton 1712
Druce: Very local and rare.

12 HERMINIUM L.
1 H. monorchis (L.) R.Br.
Musk Orchid
Native. Calcareous grassland.
Extinct, if ever present.
First record: Merrett 1666
Druce: [Druce considered the first and only record (Merrett 1666) to be extremely doubtful].

13 PLATANTHERA Rich.
1 P. chlorantha (Custer) Reichb. (28)
Greater Butterfly-orchid

Native. Coppiced woodland and woodland rides.
Rare. Found mainly in ancient or well established woodlands throughout the county but never in large numbers. Also occasionally found in abandoned quarries, such as the Plens nature reserve at Desborough, where a few plants have appeared following scrub clearance.
First record: Possibly Baker 1822
Druce: (Habenaria virescens) Widely distributed but not common.

2 P. bifolia (L.) Rich.
Lesser Butterfly-orchid
Native. Woodlands.
Probably extinct. Only recorded in Whittlewood Forest, where it is no longer to be found, and very possibly at Bedford

Purlieus in the 1960s, but this latter record was never confirmed.

First record: Druce 1877

Druce: (Habenaria bifolia) Rare or overlooked.

14 ANACAMPTIS Rich.
1 A. pyramidalis (L.) Rich.   (13)
Pyramidal Orchid

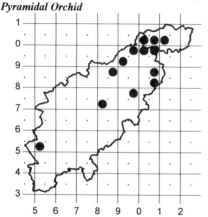

Native. Calcareous pasture.

Very rare. Confined to a few sites almost entirely in the north. It is decreasing as suitable sites disappear although it can be locally common in particularly favourable circumstances, such as at Barnack Hills and Holes and Collyweston Deeps nature reserves. In 1992 it flowered on the lawn of Ashton Wold for the first time. There are also new records from Clopton, where it had previously been recorded on the roadside in the late 1940s before it was eliminated by mowing. It is also recorded from Bedford Purlieus, near Weekley Hall Woods, Cranford Quarry and Woodford Halse. A white flowered atypical form was found in Hardwick Woods in 1970.

First record: Pitt 1813

Druce: (Orchis pyramidalis) Local, roadsides and calcareous fields.

16 GYMNADENIA R.Br.
1 G. conopsea (L.) R.Br.
Fragrant Orchid

First record: Gulliver 1841

Druce: (Habenaria gymnadenia) Local, on limestone and basic marshes.

a subsp. **conopsea**
Native. Limestone pasture, old quarries etc.
Extremely rare. It has recently been recorded at only two sites within a few miles of one another in the north of the county - Barnack Hills and Holes national nature reserves, where it is one of the more common of the orchids, and Collyweston Deeps, where it is quite uncommon.

b subsp. **densiflora** (Wahlenb.) Camus, Bergon & A.Camus
Extremely Rare. Marshes and chalk grassland.
Only recorded from Barnack Hills and Holes, where a single example was seen on a north facing slope in 1994; and Sutton Bog. It was present at Wittering Marsh during the 1960s.

16 x 18   **GYMNADENIA x DACTYL-ORHIZA = X DACTYLODENIA** Garay & H.Sweet
1 x 1   **G. conopsea x D. fuchsii = X Dactylodenia st-quintinii** (Godfery) J.Duvign.
Native. Marshes.
One plant at Sutton Bog, 1981. The parent could only have been *Gymnadenia conopsea* subsp. *densiflora*.

17 COELOGLOSSUM Hartman
1 C. viride (L.) Hartman
Frog Orchid
Native. Grassland.
Extremely rare. Only recorded from Barnack Hills and Holes national nature reserve where it grows only in small numbers, and at an isolated area of unimproved grassland with an unsecured future, where it may now be extinct as it has not been seen recently.

First record: Morton 1712

Druce: (Habenaria viride) Very rare.

18 DACTYLORHIZA Necker ex Nevski
1 D. fuchsii (Druce) Soó   (89)
Common Spotted-orchid
Native. Woodland and pastures.

Occasional. Probably the commonest orchid in Northamptonshire, being found throughout the county in old quarries, woodland (ancient and secondary), unimproved and regenerating grasslands. Although generally found in small numbers it occasionally can reach numbers in excess of 1000 on quite small sites.

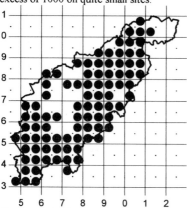

5 6 7 8 9 0 1 2

First record: Clare 1820

Druce: (Orchis fuchsii) Rather common on clay in woods and damp places.

1 x 4 D. fuchsii x D. praetermissa = D. x grandis (Druce) P.Hunt

Native. Marshy meadows.

Extremely rare. It has been recorded from Lyveden and Bonemills Hollow, and there is an old record from Wittering, but it may be present elsewhere and overlooked as the two parents quite often grow together.

Druce: (Orchis mortonii) [No status given but recorded from seventeen localities which is more than one parent D. praetermissa].

2 D. maculata (L.) Soó
Heath Spotted-orchid

a subsp. **ericetorum** (E.F.Linton) P.Hunt & Summerh.

Native. Damp pasture.

Extremely rare, being confined to one site on unimproved farmland in the centre of the county where, although it is well established at this location, its future is not secure, and one site in the Soke of Peterborough.

First record: (Orchis maculata) Druce 1911
Druce: Very local.

3 D. incarnata (L.) Soó
Early Marsh-orchid

a subsp. **incarnata**   (7)

Native. Marshes.

Very rare. Restricted to marshes or wet flushes at Aldwincle, Bulwick, Charlton and Cosgrove; and marshy areas in old quarries such as Cranford, possibly its only hope for future survival.

First record: 1880

Druce: (Orchis incarnata) Rare, confined to marshes.

c subsp. **pulchella** (Druce) Soó

Native. Acid grassland.

In the summer of 1993 a solitary specimen answering the description of this sub-species was found in uncut grass, within the conservation area in Hazel Wood, Corby, within a few hundred yards of the town centre. It did not reappear in 1994.

4 D. praetermissa (Druce) Soó   (13)
Southern Marsh-orchid

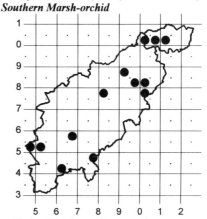

5 6 7 8 9 0 1 2

Native. Marshes and wet meadows.

Very rare. It is only known at Grafton Regis Meadow, Syresham Marsh, Woodford Halse railway cutting, Boddington Meadow Wildlife Trust reserve and Bugbrooke in the south of the county and at Aldwincle Marsh, Titchmarsh Old Fish Ponds, Wittering, Lyveden, Brigstock Country Park, Bonemills Hollow and Wansford Pasture nature reserve in the north. At Wansford *D. praetermissa* and *D. praetermissa var. junialis* (Vermeulen) Senghas (Leopard Marsh Orchid) grow in approximately equal numbers.

First record: Druce 1913 - the first record in Britain

Druce: [No status given].

20 ORCHIS L.
2 O. mascula (L.) L. (44)
Early-purple Orchid

5 6 7 8 9 0 1 2

Native. Open woodlands.
Occasional, often occurring as solitary plants or in very small groups but can occasionally be frequent in its habitat. It occurs throughout the county in ancient woodland or plantations that were formerly ancient woodlands. It also occurs on open ground at Barnack Hills and Holes national nature reserve.
First record: Clare 1821
Druce: Rather common and widely distributed.

3 O. morio L. (9)
Green-winged Orchid
Native. Pastures, generally on calcareous soil.
Very rare. It is found on a few isolated sites in the county. It has suffered more than *O. mascula* from habitat destruction in the name of agricultural improvement and it is probably still decreasing in numbers although it has recently been found at a few sites in the cuttings of the old Great Central Railway where its future may be more secure. Colour variations are not uncommon with both pink and white flowers occurring in populations.Within the county *Orchis morio* is approaching the northern limit of its range.
First record: Baker 1822
Druce: Locally abundant on mainly calcareous pastures.

4 O. ustulata L.
Burnt Orchid
Native. Grassy places on calcareous soil. Probably extinct. Only ever known from the roadside verges between Duddington and Collyweston and in the area of Barnack and Sutton in the Soke of Peterborough. It was last recorded at Southorpe in the 1956 by J. Gilbert.
First record: Morton 1712
Druce: Very rare.

21 ACERAS R.Br.
1 A. anthropophorum (L.) W.T.Aiton
Man Orchid
Native. Limestone pasture and old quarries. Extremely rare, but can be abundant where it occurs. The only recent records are from Bedford Purlieus and the nature reserves at Collyweston Deeps, Castor Hanglands and Barnack Hills and Holes. At the latter it has been estimated that the flower spikes can amount to over a thousand a year.
First record: Rev M.J. Berkeley c1850
Druce: Very local. Extraordinarily plentiful in 1928.

23 OPHRYS L.
1 O. insectifera L.
Fly Orchid
Native. Woodland on calcareous soil. Extremely rare, being recorded only in Wakerley Woods, Bedford Purlieus, Collyweston and Easton Hornstocks, but it may be under-recorded as it is extremely difficult to find.
First record: Morton (NHN) 1712
Druce: (Ophrys muscifera) Very rare.

2 O. sphegodes Miller
Early Spider-orchid
Native. Old quarries of limestone. Extinct. The last record was in 1852, at Thornhaugh.
First record: Dr. Bowles 1650
Druce: Very rare, if not extinct.

3 O. apifera Hudson (36)
Bee Orchid
Native. Short and rough grassland. Occasional, but slowly spreading as it colonises new sites such as abandoned quarries and other newly disturbed ground

308

with a high lime content. It can be very erratic in numbers from year to year. *O. apifera* var. *flavescens* and a form approaching var. *trollii* have both been recorded in the county, although only the former in recent years. The former was recorded near Weekley Hall Wood between 1992 and 1994 and the latter from the MOD area in Yardley Chase in the 1980s.

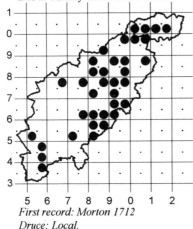

First record: Morton 1712
Druce: Local.

References
Allen D.E. *The Flora of the Rugby District* Rugby 1957
Clapham A.R. Tutin T.G. Warburg E.F. *Excursion Flora of the British Isles* Cambridge University Press 1981
Clapham A.R. Tutin T.G. Warburg E.F. *Flora of the British Isles* Cambridge University Press 1962
Clement E.J. Foster M.C. *Alien Plants of the British Isles* Botanical Society of the British Isles 1994
Dony J.G. Jury S.L. Perring F.H. *English Names of Wild Flowers Edition Two* Botanical Society of the British Isles 1974
Graham G.G. Primavesi A.L. *Roses of Great Britain and Ireland* Botanical Society of the British Isles 1993
Jermy A.C. Chater A.O. David R.W. *Sedges of the British Isles* Botanical Society of the British Isles 1982
Journals of the Northamptonshire Natural History Society and Field Club 1959-1990

Kent D.H. *List of Vascular Plants of the British Isles* Botanical Society of the British Isle 1992
Perring F.H. Walters S.M. (Editors) *Atlas of the British Flora* Thomas Nelson, Botanical Society of the British Isles 1963
Rees J.S. *A Flora of Oundle* Oundle School Natural History Society 1970
Rich T.C.G. *Crucifers of Great Britain and Ireland* Botanical Society of the British Isle 1991
Stace C. *New Flora of the British Isle* Cambridge University Press 1991
Stewart A. Pearman D.A. Preston C.D. (Editors) *Scarce Plants in Britain* Joint Nature Conservation Committee 1994
and of course
Druce G.C. *The Flora of Northamptonshire* T. Buncle and Co. 1930

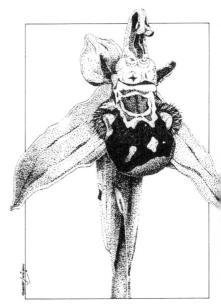

Ophrys apifera

Bee orchid (drawing by Rob Wilson)

The Flora of
NORTHAMPTONSHIRE
and the Soke of Peterborough~

Presumed Extinct Species

Vice-County 32 - *Northamptonshire and the Soke of Peterborough*

A record of species which are native to Northamptonshire and the Soke of Peterborough and thought to be extinct. Those names printed in italics are of species for which there are no records after the publication of Druce's *Flora of Northamptonshire* in 1930. Other species listed have not been reported in the county since 1970 or cannot be found at their recorded sites, even after deliberate searching. Hybrids are not included in this list. Species in brackets were only ever doubtfully present in the county.

Ajuga chamaepitys
Allium oleraceum
Arnoseris minima
Botrychium lunaria
Bupleurum tenuissimum
Cardamine impatiens
Carduus tenuiflorus
Carex dioica
Carex echinata
Carex laevigata
Centaurea cyanus
Ceratophyllum submersum
Chamaemelum nobile
Chenopodium vulvaria
Cirsium dissectum
Clinopodium calamintha
Colchicum autumnale
(Crepis foetida)
Cynoglossum germanicum
Cystopteris fragilis
Daphne mezereum
Drosera rotundifolia
Eleocharis multicaulis
Eleocharis quinqueflora
Eleogiton fluitans
Epipactis palustris
(Eriophorum gracile)
Eriophorum latifolium
Erodium moschatum
Eryngium campestre
Festuca filiformis
Filago gallica
Filago minima

Fritillaria meleagris
Galeopsis angustifolia
Galium pumilum
Galium sterneri
Gentianella anglica
Gentianella campestris
Gymnocarpium dryopteris
Gymnocarpium robertianum
Hypericum montanum
Hypochaeris glabra
Impatiens noli-tangere
Jasione montana
Juncus squarrosus
Juniperus communis
Linum perenne subsp. anglicum
Lycopodium clavatum
Lythrum portula
Marrubium vulgare
Mentha suaveolens
Misopates orontium
Moenchia erecta
Montia fontana
Nardus stricta
Oenanthe crocata
Oenanthe lachenalii
Ophrys sphegodes
Orchis ustulata
Oreopteris limbosperma
Osmunda regalis
Papaver hybridum
Parnassia palustris
Pedicularis sylvatica
Persicaria laxiflora

Persicaria minor
Pilularia globulifera
Plantago coronopus
Platanthera bifolia
Polygala vulgaris subsp. collina
Polygonatum multiflorum
Potamogeton acutifolius
Potamogeton alpinus
Potamogeton friesii
Potamogeton gramineus
Potamogeton trichoides
Potentilla palustris
Prunus cerasus
(Sagina subulata)
Salvia pratensis
Scleranthus perennis
Solidago virgaurea
Sparganium natans
Stachys germanica
Stratiotes aloides
Teesdalia nudicaulis
Tephroseris integrifolia subsp integrifolia
Teucrium scordium
Thelypteris palustris
Trifolium scabrum
Ulex minor
Utricularia minor
Utricularia vulgaris
Valerianella carinata
Valerianella rimosa

The Flora of
NORTHAMPTONSHIRE
and the Soke of Peterborough~

Extremely Rare Species

Vice-County 32 - *Northamptonshire and the Soke of Peterborough*

A record of species which are native to Northamptonshire and the Soke of Peterborough and recorded from three or less sites. Hybrids are not included in this list.

Agrimonia procera
Agrostemma githago
Alchemilla xanthochlora
Anagallis arvensis subsp. caerulea
Anagallis tenella
Antennaria dioica
Anthriscus caucalis
Aphanes inexspectata
Arabis hirsuta
Astragulus danicus
Baldellia ranunculoides
Blechnum spicant
Blysmus compressus
Bromus hordeaceus subsp. thominei
Bromus racemosus
Carex binervis
Carex distans
Carex divulsa subsp. leersii
Carex ericetorum
Carex hostiana
Carex muricata subsp. lamprocarpa
Carex pulicaris
Carex rostrata
Carex vesicaria
Carex viridula subsp. oedocarpa
Centaurium pulchellum
Cephalanthera damasonium
Cephelanthera longifolia
Cerastium pumilum
Coeloglossum viride
Convallaria majalis
Cyperus longus
Dactylorhiza incarnata subsp. pulchella
Dactylorhiza maculata subsp. ericetorum

Epilobium lanceolatum
Epilobium roseum
Equisetum sylvaticum
Erica cinerea
Erica tetralix
Euphorbia lathyris
Euphorbia platyphyllos
Euphrasia pseudokerneri
Frangula alnus
Fumaria densiflora
Fumaria muralis subsp. muralis
Galium parisiense
Genista anglica
Geum rivale
Gnaphalium sylvaticum
Gymnadenia conopsea subsp. conopsea.
Gymnadenia conopsea subsp. densiflora
Helleborus viridis subsp. occidentalis
Hieracium umbellatum
Hordelymus europaeus
Hottonia palustris
Hydrocharis morsus-ranae
Hypericum androsaemum
Hypochaeris maculata
Juncus bulbosus
Juncus gerardii
Lemna minuta
Lepidium heterophyllum
Littorella uniflora
Luronium natans
Luzula forsteri
Melampyrum cristatum
Melampyrum pratense
Melica nutans
Menyanthes trifoliata
Minuartia hybrida

Monotropa hypopitys
Myosurus minimus
Myriophyllum alterniflorum
Myriophyllum verticillatum
Ophrys insectifera
Ornithopus perpusillus
Pedicularis palustris
Petroselinum segetum
Pinguicula vulgaris
Poa humilis
Poa palustris
Persicaria bistorta
Potamogeton coloratus
Potamogeton praelongus
Pulsatilla vulgaris
Pyrus pyraster
Ranunculus hederaceus
Ranunculus lingua
Ranunculus sardous
Sagina nodosa
Salix pentandra
Scandix pecten-veneris
Schoenoplectus tabernaemontani
Schoenus nigricans
Sium latifolium
Sonchus palustris
Spergularia rubra
Spiranthes spiralis
Spirodela polyrhiza
Stellaria neglecta
Stellaria palustris
Teucrium scorodonia
Thymus pulegioides
Trifolium ochroleucon
Ulmus plotii
Umbilicus rupestris
Viola canina subsp. canina
Viola tricolor

The Flora of
NORTHAMPTONSHIRE
and the Soke of Peterborough~

Rare Species

Vice-County 32 - Northamptonshire and the Soke of Peterborough

A record of species which are native to Northamptonshire and the Soke of Peterborough and are restricted to fifteen or less, but more than three sites.

Adoxa moschatellina
Aira caryophyllea
Aira praecox
Alisma lanceolatum
Allium vineale
Alopecurus aequalis
Anacamptis pyramidalis
Anchusa arvensis
Anthemis arvensis
Anthriscus caucalis
Apium inundatum
Aquilegia vulgaris
Asperula cynanchica subsp.
cynanchica
Astragalus danicus
Azolla filiculoides
Berberis vulgaris
Bidens cernua
Blackstonia perfoliata
Brassica nigra
Bromus lepidus
Bromus racemosus
Calamagrostis canescens
Callitriche hamulata
Callitriche obtusangula
Calluna vulgaris
Campanula glomerata
Cardamine amara
Carex caryophyllea
Carex divulsa subsp. divulsa
Carex pallescens
Carex panicea
Carex viridula subsp.
brachyrrhyncha
Carlina vulgaris
Cerastium diffusum
Cerastium semidecandrum
Chenopodium hybridum
Chrysosplenium oppositifolium

Clinopodium acinos
Clinopodium ascendens
Coronopus didymus
Crepis biennis
Cuscuta epithymum
Cuscuta europaea
Cynoglossum officinale
Dactylorhiza praetermissa
Danthonia decumbens
Datura stramonium
Deschampsia flexuosa
Descurainia sophia
Dipsacus pilosus
Dryopteris affinis subsp. borreri
Dryopteris carthusiana
Elymus caninus
Epilobium palustre
Epipactis purpurata
Eriophorum angustifolium
Euphorbia amygdaloides
Euphorbia lathyris
Filago vulgaris
Gagea lutea
Galeopsis bifida
Galeopsis speciosa
Genista tinctoria subsp. tinctoria
Gentianella amarella subsp.
amarella
Geranium columbinum
Geranium rotundifolium
Helianthemum nummularium
Helictotrichon pratense
Helleborus foetidus
Helleborus viridis
Hippocrepis comosa
Hydrocotyle vulgaris
Hypericum humifusum
Hypericum pulchrum
Iris foetidissima

Isolepis setacea
Juncus compressus
Koeleria macrantha
Lathraea squamaria
Lathyrus linifolius
Lathyrus nissolia
Lathyrus sylvestris
Lepidium ruderale
Limosella aquatica
Linaria repens
Lithospermum arvense
Lotus glaber
Luzula sylvatica
Lysimachia vulgaris
Mercurialis annua
Molinia caerulea
Neottia nidus-avis
Nepeta cataria
Nymphoides peltata
Oenanthe fistulosa
Oenanthe fluviatilis
Onobrychis viciifolia
Orchis morio
Orobanche elatior
Orobanche minor
Poa angustifolia
Polygala serpyllifolia
Polypodium interjectum
Polystichum aculeatum
Polystichum setiferum
Populus nigra subsp. betulifolia
Potamogeton compressus
Potamogeton obtusifolius
Potamogeton pusillus
Potentilla anglica
Prunus domestica subsp. institia
Quercus petraea
Ranunculus arvensis

Ranunculus ficaria subsp.
bulbilifer
Ranunculus fluitans
Ranunculus hederaceus
Ranunculus parviflorus
Ranunculus peltatus
Ranunculus pencillatus subsp.
pseudofluitans
Rorippa sylvestris
Rumex maritimus
Rumex pulcher
Salix aurita
Salvia verbenaca
Sambucus ebulus
Samolus valerandi

Scabiosa columbaria
Scirpus sylvaticus
Scleranthus annuus
Sedum telephium
Senecio sylvaticus
Serratula tinctoria
Silene noctiflora
Sisymbrium altissimum
Sorbus torminalis
Spergula arvensis
Stachys arvensis
Stellaria pallida
Thymus polytrichus subsp.
britannicus
Torilis nodosa

Trifolium arvense
Trifolium micranthum
Trifolium striatum
Triglochin palustris
Tulipa sylvestris
Ulmus minor subsp. angustifolia
Ulmus vegeta
Valerianella dentata
Verbascum nigrum
Verbena officinalis
Veronica montana
Veronica scutellata
Vicia sylvatica
Viscum album

Goldenrod and weasel's snout, two plants now extinct in Northamptonshire and the
Soke of Peterborough   (drawings by Rosemary Parslow)

The Flora of
NORTHAMPTONSHIRE
and the Soke of Peterborough~

Gazeteer

of Place Names

This gazetteer is intended as an aid to the location of the place names given in the text of the systematic flora. The names of towns and villages are generally those used on the current edition of the 1:50,000 Ordnance Survey maps of the area; while other names can often be located on larger scale maps. Except for the Wildlife Trust nature reserves, there is no inferred right of access to any of the sites listed here; neither is there any inference that the site still contains anything of botanical interest. The map references given, which are normally of the centre of the site, may in certain instances only direct the reader to the general locality even though a specific site is named, and in a few instances, where it has been thought desirable, sites have been omitted. Sites in italics are outside the boundaries of Northamptonshire and the Soke of Peterborough.

Abington Park	part of Northampton	SP778615
Ailsworth	village 7 km W of Peterborough	TL117989
Ailsworth Heath	N of Ailsworth village, adjoining Castor Hanglands and part of Castor Hanglands national nature reserve	TF115020
Alder Wood Meadow, Rushton	neutral grassland 6 km NW of Kettering	SP840846
Aldwincle	village in the Nene valley 14 km E of Kettering	TL005819
Apethorpe	village 11 km S of Stamford	TL024957
Ash Coppice	part of Carlton Purlieus, 4 km W of Corby	SP842875
Ashby St Ledgers	village and park 5km N of Daventry	SP573683
Ashley	village above the Welland valley, 11 km W of Corby	SP795910
Ashton Wold	woodland, part ancient, SE of Oundle	TL090875
Ashton, near Oundle	estate village 16 km E. of Corby	TL055882
Aston-le-walls	village 16 km NW of Brackley	SP496508
Aynho	village in extreme SW of county, 8 km W of Brackley	SP515330
Aynho Wharf	Oxford Canal wharf 1 km W of Aynho	SP499323
Badby	village 4 km S of Daventry	SP560590
Badby Downs	area of land to the SW of Badby Wood	SP558580
Badby Woods	Ancient woodland 4 km S of Daventry with Victorian planting and a more recent mixed plantation on the eastern side. A famous Bluebell wood.	SP567583
Badsaddle Wood	SSSI, small remnant of ancient woodland 7 km SW of Kettering	SP83-72-
Bainton	village 11 km NW of Peterborough	TF094060
Barby	village 6 km SE of Rugby	SP543704
Barford Bridge	bridge over River Ise on A6003 north of Kettering	SP860831
Barnack	village 13 km NW of Peterborough	TF072050

Barnack Hills and Holes	National nature reserve, site of mediaeval limestone quarry, S of Barnack	TF075046
Barnwell Castle	mediaeval castle N of Barnwell village	TL050853
Barnwell Wold	mixed woodland 8 km NE of Thrapston	TL079815
Barrowden	village on Rutland bank of Welland N of Wakerley	SK948002
Barton Seagrave	large village on SE outskirts of Kettering	SP888771
Bearshank Wood	woodland	SP994861
Bedford Purlieus	ancient woodland 15 km W of Peterborough	TL040995
Biggin	park 3km W of Oundle, now part of Oundle golf course	TL010892
Billing Lings	area on E edge of Northampton	SP800635
Blackmile Lane	lane on northern outskirts of Grendon	SP895609
Blisworth	large village on A43 7 km S of Northampton	SP728544
Boddington Meadow	Wildlife Trust reserve half way between Daventry and Banbury	SP494532
Boddington Reservoir	small reservoir serving the Oxford Canal 1 km E of Upper Boddington. (SP500527). It lies between Boddington Meadow and Byfield Pool reserves	SP497530
Borough Fen	fen with duck decoy N of Peterborough	TF200080
Borough Hill	on E edge of Daventry, former BBC transmission station	SP585625
Boughton	village on N edge of Northampton	SP753659
Boughton Estates	estate of the Duke of Buccleuch 4 km NE of Kettering	SP900815
Boughton Park	part of Boughton Estate (see above)	SP895815
Bowd Lane Wood	ancient woodland 10 km NW of Kettering	SP807867
Bozeat	large village 9 km S of Wellingborough	SP906592
Bozenham Mill	on the River Tove 7 km E of Towcester	SP767482
Brackley	small town close to Oxfordshire border in SW	SP587375
Brampton Golf Course	golf course on N outskirts of Northampton	SP725647
Brampton Valley Way	footway along the line of former Northampton to Market Harborough (Leicestershire) railway	SP734680-SP739864
Braunston	canal village 5km NW of Daventry	SP545662
Brigstock Country Park	former quarries beside A6116 E of Brigstock	SP955850
Bringhurst	small village in Leicestershire close to the county boundary, the River Welland	SP842922
Brixworth	village 9km N of Northampton	SP748705
Brockhall	emparked village 12 km W of Northampton	SP633626
Broughton	village 4 km SW of Kettering	SP835756
Broughton Spinney	pocket park close to Broughton church	SP837757
Bucknell Wood	mixed conifer/broad-leaved Forestry Commision woodland	SP652447
Bugbrooke	large village 8km W of Northampton	SP690574
Bulwick	village 8 km NE of Corby	SP962942
Burghley House	stately home with parkland 2 km SE of Stamford	TF048061
Burton Latimer	small town 5 km SE of Kettering	SP900745
Byfield Pool	Canal reservoir linked to Boddington Reservoir (qv), and a Wildlife Trust reserve.	SP500527

Caldecot	village in Rutland 5 km N of Corby and close to the county boundary, the River Welland.	SP868936
Canon's Ashby	village 14km N of Brackley	SP577505
Car Dyke	drainage canal 4 km N and E of Peterborough	TF180040
Castle Ashby	village 10 km E of Northampton, adjacent to park	SP860593
Castlethorpe	*in north Buckinghamshire*	*SP800445*
Castor Hanglands	National nature reserve 8 km W of Peterborough, ancient woodland	TF120015
Cat's Water	watercourse E of Peterborough	
Chacombe	village 4 km NE of Banbury	SP491440
Charlton	village 6km W of Brackley, former limestone quarry	SP527360
Charwelton	village in the west, 7 km S of Daventry	SP535560
Chipping Warden	village in SW of county	SP498488
Church Brampton	village on NW edge of Northampton 6 km from centre	SP720658
Church Charwelton	deserted village 7 km S of Daventry, important ponds	SP544555
Church Wood	conifer wood 7 km S of Daventry	SP570549
Clipston	village 6 km S of Market harborough	SP711816
Clopton	village close to Cambridgeshire boundary 19 km E of Kettering	TL065800
Cogenhoe	village on S rim of River Nene 7 km E of Northampton	SP825606
Cold Oak Copse	originally part of Yardley Chase	SP87-57-
Collingtree	village immediately S of Northampton	SP751557
Collingtree Golf Course	golf course on S outskirts of Northampton	SP755555
Collyweston	village close to Leicestershire border 6 km SW of Stamford	SK996028
Collyweston Deeps	Wildlife Trust reserve, grassland on former stone quarries	TF004038
Collyweston Great Wood	National nature reserve ancient woodland 7 km S of Stamford	TF006008
Corby	town 10 km N of Kettering, until 1980 centre of iron smelting in county	SP88-88-
Cosgrove	village near county border and immediately N of Milton Keynes	SP795426
Cosgrove Pits	gravel pits on Buckinghamshire boundary 17 km S of Northampton	SP798424
Coton Park	The grounds of Coton Manor	SP673716
Cotterstock	village 2 km N of Oundle	TL049906
Cottesbrooke	village 16 km SW of Kettering	SP710735
Cottesbrooke Hall	country estate 17 km SW of Kettering	SP711739
Cottingham Quarry	former quarry 3 km W of Corby	SP846896
Courteenhall	village in park of same name 7 km S of Northampton	SP760530
Cowthick Plantation	plantation in former ironstone quarry N of Stanion	SP920873
Cranford	twin villages 6 km E of Kettering	SP925770
Cranford Quarry	former ironstone quarries, partially infilled	SP930762
Cranford Wood	small ancient woodland on S boundary of Rockingham Forest	SP937792

Cransley Reservoir	former water supply reservoir, now used for leisure activities, 4 km W of Kettering	SP830781
Crick	village 14km NW of Daventry	|SP589725
Croughton	village 6 km SW of Brackley	SP547335
Dallington	district of Northampton	SP740615
Dane Hole	wooded steep sided valley N of Hellidon	SP521588
Daventry	town 18 km W of Northampton	SP57-62-
Daventry Country Park	land around Daventry reservoir	SP580638
Daventry Reservoir	Canal reservoir, see Daventry country park	SP580638
Deanshanger	large village 17 km E of Brackley	SP761400
Deanshanger Gravel Pits	former gravel pits, one is now a trout farm	SP772389
Delapre Abbey	large house in grounds in S Northampton	SP760591
Denford	village in Nene valley 12 km E of Kettering	SP991766
Desborough	small town 8 km NW of Kettering	SP803831
Dingley	village and park 4 km E of Market Harborough	SP770880
Ditchford	4 km E of Wellingborough	SP930682
Draughton	small village 11 km W of Kettering	SP762767
Drayton	village in Rutland near Northamptonshire border	SP830922
Drayton House	stately home with park 1 km W of Lowick	SP963800
Drayton Reservoir	reservoir to the north of Daventry	SP56-64-
Duddington	village close to Rutland boundary 7 km SW of Stamford	SK990008
Duston	W district of Northampton 3 km from town centre	SP725810
Duston Mill	mill to W of Northampton, near A45 ring road	SP729596
Earls Barton	small town in the Nene valley between Northampton and Wellingborough	SP852638
East Carlton	village 11 km NW of Kettering, 5 km W of Corby	SP831892
East Carlton Country Park	Borough Council run park on E side of village,	SP835893
East Haddon	village 11 km NW of Northampton	SP667682
Easton Hillside	steep hillside with spinney 1 km N of Easton on the Hill	TF013054
Easton Hornstocks	National nature reserve ancient woodland 7 km S of Stamford, extensively quarried	TF015005
Easton Maudit	small village 9 km S of Wellingborough	SP888587
Easton on the Hill	village 3 km SW of Stamford	TF012043
Ecton	village on NE side of Northampton 6 km from town centre	SP827636
Elkington	hamlet close to NW county border	SP626765
Evenley	village on Oxfordshire border 3 km S of Brackley	SP587348
Evenley Camp	site mentioned by Druce, the exact locality of which is uncertain but it is thought to be the site of the old fish ponds at the map reference given	SP573344
Everdon Stubbs	Woodland Trust ancient woodland 6 km SE of Daventry	SP605566
Eydon	village 14 km NW of Brackley	SP543503
Farthinghoe	village 6km NW of Brackley	SP536398
Farthingstone	village 8 km SE of Daventry	SP613550
Farthingstone Castle Dykes	Earthworks of mediaeval castle 1 km N of Farthingstone church	SP617566

Fawsley	deserted village 5 km S of Daventry in Fawsley Park	SP561567
Fengate	area on the E outskirts of Peterborough immediately N of the River Nene	TL205985
Fermyn Woods	woodland, part of Rockingham Forest 8 km SE of Corby	SP965865
Ferry Meadows	country park with flooded gravel pits, adjacent to River Nene W of Peterborough	TL145975
Finedon	small town 8 km SE of Kettering	SP920720
Finedon Cally Banks	former ironstone railway line W of Finedon	SP908718
Finedon Pits	one time derelict ironstone sidings now a country park	SP892725
Finedon Sidings	waste area near main railway line, now an industrial site	SP895725
Fineshade Wood	ancient woodland, part now conifers managed by Forestry Commision, 10 km SW of Stamford	SP98-98-
Flag Fen	Archeological site on the edge of the Fens and on the W edge of Peterborough	TF000230
Force Leap	marsh 6 km W of Brackley and E of Charlton	SP53-36-
Fotheringhay	village 14 km SW of Peterborough	TL060931
Fotheringhay Castle	Site of former mediaeval castle, the final prison of Mary Queens of Scots, on the edge of the village of Fotheringhay and 6 km north of Oundle	Tl060932
Foxhall Quarry	former quarry	SP78-78-
Foxton	village in Leicestershire	SP700900
Gaultney Wood	ancient woodland 3 km E of Desborough	SP820837
Gayton	village 8 km SW of Northampton	SP704547
Geddington	village 5 km NE of Kettering	SP895830
Geddington Chase	ancient woodland with some areas replanted with conifers after 1945	SP910845
Glapthorn	village 11 km E of Corby	TL024903
Glapthorn Cow Pasture	Wildlife Trust reserve, secondary woodland 9 km E of Corby	TL003905
Glendon Hall	former estate 4 km NW of Kettering	SP845813
Grafton Park Wood	woodland to 7 km east of Ketttering	SP935814
Grafton Regis	small village 14 km S of Northampton	SP757467
Grafton Regis Meadow	Wildlife Trust meadow adjoining Grand Union Canal	SP765466
Grand Union Canal	major canal that runs through the county from Cosgrove to just north of Braunston, where it links with the Oxford Canal before continuing towards Birmingham, with branches to Buckingham, the River Nene at Northampton and Leicester	
Gray's Pits	shallow quarry (disused) for very fine calcareous sand at Burton Latimer	SP892756
Great Addington	village on the rim of the Nene valley 10 km SE of Kettering	SP958751
Great Billing	eastern suburb of Northampton	SP808629
Great Doddington	village 3 km SW of Wellingborough	SP882648
Great Doddington Marsh	marshy field beside River Nene S of Great Doddington	SP881643

Great Harrowden	small village centred on the Kettering to Wellingborough road 4 km N of Wellingborough	SP880708
Great Morton Sale	woodland adjoining disused quarry south of Bedford Purlieus	TL037972
Great Oakley Meadow	Wildlife Trust local nature reserve flower rich meadow on outskirts of Corby	SP863855
Great Oxendon	village 11 km NW of Kettering	SP732834
Greatworth	village 6 km NW of Brackley	SP552424
Grendon	village 8 km S of Wellingborough	SP878603
Guilsborough	village 14 km NE of Daventry	SP675730
Hall Lane Quarry	near Kettering	
Hanslope	village in Buckinghamshire close to county border	SP803450
Hardwick	tiny village 4 km NW of Wellingborough	SP851698
Hardwick Woods	Forestry Commision woodland mostly conifers on site of ancient woodland	SP828706
Harlestone	village on A428 6 km NW of Northampton	SP703646
Harlestone Firs	woodland mostly conifer plantation covering Harlestone Heath and Dallington Heath	SP714640
Harlestone Heath	former heathland, part of the area of woodland now known as Harlestone Firs.	SP714640
Harpers Brook	tributary of River Nene rising N of Desborough and entering the river at Thrapston	
Harpole	village 6 km W of Northampton	SP691607
Harrington	village 9 km W of Kettering with former World War 2 airfield south.of village	SP774800
Harringworth	village in Welland valley 10 km NE of Corby	SP916974
Harringworth Meadow	riverside meadow N of Harringworth	SP920974
Hazel Wood, Corby	relic of ancient woodland in the centre of Corby	SP877886
Hazelborough Forest	ancient woodland 9 km NE of Brackley	SP65-42-
Helmdon	village 7 km N of Brackley, former ironstone quarry	SP587438
Helpston	village 10 km NW of Peterborough, birthplace of John Clare, poet	TF122053
Hen Wood	woodland	SP596556
High Wood	Wildlife Trust reserve, notable for its cherry trees and attached grassland	SP591548
Higham Ferrers	small town adjoining Rushden, and 7 km SE of Wellingborough	SP961685
Hinton-in-the-Hedges	small village 3 km W of Brackley	SP560369
Hogs Hole, Moulton	small, very wet spinney on Moulton Farm Estates	SP781672
Holcot Causeway	causeway across Pitsford reservoir on the Holcot - Brixworth road, about 10 km N of Northampton	SP783701
Hollowell	village 11 km NW of Northampton	SP690720
Hollowell Reservooir	immediately north of Hollowell village and 12 km NW of Northampton	SP688730
Honey Hill	hill 3 km S of Welford	SP638769
Horn Wood	woodland belonging to Yardley Chase	SP89-57-
Horton	small village 9 km SE of Northampton	SP820543
Hunsbury Hill	site of iron age fort and more recently ironstone quarrying, now a public park	SP738583

Irchester	small town 4 km SE of Wellingborough	SP925655
Irchester Country Park	former ironstone quarry planted with conifers etc.	SP915660
Irthlingborough	small town 6 km NE of Wellingborough	SP945705
Kelmarsh	small estate village adjoining grounds of Kelmarsh hall, 13 km W of Kettering	SP737793
Kelmarsh Hall	13 km W of Kettering	SP735795
Kettering	town in E of county 20 km N of Northampton	SP86-78-
Kettering Furnaces	former ironworks on NW edge of Kettering	SP862803
Kettering Tip	N of Kettering, off Weekley Wood Lane	SP874810
Kettering Town Football Ground	in N part of Kettering	SP865800
Kilsby Landfill Site	landfill site with lake	SP565696
King's Cliffe	village 10 km S of Stamford	TL005973
King's Wood, Corby	Local nature reserve, ancient woodland, reduced in size	SP866871
Kings Sutton	village on SW boundary 8 km W of Brackley	SP502364
Kings Sutton Bog	marsh near village of Kings Sutton	
Kingsthorpe	region of N Northampton	SP75-68-
Kingsthorpe Scrub Field	once part of Northampton Golf Course, ploughed in 1980	SP765642
Kirby Hall	16th C building, with restored gardens	SP925927
Kislingbury	village 6 km W of Northampton	SP698595
Lamport	village 11 km SW of Kettering	SP758745
Laundimer Wood	woodland, now mainly conifer plantations, 6 km E of Corby	SP93-87-
Laxton	village 8 km NE of Corby	SP950961
Lilford Estate	5 km S of Oundle, formerly home of Thomas Littleton Powys, 4th Lord Lilford, and eminent ornithologist	TL030838
Lings Wood	Wildlife Trust reserve, former common land, now planted with conifers	SP803638
Litchborough Churchyard	in centre of village, notable for wall plants	SP632532
Little Creaton	hamlet 12 km NW of Northampton	SP710714
Little Houghton	village close to SE outskirts of Northampton	SP803596
Little Preston	hamlet 8 km S of Daventry	SP587541
Loddington	village 5 km E of Kettering	SP815784
Long Buckby	small town on Northampton loop of British Rail 14 km NW of Northampton	SP627675
Long Furlong	wood near Yardley Chase, adjoining Old Pastures Wood	SP565884
Lower Benefield	village 9 km E of Corby	SP988885
Lowick	village 2 km NW of Thrapston	SP977810
Lyveden New Bield	unfinished 17th century large summer house S of Brigstock - Oundle road, owned by the National Trust	SP986852
Maidwell	village 12 km W of Kettering	SP74-87-
Maidwell Dales	wet woodland area W of Maidwell village	SP733768
Mallows Cotton	site of mediaeval village W of Raunds	SP976733
Mantles Heath	ancient woodland on Knightley Way	SP598552

Marholm	village close to W outskirts of Peterborough	TF146020
Market Harborough	town in Leicestershire	SP73-87-
Maxey	village 11 km NW of Peterborough	TF128081
Mears Ashby	village 10 km NE of Northampton	SP839667
Middle Bridge, Drayton	bridge over the River Welland	SP837910
Milton Keynes	new town in Buckinghamshire	SP85-39-
Milton Malsor	village 5 km S of Northampton	SP736557
Morton Pinkney	village 12 km N of Brackley	SP575493
Moulton	village within NE boundary of Northampton	SP783663
Naseby Reservoir	11 km SW of Market Harborough	SP669775
Nassington	small village 12 km W of Peterborough	TL071978
Nene Washes	area between River Nene and nearby drains in Soke	TL27-99-
Newbottle	hamlet 8 km SE of Banbury	SP524369
Newbottle Spinney	spinney W of Newbottle and 7 km SE of Banbury, a Wildlife Trust reserve	SP517365
Newnham Hill	to S of Daventry	SP575608
Newton Field Centre	former church of Newton-in-the-Willows, now a field study centre	SP885833
Newton Quarry	area of former ironstone quarry planted with conifers	SP873840
Nobottle Wood	woodland	SP676633
Northamptom Racecourse	former racecourse close to the centre of Northampton	SP760617
Northampton	County town situated on River Nene	SP75-60-
Northampton General Hospital	in the centre of Northampton	SP764604
Northampton Golf Links	former heathland	SP768631
Norton	village E of Daventry	SP602638
Old Dry Hills	woodland, part of Laundimer Woods	SP943867
Old Pastures Wood	woodland near Yardley Chase, adjoining Long Furlong	SP887560
Old Pond Close	woodland, part of Yardley Chase on B5388 S of Yardley Hastings	SP877550
Old Sulehay Forest	ancient woodland	TL063986
Old Water Mill	site of former watermill, now an industrial site on E boundary of Desborough	SP817835
Onley	near the county boundary immediately S of Rugby	SP515714
Oundle	small town in the NE in valley of River Nene	TL040882
Oundle Gravel Pits	now a country park and marina beside the River Nene immediately S of Oundle	TL03-87-
Overstone	village on NE edge of Northampton, 8 km from centre	SP810665
Oxford Canal	18th century canal which enters the county in the extreme S and leaves runs close to much of the W boundary, leaving and re-entering the county several times. Straightening of the northern part of the canal left a number of disused arms.	
Oxney Lode	artificial water course E of Peterborough	TF226012
Peakirk	village 8 km N of Peterborough	TF168066
Perio Dykes	W of Perio Mill	TL033924
Perio Mill	mill on River Nene 4 km N of Oundle	TL043924

Peter's Pond	pond near Easton on the Hill	TL005052
Peterborough	Cathedral city, recently much expanded, on River Nene	TL19-99-
Piddington	village close to Salcey Forest 8 km SE of Northampton	SP803546
Pilsgate	village 3 km SE of Stamford	TF066056
Pipewell Rd. Rubbish Tip	former ironstone quarry near Desborough	SP808837
Pipewell Woods	group of ancient woods including Pipewell Wood, Monks Arbour Wood	SP835861
Pitsford Reservoir	man-made freshwater lake, largest in county	SP700780
Plumpton Woods	Forestry Commision plantation, mostly conifers	SP603494
Potterspury	village on Watling Street 18 km S of Northampton, some Roman occupation	SP759431
Preston Capes	village 8 km S of Daventry	SP575548
Racecourse Road	road running E from Easton on the Hill on the site of Stamford Racecourse	TF016043 - TF035042
Rainsborough Camp	iron age hill fort 1 km S of Charlton	SP526348
Ramsden Corner	Wildlife Trust reserve, some woodland and wet heath	SP625563
Raunds	small town 12 km NE of Wellingborough	SP998729
Ravensthorpe Reservoir	immediately E of Ravensthorpe village, and 12 km NW of Daventry	SP678706
Redhill Wood	mostly scrubbed over open woodland	SP508508
Ring Haw	former quarry near Yarwell	TL05-97-
Ringstead	village on River Nene rim, 13 km SE of Kettering	SP988752
River Cherwell	tributary of River Thames rising near Charwelton and flowing South	
River Ise	tributary of River Nene rising N of Naseby and flowing to Wellingborough	
River Nene	major river that rises at Arbury Hill near Daventry and near Naseby and flows NE through the county	
River Tove	tributary of the River Ouse that rises near Weedon Lois and flows into the Ouse at Cosgrove	
River Welland	River forming long stretches of the NW boundary	
Roade	large village 9 km S of Northampton	SP755577
Rockingham Castle	Norman castle, now a residence on rim of Welland valley	SP867913
Rockingham Forest	former Royal forest in the N of the county containing a number of major blocks of woodland including Fineshade, Wakerley, and King's Wood, Easton Hornstocks and Geddington Chase	SP9--9--
Rockingham Park	surrounding the castle	SP86-91-
Rothersthorpe	village 10 km SW of Northampton	SP715566
Rothwell	small town 5 km E of Kettering	SP815811
Rothwell Gullet	Wildlife Trust reserve, former ironstone gullet N of Rothwell	SP808818
Rush Mills	S of Northampton on the River Nene	SP78-60-
Rushden	small town close to Bedfordshire boundary 8 km E of Wellingborough	SP95-66-
Rushmere	district of SE Northampton in valley of River Nene	SP778602

Rushton	village 6 km NW of Kettering	SP841828
Saint Andrew's Hospital	private nursing home with extensive grounds in Northampton	SP770606
Saint James End	part of Northampton	SP74-60-
Saint Luke's Meadow	beside the River Welland near Duddington	SP973996
Salcey Forest	ancient woodland, now Forestry Commision planted with conifers, includes a Wildlife Trust reserve	SP80-50-
Samuel Lloyd School	school in Corby	SP892897
Sane Copse	SSSI, part of Yardley Chase	SP542855
Short Wood	Wildlife Trust reserve, ancient coppiced woodland	TL015913
Short Wood Pond	in Short Wood	
Sibbertoft	village 7 km SW of Market Harborough	SP680826
Souther Wood	woodland 12 km NE of Kettering, ancient but with many conifers	SP980840
Southey Wood	woodland, mostly conifer 10 km NW of Peterborough	TF106030
Southorpe	village 11 km W of Peterborough	TL082030
Southorpe Bog	area of marsh between Barnack and Wittering	TF066028
Southorpe Marsh	former marshland	TF02-06-
Southorpe Paddock	Wildlife Trust reserve, calcareous grassland, S of Southorpe	TL084022
Spratton	village 10 km N of Northampton on A50	SP717700
Stamford	small town on A1 (now in Lincolnshire), 18 km NW of Peterborough	TL03-07-
Stanford reservoir	Wildlife Trust reserve, man-made freshwater lake across Leicestershire boundary	SP802806
Stanion	village 3 km SE of Corby	SP916869
Stanwick	village on rim of Nene valley 13 km SE of Kettering	SP980713
Staverton	village 3 km SW of Daventry	SP542611
Stoke Albany	village on rim of Welland valley 11 km NW of Kettering	SP806879
Stoke Doyle	village on valley side of River Nene 17 km NE of Kettering	TL024863
Stoke Pavilions	only remaining part of Stoke Hall	SP741487
Stoke Wood	ancient woodland, now a Woodland Trust and Wildlife Trust reserve, 2 km north of Desborough	SP800864
Sudborough	village 11 km NE of Kettering	SP967821
Sudborough Meadow	area W of Lady Wood and Souther Wood	SP968846
Sulby	area close to Leicestershire border, a diffuse hamlet	SP659819
Summer Leys Country Park	country park and former gravel pit	SP880637
Sutton	village W of Peterborough	TL097987
Sywell	village 9 km NE of Northampton	SP821672
Sywell Country Park	see Sywell reservoir	SP833655
Sywell Reservoir	now a country park, 9 km NE of Northampton	SP833655
Sywell Wood	Ancient woodland 10 km NE of Northampton	SP830692
Tailby's Meadow,	Wildlife Trust local nature reserve grassland reserve in Desborough	SP815826
Tansor	small village 16 km SW of Peterborough	TL053910
The Coombes, Sibbertoft	area of wooded hillside	SP683836

The Plens	former ironstone quarry, now Wildlife Trust reserve on the N boundary of Desborough	SP807837
Theddingworth Bridge	bridge over the River Welland at Theddingworth	SP670854
Thornby Hall	on edge of Thornby village, 19 km W of Kettering	SP670756
Thornhaugh	village W of A1 1 km N of Wansford	TF005067
Thoroughsale Wood,	relic of ancient woodland in the centre of Corby	SP875893
Thorpe Malsor	village 3 km W of Kettering	SP814790
Thorpe Mandeville	village 8 km NE of Banbury	SP553449
Thrapston	small town 13 km E of Kettering	SP997786
Thrupp Grounds	farm to S of Grand Union Canal	SP604655
Tiffield Quarry	former quarry 3 km SW of Blisworth	SP707513
Tinwell	village in Rutland	TF005064
Titchmarsh	village on rim of Nene valley, 15 km E of Kettering	TL023797
Titchmarsh Heronry	Wildlife Trust reserve, now including adjacent lakes in river Nene valley	TL007804
Titchmarsh Reserve	Wildlife Trust reserve, former gravel workings which contains Titchmarsh Heronry	TL007815
Towcester	small town 13 km SW of Northampton	SP695483
Twywell	village 8 km E of Kettering	SP952782
Twywell Gullet	former ironstone quarry SW of Twywell, now a nature reserve	SP945775
Ufford	village in Soke of Peterborough	TF095040
Upper Catesby	small village on W boundary, 9 km SW of Daventry	SP527594
Upton	small village 4 km W of Northampton	SP718602
Upton Hall	in grounds adjoining Upton, now a school	SP718600
Upton Mill Lane	running from A45 at Upton to mill on River Nene	SP720622-SP721592
Wadenhoe	village in Nene valley	TL012820
Wakerley Great Wood	part of Wakerley Woods	SP961983
Wakerley Spinney	ancient woodland mostly replanted with conifers	SP965986
Wakerley Woods	area of ancient woodland, mainly replanted with conifers	SP95-97-
Wakerley	village on Welland valley in NE	SP954995
Walcot Hall	estate on edge of Barnack Hills and Holes	TF080041
Walgrave	village 9 km SW of Kettering	SP802720
Walton Grounds	Wildlife Trust reserve in valley in extreme SW	SP509347
Wansford	village on A1 in N of county	TL072994
Wansford Pasture	Wildlife Trust grassland reserve with wet flushes	TL070994
Wansford Quarry	old quarry adjoining Old Sulehay Forest	TL055983
Warkton	small village 2 km E of Kettering	SP893798
Watford	small village 7 km NE of Daventry	SP603681
Weedon	village 12 km W of Northampton	SP630595
Weekley	village on Boughton Estate 3km NE of Kettering	SP888808
Weekley Hall Wood	ancient woodland partially destroyed by quarrying	SP870820
Weekley Wet Beds	osier bed beside River Ise and near Weekley	SP892805
Weekley Wood Lane	lane linking A43 and A6003 north of Kettering now redeveloped as part of Kettering northern relief road	SP866811 -SP887812
Weldon	village 5 km E of Corby	SP929896
Weldon Park Wood	woodland 2 km E of Weldon	SP900945

Welford	village close to Leicestershire boundary, 11 km SW of Market Harborough	SP642804
Welford Reservoir	Canal reservoir immediately NE of Welford and feeding the Welford arm of the Grand Union canal	SP650810
Welham	village in Leicestershire close to county border	SP765925
Wellingborough	town on River Nene in S, 15 km NE of Wellingborough	SP89-68-
Wellingborough Bowling Greens	park in the centre of Wellingborough	SP894674
West Haddon	village on W side 11 km NE of Daventry	SP631719
Weston by Welland	village 10km W of Corby	SP778914
Whilton	village E of Daventry	SP636647
Whistley Wood	woodland in S of county	SP61-41-
Whiston	village 8 km SW of Wellingborough	SP850605
White Water	reservoir on the boundary between Northamptonshire and the Soke of Peterborough	TF035033
Whitfield	small village close to county boundary and 6 km NE of Brackley	SP608395
Whittlebury	forest village close to SW boundary, 12 km NE of Brackley	SP691437
Whittlebury Forest	see Whittlewood Forest - this name is used by Druce	
Whittlewood Forest	a circle of ancient woods, formerly enclosed, surrounding what used to be open lawn but is now mainly ploughed farmland.	SP73-43-
Whitworth's Mill	flour mill beside the River Nene on the S boundary of Wellingborough	SP903666
Wicken	small village 16 km E of Brackley	SP747395
Wicken Wood	part of Whittlewood Forest	SP730405
Wicksteed's Park	pleasure park on the S edge of Kettering	SP880770
Wilby	village on W edge of Wellingborough	SP867662
Wilby Brook	flows from N of Mears Ashby into the River Nene	
Winwick	tiny village 12 km NE of Daventry	SP627738
Wollaston	small town 5 km S of Wellingborough	SP909630
Wollaston Hall	small Wildlife Trust reserve on edge of Wollaston	SP910634
Wood Lane Tip	former ironstone gullet to N of Kettering, now infilled	SP875809
Woodend	hamlet 12 km N of Brackley	SP616492
Woodford	village on side of Nene valley, 10 km E of Kettering	SP965770
Woodford Halse	village 10 km S of Daventry	SP544528
Woodford Spinney	also known as the Shrubbery, probably ancient but with some planting	SP973772
Woodnewton	village 12 km S of Stamford	TL033946
Wothorpe	village 2 km S of Stamford	TF024053
Yardley Chase	group of Forestry Commision woodlands partly coniferized 11 km SE of Northampton	SP84-55-
Yardley Gobion	village 16 km SE of Northampton	SP765447
Yardley Hastings	village 11 km S of Wellingborough	SP866570
Yarwell	village in Nene valley 9 km S of Stamford	TL070978
Yelvertoft	village 15 km N of Daventry	SP597756

The Flora of
NORTHAMPTONSHIRE
and the Soke of Peterborough~

Index

C

330